LYCURGUS

THE SPEECH
AGAINST LEOCRATES

LYCURGUS

THE SPEECH AGAINST LEOCRATES

EDITED BY

A. PETRIE, M.A.

PROFESSOR OF CLASSICS, NATAL UNIVERSITY COLLEGE
(UNIVERSITY OF S. AFRICA); FORMERLY LECTURER
IN GREEK IN THE UNIVERSITY OF ABERDEEN;
SOMETIME SCHOLAR OF TRINITY COLLEGE,
CAMBRIDGE

CAMBRIDGE

AT THE UNIVERSITY PRESS

1922

CAMBRIDGE
UNIVERSITY PRESS

University Printing House, Cambridge CB2 8BS, United Kingdom

Published in the United States of America by Cambridge University Press, New York

Cambridge University Press is part of the University of Cambridge.

It furthers the University's mission by disseminating knowledge in the pursuit of
education, learning and research at the highest international levels of excellence.

www.cambridge.org
Information on this title: www.cambridge.org/9781107669451

© Cambridge University Press 1922

This publication is in copyright. Subject to statutory exception
and to the provisions of relevant collective licensing agreements,
no reproduction of any part may take place without the written
permission of Cambridge University Press.

First published 1922
First paperback edition 2014

A catalogue record for this publication is available from the British Library

ISBN 978-1-107-66945-1 Paperback

Cambridge University Press has no responsibility for the persistence or accuracy of
URLs for external or third-party internet websites referred to in this publication,
and does not guarantee that any content on such websites is, or will remain, accurate
or appropriate.

PREFACE

THE *Leocrates* of Lycurgus has remained, in England, in comparative obscurity, not having attracted an editor since John Taylor[1] edited it at Cambridge, along with the *Midias* of Demosthenes, in 1743. Yet the speech is by no means without its merits. It forms, in many ways, an excellent introduction to Attic oratory for younger students. It is easier than Demosthenes, and there is no complex political situation to expound: the issue is simple and direct. And it has a greater variety of interest than either Demosthenes or Lysias. Its very fault of diffuseness, from the purely forensic standpoint, becomes, from an educative point of view, its great virtue. Lycurgus' excursions into ancient history, legend, and the poets, provide, in Livy's phrase, so many *deverticula amoena* where the student finds refreshment with instruction.

The text of the present edition will be found to adhere, in the main, to that of Blass, whose critical commentary I have supplemented with those of Scheibe, Rehdantz and Thalheim. I have not hesitated, however, to depart from Blass where the concessions which he makes to considerations of hiatus—an unusually precarious guide in the case of Lycurgus—or of the *numeri*, to which he assigns such considerable weight, are in conflict with the

---

[1] 1704–1766. Fellow of St John's, and successively Librarian (1731–4) and Registrary (1734–51) of the University.—Sandys, *H.C.S.*, vol. II. p. 414.

clear testimony of the MSS. While I have not aimed at producing a critical edition, in the strict sense of the term, a considerable amount of attention has been devoted to textual points throughout. These have been noticed, wherever it could be done conveniently, in the body of the notes: passages requiring somewhat fuller discussion have been collected in a separate appendix.

With regard to the notes, my first and greatest obligation is to the elaborate edition of Rehdantz (Leipzig, 1876), of which any subsequent editor of Lycurgus is bound to take account. I have also had before me the brief but useful notes of E. Sofer (Leipzig and Berlin, 1905). Among the older editions, I have inspected Dobson's *Attic Orators* (vol. IV), Baiter and Sauppe, and the acute commentary of van den Es.

For the material of the *Introduction*, in addition to the relevant portions of Blass and Rehdantz, I have consulted works of general reference such as Gilbert's *Antiquities*, Jebb's *Attic Orators*, Prof. E. A. Gardner's *Ancient Athens*, Bury's *History of Greece*, and the Cambridge *Companion*. I have been able to make use of Prof. J. F. Dobson's *The Greek Orators* for matters connected with Lycurgus' style, and I am indebted to Mr Wyse's introduction to his monumental edition of Isaeus for information regarding the manuscript tradition for the minor orators.

I have had the advantage of discussing several points with my friends and former class-fellows, Mr W. M. Calder, Professor of Greek in the University of Manchester, and Mr J. Fraser, now Professor of Celtic in the University of Oxford; and

PREFACE

with a former Cambridge teacher, Mr L. Whibley, Fellow of Pembroke College, to all of whom I here wish to make acknowledgment. Prof. Calder has further kindly undertaken the revision of the proof-sheets, while my obligations to the readers of the University Press may be taken for granted. To Dr P. Giles, Master of Emmanuel College, Cambridge, and recently Vice-Chancellor of the University, I owe a special word of thanks for much kindness and encouragement. For the statements contained in the book, I alone, of course, am responsible.

A. P.

NATAL UNIVERSITY COLLEGE,
Christmas, 1921

ERRATUM

p. 152, l. 7 from bottom. For *Branchidae* read *Didyma*.

CONTENTS

	PAGE
INTRODUCTION	xi
(i) LYCURGUS: HIS LIFE AND PUBLIC ADMINISTRATION	xi
(ii) THE SPEECH AGAINST LEOCRATES .	xxvi
(iii) ANALYSIS OF THE SPEECH . .	xxxi
(iv) LYCURGUS AS AN ORATOR . .	xxxiii
(v) SOURCES OF THE TEXT . . .	xl
TEXT	1
NOTES	59
CRITICAL APPENDIX . . .	230
INDEX A	239
B	241
C	243
D	246

ὁ δὲ Λυκούργειός (sc. λόγος) ἐστι διαπαντὸς αὐξητικὸς καὶ διηρμένος καὶ σεμνός, καὶ ὅλως κατηγορικός, καὶ φιλαλήθης καὶ παρρησιαστικός· οὐ μὴν ἀστεῖος οὐδὲ ἡδύς, ἀλλ' ἀναγκαῖος. τούτου χρὴ ζηλοῦν μάλιστα τὰς δεινώσεις.

DIONYSIUS HALICARNASSENSIS, *Veterum Censura*, v. 3.

πολὺ δὲ τὸ τραχὺ καὶ σφοδρὸν ἔχει χωρὶς ἐπιμελείας...χρῆται δὲ πολλαῖς πολλάκις καὶ ταῖς παρεκβάσεσιν, ἐπὶ μύθους καὶ ἱστορίας καὶ ποιήματα φερόμενος.

HERMOGENES, *De Formis Oratoriis*, B. 11.

τὸ γὰρ μετὰ πολλῶν παραδειγμάτων διδάσκειν ῥᾳδίαν ὑμῖν τὴν κρίσιν καθίστησι.

LYCURGUS, *Contra Leocratem*, 124.

INTRODUCTION

(i) LYCURGUS: HIS LIFE AND PUBLIC ADMINISTRATION[1]

Lycurgus, son of Lycophron, was born at Athens about the year 390 B.C., being thus a few years older than Demosthenes[2]. He belonged to the noble family of the Eteobutadae, which traced its descent from the hero Butes, brother of Erechtheus, and in which the priesthoods

Birth and Family

---

[1] Our chief authorities are the *Life* in *The Lives of the Ten Orators*, attributed to Plutarch, and the decree of the orator Stratocles in connexion with Lycurgus appended thereto. A fragment of this decree (archonship of Anaxicrates, 307/6—C. I. A. II. 240) is extant, and confirms, as far as it goes, the version of Pseudo-Plutarch: the stone was probably more concise, on the whole, though the surviving fragment does not positively justify this assumption. The decree in Ps.-Plut. was most likely derived from Caecilius of Calacte (a rhetorician of the time of Augustus), who in his turn was probably dependent on a copy made by Heliodorus (*fl. c.* 160 B.C.). A *Life* of Lycurgus was written by Philiscus of Miletus (a pupil of Isocrates), and afterwards by the above-mentioned Caecilius, from the latter of whom a great part of the Ps.-Plutarchic *Life* appears to have been derived. [A commentary on the Ps.-Plut. *Life* was written by M. H. E. Meier (in Kiessling's ed. of the fragments of Lycurgus, 1847): the decree of Stratocles has been elucidated by C. Curtius, *Philologus*, XXIV. 83 sqq.]

[2] Argt. to Dem. *Against Aristogiton* (Libanius). Some place his birth as early as 396 B.C., or twelve years before the accepted date of the birth of Demosthenes.

of Poseidon Erechtheus and of Athena Polias were hereditary offices. Of his father nothing is known except his name; his grandfather, also a Lycurgus, had been among the victims of the Thirty[1]. The records of the family were rich in public honours, in life and in death, and Lycurgus was thus marked out, alike by inherited character and ancestral tradition, for a distinguished career.

The public service of Lycurgus is associated with the period in the history of Athens immediately following the battle of Chaeronea, 338 B.C., which made Philip of Macedon controller of the destinies of Greece. Demosthenes, the great orator, had been the heart and soul of the Athenian resistance to 'the Macedonian barbarian,' and Lycurgus had exerted his influence in the same direction. How far, if at all, he used his oratory for political purposes, we do not know. We hear of him accompanying Demosthenes on an embassy to the Peloponnese, in 343 B.C., to stir up opposition to Philip[2]; and he had at any rate made himself sufficiently prominent among the anti-Macedonian party to be one of those whose surrender was demanded by Alexander after the subjugation of Thebes, 335 B.C. Fortunately for Athens, the demand was refused; or rather Alexander allowed himself to be placated through the intervention of Demades, whose Macedonian sympathies were well known, and the demand was withdrawn.

A supporter of Demosthenes

Surrender demanded by Alexander

Philip's treatment of Athens after Chaeronea was so unexpectedly lenient as to confirm, to some extent, the genuineness of the friendly feeling which he had always professed towards her, and to disprove the

[1] The Greek of Ps.-Plut. (*Vit.* § 1) is ambiguous, but Lycurgus, *avus*, is evidently intended.

[2] Dem. *Phil.* III. § 72 (acc. to some MSS.).

INTRODUCTION   xiii

sinister motives attributed to him by ultra-patriots like Demosthenes. Philip undertook to restore the Athenian prisoners without ransom and not to march into Attica. Oropus was to belong to Athens, the Thracian Chersonese to Macedonia. Athens was to dissolve what remained of her confederacy, and become
<small>Philip deals leniently with Athens</small> a member of the new Hellenic league of which Macedon was to be the head. Whatever Philip's motives may have been in granting such generous terms to the city which had been such a persistent obstacle to Macedonian expansion—and the fact that Athens could still offer considerable resistance by sea may have weighed with him, apart from any natural feelings of clemency—the Athenians undoubtedly had reason to congratulate themselves on the result.

Philip was murdered in 336 B.C., and for the next thirteen years the eyes of the Greek world were fixed
<small>Alexander in the East</small> upon his all-conquering son pursuing his dazzling conquests in the East. Beside these, the ordinary domestic matters of the individual Greek states, however much notice they might have attracted in the old order of things, were almost, and naturally, without significance. We are permitted to see, however, that once again Athens showed remarkable powers of recovery, and that in the interval between the fall of Thebes and the death of Alexander she did much to rehabilitate her resources
<small>Athens recovers</small> which had been sorely taxed by the long war with Philip. There was little enthusiasm, it is true, on the part of Athens for the Macedonian hegemony, but neither was it expedient to break with the northern power, as even the more irreconcileable of the anti-Macedonians saw: it was clearly her policy to set her house in order, with a view to bettering her position when the favourable

moment arrived[1]. Her revenues had to be nursed, her navy strengthened, and her self-respect as a great power restored. The success she achieved in all these directions was largely due to the energy and wholehearted enthusiasm of Lycurgus.

At Athens, in the Demosthenic period, the question of finance was naturally of the first importance; and 'finance,' for an Athenian statesman, had come to mean, above all things, the administration of the so-called 'Theoric Fund.' This fund, the avowed purpose of which, as its name implies, was the providing of 'spectacle-money,' had developed from the practice, by whomsoever introduced—it has been attributed to Pericles, who had to find means of competing with the private wealth of Cimon[2]—of furnishing the poorer citizens with the price of their theatre ticket. It was a practice which, once begun, rapidly outran, as might be expected, the limits which we may believe its author proposed for it. At all events, by the middle of the fourth century B.C., we find that the entire surplus revenues of the state, after the expenses of administration have been provided for, are declared to be 'theoric,' and the Theoric Fund is administered by a specially elected board (οἱ ἐπὶ τὸ θεωρικόν), who, according to Aeschines, though it suits his purpose to

The Theoric Fund

---

[1] She stood aloof from the anti-Macedonian movement in the Peloponnese, which was crushed by Antipater in 331 (or 330) B.C. (battle of Megalopolis).

[2] Plut. *Vit. Per.* IX. ἄλλοι δὲ πολλοὶ πρῶτον ὑπ' ἐκείνου (sc. τοῦ Περικλέους) φασὶ τὸν δῆμον ἐπὶ κληρουχίας καὶ θεωρικὰ καὶ μισθῶν διανομὰς προαχθῆναι...καὶ ταχὺ θεωρικοῖς καὶ δικαστικοῖς λήμμασιν...συνδεκάσας τὸ πλῆθος. The principle was extended (some think, instituted) by Cleophon, who introduced the διωβελία or 'two-obol payment,' and later by Agyrrhius.

INTRODUCTION xv

exaggerate their powers when he makes the statement, 'had in their hands practically the entire administration of the city[1].' The Theoric Board, as we know it, was probably instituted under the regime of Eubulus—the greatest name in Athenian fourth century finance before Lycurgus—and held office from one Panathenaea to the following.

The Theoric Board

But the principle involved in the Theoric Fund, if it answered well enough in time of peace, could hardly do otherwise than make for inefficiency when a special military effort required to be put forth. This is the lesson conveyed by much of Athens' small achievement in her fourth century foreign policy. In spite of this, however, any proposal to divert the Fund to military purposes was certain to raise a storm of opposition, and indeed appears to have entailed very serious danger to its mover, even if we do not go the length of accepting Libanius' statement that the death penalty for such a proposal was prescribed by law[2]. The test case brought by Apollodorus about the year 350 B.C. had ended in his conviction for having introduced an illegal measure[3]. Demosthenes himself, while cautiously hinting at the expediency of applying the Fund to war purposes, definitely declines to make a formal proposal[4]. Not until 339/8 did Demosthenes see his dream realised:

The Fund safeguarded

Demosthenes gets it applied to war purposes

---

[1] Aeschin. *Ctes.* § 25 οἱ ἐπὶ τὸ θεωρικὸν κεχειροτονημένοι... σχεδὸν τὴν ὅλην διοίκησιν εἶχον τῆς πόλεως.

[2] Argt. to Dem. *Ol.* I.: νόμον ἔθεντο περὶ τῶν θεωρικῶν τούτων χρημάτων, θάνατον ἀπειλοῦντα τῷ γράψαντι μετατεθῆναί τε ταῦτ' εἰς τὴν ἀρχαίαν τάξιν καὶ γενέσθαι στρατιωτικά. The law, acc. to *Schol.* on Dem. I. 1, was introduced by Eubulus himself after the prosecution of Apollodorus.

[3] [Dem.] *C. Neaeram* § 5.

[4] Dem. *Ol.* I. § 19 τί οὖν; ἄν τις εἴποι, σὺ γράφεις ταῦτ' εἶναι στρατιωτικά; μὰ Δί' οὐκ ἔγωγε.

emboldened by the passing of his naval reforms, he now proposed that the theoric monies should be applied to military purposes, and he must have regarded his success as one of the triumphs of his policy[1].

Eubulus had been at the head of Athenian finance—presumably as President of the Theoric Board—for some fifteen years, 354-339: in 338 he was replaced by a nominee of the war party, which had now come into power, in the person of Lycurgus. The reform of Demosthenes in respect of the theoric monies was probably responsible for a radical change in the financial administration, and for the creation of a new finance official, or at any rate an official with a new title—the ταμίας τῶν στρατιωτικῶν—whom we now hear of for the first time. Lycurgus, however, is called by the Pseudo-Plutarch ταμίας τῆς κοινῆς προσόδου— 'steward of the public revenue,' 'Chancellor of the Exchequer'—a title which, while no doubt sufficiently representing his position, is probably not official[2].

Lycurgus succeeds Eubulus

'Steward of the Public Revenue'

[1] Philoch. *fr.* 135 τὰ δὲ χρήματ' ἐψηφίσαντο πάντ' εἶναι στρατιωτικά, Δημοσθένους γράψαντος (archonship of Lysimachides, 339/8).

[2] What definite office, or offices, Lycurgus held during his 'politico-financial ascendancy' is largely a matter of conjecture. From other language of Ps.-Plut. *Vit.* § 3 πιστευσάμενος τὴν διοίκησιν τῶν χρημάτων, Hyper. *fr.* 121 (Blass) ταχθεὶς ἐπὶ τῇ διοικήσει τῶν χρημάτων, Diod. XVI. 88 δώδεκα ἔτη τὰς προσόδους τῆς πόλεως διοικήσας, it has been suggested that his office was ὁ ἐπὶ τῇ διοικήσει, which probably did not exist so early, the first ἐπὶ τῇ διοικήσει mentioned in inscrr. being Lycurgus' own son Habron (not before 307 B.C.). Again, from Ps.-Plut. *Vit.* § 5 ἐπὶ τὴν τοῦ πολέμου παρασκευὴν χειροτονηθείς (cf. the *Rogatio Stratoclis* appended, 852 c), it has been inferred that

INTRODUCTION xvii

Lycurgus' twelve years of office, 338-326 B.C.
In the capacity so described Lycurgus acted for a period of twelve years, from 338 to 326. His appointment apparently ran 'from Panathenaea to Panathenaea[1],' so that his administration included three such terms of office, in the first (338–334) and the third (330–326) of which Lycurgus administered in his own name; in the second (334–330), under the name of a deputy, who was probably his own son Habron, this device being necessitated by legal restrictions on the length of tenure of the office by the same individual[2]. The

Lycurgus was στρατηγὸς ἐπὶ τὴν παρασκευήν, an official whom we do not meet with in inscrr. before the third cent., and who must almost certainly have been mentioned by Arist. 'Αθ. Πολ. 61. The words αἱρεθεὶς ὑπὸ τοῦ δήμου (*Rog. Strat.* 852 B) are too vague to allow of any certain inference. It may be that Lycurgus held special commissions for the execution of some of his duties. If he did hold a definite office, it was most likely that of ταμίας τῶν στρατιωτικῶν, or president of οἱ ἐπὶ τὸ θεωρικόν, who still existed, though no doubt with diminished powers. Cf. Gilbert, *Const. Antiqq.* pp. 245 sqq. and notes.

[1] As in the case of οἱ ἐπὶ τὸ θεωρικὸν and the ταμίας τῶν στρατιωτικῶν.

[2] [Plut.] *Vit. Lyc.* § 3 ταμίας ἐγένετο ἐπὶ τρεῖς πενταετηρίδας... τὸ μὲν πρῶτον αἱρεθεὶς αὐτός, ἔπειτα τῶν φίλων ἐπιγραψάμενός τινα αὐτὸς ἐποιεῖτο τὴν διοίκησιν, διὰ τὸ φθάσαι νόμον εἰσενεγκεῖν, μὴ πλείω ε′ ἐτῶν διοικεῖν τὸν χειροτονηθέντα ἐπὶ τὰ δημόσια χρήματα. I have followed Blass in understanding μὴ πλείω ε′ ἐτῶν to mean 'not for two successive penteterids,' and not 'for not more than five years,' absolutely. On the second interpretation, Lycurgus would have administered by deputy in both his second and third terms. Blass further holds that C.I.A. II. 834[b] 1, 11 proves that Lycurgus acted in his own name in his third penteterid as well: his vicarious administration would therefore apply to his second (334–330). His son Habron had a distinguished public career ([Plut.] *Vit. Lyc.* § 33), being ταμίας τῶν στρ. in 306/5, and also ὁ ἐπὶ τῇ διοικήσει (C.I.A. II. 167), which

powers which his appointment conferred on him, whether they exceeded or not those of the ταμίας τῶν στρατιωτικῶν—and the latter, we know, were of a much more minute and far-reaching nature than the title of the office would imply[1]—must have been such
His powers as to place in his hands the control of the whole financial administration, though he was no doubt associated with the Council and specific financial bodies (the ἀποδέκται, πωληταί, etc.) in carrying out the details of his office.

Under the direction of Lycurgus Athenian finance took a new lease of life. Boeckh[2] calls him 'almost the only real
Genius for Finance financier that antiquity produced.' He is credited with having doubled the annual revenue, raising it from 600 to 1200 talents[3].

---

would lend colour to the assumption that he acted for his father. The author of the law referred to would appear, from the context, to have been Lycurgus himself, but this is hardly likely (cf. Meier, p. XVI.). The time-limit appears to have been already in force in the time of Eubulus.

[1] Gilbert, *C.A.*, p. 247.
[2] *Staatsh.* I. 569.
[3] [Plut.] *Vit. Lyc.* § 30 τὸ μέγιστον χίλια διακόσια τάλαντα προσόδου τῇ πόλει κατέστησε, πρότερον ἑξήκοντα προσιόντων. [ἑξήκοντα is incredibly low, and ἑξακοσίων (Reiske) is generally accepted: τετρακοσίων καὶ ἑξήκοντα (cf. [Dem.] *Phil.* IV. § 38) Meursius]. At the beginning of the Peloponnesian War, the entire revenues, acc. to Xen. *Anab.* VII. I. 27, amounted to 'quite 1000 talents' (οὐ μεῖον χιλίων ταλάντων). Of this total, 460 were tribute [Pericles (Thuc. II. 13), however, makes the tribute yield 600 t. 'on an average,' 431 B.C.]: the other receipts, therefore, amounted to about 540 t. After the doubling of the tribute in 425 B.C., when, acc. to Andocides (III. 9), it produced more than 1200 t., we still get a rough total of 600 t. for the ordinary revenue, if we assume some exaggeration in Aristophanes' estimate of the total revenue as 2000 t. (*Vesp.* 656 sqq., 422 B.C.).

INTRODUCTION   xix

The total of 18,900 talents[1], which is said to have
passed through his hands during his twelve years'
tenure of office, would give an even considerably greater
average annual revenue of 1575 tal. His character for
integrity is shown by the fact that he was entrusted
by private individuals with sums amounting to 650 tal.
Pausanias states that Lycurgus 'put into the public
treasury 6500 talents more than Pericles, the son of
Xanthippus, got together[2].' These figures, even with

These figures, of course, refer to a date a century earlier
than Lycurgus' administration. From Ps.-Plut.'s statement
(supposing ἑξακοσίων to be right), it might be inferred that
the ordinary revenue had remained more or less constant,
but it must be remembered that the value of money had
fallen considerably in the interval. Gilbert (p. 358) points
out that, if this be taken into account, the figures with
which Lycurgus is credited are not so much at variance
with those of the fifth cent. as at first sight appears, and
adds that, even under the rule of Demetrius of Phalerum,
the revenues still amounted to 1200 t. per annum.

[1] There is some discrepancy between the figures of the
Life and those of the decree of Stratocles in Ps.-Plut.:

(i) [Plut.] *Vit. Lyc.* § 3 ταμίας ἐγένετο...ταλάντων ‚ιδ
(14,000) ἢ ὥς τινες ‚ιηχν' (18,650), *ib.* § 7 πιστευσάμενος δὲ
ἐν παρακαταθήκῃ παρὰ τῶν ἰδιωτῶν σν' (250) τάλαντα ἐφύ-
λαξε.

(ii) *Rog. Strat.* ap. [Plut.] 852 B διανείμας ἐκ τῆς κοινῆς
προσόδου μύρια καὶ ὀκτακισχίλια καὶ ἐνακόσια τάλαντα, πολλὰ
δὲ τῶν ἰδιωτῶν διὰ πίστεως λαβὼν...τὰ πάντα ἑξακόσια πεντή-
κοντα τάλαντα.

Rehdantz (p. 7, n. 29) plausibly remarks that it almost looks
as if the first estimate of Ps.-Plut., viz. 14,000 t., represents
the round product of 12 × 1200; while the second (18,650)
may have arisen from an accidental combination of the
inscriptional μύρια καὶ ὀκτακισχίλια with ἑξακόσια πεντή-
κοντα (the latter being the amount of private deposits), or
from the subtraction of 250 (the amount of private money
given in the *Life*) from the 18,900 t. of the inscr.

[2] Nothing can be deduced, from Pausanias' statement

the reservations that must be made for comparative purposes[1], are surprising, and speak of no ordinary financial genius.

The healthy state of the Athenian revenues was reflected in notable improvements connected with the fleet and its housing. Lycurgus put in commission no fewer than 400 triremes, some of which were overhauled and others built from the keel[2]. Ship-sheds which had long been planned, and work on which had been interrupted from time to time by the pressing military exigencies of the moment, were now completed[3]. Now, too, was finished the famous σκευοθήκη or arsenal, which was begun in 347 under the administration of Eubulus[4]. It was designed to be a storehouse for the rigging belonging to the ships at Zea, the largest of the naval harbours. The architect was Philo, who later built the great portico of the Hall of the Mysteries at Eleusis, and the specifications for the building have been pre-

Naval improvements

(1. 29. 16), as to the comparative annual revenues for Lycurgus and Pericles, as we do not know either the amount of the total contribution which Pausanias postulates for the one or the other, or the *terminus a quo* which he contemplates for Pericles' administration. Assuming, however, that Pausanias makes Lycurgus' total contribution 18,900 t., we shall then have 18,900—6500=12,400 t. as the amount 'got together' by Pericles. Taking twelve years of Pericles' administration, we would get an average annual revenue of, say, 1030 t., which agrees fairly well with Xenophon's estimate of 'quite 1000 talents' (see note 3, p. xviii).

[1] See n. 3, p. xviii.

[2] The normal strength of the fleet was 300 triremes: Xen. *Anab.* VII. 1. 27, Ar. *Ach.* 544/5.

[3] The galley-slips numbered 372, and were distributed as follows: Munychia 82, Zea 196, Cantharus 94.

[4] Cf. Aeschin. *Ctes.* § 25 οἱ ἐπὶ τὸ θεωρικὸν κεχειροτονημένοι...νεώριον καὶ σκευοθήκην ᾠκοδόμουν.

INTRODUCTION xxi

served to us in an inscription[1]. 'Its length was to be 400 feet, its breadth 55...The roof was of tiles, supported on wooden beams and rafters...The whole was divided into a nave and two aisles by two rows of columns; and the aisles were to be provided with every convenience for storing ships' gear....The evident intention was that the building should constantly remain open to public inspection, and that all storage room should be arranged so that its contents were easily visible from the central nave. Even ventilation is provided for in the specification[2].' At the same time the military needs of the state were not neglected, and a plentiful supply of arms and weapons was stored in the acropolis[3].

The Skeuo-theke of Philo

Hardly less important than the naval improvements of Lycurgus, whose post 'practically included the functions of a minister of public works[4],' were the building enterprises which he carried through: it seemed as though the age of Pericles had been revived for Athens. He rebuilt and planted the Lycean gymnasium, where Aristotle taught his 'peripatetic' disciples, and provided it with a palaestra. On the left bank of the Ilissus, he constructed the Panathenaic Stadium, originally, we may believe, laid out by Pisistratus, and destined to be embellished at a later date with the marble seats of Herodes Atticus. Most notable of all, however, was the reconstruction of the Theatre of Dionysus, which Lycurgus carried out as President. The remains of the theatre buildings as they are to-day—notably the marble thrones composing the lowest row of seats, and perhaps the tiers of seats which rise

Public buildings

The Stadium

---

[1] Dittenberger, *Syll.*² 852.
[2] Prof. E. A. Gardner, *Ancient Athens*, pp. 557–9.
[3] *Rog. Strat. ap.* [Plut.] 852 C.
[4] Bury, *H. G.* (1900), p. 826.

above them—are to a large extent the remains of the

Restoration of Dionysiac Theatre

restored theatre of Lycurgus[1]. 'From the age of Pericles to that of Hadrian there was probably no other man who left so lasting an impression [as Lycurgus] upon Athenian architecture[2].'

'The two chief monuments of the Lycurgean epoch—the Panathenaic Stadion and the theatre of Dionysus—

Lycurgus fosters the state religion

were, it must always be remembered, religious, not secular, buildings[3].' The personal piety of Lycurgus was reflected in the solicitous concern for the worship of the gods which marked his administration. Religious festivals which had fallen into desuetude were revived on a more splendid scale. 'He provided for the state gold and silver vessels for use in the processions, and all-gold Victories[4].' More interesting for us and eminently characteristic of the man was the reverence shown

[1] For a discussion of how far the extant stage-buildings (apart from acknowledged later alterations) are the work of Lycurgus' time, see Prof. E. A. Gardner, *Ancient Athens*, c. x. As against Prof. Dörpfeld, who 'regards the whole of the earliest extant scena, foundation, stylobate, and columns alike, as belonging to one time, and that the time of Lycurgus,' he lays stress on the fact that Lycurgus 'only finished what others had begun' (cf. [Plut.] *Vit.* § 6 τὸ ἐν Διονύσου θέατρον ἐπιστατῶν ἐπετέλεσεν, Rog. *Strat.* 852 C ἡμίεργα παραλαβὼν...τὸ θέατρον τὸ Διονυσιακὸν ἐξηργάσατο καὶ ἐπετέλεσεν), and thinks that there is 'no insuperable difficulty in assigning the main plan of the extant buildings to about the same time as the later temple of Dionysus [near the theatre]—perhaps as early as 420 B.C. 'If this be the case,' he adds, 'then we have actually some remains of the stage on which the plays of Sophocles, and Euripides, and Aristophanes were first produced.'

[2] E. A. Gardner, *op. cit.*, p. 399.
[3] Bury, *H. G.* (1900), p. 828.
[4] [Plut.] *Vit.* § 8, Paus. I. 29. 16.

INTRODUCTION xxiii

for the great tragedians—Aeschylus, Sophocles, and Euripides. Lycurgus proposed that bronze statues of them should be set up in the theatre[1], and caused authorised texts of their plays to be prepared and deposited in the public archives, so as to serve as a check on the alterations and interpolations of actors which even at this early date had begun to disfigure them. The official copy of Lycurgus, who thus rendered a service to scholarship, afterwards passed into the library of Alexandria.

Statues
of the great
tragedians

But Lycurgus found scope for his energy in other directions which harmonized with his whole character and with the family traditions under which he had been born and educated. His aristocratic extraction, lofty patriotism, and fervently religious ideals combined to make him a sort of *censor morum*, who 'conceived it as his mission to raise the standard of public and private life[2].' He was an Aristides and a Cato in one. 'He charged himself,' says his biographer, 'with the guardianship of the city and the arrest of malefactors[3],' and doubtless made for himself as many enemies as others have done who have undertaken a similar rôle. By enacting sumptuary laws, and prosecuting relentlessly those whom he conceived to fail in the sacred duty of patriotism, he won for himself the reputation of a second Draco: it was said of him that 'he drew his laws against evil-doers with a pen dipped not in ink, but in death[4].' Diodorus characterizes him

Social
reformer

Public
prosecutor

---

[1] The proposal was opposed by Philinus, a contemporary orator.   [2] J. F. Dobson, *The Greek Orators*, p. 272.

[3] [Plut.] *Vit.* § 10.

[4] *Ibid.* οὐ μέλανι, ἀλλὰ θανάτῳ χρίοντα τὸν κάλαμον κατὰ τῶν πονηρῶν. The credit of the famous *mot* appears to belong to Demades, who said of Draco ὅτι δι' αἵματος, οὐ διὰ μέλανος τοὺς νόμους ἔγραψεν, Plut. *Vit. Sol.* 17.

as 'a very bitter prosecutor[1],' and quotes in his support a vigorous extract from Lycurgus' speech against Lysicles, who had been a general at Chaeronea. Almost all his prosecutions were successful.

Lycurgus enforced his reforms by the severe simplicity of his own private life. Like Socrates, though better off than he, he wore the same dress summer and winter, and shoes only when the weather required them. His reputation for rectitude was such that 'the fact that Lycurgus said so was thought to be a help to a defendant in the law-courts[2].'

Austere private life

The qualities which made the name of Lycurgus feared as much as respected—his outspokenness[3] and unbending integrity—did not fail to meet with recognition from his countrymen, who could at least appreciate what they were too often reluctant to imitate. 'He was repeatedly crowned by the people and awarded statues[4].' These honours, we may believe, had not fallen to him unchallenged, but, like Demosthenes in competition with Cephalus[5], he could boast that, though often prosecuted, he had never been convicted[6]. We are told that he caused a list of all the monies he had disbursed to be inscribed on a pillar and set up in front of the palaestra

Honoured by his countrymen

---

[1] Diod. XVI. 88 οὗτος γὰρ (sc. ὁ Λυκοῦργος) τῶν τότε ῥητόρων μέγιστον ἔχων ἀξίωμα...πικρότατος ἦν κατήγορος. γνοίη δ᾽ ἄν τις αὐτοῦ τὴν ἐν τοῖς λόγοις ἀξίαν καὶ πικρίαν ἐν οἷς τοῦ Λυσικλέους κατηγορῶν λέγει.

[2] [Plut.] *Vit.* § 13. Cf. also the compliments paid him by Hyper. *Eux.* § 12 (col. 9) and by Demosthenes in Rutilius Lupus, *De Fig.* 2. § 4.

[3] He was παρρησιαστὴς διὰ τὴν εὐγένειαν [Plut.] *Vit.* § 26.

[4] *Ib.* § 40.

[5] Dem. *De Cor.* § 251.

[6] [Plut.] *Vit.* § 31 καὶ μηδένα ἀγῶνα ἁλούς, καίτοι πολλῶν κατηγορησάντων.

INTRODUCTION xxv

which he himself had built, for public inspection, and that no one was able to convict him of peculation[1].

His last recorded act, if we may trust his biographer, was in keeping with the fearlessness which had characterized his life. At the point of death he had himself carried to the Metroum and the Council-chamber to render an account of his administration; and after dissipating the charges brought against him by his only accuser—Menesaechmus, who had been one of his victims—he was conveyed back to his house and expired, 324 B.C.[2] Like several of his ancestors, he was honoured with a public funeral, and his tomb was 'opposite Athena Paeonia, in the garden of Melanthius the philosopher[3].'

Death of Lycurgus

After his death, his old enemy Menesaechmus, who had succeeded him in his office, accused him of having left a deficit. The sons were made answerable for the father's alleged shortcomings, and, being unable to pay, were thrown into prison. Demosthenes, then in exile, honoured the memory of his former political supporter by interceding for his children. The letter of Demosthenes may be spurious[4]; but we know that a pupil of Theophrastus, named Democles, as well as the orator Hyperides, pleaded their cause, with the result that they were set at liberty[5].

Demosthenes befriends his children

[1] *Ib.* § 50.
[2] This is the generally accepted date (after Suidas), and is supported by the action recorded of Demosthenes in regard to his children; some give 322 B.C., the year which witnessed the deaths of Demosthenes himself, and of Aristotle.
[3] [Plut.] *Vit.* § 29. Cf. Paus. I. 29. 16, who saw it in the (outer) Ceramicus, on the way to the Academy.
[4] Dem. *Ep.* III.
[5] A fragment of Hyperides' speech has been preserved (*fr.* 121 Blass), which may be quoted as summing up

xxvi INTRODUCTION

Some seventeen years after his death, a decree conferring honours on Lycurgus was passed on the motion of the orator Stratocles. By this decree, which, as has been mentioned, is one of our chief authorities for the administration of Lycurgus, it was provided that a bronze statue of him should be erected in the Ceramicus[1], and that the right of maintenance at the state expense should belong, in perpetuity, to the eldest of his descendants[2]. The decree of Stratocles was apparently appealed to by Lycurgus' son, Lycophron, in claiming that honour on the death, without issue, of his elder brothers, Habron and Lycurgus.

The decree of Stratocles

(ii) THE SPEECH AGAINST LEOCRATES

Fifteen speeches passed current in antiquity under the name of Lycurgus, almost all of which, as far as our knowledge goes, date from between the battle of Chaeronea and his death[3]. The titles of some of them

Lycurgus' life and work: τίνα φήσουσιν οἱ παριόντες αὐτοῦ τὸν τάφον; οὗτος ἐβίω μὲν σωφρόνως, ταχθεὶς δ' ἐπὶ τῇ διοικήσει τῶν χρημάτων εὗρε πόρους, ᾠκοδόμησε δὲ τὸ θέατρον, τὰ νεώρια, τριήρεις ἐποιήσατο, λιμένας· τοῦτον ἡ πόλις ἡμῶν ἠτίμωσε καὶ τοὺς παῖδας ἔδησεν αὐτοῦ.

[1] I.e. in the inner Ceramicus (Agora), at its southern end, where the statue was seen by Pausanias (I. 8. 2): ἐνταῦθα Λ. τε κεῖται χαλκοῦς ὁ Λυκόφρονος. A fragment of the base has been discovered, C. I. A. IV. 1363^b: -ΚΟΦΡΟ-ΝΟΣΒΟ[υτάδης].

[2] The statement of Ps.-Plut. (*Vit.* § 41) that *Lycurgus himself* received this honour *by virtue of the same decree* (i.e. the decree of S.), must be a blunder. Cf. Meier and Blass, *ad loc.*

[3] [Plut.] *Vit.* § 39 φέρονται δὲ τοῦ ῥήτορος λόγοι πεντεκαίδεκα. The list of Suidas gives either fifteen or fourteen, according as the title ἀπολογία πρὸς τὸν αὐτὸν (sc. τὸν

INTRODUCTION xxvii

have obvious reference to matters connected with his administration (e.g. περὶ τῆς διοικήσεως,

The speeches of Lycurgus περὶ τῆς ἱερείας (?), περὶ τῆς ἱερωσύνης (?));

the title of one at least is obscure (πρὸς τὰς μαντείας); eight out of the fifteen speeches are concerned with the prosecution of individuals on various charges. He was associated with Demosthenes in the prosecution of Aristogiton; he appeared against Hyperides in the cases of Euxenippus and Lycophron; and he spoke against the orator Demades. The prosecution of Lysicles, one of the generals at Chaeronea, has been already referred to[1]. The impeachments of Autolycus[2] and Leocrates had this much in common, that they were both concerned with matters arising out of the panic which the news of Chaeronea produced at Athens. Only the speech against Leocrates has been preserved to us entire: of the others we have only inconsiderable fragments[3].

The case against Leocrates turned on the fact that he had fled from Athens at the news of the defeat at

The case of Leocrates Chaeronea, and sailed to Rhodes. After some stay there, he betook himself to Megara, where he engaged in trade for some five or six years. Thereafter he returned to Athens, expecting, presumably, that his desertion would have been forgotten in the interval; but Lycurgus impeached him for treason (εἰσαγγελία προδοσίας).

Such, in brief, were the circumstances; but one or two points call for somewhat closer attention. Rehdantz (among others) raises the question, When exactly did

Δημάδην) ὑπὲρ τῶν εὐθυνῶν is taken to represent two speeches or one. Cf. Blass, *App. ad Lyc.*, p. XLII.

[1] *Supra*, p. xxiv. [2] *C. Leocr.* § 53.

[3] These, along with fragments of Lycurgus' laws and decrees, have been collected by Blass in his edition of the *Leocrates*.

P. L.   c

INTRODUCTION

Leocrates' desertion take place? and under what law was he chargeable? Autolycus, says Lycurgus, was condemned because, though he remained himself, he was responsible for having removed his wife and sons to a place of safety[1]. Following upon this, apparently, the people passed a decree pronouncing absconders generally to be amenable to the charge of treason[2]. Lycurgus, however, makes no use of this decree against Leocrates, presumably because the latter's flight had taken place previous to its passing. Autolycus himself had been condemned on the strength of a decree passed immediately on receipt of the news of Chaeronea, directing that the women and children should be brought inside the walls, and empowering the generals to take such measures as they thought fit for the defence of the city[3]. By this same decree, presumably, Leocrates stood or fell. Did his flight take place before, or after, it was passed? It was obviously in the interest of the prosecutor to establish, as clearly as possible, that the decree was operative before Leocrates absconded; it was equally in his interest, on the other hand, if this was not the case, not to condescend too precisely on the *time* relation, but to contrive to create a presumption that a positive enactment had been transgressed. That Leocrates had really the better of the argument in this matter may be deduced from the circumstance that it is this second line that the orator takes. He dexterously first draws attention to the resolutions adopted at the first Assembly after the battle, and then proceeds: Λεωκράτης δὲ τούτων οὐδενὸς φροντίσας, συσκευασάμενος ἃ εἶχε χρήματα...ᾤχετο φεύγων[4], thus establishing, by implication, the connexion which he desired, but which

Margin: When did Leocrates' flight take place?

Margin: Line taken by Lycurgus

---
[1] C. Leocr. § 53.   [2] Ibid.
[3] Ib. § 16 (decree of Hyperides).   [4] § 17.

INTRODUCTION xxix

we have reason to suppose the facts did not justify, between the decree and Leocrates' flight.

But while Lycurgus is thus at pains to correlate Leocrates' action with a positive measure forbidding it, and indeed appears to have felt that such a correlation was essential to his success, from the point of view of the jury, we cannot doubt that, from his own and higher point of view, the existence of an express **Lycurgus'** legal enactment which he could appeal to **view of the** was entirely a secondary consideration. It **offence** was enough that Leocrates had failed in patriotism—that 'being a man he had not rendered to his country the price of his nurture[1]'—and failure in patriotism constituted, in the eyes of his accuser, the greatest crime of which a citizen could be capable. And here it may be remarked that, to our ideas, Leocrates' offence was nothing worse than cowardice—the term, indeed, which Lycurgus' biographer applies to it[2]—and Aeschines, who refers to the prosecution of Leocrates, speaks of his sailing to Rhodes ὅτι τὸν φόβον ἀνάνδρως ἤνεγκε, 'because he endured not the panic like a man[3].' But to Lycurgus it was the grossest treason: his whole speech is directed to showing that it was so to be regarded, and deserved to be visited with the appropriate penalties. And further, it must be remembered that the Assembly, before which Lycurgus' εἰσαγγελία was brought[4], must have decided that he had a *vera causa* in prosecuting for treason.

[1] § 53 ἀνὴρ ὢν οὐκ ἀπέδωκε τὰ τροφεῖα τῇ πατρίδι.
[2] [Plut.] *Vit.* § 45 ὁ δ' εὐθύνας (sc. ἐγράψατο s. εἷλε) Ἀριστογείτονα καὶ Λεωκράτην καὶ Αὐτόλυκον δειλίας.
[3] *C. Ctes.* § 252.
[4] So Rehdantz, *Einl.* § 13. An εἰσαγγελία might be brought either before the Council or the Assembly: the subsequent procedure, in either case, was practically the same, if the penalty involved exceeded the competence of the Council (see notes to § 1 of the speech): cf. Gilbert, pp. 305–6.

The case was heard, in the ordinary course of things, before a Heliastic court, consisting probably of 1000 dicasts[1], in the summer of 330 B.C., shortly before the final trial of strength between Aeschines and Demosthenes[2]. The speech of Lycurgus has been well described as 'a solemn and earnest protest on behalf of public spirit. There is not a trace of personal feeling, there is no attempt to disparage the man's private life. But the tone throughout is that of a lofty and inexorable indignation[3].'

The trial

Leocrates was acquitted by a single vote[4], and Lycurgus had to be content with a moral triumph. Considering, however, that the defendant had much in favour—that time must have dulled the memory of his offence, that he was not without influential advocates[5], and that the trial took place at a time 'when the common temper of the city was with the accused'—the result was 'a remark-

The result

---

[1] Strictly 1001, to prevent a tie in the voting: cf. Arist. Ἀθ. Πολ. 53. 3, Dem. XXIV. 9 and *Schol.* διὰ τοῦτο δὲ ὁ εἷς προσετέθη ἀεὶ τοῖς δικασταῖς, κ.τ.λ.

[2] The determination of the date of the trial is naturally bound up with the duration of Leocrates' sojourn abroad. Lycurgus makes him stay at Megara, § 21 πλείω ἢ πέντε ἔτη, § 56 πέντε ἔτη, § 145 πλείω πέντ' ἢ ἓξ ἔτη. Also § 58 ἓξ ἔτη συνεχῶς ἀποδημήσας presumably refers to Megara only. Taking these figures in conjunction with § 45 ὀγδόῳ ἔτει τὴν πατρίδα αὐτῶν προσαγορεύων, we must assume that Leocrates stayed for about two years at Rhodes, i.e. he was abroad *eight* years all told. The language of Aeschines (*Ctes.* § 252) ἕτερος δ' ἐκπλεύσας ἰδιώτης εἰς Ῥόδον...πρῴην ποτ' ('only the other day') εἰσηγγέλθη κ.τ.λ., would seem to fix the speech to the earlier part of 330 B.C.

[3] Jebb, *Attic Orators*, vol. II. p. 376.

[4] Aeschin. *C. Ctes.* § 252 ...καὶ ἴσαι αἱ ψῆφοι αὐτῷ ἐγένοντο· εἰ δὲ μία μόνον μετέπεσεν, ὑπερώριστ' ἂν ἢ ἀπέθανεν.

[5] § 139.

INTRODUCTION xxxi

able testimony to the character and to the eloquence of the accuser[1].'

(iii) ANALYSIS

No very precise analysis of the speech, according to the recognised divisions, can be attempted. We can distinguish, it is true, the regular introduction (προοίμιον), narrative (διήγησις), and epilogue (ἐπίλογος); but in the third department of proof (πίστις), Lycurgus allows himself a wide latitude[2]. Still even here we can follow him with some certainty, till the main refutation of the adversary's arguments (λύσις τῶν κεφαλαίων) concludes at § 74: thereafter follows a congeries of appeals to, and examples from, ancient history, the poets, etc., which it is almost impossible to reduce to order, until we come to the epilogue (§§ 149, 150).

Introduction. I pray the gods that I may be a worthy prosecutor (§§ 1–2); the rôle of public prosecutor is unpopular, but I must undertake it: I am not actuated by any personal spite (§§ 3–6); the case before you is unique in the history of crime, and you must give a righteous verdict, with the example of the Areopagus before you. Your decision will be talked of among the Greeks (§§ 7–15).

Narrative. Leocrates' flight to Rhodes, and evidence therefor (§§ 16–20); his migration to Megara, and

[1] Jebb, *Attic Orators*, II. p. 381.
[2] Cf. A. G. Becker in Dobson, *Attic Orators*, vol. IV., where, in reference to technical arrangement, he remarks: 'non semel factum est, ut optimus quisque orator, artis praecepta relinquens, suum sibi eligeret ordinem, quod imprimis conspicuum est in Demosthene...quae artificia Lycurgus vel ignoravit vel contempsit. et in hac gravissima Leocratis accusatione iudicum animos ad suam sententiam pertrahere speravit vi veritatis, sensu recti, et orationis gravitate.'

INTRODUCTION

residence there. Evidence (§§ 21–24); his removal of his family *sacra* from their native soil, and export of corn to Leucas (§§ 25–27).

Argument. The fairness of my procedure is seen in my challenge to the defendant to surrender his slaves, which he declined. He stands self-condemned (§§ 28–36).

Elaboration of the narrative: the pitiable plight of Athens after Chaeronea (§§ 37–45); praise of the men who fell in the battle there (§§ 46–51); acquittal is impossible in the face of precedents (§§ 52–54).

Anticipation of adversary's arguments: (*a*) that he sailed as a merchant (§§ 55–58); (*b*) that he held no position of trust (§§ 59–62); (*c*) that the results described could not have depended upon his single action (§§ 63–67); (*d*) that departure from the city does not necessarily constitute desertion, as witness the case of our ancestors before Salamis (§§ 68–74).

Appeals to ancestral usage, ancient history, etc.:
The attitude of our ancestors to such cases shown by the sanctity they attached to oaths (§§ 75–82). Their love of country shown by the self-sacrifice of Codrus (§§ 83–89). Leocrates will quote the fact of his standing his trial as a proof of his innocence, but as a matter of fact he has been brought here by Providence: remember Callistratus (§§ 90–93). The gods reward piety —'the Place of the Pious' (§§ 94–97). Patriotism inculcated by the poets—Euripides' *Erechtheus*, Homer and Tyrtaeus: the spirit of their poetry displayed at Marathon and Thermopylae (§§ 98–110). Severity of our ancestors towards traitors—Phrynichus, Hipparchus, absconders to Decelea, the man who died at Salamis: decree of Demophantus (§§ 111–127). Salutary example of Sparta (§§ 128–130). Leocrates was false even to the natural instincts of the brute creation (§§ 131–134). His advocates are equally culpable. His own father would have condemned him. They should

INTRODUCTION xxxiii

not presume to secure the acquittal of the guilty on the strength of their own public services (§§135–140). It is a pity your wives and children could not be present in court at a case like this: Leocrates is no ordinary offender (§§ 141–145). He is guilty of the most heinous crimes: it rests with you to punish him (§§ 146–148).

Epilogue. I have done my duty: remember that the land, its trees and its harbours, appeal to you; and pass an exemplary sentence (§§ 149–150).

(iv) LYCURGUS AS AN ORATOR

Lycurgus is reputed to have been a pupil of Isocrates[1]:

A pupil of Isocrates

he was certainly familiar with the great master's works. A training in the epideictic school was not the best preparation for one who needed oratory only for practical purposes; but the influence of the master was sufficiently strong to make the style of the pupil Isocratic at the base. Occasional sentences[2]—and even paragraphs[3]—of the *Leocrates* are cast in an unmistakably Isocratic mould.

---

[1] [Plut.] *Vit.* § 2, where it is also stated that he first studied philosophy as a pupil of Plato.

[2] Cf. § 3 ἐβουλόμην δ᾽ ἄν...ὥσπερ ὠφέλιμόν ἐστι...οὕτω κ.τ.λ., with Isocr. VIII. (*De Pace*) § 36 ἠβουλόμην δ᾽ ἄν, ὥσπερ προσῆκόν ἐστιν...οὕτω κ.τ.λ. and XV. (*Antid.*) § 114; § 7 with Isocr. VII. (*Areopag.*) § 43; § 48 τοιαύταις δὲ γνώμαις χρησάμενοι κ.τ.λ., with Isocr. IV. (*Paneg.*) § 92, and VI. (*Archid.*) § 100; § 70 μόνοι δ᾽ ἀμφοτέρων περιγεγόνασι...ὡς ἑκατέρων προσῆκε, with Isocr. IV. (*Paneg.*) § 72 ἀμφοτέρων κρατήσαντες ὡς ἑκατέρων προσῆκεν; and § 136 εἴ τις ἄρ᾽ ἔστιν αἴσθησις κ.τ.λ., with Isocr. IX. (*Evag.*) § 2, XIV. (*Plataic.*) § 61, XIX. (*Aeginet.*) § 42.

[3] Cf. the whole passage §§ 46–51, which is 'nothing but a condensed funeral speech on those who died at Chaeronea' (J. F. Dobson, *The Greek Orators*, p. 278), and contains, as might be expected, numerous echoes of Isocrates.

To the epideictic style are also to be referred the use of abstracts in the plural¹, of pairs of synonyms², and such phrases as τὰ κοινὰ τῶν ἀδικημάτων (for τὰ κοινὰ ἀδικήματα), τὰ κάλλιστα τῶν ἔργων, etc.³ A noticeable feature is the use of prepositions for the simple (mostly subjective) genitive, in such expressions as τὰ ἐκ τῶν νόμων ἐπιτίμια, ἡ παρὰ τῶν θεῶν βοήθεια, ἡ ὑπὲρ τῶν τοιούτων τιμωρία, etc.⁴

Epideictic features

'His vocabulary and his metaphors,' says Jevons⁵, 'are poetical to an extent which would have been more intelligible in the immaturity of Attic oratory than it is at its close.' This is true, within limits. His metaphors certainly are striking, and his bold personifications, in particular, would have offended the taste of more fastidious stylists⁶. But his vocabulary can hardly be said to be poetical in the sense that it contains a great, or even a considerable, number of words which would not be admitted in good prose⁷.

Poetic flavour

---

¹ Cf. § 18 εὐτυχίαι, §§ 20, 139 χάριτες, §§ 37, 43 φόβοι, § 48 εὔνοιαι, § 78 ἀδικίαι, § 126 τιμωρίαι.

² Cf. § 3 (also § 150) διαφυλάττει καὶ διασώζει, § 91 τοῦ ἀκλεοῦς καὶ ἀδόξου θανάτου, § 141 ἐν ὀφθαλμοῖς ὄντες καὶ ὁρώμενοι.

³ Cf. §§ 6, 48, 102, 104, etc.

⁴ Cf. §§ 4, 9, 15, 26, 79, 97, etc.

⁵ *Greek Literature*⁴, p. 447.

⁶ Cf. § 17, 'he pitied not the harbours of the city...he felt no shame before the walls of his country' (also § 21); § 25, 'he required the sacred things to share his exile'; § 43, 'the country was contributing its trees, the dead their tombs, and the temples their arms'; § 50, 'their lives are their country's crown of glory'; § 61, 'it is death for a city to be laid desolate'; § 150, 'the country and its trees supplicate you: the harbours implore you.'

⁷ The only individual words of a poetic cast which I have been able to discover (excluding the language of the oaths at §§ 77, 81) are: §§ 4, 8, 65 ἐπιτίμιον, §§ 7, 62, 110 αἰών

INTRODUCTION xxxv

In the matter of hiatus, Lycurgus is very inconsistent. In some cases he has obviously been at pains to avoid it by a slight disturbance of the natural order of the words[1]; in others, the little care which would have avoided it has not been exercised[2]; and, generally speaking, open positions, at which Isocrates[3] would have shuddered, are frequent[4]. Attention has been drawn to his lack of skill, or of care, in the connecting of his clauses, and to clumsiness in the building up of his sentences[5]. The καίτοι, which is his favourite instrument for introducing his premises, recurs with somewhat monotonous regularity[6].

Variable in hiatus

All this amounts to saying that, judged by Isocratic, or even less exacting, standards, Lycurgus is inartistic.

(used also by Isocr.), § 82 εὔκλεια, § 99 ἰών (perhaps a quotation), § 130 φιλοψυχεῖν (quoted also from Dem. and Lysias); and the phrase ἐπὶ γήρως ὁδῷ (quoted also from Hyper. v. col. 22).

[1] Cf. § 7 οὐ μικρόν τι μέρος συνέχει τῶν τῆς πόλεως, οὐδ' ἐπ' ὀλίγον χρόνον (where συνέχει | οὐδ' is avoided), § 58 ἄξιον ἐστὶν οὐ μόνον αὐτῷ διὰ τὴν πρᾶξιν ὀργίζεσθαι ταύτην (ὀργίζεσθαι | αὐτῷ), § 83 τοῦτο γὰρ ἔχει μέγιστον ἡ πόλις ὑμῶν ἀγαθόν (ἔχει | ἡ), etc.

[2] Cf. e.g. § 20 πολλοὶ ἐπείσθησαν τῶν μαρτύρων ἢ ἀμνημονεῖν κ.τ.λ., where πολλοὶ τῶν μ. ἐπείσθησαν might have been said.

[3] ὁ φοβούμενος φωνῆεν φωνήεντι συγκροῦσαι (Plut. De Glor. Athen. c. 8).

[4] Cf. e.g. § 52 τοὺς τὰ τῶν ἄλλων φονικὰ ἀδικήματα ὁσιώτατα δικάζοντας, § 65 οὐδὲ τὸν μὲν μεγάλα ἱεροσυλήσαντα ἀπέκτεινον, τὸν δὲ μικρὰ ἐλάττονι τιμωρίᾳ ἐκόλαζον, § 113 τά γε ὀστᾶ αὐτοῦ ἀνορύξαι καὶ ἐξορίσαι ἔξω τῆς Ἀττικῆς, § 117, etc.

[5] J. F. Dobson, *The Greek Orators*, p. 277. He notices the successive γάρ's in §§ 49–50 (to which § 98 might be added), and the accumulation of participles (five) in § 93.

[6] Cf. §§ 37, 39, 44, 52 sq., 74 sq., 77, etc.

The ancient critics justly complained of the inelegance and harshness of his diction[1]. The truth seems to be that Lycurgus cared too much about what he said to care a great deal about how he said it. While he inevitably reproduced some characteristic features of his master's style, he did not 'swallow Isocrates whole,' as Demosthenes was said[2] to have done Isaeus. What artistic skill he did attain appears to have been the result of hard work. 'Not being well gifted,' says his biographer, 'for extempore speaking, he practised night and day; on his couch there was only a sheep-skin and a pillow that he might be easily awakened to his task[3].' We may even suspect that, in his heart, Lycurgus despised the artifices of rhetoric; he was content with a tolerable standard of technical proficiency and relied on the *vis veritatis* to do the rest.

Lycurgus not an artist in style

In addition to the influence of Isocrates, however, Lycurgus' oratory was moulded by other influences which are to be referred rather to the character of the man himself. By birth, education and family tradition, Lycurgus had almost a greater affinity with the elder Athens than with his own, and this affinity reacted on his style. In several ways he claims kin, more than any of the other orators, with Antiphon. In dignity, in a certain aristocratic aloofness, and deep religious feeling, he furnishes striking points of coincidence with the earlier orator, to whose antithetical style he now and again appears to revert. 'Engrafted on the smooth luxuriance of Isocrates, we find once more the archaic, somewhat

Resemblance to Antiphon

---

[1] Dionysius, *Vett. Cens.* v. 3 οὐ μὴν ἀστεῖος οὐδὲ ἡδύς, ἀλλ' ἀναγκαῖος; Hermogenes, περὶ ἰδ., B. 11 πολὺ δὲ τὸ τραχὺ καὶ σφοδρὸν ἔχει χωρὶς ἐπιμελείας.

[2] By the orator Pytheas (Dionysius, *Isaeus*, c. 4).

[3] [Plut.] *Vit.* § 24.

INTRODUCTION xxxvii

rigid stateliness of Antiphon ... The combination of these manners, the Isocratic and the archaic, has an effect which is not harmonious—Lycurgus lacked the force to fuse them[1].' In regard to evolution of style, Lycurgus is thus the child of two distinct epochs.

In the handling of his case Lycurgus, to our ideas, sins gravely against relevancy and a proper sense of proportion. Yet he lectures the jury on the very subject of irrelevant pleading[2]. He undertakes to keep to

His discursiveness
the point in his own case, and at the end of the speech gives himself credit for having done so[3]. And his claim must be allowed, in so far as the absence of any personal abuse of his opponent is concerned: there is no trace of the offensive personalities that mark the passages of arms between Aeschines and Demosthenes. But he has rather an odd conception of what is relevant to the establishing of his case. After he has done so, to all intents and purposes[4], he proceeds to accumulate instances of treason and its punishment, or of patriotism and its reward, which, so far as they have a bearing on the case at all, serve simply to point the moral: 'Leocrates is a traitor and must be punished.' As he himself puts

Lycurgus an educator
it: 'Instruction by means of numerous examples will make your decision easy[5].' Armed with this doctrine, Lycurgus ranges over a wide field for his illustrations. The half-apology with which he introduces some of these betrays some uneasiness in his own mind about their appropriateness[6]; but Lycurgus is an educator as well as an orator—'it will be fitting for all the younger men to hear them[7]'—

[1] Jebb, *Attic Orators*, vol. II. 377.   [2] §§ 11 sqq.   [3] § 149.
[4] He has practically proved his case by § 36.
[5] § 124.   [6] Cf. §§ 95, 98.
[7] § 95 εἰ γὰρ καὶ μυθωδέστερόν ἐστιν, ἀλλ' ἁρμόσει καὶ νῦν ἅπασι τοῖς νεωτέροις ἀκοῦσαι.

and herein his 'instruction by examples' finds its justification[1].

A considerable portion of the speech may fairly be described as a eulogy of the Athens of an earlier day. Lycurgus' excursions into ancient history provide some rather startling details[2], which, while not enhancing the general reputation of the orators for historical accuracy, must be set down, in this case, as interesting and venial slips of memory where there is no intention to falsify. The atmosphere of religion which pervades the speech, and in particular the doctrine which he expounds, more than once[3], touching the divine punishment of sin, reveal a quality of mind which, as already remarked, has much in common with Antiphon, and even with Aeschylus. The extent, indeed, of his moral and religious affinities with the older poet-moralists is attested—in addition to the more practical ways in which he sought to honour them[4]—by his intimate acquaintance with their works and the length at which he quotes them. Aeschines, it is true, indulges in quotation, and Demosthenes retaliates in kind: both, however, show regard for relevancy and proportion. But Lycurgus, 'like a bath-man[5],' deluges his hearers with fifty-five lines of Euripides, and not content with that, inflicts upon them, after another six lines of Homer,

Lycurgus as historian

Moral and religious tone

Lycurgus and the poets

---

[1] For his didactic tone, cf. § 4 τρία γάρ ἐστι τὰ μέγιστα, ἃ διαφυλάττει...τὴν δημοκρατίαν, § 10 δύο γάρ ἐστι τὰ παιδεύοντα τοὺς νέους: also §§ 6, 64, 79.

[2] E.g. § 70 (Eteonicus Spartan commander at Salamis), § 71 (stoning of Alexander of Macedon), § 128 (Pausanias 'king' of Sparta), etc.; cf. Macan, *Herod.* VII–IX, vol. II. pp. 39–41.

[3] Cf. §§ 79, 91–93.   [4] Cf. p. xxiii, *supra*.

[5] Plato, *Rep.* I. 344 D (of Thrasymachus) ὥσπερ βαλανεύς...καταντλήσας...ἀθρόον καὶ πολὺν τὸν λόγον.

INTRODUCTION xxxix

thirty-two lines of Tyrtaeus. Only the most long-suffering jury, one would imagine, would have tolerated such liberties, unless indeed the gratification of their *amour propre* as Athenians may be supposed to have been a reasonable off-set to utter boredom. To Lycurgus himself, of course, the question of the relevancy, or otherwise, of it all never occurred: it has all, to him, a vital bearing on the issue: he is in deadly earnest all the time, and communicates something of his white heat to his hearers.

But though Lycurgus' *laudatio temporis acti* may have been, quite incidentally, pleasing enough to the judges, he would never have stooped to flatter them. Like a good aristocrat, he confesses to an admiration for Sparta, and adduces from there examples of 'law and order' which we may suspect were not entirely congenial to his audience[1]. He addresses to the jury some home truths with regard to the irrelevant pleading which they countenance, and takes occasion, as a speaker who was concerned with securing a verdict at all costs would hardly have done, to eulogise the court of the Areopagus, which, however venerable and venerated even by the Athenians of his own day, was anything but a democratic institution[2].

Praise of Sparta and the Areopagus

Lycurgus' own character, as has been well observed, is the best comment on his oratory[3]. The ancient critics, while justly noting his faults—the harshness of his diction, his tendency to repeat himself, and his 'penchant for legend, tales and poetry[4]'—allowed him the qualities of dignity and impressiveness, and recognised his passion

Ancient critics on Lycurgus

---

[1] § 128 καὶ μή μοι ἀχθεσθῆτε...εἰ πολλάκις μέμνημαι τῶν ἀνδρῶν τούτων.

[2] §§ 12, 52.   [3] Jebb, *Attic Orators*, vol. II. p. 376.

[4] Hermogenes, περὶ ἰδεῶν, B. 11.

INTRODUCTION

for truth and outspokenness[1]. Dio Chrysostom credits him with 'a certain simplicity and nobility of manner,' and Dionysius lays his finger on what is perhaps his outstanding quality when he says: τούτου χρὴ ζηλοῦν μάλιστα τὰς δεινώσεις. By δείνωσις was meant 'the power to bring out the enormity of a wrong,' and the full import of the term cannot be better conveyed than

His δείνωσις in the words of another great literary critic, Quintilian[2]: 'in hoc eloquentiae vis est ut iudicem non in id tantum compellat, in quod ipsa rei natura ducetur, sed aut qui non est, aut maiorem quam est, faciat adfectum. *haec est illa, quae* dinosis *vocatur, rebus indignis asperis invidiosis addens vim oratio.*' As examples of this may be quoted Lycurgus' description of the flight of Leocrates (§ 17), or his powerful picture of the plight of Athens after Chaeronea (§§ 39 sqq.).

(v) SOURCES OF THE TEXT

The manuscript tradition for Lycurgus is substantially the same as for the rest of the minor orators. The chief MS. is the *Codex Crippsianus*, denoted by the letter A, in the British Museum (Brit. Mus. Burneianus 95), and dated to the thirteenth century A.D.[3] It derives its name from John Marten Cripps, who was associated with Edward Daniel Clarke (1769-1822, Jesus College, Cambridge) in travels in the east about the beginning of the nineteenth century; and it was obtained from the famous monastery of Batopedion,

[1] Dionysius, *Vett. Cens.* v. 3 διῃρμένος...σεμνός...φιλαλήθης...παρρησιαστικός.
[2] VI. 2. 24.
[3] An exhaustive description of A will be found in the introduction to Wyse's *Isaeus*, to which I am indebted for the brief account of it given here.

INTRODUCTION xli

on Mount Athos. Ultimately it came into the possession of Charles Burney, on whose death in 1817 it passed into the British Museum. The MS. is on vellum, in folio (ff. 170), and contains, in order, Andocides, Isaeus, Dinarchus, Antiphon, Lycurgus, Gorgias (Helen and Palamedes), Alcidamas (Ulysses), Lesbonax, Herodes. It has been corrected both by the scribe himself (A^1), and by at least one later hand (A^2), which latter, once believed to stop at a point in Antiphon, can be detected (acc. to Thalheim) in §§ 70–86 of Lycurgus. 'The *Codex Crippsianus* is an inferior MS., remarkable neither for age nor integrity, but infected with nearly all the vices to which MSS. are liable[1],' one of the chief being the omission of small single words. It was collated by F. Osann for his edition of Lycurgus published at Jena in 1821, and subsequently by Bekker and Dobson for their respective editions of the Attic orators, 1822–3 and 1828. More recently, the MS. has been examined by (among others) Jernstedt, Blass and Thalheim.

It has now been proved that B = Laurentianus (also obtained from Batopedion, by Janus Lascaris, French Ambassador at Venice, 1503–9), L = Marcianus, M = Brit. Mus. Burneianus 96, P = Ambrosianus, Z = Vratislaviensis (Breslau Public Library), all of the fifteenth century, are derived from A. The dependence of B on A, first argued by Thalheim, was confirmed by Jernstedt, Blass and Buermann: B was shown by H. Reutzel to be the source of LMZ: M was copied from L, Z from M, and M was very probably the source of P. LMP were all written at Florence about the end of the fifteenth century. L 'still possesses a certain historical interest as the source of the Aldine edition of 1513, which repeats all its lacunae and many of its peculiar readings[2].'

[1] *Op. cit.* p. xxxvi. [2] *Op. cit.* p. iv.

INTRODUCTION

The only other MS. of equal authority to A is the *Codex Oxoniensis* N = Bodleianus Misc. 208, of the end of the fourteenth century, which, however, is not complete for Lycurgus, containing only §§ 1–34. 4 προδοσίας and §§ 98. 4 τὸν Ποσειδῶνος—147. 5 ἐγκατα[λιπών. N and A descend from a common archetype, which Blass (but probably without justification) describes as 'multis locis sive correctum sive varia lectione auctum[1].' N has also been corrected (but to a lesser extent than A), both by the first hand (N[1]) and by a later conjectural critic of some learning (N[2]). The readings of N agree in the main with those of A[1], as against A pr. N and A[1] may therefore be regarded, on the whole, as preserving the text of the archetype, but A[1] is not always trustworthy. N has been collated both by Blass and by Thalheim.

'The *editio princeps* of 1513 was not only derived from an inferior MS. but teemed with typographical errors ... The efforts of three centuries were spent on purging the text of the Aldine[2].' This remark is no doubt eminently true of the speech of Lycurgus. The text of the *Leocrates*, though purified to a great extent by the labours of successive scholars, from Taylor and Reiske onwards, still provides a considerable field for the textual critic, though the field has been narrowed since van den Es, in 1854, concluded his critical notes with the following suggestive observation: 'ne quis in una oratione tot vitia miretur. notum est Lycurgi Leocrateam ludi magistris in deliciis esse habitam: veterum scripta autem nulla plus mendorum contraxerunt, quam quae ab iis terebantur et explicabantur; frequentius etiam in discipulorum usum describebantur eoque paullatim magis atque magis corrumpebantur.'

[1] Praef. ad Lycurgum, p. iv.
[2] Wyse, *op. cit.* p. xxxvi.

ΚΑΤΑ ΛΕΩΚΡΑΤΟΥΣ

ΥΠΟΘΕΣΙΣ

Μετὰ τὰ ἐν Χαιρωνείᾳ δεινὰ ψήφισμα ποιεῖ ὁ τῶν Ἀθηναίων δῆμος, ὥστε μήτε τινὰ ἔξω γενέσθαι τῆς πόλεως, μήτε μὴν ἐκθέσθαι παῖδας καὶ γυναῖκας. Λεωκράτης οὖν τις ἐξελθὼν τῆς πόλεως, καὶ ἀφικόμενος ἐν Ῥόδῳ καὶ πάλιν ἐν Μεγάροις, ἦλθεν ἐν Ἀθήναις· καὶ παρρησιαζομένου αὐτοῦ κατηγορίαν ποιεῖται ὁ Λυκοῦργος αὐτοῦ ὡς προδότου. Ἡ δὲ στάσις ὅρος ἀντονομάζων· ὁμολογεῖ γὰρ καὶ ὁ Λεωκράτης ἀπολιπεῖν τὴν πόλιν, οὐ μέντοι προδιδόναι. ἄλλοι στοχασμὸν ἀπὸ γνώμης, ὡς τοῦ μὲν ἐξελθεῖν ὁμολογουμένου, ἀμφιβαλλομένης δὲ τῆς προαιρέσεως, ποίᾳ γνώμῃ ἐξῆλθεν, εἴτ' ἐπὶ προδοσίᾳ εἴτ' ἐπὶ ἐμπορίᾳ. ἄλλοι δὲ ἀντίστασιν· λέγει γὰρ οὐκ ἐπὶ προδοσίᾳ τῆς πόλεως ἐξελθεῖν, ἀλλ' ἐπὶ ἐμπορίᾳ. ἔοικε δὲ ἡ τοῦ λόγου ὑπόθεσις τῇ τοῦ κατὰ Αὐτολύκου.

Δικαίαν, ὦ Ἀθηναῖοι, καὶ εὐσεβῆ καὶ ὑπὲρ ὑμῶν καὶ ὑπὲρ τῶν θεῶν τὴν ἀρχὴν τῆς κατηγορίας Λεωκράτους τοῦ κρινομένου ποιήσομαι. εὔχομαι γὰρ τῇ Ἀθηνᾷ καὶ τοῖς ἄλλοις θεοῖς καὶ τοῖς ἥρωσι τοῖς κατὰ τὴν πόλιν καὶ τὴν χώραν ἱδρυμένοις, εἰ μὲν εἰσήγγελκα Λεωκράτη δικαίως καὶ κρίνω τὸν προδόντ' αὐτῶν καὶ τοὺς νεὼς καὶ τὰ ἕδη καὶ τὰ τεμένη καὶ τὰς ἐν τοῖς νόμοις τιμὰς καὶ θυσίας τὰς ὑπὸ τῶν ὑμετέρων προγόνων παραδεδομένας, ἐμὲ 2 μὲν ἄξιον ἐν τῇ τήμερον ἡμέρᾳ τῶν Λεωκράτους ἀδικημάτων κατήγορον πυιῆσαι, ὃ καὶ τῷ δήμῳ καὶ τῇ πόλει συμφέρει, ὑμᾶς δ' ὡς ὑπὲρ πατέρων καὶ παίδων καὶ γυναικῶν καὶ πατρίδος καὶ ἱερῶν βουλευομένους, καὶ ἔχοντας ὑπὸ τῇ ψήφῳ τὸν προδότην ἁπάντων τούτων, ἀπαραιτήτους δικαστὰς καὶ νῦν καὶ εἰς τὸν λοιπὸν χρόνον γενέσθαι τοῖς τὰ τοιαῦτα καὶ τηλικαῦτα παρανομοῦσιν· εἰ δὲ μήτε τὸν προδόντα τὴν πατρίδα μήτε τὸν ἐγκαταλιπόντα τὴν πόλιν καὶ τὰ ἱερὰ εἰς τουτονὶ τὸν ἀγῶνα καθίστημι, σωθῆναι αὐτὸν ἐκ τοῦ κινδύνου καὶ ὑπὸ τῶν θεῶν καὶ ὑφ' ὑμῶν τῶν δικαστῶν.

Ἐβουλόμην δ' ἄν, ὦ ἄνδρες, ὥσπερ ὠφέλιμόν ἐστι τῇ πόλει εἶναι τοὺς κρίνοντας ἐν ταύτῃ τοὺς παρανομοῦντας, οὕτω καὶ φιλάνθρωπον αὐτὸ παρὰ τοῖς πολλοῖς ὑπειλῆφθαι· νῦν δὲ περιέστηκεν εἰς τοῦτο, ὥστε τὸν ἰδίᾳ κινδυνεύοντα καὶ ὑπὲρ τῶν κοινῶν ἀπεχθανόμενον οὐ φιλόπολιν, ἀλλὰ φιλοπράγμονα δοκεῖν εἶναι, οὐ δικαίως οὐδὲ συμφερόντως τῇ πόλει. τρία γάρ ἐστι τὰ μέγιστα, ἃ διαφυλάττει καὶ διασῴζει τὴν δημοκρατίαν καὶ τὴν τῆς πόλεως εὐδαιμονίαν, πρῶτον μὲν ἡ τῶν νόμων τάξις, δεύτερον δ' ἡ τῶν δικαστῶν ψῆφος, τρίτον δ' ἡ τούτοις τἀδικήματα παραδιδοῦσα κρίσις. ὁ μὲν γὰρ νόμος πέφυκε προλέγειν ἃ μὴ δεῖ πράττειν, ὁ δὲ κατήγορος μηνύειν τοὺς ἐνόχους τοῖς ἐκ τῶν νόμων ἐπιτιμίοις καθεστῶτας, ὁ δὲ δικαστὴς κολάζειν τοὺς ὑπ' ἀμφοτέρων τούτων ἀποδειχθέντας αὐτῷ, ὥστ' οὔθ' ὁ νόμος οὔθ' ἡ τῶν δικαστῶν ψῆφος ἄνευ τοῦ παραδώσοντος αὐτοῖς τοὺς ἀδικοῦντας ἰσχύει. Ἐγὼ δ', ὦ Ἀθηναῖοι, εἰδὼς Λεωκράτην φυγόντα μὲν τοὺς ὑπὲρ τῆς πατρίδος κινδύνους, ἐγκαταλιπόντα δὲ τοὺς αὑτοῦ πολίτας, προδεδωκότα δὲ πᾶσαν τὴν ὑμετέραν δύναμιν, ἅπασι δὲ τοῖς γεγραμμένοις ἔνοχον ὄντα, ταύτην τὴν εἰσαγγελίαν ἐποιησάμην, οὔτε δι' ἔχθραν οὐδεμίαν οὔτε διὰ φιλονεικίαν οὐδ' ἡντινοῦν τοῦτον τὸν ἀγῶνα προελόμενος, ἀλλ' αἰσχρὸν εἶναι νομίσας τοῦτον περιορᾶν εἰς τὴν ἀγορὰν ἐμβάλλοντα καὶ τῶν κοινῶν ἱερῶν μετέχοντα, τῆς τε πατρίδος ὄνειδος καὶ πάντων ὑμῶν γεγενημένον. πολίτου γάρ ἐστι δικαίου, μὴ διὰ τὰς ἰδίας ἔχθρας εἰς τὰς κοινὰς κρίσεις καθιστάναι τοὺς τὴν πόλιν μηδὲν ἀδικοῦντας, ἀλλὰ τοὺς εἰς τὴν πατρίδα τι παρανομοῦντας ἰδίους ἐχθροὺς εἶναι νομίζειν, καὶ τὰ κοινὰ τῶν ἀδικημάτων κοινὰς καὶ τὰς προφάσεις ἔχειν τῆς πρὸς αὐτοὺς διαφορᾶς. Ἅπαντας μὲν οὖν χρὴ νομίζειν μεγάλους εἶναι τοὺς δημοσίους ἀγῶνας, μάλιστα δὲ τοῦτον ὑπὲρ οὗ νῦν μέλλετε τὴν ψῆφον φέρειν. ὅταν μὲν γὰρ τὰς τῶν παρανόμων γραφὰς δικάζητε, τοῦτο μόνον ἐπανορθοῦτε καὶ ταύτην τὴν πρᾶξιν κωλύετε, καθ' ὅσον ἂν τὸ ψήφισμα μέλλῃ βλάπτειν τὴν πόλιν· ὁ δὲ νῦν ἐνεστηκὼς ἀγὼν οὐ μικρόν τι μέρος συνέχει τῶν τῆς πόλεως οὐδ' ἐπ' ὀλίγον χρόνον, ἀλλ' ὑπὲρ ὅλης τῆς πατρίδος καὶ κατὰ παντὸς τοῦ αἰῶνος ἀείμνηστον καταλείψει τοῖς ἐπιγιγνομένοις

8 τὴν κρίσιν. οὕτω γάρ ἐστι δεινὸν τὸ γεγενημένον ἀδίκημα καὶ τηλικοῦτον ἔχει τὸ μέγεθος, ὥστε μήτε κατηγορίαν [μήτε τιμωρίαν] ἐνδέχεσθαι εὑρεῖν ἀξίαν μήτ' ἐν τοῖς νόμοις ὡρίσθαι τιμωρίαν [ἀξίαν] τῶν ἁμαρτημάτων. τί γὰρ χρὴ παθεῖν τὸν ἐκλιπόντα μὲν τὴν πατρίδα, μὴ βοηθήσαντα δὲ τοῖς πατρῴοις ἱεροῖς, ἐγκαταλιπόντα δὲ τὰς τῶν προγόνων θήκας, ἅπασαν δὲ τὴν πόλιν ὑποχείριον τοῖς πολεμίοις παραδόντα; τὸ μὲν γὰρ μέγιστον καὶ ἔσχατον τῶν τιμημάτων, θάνατος, ἀναγκαῖον μὲν ἐκ τῶν νόμων ἐπιτίμιον, ἔλαττον δὲ τῶν 9 Λεωκράτους ἀδικημάτων καθέστηκε. παρεῖσθαι δὲ τὴν ὑπὲρ τῶν τοιούτων τιμωρίαν συμβέβηκεν, ὦ ἄνδρες, οὐ διὰ ῥᾳθυμίαν τῶν τότε νομοθετούντων, ἀλλὰ διὰ τὸ μὴ ἐν τοῖς πρότερον χρόνοις γεγενῆσθαι τοιοῦτον μηδέν, μηδ' ἐν τοῖς μέλλουσιν ἐπίδοξον εἶναι γενήσεσθαι. διὸ καὶ μάλιστ', ὦ ἄνδρες, δεῖ ὑμᾶς γενέσθαι μὴ μόνον τοῦ νῦν ἀδικήματος δικαστάς, ἀλλὰ καὶ νομοθέτας. ὅσα μὲν γὰρ τῶν ἀδικημάτων νόμος τις διώρικε, ῥᾴδιον τούτῳ κανόνι χρωμένους κολάζειν τοὺς παρανομοῦντας· ὅσα δὲ μὴ σφόδρα περιείληφεν, ἑνὶ ὀνόματι προσαγορεύσας, μείζω δὲ τούτων τις ἠδίκηκεν, ἅπασι δ' ὁμοίως ἔνοχός ἐστιν, ἀναγκαῖον τὴν ὑμετέραν κρίσιν κατα-
10 λείπεσθαι παράδειγμα τοῖς ἐπιγιγνομένοις. εὖ δ' ἴστε, ὦ ἄνδρες, ὅτι οὐ μόνον τοῦτον νῦν κολάσετε κατεψηφισμένοι, ἀλλὰ καὶ τοὺς νεωτέρους ἅπαντας ἐπ' ἀρετὴν προτρέψετε. δύο γάρ ἐστι τὰ παιδεύ-

ΚΑΤΑ ΛΕΩΚΡΑΤΟΥΣ 5

οντα τοὺς νέους, ἥ τε τῶν ἀδικούντων τιμωρία, καὶ ἡ τοῖς ἀνδράσι τοῖς ἀγαθοῖς διδομένη δωρεά· πρὸς ἑκάτερον δὲ τούτων ἀποβλέποντες, τὴν μὲν διὰ τὸν φόβον φεύγουσι, τῆς δὲ διὰ τὴν δόξαν ἐπιθυμοῦσι. 4 διὸ δεῖ, ὦ ἄνδρες, προσέχειν τούτῳ τῷ ἀγῶνι, καὶ μηδὲν περὶ πλείονος ποιήσασθαι τοῦ δικαίου.

Ποιήσομαι δὲ κἀγὼ τὴν κατηγορίαν δικαίαν, 11 οὔτε ψευδόμενος οὐδὲν οὔτ' ἔξω τοῦ πράγματος λέγων. οἱ μὲν γὰρ πλεῖστοι τῶν εἰς ὑμᾶς εἰσιόντων πάντων ἀτοπώτατον ποιοῦσιν· ἢ γὰρ συμβουλεύουσιν ἐνταῦθα περὶ τῶν κοινῶν πραγμάτων, ἢ κατηγοροῦσι καὶ διαβάλλουσι πάντα μᾶλλον ἢ περὶ οὗ μέλλετε τὴν ψῆφον φέρειν. ἔστι δ' οὐδέτερον τούτων χαλεπόν, οὔθ' ὑπὲρ ὧν μὴ βουλεύεσθε γνώμην ἀποφήνασθαι, οὔθ' ὑπὲρ ὧν μηδεὶς ἀπολογήσεται κατηγορίαν εὑρεῖν. ἀλλ' οὐ δίκαιον 12 ὑμᾶς μὲν ἀξιοῦν δικαίαν τὴν ψῆφον φέρειν, αὐτοὺς δὲ μὴ δικαίαν τὴν κατηγορίαν ποιεῖσθαι. τούτων δ' αἴτιοι ὑμεῖς ἐστε, ὦ ἄνδρες· τὴν γὰρ ἐξουσίαν ταύτην δεδώκατε τοῖς ἐνθάδ' εἰσιοῦσι, καὶ ταῦτα κάλλιστον ἔχοντες τῶν Ἑλλήνων παράδειγμα τὸ ἐν Ἀρείῳ πάγῳ συνέδριον, ὃ τοσοῦτον διαφέρει τῶν ἄλλων δικαστηρίων, ὥστε καὶ παρ' αὐτοῖς ὁμολογεῖσθαι τοῖς ἁλισκομένοις δικαίαν ποιεῖσθαι τὴν κρίσιν. πρὸς ὃ δεῖ καὶ ὑμᾶς ἀποβλέποντας 13 μὴ ἐπιτρέπειν τοῖς ἔξω τοῦ πράγματος λέγουσιν· οὕτω γὰρ ἔσται τοῖς τε κρινομένοις ἄνευ διαβολῆς ὁ ἀγών, καὶ τοῖς διώκουσιν ἥκιστα συκοφαντεῖν, καὶ ὑμῖν εὐορκοτάτην ⟨τὴν⟩ ψῆφον ἐνεγκεῖν. ἀδύνατον γάρ ἐστιν ἄνευ τοῦ ⟨τοιούτου⟩ λόγου, μὴ δικαίως δεδιδαγμένους δικαίαν θέσθαι τὴν ψῆφον.

14 Δεῖ δ', ὦ ἄνδρες, μηδὲ ταῦτα λαθεῖν ὑμᾶς, ὅτι 5 οὐχ ὅμοιός ἐστιν ὁ ἀγὼν περὶ τούτου καὶ τῶν ἄλλων ἰδιωτῶν. περὶ μὲν γὰρ ἀγνῶτος ἀνθρώπου τοῖς Ἕλλησιν ἐν ὑμῖν αὐτοῖς ἐδοκεῖτ' ἂν ἢ καλῶς ἢ καὶ φαύλως ἐψηφίσθαι· περὶ δὲ τούτου ὅ τι ἂν βουλεύσησθε, παρὰ πᾶσι τοῖς Ἕλλησιν ἔσται λόγος, οἳ ἴσασι τὰ τῶν προγόνων τῶν ὑμετέρων ἔργα ἐναντιώτατα τοῖς τούτῳ διαπεπραγμένοις ὄντα. ἐπιφανὴς γάρ ἐστι διὰ τὸν ἔκπλουν τὸν εἰς Ῥόδον καὶ τὴν ἀπαγγελίαν ἣν ἐποιήσατο καθ' ὑμῶν πρός τε τὴν πόλιν τὴν τῶν Ῥοδίων καὶ τῶν 15 ἐμπόρων τοῖς ἐπιδημοῦσιν ἐκεῖ, οἳ πᾶσαν τὴν οἰκουμένην περιπλέοντες δι' ἐργασίαν ἀπήγγελλον ἅμα περὶ τῆς πόλεως ἃ Λεωκράτους ἠκηκόεσαν. ὥστε περὶ πολλοῦ ποιητέον ἐστὶν ὀρθῶς βουλεύσασθαι περὶ αὐτοῦ. εὖ γὰρ ἴστε, ὦ Ἀθηναῖοι, ὅτι ᾧ πλεῖστον διαφέρετε τῶν ἄλλων ἀνθρώπων, τῷ πρός τε τοὺς θεοὺς εὐσεβῶς καὶ πρὸς τοὺς γονεῖς ὁσίως καὶ πρὸς τὴν πατρίδα φιλοτίμως ἔχειν, τούτου πλεῖστον ἀμελεῖν δόξαιτ' ἄν, εἰ τὴν παρ' ὑμῶν οὗτος διαφύγοι τιμωρίαν.

16 Δέομαι δ' ὑμῶν, ὦ Ἀθηναῖοι, ἀκοῦσαί μου τῆς 6 κατηγορίας διὰ τέλους, καὶ μὴ ἄχθεσθαι, ἐὰν ἄρξωμαι ἀπὸ τῶν τῇ πόλει τότε συμβάντων, ἀλλὰ τοῖς αἰτίοις ὀργίζεσθαι καὶ δι' οὓς ἀναγκάζομαι νῦν

μεμνῆσθαι περὶ αὐτῶν. Γεγενημένης γὰρ τῆς ἐν Χαιρωνείᾳ μάχης καὶ συνδραμόντων ἁπάντων ὑμῶν εἰς τὴν ἐκκλησίαν ἐψηφίσατο ὁ δῆμος, παῖδας μὲν καὶ γυναῖκας ἐκ τῶν ἀγρῶν εἰς τὰ τείχη κατακομίζειν, τοὺς δὲ στρατηγοὺς τάττειν εἰς τὰς φυλακὰς τῶν Ἀθηναίων καὶ τῶν ἄλλων τῶν οἰκούντων Ἀθήνησι, καθ' ὅ τι ἂν αὐτοῖς δοκῇ. Λεωκράτης 17 δὲ τούτων οὐδενὸς φροντίσας, συσκευασάμενος ἃ εἶχε χρήματα, μετὰ τῶν οἰκετῶν ἐπὶ τὸν λέμβον κατεκόμισε, τῆς νεὼς ἤδη περὶ τὴν ἀκτὴν ἐξορμούσης, καὶ περὶ δείλην ὀψίαν αὐτὸς μετὰ τῆς ἑταίρας Εἰρηνίδος κατὰ μέσην τὴν ἀκτὴν διὰ τῆς πυλίδος ἐξελθὼν πρὸς τὴν ναῦν προσέπλευσε καὶ ᾤχετο φεύγων, οὔτε τοὺς λιμένας τῆς πόλεως ἐλεῶν, ἐξ ὧν ἀνήγετο, οὔτε τὰ τείχη τῆς πατρίδος αἰσχυνόμενος, ὧν τὴν φυλακὴν ἔρημον τὸ καθ' αὑτὸν μέρος κατέλειπεν· οὐδὲ τὴν ἀκρόπολιν καὶ τὸ ἱερὸν τοῦ Διὸς τοῦ σωτῆρος καὶ τῆς Ἀθηνᾶς τῆς σωτείρας ἀφορῶν καὶ προδιδοὺς ἐφοβήθη, οὓς αὐτίκα σώσοντας ἑαυτὸν ἐκ τῶν κινδύνων ἐπικαλέσεται. καταχθεὶς δὲ καὶ ἀφικόμενος εἰς Ῥόδον, ὥσπερ 18 τῇ πατρίδι μεγάλας εὐτυχίας εὐαγγελιζόμενος, ἀπήγγειλεν ὡς τὸ μὲν ἄστυ τῆς πόλεως ἑαλωκὸς καταλίποι, τὸν δὲ Πειραιέα πολιορκούμενον, αὐτὸς δὲ μόνος διασωθεὶς ἥκοι· καὶ οὐκ ᾐσχύνθη τὴν τῆς πατρίδος ἀτυχίαν αὐτοῦ σωτηρίαν προσαγορεύσας. οὕτω δὲ σφόδρα ταῦτ' ἐπίστευσαν οἱ Ῥόδιοι, ὥστε τριήρεις πληρώσαντες τὰ πλοῖα κατῆγον, καὶ τῶν ἐμπόρων καὶ τῶν ναυκλήρων οἱ παρεσκευασμένοι δεῦρο πλεῖν αὐτοῦ τὸν σῖτον ἐξείλοντο καὶ τἆλλα χρήματα διὰ τοῦτον. Καὶ ὅτι ταῦτ' ἀληθῆ λέγω, ἀναγνώσεται ὑμῖν τὰς μαρτυρίας ἁπάντων, πρῶτον μὲν τὰς τῶν γειτόνων καὶ τῶν ἐν τῷ τόπῳ τούτῳ κατοικούντων, οἳ τοῦτον ἴσασιν ἐν τῷ πολέμῳ φυγόντα καὶ ἐκπλεύσαντα Ἀθήνηθεν, ἔπειτα τῶν παραγενομένων εἰς Ῥόδον, ὅτε Λεωκράτης ταῦτ' ἀπήγγελλε, μετὰ δὲ ταῦτα τὴν Φυρκίνου μαρτυρίαν, ὃν καὶ ὑμῶν ⟨ἴσασιν⟩ οἱ πολλοὶ κατηγοροῦντα ἐν τῷ δήμῳ τούτου, ὡς καὶ μεγάλα βεβλαφὼς εἴη τὴν πεντηκοστήν, μετέχων αὐτῆς.

Πρὸ δὲ τοῦ ἀναβαίνειν τοὺς μάρτυρας βραχέα βούλομαι διαλεχθῆναι ὑμῖν. οὐ γὰρ ἀγνοεῖτε, ὦ ἄνδρες, οὔτε τὰς παρασκευὰς τῶν κρινομένων, οὔτε τὰς δεήσεις τῶν ἐξαιτουμένων, ἀλλ' ἀκριβῶς ἐπίστασθε, ὅτι χρημάτων ἕνεκα καὶ χάριτος πολλοὶ ἐπείσθησαν τῶν μαρτύρων ἢ ἀμνημονεῖν ἢ μὴ ἐλθεῖν ἢ ἑτέραν πρόφασιν εὑρεῖν. ἀξιοῦτε οὖν τοὺς μάρτυρας ἀναβαίνειν καὶ μὴ ὀκνεῖν, μηδὲ περὶ πλείονος ποιεῖσθαι τὰς χάριτας ὑμῶν καὶ τῆς πόλεως, ἀλλ' ἀποδιδόναι τῇ πατρίδι τἀληθῆ καὶ τὰ δίκαια, καὶ μὴ λείπειν τὴν τάξιν ταύτην, μηδὲ μιμεῖσθαι Λεωκράτην, ἢ λαβόντας τὰ ἱερὰ κατὰ τὸν νόμον ἐξομόσασθαι. ἐὰν δὲ μηδέτερον τούτων ποιῶσιν, ὑπὲρ ὑμῶν καὶ τῶν νόμων καὶ τῆς δημοκρατίας κλητεύσομεν αὐτούς. Λέγε τὰς μαρτυρίας.

ΚΑΤΑ ΛΕΩΚΡΑΤΟΥΣ

ΜΑΡΤΥΡΙΑΙ

8 Μετὰ ταῦτα τοίνυν, ὦ ἄνδρες, ἐπειδὴ χρόνος ἐγένετο καὶ ἀφικνεῖτο Ἀθήνηθεν πλοῖα εἰς τὴν Ῥόδον καὶ φανερὸν ἦν ὅτι οὐδὲν δεινὸν ἐγεγόνει περὶ τὴν πόλιν, φοβηθεὶς ἐκπλεῖ πάλιν ἐκ τῆς Ῥόδου καὶ ἀφικνεῖται εἰς Μέγαρα· καὶ ᾤκει ἐν Μεγάροις πλείω ἢ πέντε ἔτη προστάτην ἔχων Μεγαρέα, οὐδὲ τὰ ὅρια τῆς χώρας αἰσχυνόμενος, ἀλλ' ἐν γειτόνων τῆς ἐκθρεψάσης αὐτὸν πατρίδος μετοικῶν. καὶ οὕτως αὐτοῦ κατεγνώκει ἀίδιον φυγήν, ὥστε μεταπεμψάμενος ἐντεῦθεν Ἀμύνταν τὸν τὴν ἀδελφὴν ἔχοντα αὐτοῦ τὴν πρεσβυτέραν καὶ τῶν φίλων Ἀντιγένην Ξυπεταιόνα, καὶ δεηθεὶς τοῦ κηδεστοῦ πρίασθαι παρ' αὐτοῦ τἀνδράποδα καὶ τὴν οἰκίαν, ἀποδόσθαι ταλάντου, κἀπὸ τούτου προσέταξε τοῖς τε χρήσταις ἀποδοῦναι τὰ ὀφειλόμενα καὶ τοὺς ἐράνους διενεγκεῖν, τὸ δὲ λοιπὸν αὐτῷ ἀποδοῦναι. διοικήσας δὲ ταῦτα πάντα ὁ Ἀμύντας, αὐτὸς πάλιν ἀποδίδοται τἀνδράποδα πέντε καὶ τριάκοντα μνῶν Τιμοχάρει Ἀχαρνεῖ τῷ τὴν νεωτέραν ἔχοντι τούτου ἀδελφήν· ἀργύριον δὲ οὐκ ἔχων δοῦναι ὁ Τιμοχάρης, συνθήκας ποιησάμενος καὶ θέμενος παρὰ Λυσικλεῖ, μίαν μνᾶν τόκον ἔφερε τῷ Ἀμύντᾳ. ἵνα δὲ μὴ λόγον οἴησθε εἶναι, ἀλλ' εἰδῆτε τὴν ἀλήθειαν, ἀναγνώσεται καὶ τούτων ὑμῖν τὰς μαρτυρίας. εἰ μὲν οὖν ζῶν ἐτύγχανεν ὁ Ἀμύντας, ἐκεῖνον ⟨ἂν⟩ αὐτὸν παρειχόμην· νυνὶ δ' ὑμῖν καλῶ τοὺς συνειδότας. Καί μοι λέγε

ΛΥΚΟΥΡΓΟΥ

ταύτην τὴν μαρτυρίαν, ὡς ἐπρίατο παρὰ Λεωκράτους ἐν Μεγάροις τὰ ἀνδράποδα Ἀμύντας καὶ τὴν οἰκίαν.

ΜΑΡΤΥΡΙΑ

24 Ἀκούσατε δὲ καὶ ὡς ἀπέλαβε τετταράκοντα μνᾶς παρ' Ἀμύντου Φιλόμηλος Χολαργεὺς καὶ Μενέλαος ὁ πρεσβεύσας ὡς βασιλέα.

ΜΑΡΤΥΡΙΑ

Λαβὲ δέ μοι καὶ τὴν Τιμοχάρους τοῦ πριαμένου τἀνδράποδα παρ' Ἀμύντου πέντε καὶ τριάκοντα μνῶν, καὶ τὰς συνθήκας.

ΜΑΡΤΥΡΙΑ ΣΥΝΘΗΚΑΙ

25 Τῶν μὲν μαρτύρων ἀκηκόατε, ὦ ἄνδρες· ἄξιον δ' ἐστὶν ἐφ' οἷς μέλλω λέγειν ἀγανακτῆσαι καὶ μισῆσαι τουτονὶ Λεωκράτην. οὐ γὰρ ἐξήρκεσε τὸ σῶμα τὸ ἑαυτοῦ καὶ τὰ χρήματα μόνον ὑπεκθέσθαι, ἀλλὰ καὶ τὰ ἱερὰ τὰ πατρῷα, ἃ τοῖς ὑμετέροις νομίμοις καὶ πατρίοις ἔθεσιν οἱ πρόγονοι παρέδοσαν αὐτῷ ἱδρυσάμενοι, ταῦτα μετεπέμψατο εἰς Μέγαρα καὶ ἐξήγαγεν ἐκ τῆς χώρας, οὐδὲ τὴν ἐπωνυμίαν τῶν πατρῴων ἱερῶν φοβηθείς, ὅτι ἐκ τῆς πατρίδος αὐτὰ κινήσας συμφεύγειν αὐτῷ, ἐκλιπόντα τοὺς νεὼς καὶ τὴν χώραν ἣν κατεῖχεν, ἠξίωσε, καὶ ἱδρῦσθαι ἐπὶ ξένης καὶ ἀλλοτρίας, καὶ εἶναι ὀθνεῖα τῇ χώρᾳ καὶ τοῖς νομίμοις τοῖς
26 κατὰ τὴν Μεγαρέων πόλιν εἰθισμένοις. καὶ οἱ μὲν

πατέρες ὑμῶν τῇ Ἀθηνᾷ ὡς τὴν χώραν εἰληχυίᾳ ὁμώνυμον αὐτὴν τὴν πατρίδα προσηγόρευον Ἀθήνας, ἵν᾽ οἱ τιμῶντες τὴν θεὸν τὴν ὁμώνυμον αὐτῇ πόλιν μὴ ἐγκαταλίπωσι· Λεωκράτης δ᾽ οὔτε νομίμων οὔτε πατρίων οὔθ᾽ ἱερῶν φροντίσας τὸ καθ᾽ ἑαυτὸν ἐξαγώγιμον ὑμῖν καὶ τὴν παρὰ τῶν θεῶν βοήθειαν ἐποίησε. καὶ οὐκ ἐξήρκεσεν αὐτῷ τοσαῦτα καὶ τηλικαῦτα τὴν πόλιν ἀδικῆσαι, ἀλλ᾽ οἰκῶν ἐν Μεγάροις, οἷς παρ᾽ ὑμῶν ἐξεκομίσατο χρήμασιν ἀφορμῇ χρώμενος, ἐκ τῆς Ἠπείρου παρὰ Κλεοπάτρας εἰς Λευκάδα ἐσιτήγει καὶ ἐκεῖθεν εἰς Κόρινθον. καίτοι, ὦ ἄνδρες, καὶ περὶ τούτων οἱ 27 ὑμέτεροι νόμοι τὰς ἐσχάτας τιμωρίας ὁρίζουσιν, ἐάν τις Ἀθηναίων ἄλλοσέ ποι σιτηγήσῃ ἢ ὡς ὑμᾶς. ἔπειτα τὸν προδόντα μὲν ἐν τῷ πολέμῳ, σιτηγήσαντα δὲ παρὰ τοὺς νόμους, μὴ φροντίσαντα δὲ μήτε ἱερῶν μήτε πατρίδος μήτε νόμων, τοῦτον ἔχοντες ὑπὸ τῇ ὑμετέρᾳ ψήφῳ οὐκ ἀποκτενεῖτε καὶ παράδειγμα τοῖς ἄλλοις ποιήσετε; πάντων ἄρ᾽ ἀνθρώπων ῥᾳθυμότατοι ἔσεσθε, καὶ ἥκιστα ἐπὶ τοῖς δεινοῖς ὀργιζόμενοι.

9 Καὶ ταῦτα δ᾽, ὦ ἄνδρες, ἐμοῦ θεωρήσατε, ὡς 28 δικαίαν τὴν ἐξέτασιν ποιουμένου περὶ τούτων. οὐ γὰρ οἶμαι δεῖν ὑμᾶς ὑπὲρ τηλικούτων ἀδικημάτων εἰκάζοντας, ἀλλὰ τὴν ἀλήθειαν εἰδότας ψηφίζεσθαι, καὶ τοὺς μάρτυρας μὴ δώσοντας ἔλεγχον μαρτυρεῖν, ἀλλὰ δεδωκότας. προὐκαλεσάμην γὰρ αὐτοὺς πρόκλησιν ὑπὲρ τούτων ἁπάντων γράψας

ΛΥΚΟΥΡΓΟΥ

καὶ ἀξιῶν βασανίζειν τοὺς τούτου οἰκέτας, ἧς ἀκοῦσαι ἄξιόν ἐστιν. Καί μοι λέγε ταύτην.

ΠΡΟΚΛΗΣΙΣ

29 Ἀκούετε, ὦ ἄνδρες, τῆς προκλήσεως. ἅμα τοίνυν ταύτην Λεωκράτης οὐκ ἐδέχετο καὶ κατεμαρτύρει αὑτοῦ, ὅτι προδότης τῆς πατρίδος ἐστίν· ὁ γὰρ τὸν παρὰ τῶν συνειδότων ἔλεγχον φυγὼν ὡμολόγηκεν ἀληθῆ εἶναι τὰ εἰσηγγελμένα. τίς γὰρ ὑμῶν οὐκ οἶδεν, ὅτι περὶ τῶν ἀμφισβητουμένων πολὺ δοκεῖ δικαιότατον καὶ δημοτικώτατον εἶναι, ὅταν οἰκέται ἢ θεράπαιναι συνειδῶσιν ἃ δεῖ, τούτους ἐλέγχειν καὶ βασανίζειν, καὶ τοῖς ἔργοις μᾶλλον ἢ τοῖς λόγοις πιστεύειν, ἄλλως τε καὶ περὶ πραγμάτων κοινῶν καὶ μεγάλων καὶ συμφε-
30 ρόντων τῇ πόλει; ἐγὼ τοίνυν τοσοῦτον ἀφέστηκα τοῦ ἀδίκως τὴν εἰσαγγελίαν κατὰ Λεωκράτους ποιήσασθαι, ὅσον ἐγὼ μὲν ἐβουλόμην τοῖς ἰδίοις κινδύνοις ἐν τοῖς Λεωκράτους οἰκέταις καὶ θεραπαίναις βασανισθεῖσι τὸν ἔλεγχον γενέσθαι, οὑτοσὶ δὲ διὰ τὸ συνειδέναι ἑαυτῷ οὐχ ὑπέμεινεν, ἀλλ᾽ ἔφυγε. καίτοι, ὦ ἄνδρες, πολὺ θᾶττον οἱ Λεωκράτους οἰκέται καὶ θεράπαιναι τῶν γενομένων ἄν τι ἠρνήθησαν ἢ τὰ μὴ ὄντα τοῦ αὑτῶν δεσπότου
31 κατεψεύσαντο. χωρὶς τοίνυν τούτων Λεωκράτης 10 ἀναβοήσεται αὐτίκα ὡς ἰδιώτης ὢν καὶ ὑπὸ τῆς τοῦ ῥήτορος καὶ συκοφάντου δεινότητος ἀναρπαζόμενος· ἐγὼ δ᾽ ἡγοῦμαι πάντας ὑμᾶς εἰδέναι, ὅτι

ΚΑΤΑ ΛΕΩΚΡΑΤΟΥΣ

τῶν μὲν δεινῶν καὶ συκοφαντεῖν ἐπιχειρούντων ἔργον ἐστὶν ἅμα τοῦτο προαιρεῖσθαι καὶ ζητεῖν τὰ χωρία ταῦτα, ἐν οἷς τοὺς παραλογισμοὺς κατὰ τῶν ἀγωνιζομένων ποιήσονται, τῶν δὲ δικαίως τὰς κρίσεις ἐνισταμένων καὶ τοὺς ἐνόχους ταῖς ἀραῖς ἀκριβῶς ἀποδεικνύντων τἀναντία φαίνεσθαι τούτοις ποιοῦντας, ὥσπερ ἡμεῖς. οὑτωσὶ δὲ δια- 32 λογίζεσθε περὶ τούτων παρ᾽ ὑμῖν αὐτοῖς. τίνας ἀδύνατον ἦν τῇ δεινότητι καὶ ταῖς παρασκευαῖς ταῖς τοῦ λόγου παραγαγεῖν; κατὰ φύσιν τοίνυν βασανιζόμενοι πᾶσαν τὴν ἀλήθειαν περὶ πάντων τῶν ἀδικημάτων ἔμελλον φράσειν οἱ οἰκέται καὶ αἱ θεράπαιναι. ἀλλὰ τούτους Λεωκράτης παραδοῦναι ἔφυγε, καὶ ταῦτα οὐκ ἀλλοτρίους, ἀλλ᾽ αὑτοῦ ὄντας. τίνας δὲ δυνατὸν εἶναι δοκεῖ τοῖς 33 λόγοις ψυχαγωγῆσαι καὶ τὴν ὑγρότητα αὐτῶν τοῦ ἤθους τοῖς δακρύοις εἰς ἔλεον προαγαγέσθαι; τοὺς δικαστάς. ἐνταῦθα Λεωκράτης ὁ προδότης τῆς πατρίδος ἐλήλυθεν, οὐδὲν ἕτερον ἢ φοβούμενος, μὴ ἐκ τῆς αὐτῆς οἰκίας οἵ τ᾽ ἐξελέγχοντες τῷ ἔργῳ καὶ ὁ ἐξελεγχόμενος γένηται. τί γὰρ ἔδει προφάσεων ἢ λόγων ἢ σκήψεως; ἁπλοῦν τὸ δίκαιον, ῥᾴδιον τὸ ἀληθές, βραχὺς ὁ ἔλεγχος. εἰ μὲν ὁμο- 34 λογεῖ τὰ ἐν τῇ εἰσαγγελίᾳ ἀληθῆ καὶ ὅσια εἶναι, τί οὐ τῆς ἐκ τῶν νόμων τιμωρίας τυγχάνει; εἰ δὲ μή φησι ταῦτα ἀληθῆ εἶναι, τί οὐ παραδέδωκε τοὺς οἰκέτας καὶ τὰς θεραπαίνας; προσήκει γὰρ τὸν ὑπὲρ προδοσίας κινδυνεύοντα καὶ παραδιδόναι

βασανίζειν καὶ μηδένα τῶν ἀκριβεστάτων ἐλέγχων
35 φεύγειν. ἀλλ' οὐδὲν τούτων ἔπραξεν, ἀλλὰ καταμεμαρτυρηκὼς ἑαυτοῦ, ὅτι προδότης ἐστὶ τῆς πατρίδος καὶ τῶν ἱερῶν καὶ τῶν νόμων, ἀξιώσει ὑμᾶς ἐναντία ταῖς αὐτοῦ ὁμολογίαις καὶ μαρτυρίαις ψηφίσασθαι. καὶ πῶς δίκαιόν ἐστι τὸν τὴν ἐξουσίαν τῆς ἀπολογίας αὐτοῦ ἐξ ἄλλων τε πολλῶν καὶ ἐκ τοῦ μὴ δέξασθαι τὰ δίκαια περιῃρημένον, τοῦτον ἐᾶσαι ὑμᾶς αὐτοὺς ὑπὲρ τῶν ὁμολογουμένων ἀδικημάτων ἐξαπατῆσαι;
36 Περὶ μὲν οὖν τῆς προκλήσεως καὶ τοῦ ἀδικήματος, ὅτι ὁμολογούμενόν ἐστιν, ἱκανῶς ὑμᾶς ἡγοῦμαι, ὦ ἄνδρες, μεμαθηκέναι· ἐν οἷς δὲ καιροῖς 11 καὶ ἡλίκοις κινδύνοις τὴν πόλιν οὖσαν Λεωκράτης προδέδωκεν, ἀναμνῆσαι ὑμᾶς βούλομαι. Καί μοι λαβὲ τὸ ψήφισμα, γραμματεῦ, τὸ Ὑπερείδου, καὶ ἀναγίγνωσκε.

ΨΗΦΙΣΜΑ

37 Ἀκούετε τοῦ ψηφίσματος, ὦ ἄνδρες, ὅτι τὴν βουλὴν τοὺς πεντακοσίους καταβαίνειν εἰς Πειραιᾶ χρηματιοῦσαν περὶ φυλακῆς τοῦ Πειραιέως ἐν τοῖς ὅπλοις ἔδοξε, καὶ πράττειν διεσκευασμένην ὅ τι ἂν δοκῇ τῷ δήμῳ συμφέρον εἶναι. καίτοι, ὦ ἄνδρες, εἰ οἱ ἀφειμένοι τοῦ στρατεύεσθαι ἕνεκα τοῦ βουλεύεσθαι ὑπὲρ τῆς πόλεως ἐν τῇ τῶν στρατιωτῶν τάξει διέτριβον, ἆρ' ὑμῖν δοκοῦσι μικροὶ καὶ οἱ
38 τυχόντες φόβοι τότε τὴν πόλιν κατασχεῖν; ἐν

ΚΑΤΑ ΛΕΩΚΡΑΤΟΥΣ 15

οἷς Λεωκράτης οὑτοσὶ καὶ αὐτὸς ἐκ τῆς πόλεως ἀποδρὰς ᾤχετο, καὶ τὰ χρήματα τὰ ὑπάρχοντα ἐξεκόμισε, καὶ ⟨τὰ⟩ ἱερὰ τὰ πατρῷα μετεπέμψατο, καὶ εἰς τοσοῦτον προδοσίας ἦλθεν, ὥστε κατὰ τὴν τούτου προαίρεσιν ἔρημοι μὲν ⟨ἂν⟩ ἦσαν οἱ ναοί, ἔρημοι δ' αἱ φυλακαὶ τῶν τειχῶν, ἐξελέλειπτο δ' ἡ πόλις καὶ ἡ χώρα. καίτοι κατ' ἐκείνους τοὺς 39 χρόνους, ὦ ἄνδρες, τίς οὐκ ἂν τὴν πόλιν ἠλέησεν, οὐ μόνον πολίτης, ἀλλὰ καὶ ξένος ἐν τοῖς ἔμπροσθε χρόνοις ἐπιδεδημηκώς; τίς δ' ἦν οὕτως ἢ μισόδημος τότ' ἢ μισαθήναιος, ὅστις ἐδυνήθη ἂν ἄτακτον αὐτὸν ὑπομεῖναι ἰδεῖν; ἡνίκα ἡ μὲν ἧττα καὶ τὸ γεγονὸς πάθος τῷ ⟨στρατῷ⟩ προσήγγελτο, ὀρθὴ δ' ἦν ἡ πόλις ἐπὶ τοῖς συμβεβηκόσιν, αἱ δ' ἐλπίδες τῆς σωτηρίας τῷ δήμῳ ἐν τοῖς ὑπὲρ πεντήκοντ' ἔτη γεγονόσι καθειστήκεσαν, ὁρᾶν δ' ἦν ἐπὶ μὲν 40 τῶν θυρῶν γυναῖκας ἐλευθέρας, περιφόβους κατεπτηχυίας καὶ πυνθανομένας εἰ ζῶσιν, τὰς μὲν ὑπὲρ ἀνδρός, τὰς δ' ὑπὲρ πατρός, τὰς δ' ὑπὲρ ἀδελφῶν, ἀναξίως αὑτῶν καὶ τῆς πόλεως ὁρωμένας, τῶν δ' ἀνδρῶν τοὺς τοῖς σώμασιν ἀπειρηκότας καὶ ταῖς ἡλικίαις πρεσβυτέρους καὶ ὑπὸ τῶν νόμων τοῦ στρατεύεσθαι ἀφειμένους ἰδεῖν ἦν καθ' ὅλην τὴν πόλιν τότ' ἐπὶ γήρως ὁδῷ περιφθειρομένους, διπλᾶ θαἱμάτια ἐμπεπορπημένους; πολλῶν δὲ καὶ δεινῶν 41 κατὰ τὴν πόλιν γιγνομένων καὶ πάντων τῶν πολιτῶν τὰ μέγιστα ἠτυχηκότων, μάλιστ' ἄν τις ἤλγησε καὶ ἐδάκρυσεν ἐπὶ ταῖς τῆς πόλεως συμφοραῖς,

ἡνίχ' ὁρᾶν ἦν τὸν δῆμον ψηφισάμενον τοὺς μὲν
δούλους ἐλευθέρους, τοὺς δὲ ξένους Ἀθηναίους,
τοὺς δ' ἀτίμους ἐπιτίμους· ὃς πρότερον ἐπὶ τῷ
42 αὐτόχθων εἶναι καὶ ἐλεύθερος ἐσεμνύνετο. τοσαύτῃ
δ' ἡ πόλις ἐκέχρητο μεταβολῇ, ὥστε πρότερον
μὲν ὑπὲρ τῆς τῶν ἄλλων Ἑλλήνων ἐλευθερίας
ἀγωνίζεσθαι, ἐν δὲ τοῖς τότε χρόνοις ἀγαπᾶν,
ἐὰν ὑπὲρ τῆς αὐτῶν σωτηρίας ἀσφαλῶς δύνηται
⟨δια⟩κινδυνεῦσαι, καὶ πρότερον μὲν πολλῆς χώρας
τῶν βαρβάρων ἐπάρχειν, τότε δὲ πρὸς Μακεδόνας
ὑπὲρ τῆς ἰδίας κινδυνεύειν· καὶ τὸν δῆμον ὃν
πρότερον Λακεδαιμόνιοι καὶ Πελοποννήσιοι καὶ οἱ
τὴν Ἀσίαν κατοικοῦντες Ἕλληνες βοηθὸν ἐπεκαλοῦντο, τοῦτον ἔδει τότ' ἐξ Ἄνδρου καὶ Κέω καὶ
Τροζῆνος καὶ Ἐπιδαύρου ἐπικουρίαν αὐτῷ μετα-
43 πέμψασθαι. ὥστε, ὦ ἄνδρες, τὸν ἐν τοῖς τοιούτοις
φόβοις καὶ τηλικούτοις κινδύνοις καὶ τοσαύτῃ
αἰσχύνῃ ἐγκαταλιπόντα τὴν πόλιν, καὶ μήτε ⟨τὰ⟩
ὅπλα θέμενον ὑπὲρ τῆς πατρίδος, μήτε τὸ σῶμα
παρασχόντα τάξαι τοῖς στρατηγοῖς, ἀλλὰ φυγόντα
καὶ προδόντα τὴν τοῦ δήμου σωτηρίαν, τίς ἂν
ἢ δικαστὴς φιλόπολις καὶ εὐσεβεῖν βουλόμενος
ψήφῳ ἀπολύσειεν, ἢ ῥήτωρ κληθεὶς τῷ προδότῃ
τῆς πόλεως βοηθήσειε; τὸν οὐδὲ συμπενθῆσαι
τὰς τῆς πατρίδος συμφορὰς τολμήσαντα, οὐδὲ
συμβεβλημένον οὐδὲν εἰς τὴν τῆς πόλεως καὶ τοῦ
δήμου σωτηρίαν, ὅθ' ἡ μὲν χώρα τὰ δένδρα συνεβάλλετο, οἱ δὲ τετελευτηκότες τὰς θήκας, οἱ δὲ

ΚΑΤΑ ΛΕΩΚΡΑΤΟΥΣ

νεῷ τὰ ὅπλα. καίτοι κατ' ἐκείνους τοὺς χρόνους 44 οὐκ ἔστιν ἥτις ἡλικία οὐ παρέσχεν ἑαυτὴν εἰς τὴν τῆς πόλεως σωτηρίαν· ἐπεμελοῦντο γὰρ οἱ μὲν τῆς τῶν τειχῶν κατασκευῆς, οἱ δὲ τῆς τῶν τάφρων, οἱ δὲ τῆς χαρακώσεως· οὐδεὶς δ' ἦν ἀργὸς τῶν ἐν τῇ πόλει. ἐφ' ὧν οὐδενὸς τὸ σῶμα τὸ ἑαυτοῦ παρέσχε τάξαι Λεωκράτης. ὧν εἰκὸς ὑμᾶς ἀνα- 45 μνησθέντας τὸν μηδὲ συνενεγκεῖν μηδ' ἐπ' ἐκφορὰν ἐλθεῖν ἀξιώσαντα τῶν ὑπὲρ τῆς ἐλευθερίας καὶ τοῦ δήμου σωτηρίας ἐν Χαιρωνείᾳ τελευτησάντων θανάτῳ ζημιῶσαι, ὡς τὸ ἐπὶ τούτῳ μέρος ἀτάφων ἐκείνων τῶν ἀνδρῶν γεγενημένων· ὧν οὗτος οὐδὲ τὰς θήκας παριὼν ᾐσχύνθη, ὀγδόῳ ἔτει τὴν πατρίδα αὐτῶν προσαγορεύων.

12 Περὶ ὧν, ⟨ὦ⟩ ἄνδρες, μικρῷ πλείω βούλομαι 46 διελθεῖν, καὶ ὑμῶν ἀκοῦσαι δέομαι καὶ μὴ νομίζειν ἀλλοτρίους εἶναι τοὺς τοιούτους ⟨λόγους⟩ τῶν δημοσίων ἀγώνων· αἱ γὰρ τῶν ἀγαθῶν ἀνδρῶν εὐλογίαι τὸν ἔλεγχον σαφῆ κατὰ τῶν τἀναντία ἐπιτηδευόντων ποιοῦσιν. ἔτι δὲ καὶ δίκαιον τὸν ἔπαινον, ὃς μόνος ἆθλον τῶν κινδύνων τοῖς ἀγαθοῖς ἀνδράσιν ἐστί, τοῦτον, ἐπειδὴ καὶ ἐκεῖνοι εἰς τὴν κοινὴν σωτηρίαν τῆς πόλεως τὰς ψυχὰς αὐτῶν ἀνήλωσαν, ἐν τοῖς δημοσίοις καὶ κοινοῖς ἀγῶσι τῆς πόλεως μὴ παραλείπειν. ἐκεῖνοι γὰρ τοῖς 47 πολεμίοις ἀπήντησαν ἐπὶ τοῖς ὁρίοις τῆς Βοιωτίας ὑπὲρ τῆς τῶν Ἑλλήνων ἐλευθερίας μαχούμενοι, οὐκ ἐν τοῖς τείχεσι τὰς ἐλπίδας τῆς σωτηρίας

ἔχοντες, οὐδὲ τὴν χώραν κακῶς ποιεῖν προέμενοι τοῖς ἐχθροῖς, ἀλλὰ τὴν μὲν αὐτῶν ἀνδρείαν ἀσφαλεστέραν φυλακὴν εἶναι νομίζοντες τῶν λιθίνων περιβόλων, τὴν δὲ θρέψασαν αὐτοὺς αἰσχυνόμενοι περιορᾶν πορθουμένην, εἰκότως· ὥσπερ γὰρ πρὸς τοὺς φύσει γεννήσαντας καὶ τοὺς ποιητοὺς τῶν πατέρων οὐχ ὁμοίως ἔχουσιν ἅπαντες ταῖς εὐνοίαις, οὕτω καὶ πρὸς τὰς χώρας τὰς μὴ φύσει προσηκούσας, ἀλλ᾽ ὕστερον ἐπικτήτους γενομένας καταδεέστερον διάκεινται. τοιαύταις δὲ γνώμαις χρησάμενοι, καὶ τοῖς ἀρίστοις ἀνδράσιν ἐξ ἴσου τῶν κινδύνων μετασχόντες, οὐχ ὁμοίως τῆς τύχης ἐκοινώνησαν· τῆς γὰρ ἀρετῆς οὐ ζῶντες ἀπολαύουσιν, ἀλλὰ τελευτήσαντες τὴν δόξαν καταλελοίπασιν, οὐχ ἡττηθέντες, ἀλλ᾽ ἀποθανόντες ἔνθαπερ ἐτάχθησαν ὑπὲρ τῆς ἐλευθερίας ἀμύνοντες. εἰ δὲ δεῖ καὶ παραδοξότατον μὲν εἰπεῖν, ἀληθὲς δέ, ἐκεῖνοι νικῶντες ἀπέθανον. ἃ γὰρ ἆθλα τοῦ πολέμου τοῖς ἀγαθοῖς ἀνδράσιν ἐστίν, ἐλευθερία καὶ ἀρετή, ταῦτ᾽ ἀμφότερα τοῖς τελευτήσασιν ὑπάρχει. ἔπειτα δ᾽ οὐδ᾽ οἷόν τ᾽ ἐστὶν εἰπεῖν ἡττῆσθαι τοὺς ταῖς διανοίαις μὴ πτήξαντας τὸν τῶν ἐπιόντων φόβον. μόνους γὰρ τοὺς ἐν τοῖς πολέμοις καλῶς ἀποθνῄσκοντας οὐδ᾽ ἂν εἷς ἡττῆσθαι δικαίως φήσειε· τὴν γὰρ δουλείαν φεύγοντες εὐκλεᾶ θάνατον αἱροῦνται. ἐδήλωσε δ᾽ ἡ τούτων τῶν ἀνδρῶν ἀρετή· μόνοι γὰρ τῶν ἁπάντων τὴν τῆς Ἑλλάδος ἐλευθερίαν ἐν τοῖς ἑαυτῶν σώμασιν εἶχον. ἅμα

ΚΑΤΑ ΛΕΩΚΡΑΤΟΥΣ 19

γὰρ οὗτοί τε τὸν βίον μετήλλαξαν καὶ τὰ τῆς
Ἑλλάδος εἰς δουλείαν μετέπεσεν· συνετάφη γὰρ
τοῖς τούτων σώμασιν ἡ τῶν ἄλλων Ἑλλήνων
ἐλευθερία. ὅθεν καὶ φανερὸν πᾶσιν ἐποίησαν οὐκ
ἰδίᾳ πολεμοῦντες, ἀλλ' ὑπὲρ κοινῆς ἐλευθερίας
προκινδυνεύοντες. ὥστε, ὦ ἄνδρες, οὐκ ⟨ἂν⟩ αἰσχυνθείην εἰπὼν στέφανον τῆς πατρίδος εἶναι τὰς
ἐκείνων ψυχάς. καὶ δι' ἃ οὐκ ἀλόγως ⟨ἀνδρείαν⟩ 51
ἐπετήδευον, ἐπίστασθε, ὦ Ἀθηναῖοι, μόνοι τῶν
Ἑλλήνων τοὺς ἀγαθοὺς ἄνδρας τιμᾶν· εὑρήσετε
δὲ παρὰ μὲν τοῖς ἄλλοις ἐν ταῖς ἀγοραῖς ἀθλητὰς
ἀνακειμένους, παρ' ὑμῖν δὲ στρατηγοὺς ἀγαθοὺς
καὶ τοὺς τὸν τύραννον ἀποκτείναντας. καὶ τοιούτους μὲν ἄνδρας οὐδ' ἐξ ἁπάσης τῆς Ἑλλάδος
ὀλίγους εὑρεῖν ῥᾴδιον, τοὺς δὲ τοὺς στεφανίτας
ἀγῶνας νενικηκότας εὐπετῶς πολλαχόθεν ἔστι
γεγονότας ἰδεῖν. ὥσπερ τοίνυν τοῖς εὐεργέταις
μεγίστας τιμὰς ἀπονέμετε, οὕτω δίκαιον καὶ τοὺς
τὴν πατρίδα καταισχύνοντας καὶ προδιδόντας
ταῖς ἐσχάταις τιμωρίαις κολάζειν.

13 Σκέψασθε δ', ὦ ἄνδρες, ὅτι οὐδ' ἐν ὑμῖν ἐστιν 52
ἀποψηφίσασθαι Λεωκράτους τουτουί, τὰ δίκαια
ποιοῦσι. τὸ γὰρ ἀδίκημα τοῦτο κεκριμένον ἐστὶ
καὶ κατεγνωσμένον. ἡ μὲν γὰρ ἐν Ἀρείῳ πάγῳ
βουλή (καὶ μηδείς μοι θορυβήσῃ· ταύτην γὰρ
ὑπολαμβάνω μεγίστην τότε γενέσθαι τῇ πόλει
σωτηρίαν) τοὺς φυγόντας τὴν πατρίδα καὶ ἐγκαταλιπόντας τότε τοῖς πολεμίοις λαβοῦσα ἀπέκτεινε.

2—2

καίτοι, ὦ ἄνδρες, μὴ νομίζετε τοὺς τὰ τῶν ἄλλων φονικὰ ἀδικήματα ὁσιώτατα δικάζοντας αὐτοὺς ἂν εἴς τινα τῶν πολιτῶν τοιοῦτόν τι παρανομῆσαι. 53 ἀλλὰ μὴν Αὐτολύκου γε ὑμεῖς κατεψηφίσασθε, μείναντος μὲν αὐτοῦ ἐν τοῖς κινδύνοις, ἔχοντος δ' αἰτίαν τοὺς υἱεῖς καὶ τὴν γυναῖκα ὑπεκθέσθαι, καὶ ἐτιμωρήσασθε. καίτοι εἰ τὸν τοὺς ἀχρήστους εἰς τὸν πόλεμον ὑπεκθέσθαι αἰτίαν ἔχοντα ἐτιμωρήσασθε, τί δεῖ πάσχειν ὅστις ἀνὴρ ὢν οὐκ ἀπέδωκε τὰ τροφεῖα τῇ πατρίδι; ἔτι δὲ ὁ δῆμος, δεινὸν ἡγησάμενος εἶναι τὸ γιγνόμενον, ἐψηφίσατο ἐνόχους εἶναι τῇ προδοσίᾳ τοὺς φεύγοντας τὸν ὑπὲρ τῆς πατρίδος κίνδυνον, ἀξίους εἶναι νομίζων τῆς 54 ἐσχάτης τιμωρίας. ἃ δὴ κατέγνωσται μὲν παρὰ τῷ δικαιοτάτῳ συνεδρίῳ, κατεψήφισται δ' ὑφ' ὑμῶν τῶν δικάζειν λαχόντων, ὁμολογεῖται δὲ παρὰ τῷ δήμῳ τῆς μεγίστης ἄξια εἶναι τιμωρίας, τούτοις ὑμεῖς ἐναντία ψηφιεῖσθε; πάντων ἄρ' ἀνθρώπων ἔσεσθε ἀγνωμονέστατοι, καὶ ἐλαχίστους ἕξετε τοὺς ὑπὲρ ὑμῶν αὐτῶν κινδυνεύοντας.

55 Ὡς μὲν οὖν ἔνοχός ἐστι τοῖς εἰσηγγελμένοις 14 ἅπασιν, ὦ ἄνδρες, Λεωκράτης, φανερόν ἐστι· πυνθάνομαι δ' αὐτὸν ἐπιχειρήσειν ὑμᾶς ἐξαπατᾶν λέγοντα, ὡς ἔμπορος ἐξέπλευσε καὶ κατὰ ταύτην τὴν ἐργασίαν ἀπεδήμησεν εἰς Ῥόδον. ἐὰν οὖν ταῦτα λέγῃ, ἐνθυμεῖσθ' ᾧ ῥᾳδίως λήψεσθ' αὐτὸν ψευδόμενον. πρῶτον μὲν γὰρ οὐκ ἐκ τῆς ἀκτῆς κατὰ τὴν πυλίδα ἐμβαίνουσιν οἱ κατ' ἐμπορίαν

ΚΑΤΑ ΛΕΩΚΡΑΤΟΥΣ

πλέοντες, ἀλλ' εἴσω τοῦ λιμένος, ὑπὸ πάντων τῶν φίλων ὁρώμενοι καὶ ἀποστελλόμενοι· ἔπειτα οὐ μετὰ τῆς ἑταίρας καὶ τῶν θεραπαινῶν, ἀλλὰ μόνος μετὰ παιδὸς τοῦ διακονοῦντος. πρὸς δὲ τούτοις 56 τί προσῆκεν ἐν Μεγάροις τὸν Ἀθηναῖον ἔμπορον πέντε ἔτη κατοικεῖν καὶ τὰ ἱερὰ τὰ πατρῷα μετακομίζεσθαι καὶ τὴν οἰκίαν τὴν ἐνθάδε πωλεῖν, εἰ μὴ κατεγνώκει τε αὐτοῦ προδεδωκέναι τὴν πατρίδα καὶ μεγάλα πάντας ἠδικηκέναι; ὃ καὶ πάντων γένοιτ' ἂν ἀτοπώτατον, εἰ περὶ ὧν αὐτὸς προσεδόκα τεύξεσθαι τιμωρίας, ταῦθ' ὑμεῖς ἀπολύσαιτε κύριοι γενόμενοι τῆς ψήφου. χωρὶς δὲ τούτων οὐχ ἡγοῦμαι δεῖν ἀποδέχεσθαι ταύτην τὴν ἀπολογίαν. πῶς 57 γὰρ οὐ δεινὸν τοὺς μὲν ἐπὶ ἐμπορίαν ἀποδημοῦντας σπεύδειν ἐπὶ τὴν τῆς πόλεως βοήθειαν, τοῦτον δὲ μόνον ἐν τοῖς τότε καιροῖς καὶ κατ' ἐργασίαν ἐκπλεῖν, ἡνίκα οὐδ' ἂν εἷς προσκτήσασθαι οὐδὲν ἂν ἐζήτησεν, ἀλλὰ τὰ ὑπάρχοντα μόνον διαφυλάξαι; ἡδέως δ' ἂν αὐτοῦ πυθοίμην, τίν' ἐμπορίαν εἰσάγων χρησιμώτερος ἐγένετο ἂν τῇ πόλει τοῦ παρασχεῖν τὸ σῶμα τάξαι τοῖς στρατηγοῖς καὶ τοὺς ἐπιόντας ἀμύνασθαι μεθ' ὑμῶν μαχόμενος. ἐγὼ μὲν οὐδεμίαν ὁρῶ τηλικαύτην οὖσαν βοήθειαν. ἄξιον δ' ἐστὶν οὐ μόνον αὐτῷ διὰ τὴν πρᾶξιν ὀργί- 58 ζεσθαι ταύτην, ἀλλὰ καὶ διὰ τὸν λόγον τοῦτον· φανερῶς γὰρ ψεύδεσθαι τετόλμηκεν. οὔτε γὰρ πρότερον οὐδὲ πώποτε ἐγένετο ἐπὶ ταύτης τῆς ἐργασίας, ἀλλ' ἐκέκτητο χαλκοτύπους, οὔτε τότ' ἐκπλεύσας οὐδὲν εἰσήγαγεν ἐκ Μεγάρων, ἓξ ἔτη συνεχῶς ἀποδημήσας. ἔτι δὲ καὶ ⟨τῆς⟩ πεντηκοστῆς μετέχων ἐτύγχανεν, ἣν οὐκ ἂν καταλιπὼν κατ' ἐμπορίαν ἀπεδήμει. ὥστ' ἂν μέν τι περὶ τούτων λέγῃ, οὐδ' ὑμᾶς ἐπιτρέψειν αὐτῷ νομίζω.

59 Ἥξει δ' ἴσως ἐπ' ἐκεῖνον τὸν λόγον φερόμενος, 15 ὃν αὐτῷ συμβεβουλεύκασί τινες τῶν συνηγόρων, ὡς οὐκ ἔνοχός ἐστι τῇ προδοσίᾳ· οὔτε γὰρ νεωρίων κύριος οὔτε πυλῶν οὔτε στρατοπέδων οὔθ' ὅλως τῶν τῆς πόλεως οὐδενός. ἐγὼ δ' ἡγοῦμαι τοὺς μὲν τούτων κυρίους μέρος ἄν τι προδοῦναι τῆς ὑμετέρας δυνάμεως, τουτονὶ δ' ὅλην ἔκδοτον ποιῆσαι τὴν πόλιν. ἔτι δ' οἱ μὲν τοὺς ζῶντας μόνον ἀδικοῦσι προδιδόντες, οὗτος δὲ καὶ τοὺς τετελευτηκότας, 60 τῶν πατρίων νομίμων ἀποστερῶν. καὶ ὑπὸ μὲν ἐκείνων προδοθεῖσαν οἰκεῖσθαι ἂν συνέβαινε δούλην οὖσαν τὴν πόλιν, ὃν δὲ τρόπον οὗτος ἐξέλιπεν, ἀοίκητον ἂν γενέσθαι. ἔτι δ' ἐκ μὲν τοῦ κακῶς πράττειν τὰς πόλεις μεταβολῆς τυχεῖν ἐπὶ τὸ βέλτιον εἰκός ἐστιν, ἐκ δὲ τοῦ παντάπασι γενέσθαι ἀναστάτους καὶ τῶν κοινῶν ἐλπίδων στερηθῆναι. ὥσπερ γὰρ ἀνθρώπῳ ζῶντι μὲν ἐλπὶς ἐκ τοῦ κακῶς πρᾶξαι μεταπεσεῖν, τελευτήσαντι δὲ συναναιρεῖται πάντα δι' ὧν ἄν τις εὐδαιμονήσειεν, οὕτω καὶ περὶ τὰς πόλεις συμβαίνει πέρας ἔχειν τὴν 61 ἀτυχίαν, ὅταν ἀνάστατοι γένωνται. εἰ γὰρ δεῖ τὴν ἀλήθειαν εἰπεῖν, πόλεώς ἐστι θάνατος ἀνάστατον γενέσθαι. τεκμήριον δὲ μέγιστον· ἡμῶν γὰρ ἡ

πόλις τὸ μὲν παλαιὸν ὑπὸ τῶν τυράννων κατεδουλώθη, τὸ δ' ὕστερον ὑπὸ τῶν τριάκοντα, ⟨ὅτε⟩ καὶ ὑπὸ Λακεδαιμονίων τὰ τείχη καθηρέθη· καὶ ἐκ τούτων ὅμως ἀμφοτέρων ἠλευθερώθημεν καὶ τῆς τῶν Ἑλλήνων εὐδαιμονίας ἠξιώθημεν προστάται γενέσθαι. ἀλλ' οὐχ ὅσαι πώποτ' ἀνάστατοι γεγόνασι. τοῦτο μὲν γάρ, εἰ καὶ παλαιότερον εἰπεῖν ἐστι, τὴν Τροίαν τίς οὐκ ἀκήκοεν, ὅτι μεγίστη γεγενημένη τῶν τότε πόλεων καὶ πάσης ἐπάρξασα τῆς Ἀσίας, ὡς ἅπαξ ὑπὸ τῶν Ἑλλήνων κατεσκάφη, τὸν αἰῶνα ἀοίκητός ἐστι; τοῦτο δὲ Μεσσήνην πεντακοσίοις ἔτεσιν ὕστερον ἐκ τῶν τυχόντων ἀνθρώπων συνοικισθεῖσαν;

16 Ἴσως οὖν τῶν συνηγόρων αὐτῷ τολμήσει τις εἰπεῖν, μικρὸν τὸ πρᾶγμα ποιῶν, ὡς οὐδὲν ἂν παρ' ἕνα ἄνθρωπον ἐγένετο τούτων· καὶ οὐκ αἰσχύνονται τοιαύτην ἀπολογίαν ποιούμενοι πρὸς ὑμᾶς, ἐφ' ᾗ δικαίως ἂν ἀποθάνοιεν. εἰ μὲν γὰρ ὁμολογοῦσι τὴν πατρίδα αὐτὸν ἐκλιπεῖν, τοῦτο συγχωρήσαντες ὑμᾶς ἐάτωσαν διαγνῶναι περὶ τοῦ μεγέθους· εἰ δ' ὅλως μηδὲν τούτων πεποίηκεν, οὐ μανία δή που τοῦτο λέγειν, ὡς οὐδὲν ἂν ἐγένετο παρὰ τοῦτον; ἡγοῦμαι δ' ἔγωγε, ὦ ἄνδρες, τοὐναντίον τούτοις, παρὰ τοῦτον εἶναι τῇ πόλει τὴν σωτηρίαν. ἡ γὰρ πόλις οἰκεῖται κατὰ τὴν ἰδίαν ἑκάστου μοῖραν φυλαττομένη· ὅταν οὖν ταύτην ἐφ' ἑνός τις παρίδῃ, λέληθεν ἑαυτὸν ἐφ' ἁπάντων τοῦτο πεποιηκώς. καίτοι ῥᾴδιόν ἐστιν, ὦ ἄνδρες,

πρὸς τὰς τῶν ἀρχαίων νομοθετῶν διανοίας ἀπο-
65 βλέψαντας τὴν ἀλήθειαν εὑρεῖν. ἐκεῖνοι γὰρ οὐ
τῷ μὲν ἑκατὸν τάλαντα κλέψαντι θάνατον ἔταξαν,
τῷ δὲ δέκα δραχμὰς ἔλαττον ἐπιτίμιον· οὐδὲ τὸν
μὲν μεγάλα ἱεροσυλήσαντα ἀπέκτεινον, τὸν δὲ
μικρὰ ἐλάττονι τιμωρίᾳ ἐκόλαζον· οὐδὲ τὸν μὲν
οἰκέτην ἀποκτείναντα ἀργυρίῳ ἐζημίουν, τὸν δὲ
ἐλεύθερον εἶργον τῶν νομίμων· ἀλλ' ὁμοίως ἐπὶ
πᾶσι καὶ τοῖς ἐλαχίστοις παρανομήμασι θάνατον
66 ὥρισαν εἶναι τὴν ζημίαν. οὐ γὰρ πρὸς τὸ ἴδιον
ἕκαστος αὐτῶν ἀπέβλεπε τοῦ γεγενημένου πράγματος, οὐδ' ἐντεῦθεν τὸ μέγεθος τῶν ἁμαρτημάτων
ἐλάμβανον, ἀλλ' αὐτὸ ἐσκόπουν τοῦτο, εἰ πέφυκε
τὸ ἀδίκημα τοῦτο ἐπὶ πλεῖον ἐλθὸν μέγα βλάπτειν
τοὺς ἀνθρώπους. καὶ γὰρ ἄτοπον ἄλλως πως περὶ
τούτου ἐξετάζειν. φέρε γάρ, ὦ ἄνδρες, εἴ τις ἕνα
νόμον εἰς τὸ Μητρῷον ἐλθὼν ἐξαλείψειεν, εἶτ'
ἀπολογοῖτο ὡς οὐδὲν παρὰ τοῦτον τῇ πόλει ἐστίν,
ἆρ' οὐκ ἂν ἀπεκτείνατ' αὐτόν; ἐγὼ μὲν οἶμαι
δικαίως, εἴπερ ἐμέλλετε καὶ τοὺς ἄλλους σῴζειν.
67 τὸν αὐτὸν τοίνυν τρόπον κολαστέον ἐστὶ τοῦτον, εἰ
μέλλετε τοὺς ἄλλους πολίτας βελτίους ποιήσειν·
καὶ οὐ τοῦτο λογιεῖσθε, εἰ εἷς ἐστι μόνος ἄνθρωπος,
ἀλλ' εἰς τὸ πρᾶγμα. ἐγὼ μὲν γὰρ ἡγοῦμαι τὸ μὴ
πολλοὺς τοιούτους γενέσθαι ἡμέτερον εὐτύχημα
εἶναι, τοῦτον μέντοι διὰ τοῦτο μείζονος τιμωρίας
ἄξιον εἶναι τυχεῖν, ὅτι μόνος τῶν ἄλλων πολιτῶν
οὐ κοινήν, ἀλλ' ἰδίαν τὴν σωτηρίαν ἐζήτησεν.

ΚΑΤΑ ΛΕΩΚΡΑΤΟΥΣ 25

17 Ἀγανακτῶ δὲ μάλιστα, ὦ ἄνδρες, ἐπειδὰν ἀκού- 68
σω τῶν μετὰ τούτου τινὸς λέγοντος, ὡς οὐκ ἔστι
τοῦτο προδιδόναι, εἴ τις ᾤχετο ἐκ τῆς πόλεως·
καὶ γὰρ οἱ πρόγονοί ποθ᾽ ὑμῶν τὴν πόλιν καταλιπόντες, ὅτε πρὸς Ξέρξην ἐπολέμουν, εἰς Σαλαμῖνα
διέβησαν. καὶ οὕτως ἐστὶν ἀνόητος ἢ παντάπασιν
ὑμῶν καταπεφρονηκώς, ὥστε τὸ κάλλιστον τῶν
ἔργων πρὸς τὸ αἴσχιστον συμβαλεῖν ἠξίωσε. ποῦ 69
γὰρ οὐ περιβόητος ἐκείνων τῶν ἀνδρῶν ἡ ἀρετὴ
γέγονε; τίς δ᾽ οὕτως ἢ φθονερός ἐστιν ἢ παντάπασιν ἀφιλότιμος, ὃς οὐκ ἂν εὔξαιτο τῶν ἐκείνοις
πεπραγμένων μετασχεῖν; οὐ γὰρ τὴν πόλιν ἐξέ-
λιπον, ἀλλὰ τὸν τόπον μετήλλαξαν, πρὸς τὸν
ἐπιόντα κίνδυνον καλῶς βουλευσάμενοι. Ἐτεό- 70
νικος μὲν γὰρ ὁ Λακεδαιμόνιος καὶ Ἀδείμαντος ὁ
Κορίνθιος καὶ τὸ Αἰγινητῶν ναυτικὸν ὑπὸ νύκτα
τὴν σωτηρίαν αὑτοῖς ἔμελλον πορίζεσθαι· ἐγκαταλειπόμενοι δ᾽ οἱ πρόγονοι ὑπὸ πάντων τῶν
Ἑλλήνων, βίᾳ καὶ τοὺς ἄλλους ἠλευθέρωσαν,
ἀναγκάσαντες ἐν Σαλαμῖνι μεθ᾽ αὑτῶν πρὸς τοὺς
βαρβάρους ναυμαχεῖν. μόνοι δ᾽ ἀμφοτέρων περιγεγόνασι, καὶ τῶν πολεμίων καὶ τῶν συμμάχων,
ὡς ἑκατέρων προσῆκε, τοὺς μὲν εὐεργετοῦντες,
τοὺς δὲ μαχόμενοι νικῶντες. ἆρά γ᾽ ὅμοιοι τῷ
φεύγοντι τὴν πατρίδα τεττάρων ἡμερῶν πλοῦν εἰς
Ῥόδον; ἦ που ταχέως ἂν ἠνέσχετό τις ἐκείνων 71
τῶν ἀνδρῶν τοιοῦτον ἔργον, ἀλλ᾽ οὐκ ἂν κατέλευσαν τὸν καταισχύνοντα τὴν αὐτῶν ἀριστείαν.

ούτω γοῦν ἐφίλουν τὴν πατρίδα πάντες, ὥστε τὸν παρὰ Ξέρξου πρεσβευτὴν Ἀλέξανδρον, φίλον ὄντα αὐτοῖς πρότερον, ὅτι γῆν καὶ ὕδωρ ᾔτησε, μικροῦ δεῖν κατέλευσαν. ὅπου δὲ καὶ τοῦ λόγου τιμωρίαν ἠξίουν λαμβάνειν, ἦ που τὸν ἔργῳ παραδόντα τὴν πόλιν ὑποχείριον τοῖς πολεμίοις οὐ 72 μεγάλαις ἂν ζημίαις ἐκόλασαν. τοιγαροῦν τοιαύταις χρώμενοι γνώμαις ἐνενήκοντα μὲν ἔτη τῶν Ἑλλήνων ἡγεμόνες κατέστησαν, Φοινίκην δὲ καὶ Κιλικίαν ἐπόρθησαν, ἐπ' Εὐρυμέδοντι δὲ καὶ πεζομαχοῦντες καὶ ναυμαχοῦντες ἐνίκησαν, ἑκατὸν δὲ τριήρεις τῶν βαρβάρων αἰχμαλώτους ἔλαβον, ἅπασαν δὲ τὴν Ἀσίαν κακῶς ποιοῦντες περι- 73 έπλευσαν. καὶ τὸ κεφάλαιον τῆς νίκης, οὐ τὸ ἐν Σαλαμῖνι τρόπαιον ἀγαπήσαντες [ἔστησαν], ἀλλ' ὅρους τοῖς βαρβάροις πήξαντες τοὺς εἰς τὴν ἐλευθερίαν τῆς Ἑλλάδος, καὶ τούτους κωλύσαντες ὑπερβαίνειν, συνθήκας ἐποιήσαντο, μακρῷ μὲν πλοίῳ μὴ πλεῖν ἐντὸς Κυανέων καὶ Φασήλιδος, τοὺς δ' Ἕλληνας αὐτονόμους εἶναι, μὴ μόνον τοὺς τὴν Εὐρώπην, ἀλλὰ καὶ τοὺς τὴν Ἀσίαν 74 κατοικοῦντας. καίτοι οἴεσθ' ἄν, εἰ τῇ Λεωκράτους διανοίᾳ χρησάμενοι πάντες ἔφυγον, τούτων ἄν τι γενέσθαι τῶν καλῶν ἔργων, ἢ ταύτην ἂν ἔτι τὴν χώραν κατοικεῖν ὑμᾶς; χρὴ τοίνυν, ὦ ἄνδρες, ὥσπερ τοὺς ἀγαθοὺς ἐπαινεῖτε καὶ τιμᾶτε, οὕτω καὶ τοὺς κακοὺς μισεῖν τε καὶ κολάζειν, ἄλλως τε καὶ Λεωκράτην, ὃς οὔτε ἔδεισεν οὔτε ᾐσχύνθη ὑμᾶς.

18 Καίτοι ὑμεῖς τίνα τρόπον νενομίκατε περὶ τού- 75
των, καὶ πῶς ἔχετε ταῖς διανοίαις, θεωρήσατε.
ἄξιον γὰρ ὅμως καίπερ πρὸς εἰδότας διελθεῖν·
ἐγκώμιον γὰρ νὴ τὴν Ἀθηνᾶν εἰσι τῆς πόλεως
οἱ παλαιοὶ νόμοι καὶ τὰ ἔθη τῶν ἐξ ἀρχῆς ταῦτα
κατασκευασάντων, οἷς ἂν προσέχητε, τὰ δίκαια
ποιήσετε καὶ πᾶσιν ἀνθρώποις σεμνοὶ καὶ ἄξιοι
τῆς πόλεως δόξετ' εἶναι. ὑμῖν γὰρ ἔστιν ὅρκος, 76
ὃν ὀμνύουσι πάντες οἱ πολῖται, ἐπειδὰν εἰς τὸ
ληξιαρχικὸν γραμματεῖον ἐγγραφῶσι καὶ ἔφηβοι
γένωνται, μήτε τὰ ἱερὰ ὅπλα καταισχυνεῖν μήτε
τὴν τάξιν λείψειν, ἀμυνεῖν δὲ τῇ πατρίδι καὶ
ἀμείνω παραδώσειν. ὃν εἰ μὲν ὀμώμοκε Λεωκράτης, φανερῶς ἐπιώρκηκεν, καὶ οὐ μόνον ὑμᾶς
ἠδίκηκεν, ἀλλὰ καὶ εἰς τὸ θεῖον ἠσέβηκεν· εἰ δὲ
μὴ ὀμώμοκεν, εὐθὺς δῆλός ἐστι παρασκευασάμενος
⟨ὡς⟩ οὐδὲν ποιήσων τῶν δεόντων, ἀνθ' ὧν δικαίως
ἂν αὐτὸν καὶ ὑπὲρ ὑμῶν καὶ ὑπὲρ τῶν θεῶν
τιμωρήσαισθε. βούλομαι δ' ὑμᾶς ἀκοῦσαι τοῦ
ὅρκου. Λέγε, γραμματεῦ. 77

⟨ΟΡΚΟΣ

Οὐ καταισχυνῶ ὅπλα τὰ ἱερά, οὐδ' ἐγκαταλείψω τὸν
παραστάτην ὅτῳ ἂν στοιχήσω, ἀμυνῶ δὲ καὶ ὑπὲρ ἱερῶν
καὶ ὑπὲρ ὁσίων, καὶ μόνος καὶ μετὰ πολλῶν· τὴν πατρίδα
δὲ οὐκ ἐλάττω παραδώσω, πλείω δὲ καὶ ἀρείω ὅσης ἂν
παραδέξωμαι. καὶ εὐηκοήσω τῶν ἀεὶ κραινόντων, καὶ τοῖς
θεσμοῖς τοῖς ἱδρυμένοις πείσομαι καὶ οὕστινας ἂν ἄλλους
τὸ πλῆθος ἱδρύσηται ὁμοφρόνως· καὶ ἄν τις ἀναιρῇ τοὺς

θεσμούς ή μη πείθηται, ουκ επιτρέψω, αμυνώ δε και μόνος και μετά πάντων. και ιερά τα πάτρια τιμήσω. ίστορες θεοί τούτων, Άγλαυρος, Ενυάλιος Άρης, Ζεύς, Θαλλώ, Αυξώ, Ηγεμόνη.)

Καλός γ', ώ άνδρες, και όσιος ο όρκος. παρά τούτον τοίνυν άπαντα πεποίηκε Λεωκράτης. καίτοι πως αν άνθρωπος γένοιτο ανοσιώτερος ή μάλλον προδότης της πατρίδος; τίνα δ' αν τρόπον όπλα καταισχύνειέ τις μάλλον, ή ει λαβείν μη θέλοι και τους πολεμίους αμύνασθαι; πως δ' ου και τον παραστάτην και την τάξιν λέλοιπεν ο μηδέ τάξαι το σώμα παρασχών; πού δ' υπέρ οσίων και ιερών ήμυνεν αν ο μηδένα κίνδυνον υπομείνας; τίνι δ' αν την πατρίδα παρέδωκε μείζονα — προδοσία; το γαρ τούτου μέρος εκλελειμμένη τοις πολεμίοις υποχείριός εστιν. είτα τούτον ουκ αποκτενείτε τον απάσαις ταις αδικίαις ένοχον όντα; τίνας ούν τιμωρήσεσθε; τους έν τι τούτων ημαρτηκότας; ράδιον έσται παρ' υμίν άρα μεγάλα αδικείν, ει φανείσθε επί τοις μικροίς μάλλον οργιζόμενοι.

Και μην, ώ άνδρες, και τούθ' υμάς δει μαθείν, ότι το συνέχον την δημοκρατίαν όρκος εστί. τρία γάρ εστιν εξ ων η πολιτεία συνέστηκεν, ο άρχων, ο δικαστής, ο ιδιώτης. τούτων τοίνυν έκαστος ταύτην πίστιν δίδωσιν, εικότως· τους μεν γαρ ανθρώπους πολλοί ήδη εξαπατήσαντες και διαλαθόντες ου μόνον των παρόντων κινδύνων απε-

ΚΑΤΑ ΛΕΩΚΡΑΤΟΥΣ 29

λύθησαν, ἀλλὰ καὶ τὸν ἄλλον χρόνον ἀθῷοι τῶν ἀδικημάτων τούτων εἰσί· τοὺς δὲ θεοὺς οὔτ' ἂν ἐπιορκήσας τις λάθοι, οὔτ' ἂν ἐκφύγοι τὴν ἀπ' αὐτῶν τιμωρίαν, ἀλλ' εἰ μὴ αὐτός, οἱ παῖδές γε καὶ τὸ γένος ἅπαν τὸ τοῦ ἐπιορκήσαντος μεγάλοις ἀτυχήμασι περιπίπτει. διόπερ, ὦ ἄνδρες δικα- 80 σταί, ταύτην πίστιν ἔδοσαν αὑτοῖς ἐν Πλαταιαῖς πάντες οἱ Ἕλληνες, ὅτ' ἔμελλον παραταξάμενοι μάχεσθαι πρὸς τὴν Ξέρξου δύναμιν, οὐ παρ' αὑτῶν εὑρόντες, ἀλλὰ μιμησάμενοι τὸν παρ' ὑμῖν εἰθισμένον ὅρκον. ὃν ἄξιόν ἐστιν ἀκοῦσαι· καὶ γὰρ παλαιῶν ὄντων τῶν τότε πεπραγμένων ὅμως ὡς ἴχνος ἔστιν ἐν τοῖς γεγραμμένοις ἰδεῖν τὴν ἐκείνων ἀρετήν. Καί μοι ἀναγίγνωσκε αὐτόν.

ΟΡΚΟΣ

Οὐ ποιήσομαι περὶ πλείονος τὸ ζῆν τῆς ἐλευθερίας, οὐδ' 81 ἐγκαταλείψω τοὺς ἡγεμόνας οὔτε ζῶντας οὔτε ἀποθανόντας, ἀλλὰ τοὺς ἐν τῇ μάχῃ τελευτήσαντας τῶν συμμάχων ἅπαντας θάψω. καὶ κρατήσας τῷ πολέμῳ τοὺς βαρβάρους, τῶν μὲν μαχεσαμένων ὑπὲρ τῆς Ἑλλάδος πόλεων οὐδεμίαν ἀνάστατον ποιήσω, τὰς δὲ τὰ τοῦ βαρβάρου προελομένας ἁπάσας δεκατεύσω. καὶ τῶν ἱερῶν τῶν ἐμπρησθέντων καὶ καταβληθέντων ὑπὸ τῶν βαρβάρων οὐδὲν ἀνοικοδομήσω παντάπασιν, ἀλλ' ὑπόμνημα τοῖς ἐπιγιγνομένοις ἐάσω καταλείπεσθαι τῆς τῶν βαρβάρων ἀσεβείας.

Οὕτω τοίνυν, ὦ ἄνδρες, σφόδρα ἐνέμειναν ἐν 82 τούτῳ πάντες, ὥστε καὶ τὴν παρὰ τῶν θεῶν εὔνοιαν μεθ' εαυτών έσχον βοηθόν, και πάντων ⟨τῶν⟩ Ἑλλήνων ἀνδρῶν ἀγαθῶν γενομένων πρὸς τὸν κίνδυνον, μάλιστα ἡ πόλις ὑμῶν εὐδοκίμησεν. ὃ καὶ πάντων ἂν εἴη δεινότατον, τοὺς μὲν προγόνους ὑμῶν ἀποθνήσκειν τολμᾶν ὥστε μὴ τὴν πόλιν ἀδοξεῖν, ὑμᾶς δὲ μὴ κολάζειν τοὺς καταισχύναντας αὐτήν, ἀλλὰ περιορᾶν τὴν κοινὴν καὶ μετὰ πολλῶν πόνων συνειλεγμένην εὔκλειαν, ταύτην διὰ τὴν τῶν τοιούτων ἀνδρῶν πονηρίαν καταλυομένην.

83 Καίτοι, ὦ ἄνδρες, μόνοις ὑμῖν τῶν Ἑλλήνων 20 οὐκ ἔστιν οὐδὲν τούτων περιιδεῖν. βούλομαι δὲ μικρὰ τῶν παλαιῶν ὑμῖν διελθεῖν, οἷς παραδείγμασι χρώμενοι καὶ περὶ τούτων καὶ περὶ τῶν ἄλλων βέλτιον βουλεύσεσθε. τοῦτο γὰρ ἔχει μέγιστον ἡ πόλις ὑμῶν ἀγαθόν, ὅτι τῶν καλῶν ἔργων παράδειγμα τοῖς Ἕλλησι γέγονεν· ὅσον γὰρ τῷ χρόνῳ πασῶν ἐστιν ἀρχαιοτάτη, τοσοῦτον οἱ πρόγονοι ἡμῶν τῶν ἄλλων ἀνθρώπων ἀρετῇ 84 διενηνόχασιν. ἐπὶ Κόδρου γὰρ βασιλεύοντος Πελοποννησίοις γενομένης ἀφορίας κατὰ τὴν χώραν αὐτῶν ἔδοξε στρατεύειν ἐπὶ τὴν πόλιν ἡμῶν, καὶ ἡμῶν τοὺς προγόνους ἐξαναστήσαντας κατανείμασθαι τὴν χώραν. καὶ πρῶτον μὲν εἰς Δελφοὺς ἀποστείλαντες τὸν θεὸν ἐπηρώτων, εἰ λήψονται τὰς Ἀθήνας· ἀνελόντος δ' αὐτοῖς τοῦ θεοῦ, ὅτι τὴν πόλιν αἱρήσουσιν, ἂν μὴ τὸν βασιλέα τῶν Ἀθηναίων Κόδρον ἀποκτείνωσιν, ἐστράτευον ἐπὶ 85 τὰς Ἀθήνας. Κλεόμαντις δὲ τῶν Δελφῶν τις, πυ-

ΚΑΤΑ ΛΕΩΚΡΑΤΟΥΣ 31

θόμενος τὸ χρηστήριον, δι' ἀπορρήτων ἐξήγγειλε τοῖς Ἀθηναίοις· οὕτως οἱ πρόγονοι ἡμῶν ὡς ἔοικε καὶ τοὺς ἔξωθεν ἀνθρώπους εὔνους ἔχοντες διετέλουν. ἐμβαλόντων δὲ τῶν Πελοποννησίων εἰς τὴν Ἀττικήν, τί ποιοῦσιν οἱ πρόγονοι ὑμῶν, ἄνδρες δικασταί; οὐ καταλιπόντες τὴν χώραν ὥσπερ Λεωκράτης ᾤχοντο, οὐδ' ἔκδοτον τὴν θρεψαμένην καὶ τὰ ἱερὰ τοῖς πολεμίοις παρέδοσαν, ἀλλ' ὀλίγοι ὄντες κατακλησθέντες ἐπολιορκοῦντο καὶ διεκαρτέρουν εἰς τὴν πατρίδα. καὶ οὕτως ἦσαν, ὦ 86 ἄνδρες, γενναῖοι οἱ τότε βασιλεύοντες, ὥστε προῃροῦντο ἀποθνῄσκειν ὑπὲρ τῆς τῶν ἀρχομένων σωτηρίας μᾶλλον ἢ ζῶντες ἑτέραν μεταλλάξαι τινὰ χώραν. φασὶν γοῦν τὸν Κόδρον παραγγείλαντα τοῖς Ἀθηναίοις, προσέχειν ὅταν τελευτήσῃ τὸν βίον, λαβόντα πτωχικὴν στολὴν ὅπως ἂν ἀπατήσῃ τοὺς πολεμίους, κατὰ τὰς πύλας ὑποδύντα φρύγανα συλλέγειν πρὸ τῆς πόλεως, προσελθόντων δ' αὐτῷ δυοῖν ἀνδρῶν ἐκ τοῦ στρατοπέδου καὶ τὰ κατὰ τὴν πόλιν πυνθανομένων, τὸν ἕτερον αὐτῶν ἀποκτεῖναι τῷ δρεπάνῳ προσπεσόντα· τὸν 87 δὲ περιλελειμμένον, παροξυνθέντα τῷ Κόδρῳ καὶ νομίσαντα πτωχὸν εἶναι, σπασάμενον τὸ ξίφος ἀποκτεῖναι τὸν Κόδρον. τούτων δὲ γενομένων οἱ μὲν Ἀθηναῖοι κήρυκα πέμψαντες ἠξίουν δοῦναι τὸν βασιλέα θάψαι, λέγοντες αὐτοῖς ἅπασαν τὴν ἀλήθειαν· οἱ δὲ Πελοποννήσιοι τοῦτον μὲν ἀπέδοσαν, γνόντες δ' ὡς οὐκέτι δυνατὸν αὐτοῖς τὴν χώραν κατασχεῖν ἀπεχώρησαν. τῷ δὲ Κλεομάντει τῷ Δελφῷ ἡ πόλις αὐτῷ τε καὶ ἐκγόνοις ἐν πρυτανείῳ ἀίδιον σίτησιν ἔδοσαν. ἆρά γ' ὁμοίως ἐφίλουν τὴν πατρίδα Λεωκράτει οἱ τότε βασιλεύοντες, οἵ γε προῃροῦντο τοὺς πολεμίους ἐξαπατῶντες ἀποθνήσκειν ὑπὲρ αὐτῆς καὶ τὴν ἰδίαν ψυχὴν ἀντὶ τῆς κοινῆς σωτηρίας ἀντικαταλλάττεσθαι; τοιγαροῦν μονώτατοι ἐπώνυμοι τῆς χώρας εἰσίν, ἰσοθέων τιμῶν τετυχηκότες, εἰκότως· ὑπὲρ ἧς γὰρ οὕτω σφόδρα ἐσπούδαζον, δικαίως ταύτης καὶ τεθνεῶτες ἐκληρονόμουν. ἀλλὰ Λεωκράτης οὔτε ζῶν οὔτε τεθνεὼς δικαίως ἂν αὐτῆς μετάσχοι, μονώτατος ⟨δ'⟩ ἂν προσηκόντως ἐξορισθείη τῆς χώρας, ἣν ἐγκαταλιπὼν τοῖς πολεμίοις ᾤχετο· οὐδὲ γὰρ καλὸν τὴν αὐτὴν καλύπτειν τοὺς τῇ ἀρετῇ διαφέροντας καὶ τὸν κάκιστον πάντων ἀνθρώπων.

Καίτοι γ' ἐπεχείρησεν εἰπεῖν, ὃ καὶ νῦν ἴσως ἐρεῖ πρὸς ὑμᾶς, ὡς οὐκ ἄν ποτε ὑπέμεινε τὸν ἀγῶνα τοῦτον συνειδὼς ἑαυτῷ τοιοῦτόν τι διαπεπραγμένῳ· ὥσπερ οὐ πάντας καὶ τοὺς κλέπτοντας καὶ ἱεροσυλοῦντας τούτῳ τῷ τεκμηρίῳ χρωμένους. οὐ γὰρ τοῦ πράγματός ἐστι σημεῖον, ὡς οὐ πεποιήκασιν, ἀλλὰ τῆς ἀναιδείας ἣν ἔχουσιν. οὐ γὰρ τοῦτο δεῖ λέγειν, ἀλλ' ὡς οὐκ ἐξέπλευσεν οὐδὲ τὴν πόλιν ἐγκατέλιπεν οὐδ' ἐν Μεγάροις κατῴκησε· ταῦτά ἐστι τεκμήρια τοῦ πράγματος, ἐπεί γε τὸ ἐλθεῖν τοῦτον, οἶμαι θεόν τινα αὐτὸν ἐπ' αὐτὴν ἀγαγεῖν τὴν τιμωρίαν, ἵν' ἐπειδὴ τὸν εὐκλεᾶ κίνδυνον ἔφυγε, τοῦ ἀκλεοῦς καὶ ἀδόξου θανάτου τύχοι, καὶ οὓς προὔδωκε, τούτοις ὑποχείριον αὐτὸν καταστήσειεν. ἑτέρωθι μὲν γὰρ ἀτυχῶν οὔπω δῆλον, εἰ διὰ ταῦτα δίκην δίδωσιν· ἐνταῦθα δὲ παρ' οἷς προὔδωκεν φανερόν ἐστιν, ὅτι τῶν αὐτοῦ παρανομημάτων ὑπέχει ταύτην τὴν τιμωρίαν. οἱ γὰρ θεοὶ οὐδὲν πρότερον ποιοῦσιν, ἢ 92 τῶν πονηρῶν ἀνθρώπων τὴν διάνοιαν παράγουσι· καί μοι δοκοῦσι τῶν ἀρχαίων τινὲς ποιητῶν ὥσπερ χρησμοὺς γράψαντες τοῖς ἐπιγιγνομένοις τάδε τὰ ἰαμβεῖα καταλιπεῖν·

ὅταν γὰρ ὀργὴ δαιμόνων βλάπτῃ τινά,
τοῦτ' αὐτὸ πρῶτον, ἐξαφαιρεῖται φρενῶν
τὸν νοῦν τὸν ἐσθλόν, εἰς δὲ τὴν χείρω τρέπει
γνώμην, ἵν' εἰδῇ μηδὲν ὧν ἁμαρτάνει.

22 τίς γὰρ οὐ μέμνηται τῶν πρεσβυτέρων ἢ τῶν 93 νεωτέρων οὐκ ἀκήκοε Καλλίστρατον, οὗ θάνατον ἡ πόλις κατέγνω, τοῦτον φυγόντα, καὶ τοῦ θεοῦ τοῦ ἐν Δελφοῖς ἀκούσαντα, ὅτι ἂν ἔλθῃ Ἀθήναζε τεύξεται τῶν νόμων, ἀφικόμενον καὶ ἐπὶ τὸν βωμὸν τῶν δώδεκα θεῶν καταφυγόντα, καὶ οὐδὲν ἧττον ὑπὸ τῆς πόλεως ἀποθανόντα; δικαίως· τὸ γὰρ τῶν νόμων τοῖς ἠδικηκόσι τυχεῖν τιμωρίας ἐστίν. ὁ δέ γε θεὸς ὀρθῶς ἀπέδωκε τοῖς ἠδικημένοις κολάσαι τὸν αἴτιον· δεινὸν γὰρ ἂν εἴη, εἰ ταὐτὰ σημεῖα τοῖς εὐσεβέσι καὶ τοῖς κακούργοις φαίνοιτο.

94 Ἡγοῦμαι δ' ἔγωγ', ὦ ἄνδρες, τὴν τῶν θεῶν ἐπιμέλειαν πάσας μὲν τὰς ἀνθρωπίνας πράξεις ἐπισκοπεῖν, μάλιστα δὲ τὴν περὶ τοὺς γονέας καὶ τοὺς τετελευτηκότας καὶ τὴν πρὸς αὐτοὺς εὐσέβειαν, εἰκότως· παρ' ὧν γὰρ τὴν ἀρχὴν τοῦ ζῆν εἰλήφαμεν καὶ πλεῖστα ἀγαθὰ πεπόνθαμεν, εἰς τούτους μὴ ὅτι ἁμαρτεῖν, ἀλλὰ μὴ εὐεργετοῦντας τὸν αὐτῶν βίον καταναλῶσαι μέγιστον ἀσέβημά
95 ἐστι. λέγεται γοῦν ἐν Σικελίᾳ (εἰ γὰρ καὶ μυθω- 23 δέστερόν ἐστιν, ἀλλ' ἁρμόσει καὶ νῦν ἅπασι τοῖς νεωτέροις ἀκοῦσαι) ἐκ τῆς Αἴτνης ῥύακα πυρὸς γενέσθαι· τοῦτον δὲ ῥεῖν φασιν ἐπί ⟨τε⟩ τὴν ἄλλην χώραν, καὶ δὴ καὶ πρὸς πόλιν τινὰ τῶν ἐκεῖ κατοικουμένων. τοὺς μὲν οὖν ἄλλους ὁρμῆσαι πρὸς φυγήν, τὴν αὑτῶν σωτηρίαν ζητοῦντας, ἕνα δέ τινα τῶν νεωτέρων, ὁρῶντα τὸν πατέρα πρεσβύτερον ὄντα καὶ οὐχὶ δυνάμενον ἀποχωρεῖν ἀλλὰ
96 ἐγκαταλαμβανόμενον, ἀράμενον φέρειν. φορτίου δ' οἶμαι προσγενομένου καὶ αὐτὸς ἐγκατελήφθη. ὅθεν δὴ καὶ ἄξιον θεωρῆσαι τὸ θεῖον, ὅτι τοῖς ἀνδράσι τοῖς ἀγαθοῖς εὐμενῶς ἔχει. λέγεται γὰρ κύκλῳ τὸν τόπον ἐκεῖνον περιρρεῦσαι τὸ πῦρ καὶ σωθῆναι τούτους μόνους, ἀφ' ὧν καὶ τὸ χωρίον ἔτι καὶ νῦν προσαγορεύεσθαι τῶν εὐσεβῶν χῶρον· τοὺς δὲ ταχεῖαν τὴν ἀποχώρησιν ποιησαμένους καὶ τοὺς ἑαυτῶν γονεῖς ἐγκαταλιπόντας ἅπαντας
97 ἀπολέσθαι. ὥστε καὶ ὑμᾶς δεῖν τὴν παρὰ ⟨τῶν⟩ θεῶν ἔχοντας μαρτυρίαν ὁμογνωμόνως τοῦτον κο-

λάζειν, τὸν ἅπασι τοῖς μεγίστοις ἀδικήμασιν ἔνοχον ὄντα κατὰ τὸ ἑαυτοῦ μέρος. τοὺς μὲν γὰρ θεοὺς τὰς πατρίους τιμὰς ἀπεστέρησε, τοὺς δὲ γονεῖς τοῖς πολεμίοις ἐγκατέλιπε, τοὺς δὲ τετελευτηκότας τῶν νομίμων οὐκ εἴασε τυχεῖν.

Καίτοι σκέψασθε, ὦ ἄνδρες· οὐ γὰρ ἀποστήσομαι τῶν παλαιῶν· ἐφ' οἷς γὰρ ἐκεῖνοι ποιοῦντες ἐφιλοτιμοῦντο, ταῦτα δικαίως ἂν ὑμεῖς ἀκούσαντες ἀποδέχοισθε. φασὶ γὰρ Εὔμολπον τὸν Ποσειδῶνος καὶ Χιόνης μετὰ Θρᾳκῶν ἐλθεῖν τῆς χώρας ταύτης ἀμφισβητοῦντα, τυχεῖν δὲ κατ' ἐκείνους τοὺς χρόνους βασιλεύοντα Ἐρεχθέα, γυναῖκα ἔχοντα Πραξιθέαν τὴν Κηφισοῦ θυγατέρα. μεγάλου δὲ στρατοπέδου μέλλοντος αὐτοῖς εἰσβάλλειν εἰς τὴν χώραν, εἰς Δελφοὺς ἰὼν ἠρώτα τὸν θεόν, τί ποιῶν ἂν νίκην λάβοι παρὰ τῶν πολεμίων. χρήσαντος δ' αὐτῷ τοῦ θεοῦ, τὴν θυγατέρα εἰ θύσειε πρὸ τοῦ συμβαλεῖν τὼ στρατοπέδω, κρατήσειν τῶν πολεμίων, ὁ δὲ τῷ θεῷ πιθόμενος τοῦτ' ἔπραξε, καὶ τοὺς ἐπιστρατευομένους ἐκ τῆς χώρας ἐξέβαλε. διὸ καὶ δικαίως ἄν τις Εὐριπίδην ἐπαινέσειεν, ὅτι τά τ' ἄλλ' ὢν ἀγαθὸς ποιητὴς καὶ τοῦτον τὸν μῦθον προείλετο ποιῆσαι, ἡγούμενος κάλλιστον ἂν γενέσθαι τοῖς πολίταις παράδειγμα τὰς ἐκείνων πράξεις, πρὸς ἃς ἀποβλέποντας καὶ θεωροῦντας συνεθίζεσθαι ταῖς ψυχαῖς τὸ τὴν πατρίδα φιλεῖν. ἄξιον δ', ὦ ἄνδρες δικασταί, καὶ τῶν ἰαμβείων ἀκοῦσαι, ἃ πεποίηκε λέγουσαν τὴν μητέρα τῆς παιδός. ὄψεσθε γὰρ ἐν αὐτοῖς μεγαλοψυχίαν καὶ γενναιότητα ἀξίαν καὶ τῆς πόλεως καὶ τοῦ γενέσθαι Κηφισοῦ θυγατέρα.

ΡΗΣΙΣ ΕΥΡΙΠΙΔΟΥ

τὰς χάριτας ὅστις εὐγενῶς χαρίζεται,
ἥδιον ἐν βροτοῖσιν· οἳ δὲ δρῶσι μέν,
χρόνῳ δὲ δρῶσι, δυσγενέστερον ⟨λέγω⟩·
ἐγὼ δὲ δώσω τὴν ἐμὴν παῖδα κτανεῖν.
λογίζομαι δὲ πολλά· πρῶτα μὲν πόλιν 5
οὐκ ἄν τιν' ἄλλην τῆσδε βελτίω λάβοιν·
ᾗ πρῶτα μὲν λεὼς οὐκ ἐπακτὸς ἄλλοθεν,
αὐτόχθονες δ' ἔφυμεν· αἱ δ' ἄλλαι πόλεις
πεσσῶν ὁμοίαις διαφοραῖς ἐκτισμέναι
ἄλλαι παρ' ἄλλων εἰσὶν εἰσαγώγιμοι. 10
ὅστις δ' ἀπ' ἄλλης πόλεος οἰκήσῃ πόλιν,
ἁρμὸς πονηρὸς ὥσπερ ἐν ξύλῳ παγείς,
λόγῳ πολίτης ἐστί, τοῖς δ' ἔργοισιν οὔ.
ἔπειτα τέκνα τοῦδ' ἕκατι τίκτομεν,
ὡς θεῶν τε βωμοὺς πατρίδα τε ῥυώμεθα. 15
πόλεως δ' ἁπάσης τοὔνομ' ἕν, πολλοὶ δέ νιν
ναίουσι· τούτους πῶς διαφθεῖραί με χρή,
ἐξὸν προπάντων μίαν ὕπερ δοῦναι θανεῖν;
εἴπερ γὰρ ἀριθμὸν οἶδα καὶ τοὐλάσσονος
τὸ μεῖζον, οὑνὸς οἶκος οὐ πλεῖον σθένει 20
πταίσας ἁπάσης πόλεος, οὐδ' ἴσον φέρει.
εἰ δ' ἦν ἐν οἴκοις ἀντὶ θηλειῶν στάχυς

ΚΑΤΑ ΛΕΩΚΡΑΤΟΥΣ

ἄρσην, πόλιν δὲ πολεμία κατεῖχε φλόξ,
οὐκ ἄν νιν ἐξέπεμπον εἰς μάχην δορός,
θάνατον προταρβοῦσ'; ἀλλ' ἔμοιγ' ἔστω τέκνα, 25
⟨ἃ⟩ καὶ μάχοιτο καὶ μετ' ἀνδράσιν πρέποι,
μὴ σχήματ' ἄλλως ἐν πόλει πεφυκότα.
τὰ μητέρων δὲ δάκρυ' ὅταν πέμπῃ τέκνα,
πολλοὺς ἐθήλυν' εἰς μάχην ὁρμωμένους.
μισῶ γυναῖκας αἵτινες πρὸ τοῦ καλοῦ 30
ζῆν παῖδας εἵλοντ' ἢ παρῄνεσαν κακά.
καὶ μὴν θανόντες γ' ἐν μάχῃ πολλῶν μέτα
τύμβον τε κοινὸν ἔλαχον εὔκλειάν τ' ἴσην·
τῇ 'μῇ δὲ παιδὶ στέφανος εἷς μιᾷ μόνῃ
πόλεως θανούσῃ τῆσδ' ὕπερ δοθήσεται. 35
καὶ τὴν τεκοῦσαν καὶ σὲ δύο θ' ὁμοσπόρω
σώσει· τί τούτων οὐχὶ δέξασθαι καλόν;
τὴν οὐκ ἐμὴν πλὴν ⟨ᾗ⟩ φύσει δώσω κόρην
θῦσαι πρὸ γαίας. εἰ γὰρ αἱρεθήσεται
πόλις, τί παίδων τῶν ἐμῶν μέτεστί μοι; 40
οὐκοῦν ἅπαντα τοὖν γ' ἐμοὶ σωθήσεται·
ἄρξουσιν ἄλλοι, τήνδ' ἐγὼ σώσω πόλιν.
ἐκεῖνο δ' οὗ ⟨τὸ⟩ πλεῖστον ἐν κοινῷ μέρος,
οὐκ ἔσθ' ἑκούσης τῆς ἐμῆς ψυχῆς ἀνήρ,
προγόνων παλαιὰ θέσμι' ⟨ὅσ⟩τις ἐκβαλεῖ· 45
οὐδ' ἀντ' ἐλάας χρυσέας τε Γοργόνος
τρίαιναν ὀρθὴν στᾶσαν ἐν πόλεως βάθροις
Εὔμολπος οὐδὲ Θρῇξ ἀναστέψει λεὼς
στεφάνοισι, Παλλὰς δ' οὐδαμοῦ τιμήσεται.
χρῆσθ', ὦ πολῖται, τοῖς ἐμοῖς λοχεύμασιν, 50

ΛΥΚΟΥΡΓΟΥ

σώζεσθε, νικᾶτ᾽· ἀντὶ γὰρ ψυχῆς μιᾶς
οὐκ ἔσθ᾽ ὅπως ὑμῖν ἐγὼ οὐ σώσω πόλιν.
ὦ πατρίς, εἴθε πάντες οἳ ναίουσί σε
οὕτω φιλοῖεν ὡς ἐγώ· καὶ ῥᾳδίως
οἰκοῖμεν ἄν σε, κοὐδὲν ἂν πάσχοις κακόν.   55

101   Ταῦτα, ὦ ἄνδρες, τοὺς πατέρας ὑμῶν ἐπαίδευε. 25
φύσει γὰρ οὐσῶν φιλοτέκνων πασῶν τῶν γυναικῶν, ταύτην ἐποίησε τὴν πατρίδα μᾶλλον τῶν
παίδων φιλοῦσαν, ἐνδεικνύμενος ὅτι εἴπερ αἱ γυναῖκες τοῦτο τολμήσουσι ποιεῖν, τούς γ᾽ ἄνδρας
ἀνυπέρβλητόν τινα δεῖ τὴν εὔνοιαν ὑπὲρ τῆς
πατρίδος ἔχειν, καὶ μὴ φεύγειν αὐτὴν ἐγκαταλιπόντας, μηδὲ καταισχύνειν πρὸς ἅπαντας τοὺς
Ἕλληνας, ὥσπερ Λεωκράτης.

102   Βούλομαι δ᾽ ὑμῖν καὶ τῶν Ὁμήρου παρασχέ- 26
σθαι ἐπῶν· οὕτω γὰρ ὑπέλαβον ὑμῶν οἱ πατέρες
σπουδαῖον εἶναι ποιητήν, ὥστε νόμον ἔθεντο καθ᾽
ἑκάστην πεντετηρίδα τῶν Παναθηναίων μόνου τῶν
ἄλλων ποιητῶν ῥαψῳδεῖσθαι τὰ ἔπη, ἐπίδειξιν
ποιούμενοι πρὸς τοὺς Ἕλληνας, ὅτι τὰ κάλλιστα
τῶν ἔργων προῃροῦντο, εἰκότως· οἱ μὲν γὰρ νόμοι
διὰ τὴν συντομίαν οὐ διδάσκουσιν, ἀλλ᾽ ἐπιτάττουσιν ἃ δεῖ ποιεῖν, οἱ δὲ ποιηταὶ μιμούμενοι
τὸν ἀνθρώπινον βίον, τὰ κάλλιστα τῶν ἔργων
ἐκλεξάμενοι, μετὰ λόγου καὶ ἀποδείξεως τοὺς ἀν-
103 θρώπους συμπείθουσιν. Ἕκτωρ γὰρ τοῖς Τρωσὶ
παρακελευόμενος ὑπὲρ τῆς πατρίδος τάδ᾽ εἴρηκεν·

ΚΑΤΑ ΛΕΩΚΡΑΤΟΥΣ 39

ἀλλὰ μάχεσθ' ἐπὶ νηυσὶ διαμπερές. ὃς δέ κεν ὕμεων
βλήμενος ἠὲ τυπεὶς θάνατον καὶ πότμον ἐπίσπῃ,
τεθνάτω. οὔ οἱ ἀεικὲς ἀμυνομένῳ περὶ πάτρης
τεθνάμεν· ἀλλ' ἄλοχός τε σόη καὶ νήπια τέκνα,
καὶ κλῆρος καὶ οἶκος ἀκήρατος, εἴ κεν Ἀχαιοὶ
οἴχωνται σὺν νηυσὶ φίλην ἐς πατρίδα γαῖαν.

27 Τούτων τῶν ἐπῶν ἀκούοντες, ὦ ἄνδρες, οἱ πρό- 104
γονοι ὑμῶν, καὶ τὰ τοιαῦτα τῶν ἔργων ζηλοῦντες,
οὕτως ἔσχον πρὸς ἀρετήν, ὥστ' οὐ μόνον ὑπὲρ τῆς
αὑτῶν πατρίδος, ἀλλὰ καὶ πάσης ⟨τῆς⟩ Ἑλλάδος
ὡς κοινῆς ἤθελον ἀποθνήσκειν. οἱ γοῦν ἐν Μαραθῶνι παραταξάμενοι τοῖς βαρβάροις τὸν ἐξ
ἁπάσης τῆς Ἀσίας στόλον ἐκράτησαν, τοῖς ἰδίοις
κινδύνοις κοινὴν ἄδειαν ἅπασι τοῖς Ἕλλησι κτώ-
μενοι, οὐκ ἐπὶ τῇ δόξῃ μέγα φρονοῦντες, ἀλλ'
ἐπὶ τῷ ταύτης ἄξια πράττειν, τῶν μὲν Ἑλλήνων
προστάτας, τῶν δὲ βαρβάρων δεσπότας ἑαυτοὺς
καθιστάντες· οὐ γὰρ λόγῳ τὴν ἀρετὴν ἐπετήδευον,
28 ἀλλ' ἔργῳ πᾶσιν ἐπεδείκνυντο. τοιγαροῦν οὕτως 105
ἦσαν ἄνδρες σπουδαῖοι καὶ κοινῇ καὶ ἰδίᾳ οἱ
τότε τὴν πόλιν οἰκοῦντες, ὥστε τοῖς ἀνδρειοτάτοις
Λακεδαιμονίοις ἐν τοῖς ἔμπροσθε χρόνοις πολεμοῦσι πρὸς Μεσσηνίους ἀνεῖλεν ὁ θεός, παρ'
ἡμῶν ἡγεμόνα λαβεῖν καὶ νικήσειν τοὺς ἐναντίους.
καίτοι εἰ τοῖν ἀφ' Ἡρακλέους γεγενημένοιν, οἳ
ἀεὶ βασιλεύουσιν ἐν Σπάρτῃ, τοὺς παρ' ἡμῶν
ἡγεμόνας ἀμείνους ὁ θεὸς ἔκρινε, πῶς οὐκ ἀνυ-

106 πέρβλητον χρὴ τὴν ἐκείνων ἀρετὴν νομίζειν; τίς γὰρ οὐκ οἶδε τῶν Ἑλλήνων, ὅτι Τυρταῖον στρατηγὸν ἔλαβον παρὰ τῆς πόλεως, μεθ᾽ οὗ καὶ τῶν πολεμίων ἐκράτησαν καὶ τὴν περὶ τοὺς νέους ἐπιμέλειαν συνετάξαντο, οὐ μόνον εἰς τὸν παρόντα κίνδυνον, ἀλλ᾽ εἰς ἅπαντα τὸν αἰῶνα βουλευσάμενοι καλῶς. κατέλιπε γὰρ αὐτοῖς ἐλεγεῖα ποιή-
107 σας, ὧν ἀκούοντες παιδεύονται πρὸς ἀνδρείαν· καὶ περὶ τοὺς ἄλλους ποιητὰς οὐδένα λόγον ἔχοντες, περὶ τούτου οὕτω σφόδρα ἐσπουδάκασιν, ὥστε νόμον ἔθεντο, ὅταν ἐν τοῖς ὅπλοις ἐξεστρατευμένοι ὦσι, καλεῖν ἐπὶ τὴν τοῦ βασιλέως σκηνὴν ἀκουσομένους τῶν Τυρταίου ποιημάτων ἅπαντας, νομίζοντες οὕτως ἂν αὐτοὺς μάλιστα πρὸ τῆς πατρίδος ἐθέλειν ἀποθνήσκειν. χρήσιμον δ᾽ ἐστὶ καὶ τούτων ἀκοῦσαι τῶν ἐλεγείων, ἵν᾽ ἐπίστησθε οἷα ποιοῦντες εὐδοκίμουν παρ᾽ ἐκείνοις.

τεθνάμεναι γὰρ καλὸν ἐνὶ προμάχοισι πεσόντα
ἄνδρ᾽ ἀγαθόν, περὶ ᾗ πατρίδι μαρνάμενον.
ἣν δ᾽ αὐτοῦ προλιπόντα πόλιν καὶ πίονας ἀγροὺς
πτωχεύειν πάντων ἔστ᾽ ἀνιηρότατον,
πλαζόμενον σὺν μητρὶ φίλῃ καὶ πατρὶ γέροντι 5
παισί τε σὺν μικροῖς κουριδίῃ τ᾽ ἀλόχῳ.
ἐχθρὸς μὲν γὰρ τοῖσι μετέσσεται, οὕς κεν ἵκηται
χρημοσύνῃ τ᾽ εἴκων καὶ στυγερῇ πενίῃ,
αἰσχύνει δὲ γένος, κατὰ δ᾽ ἀγλαὸν εἶδος ἐλέγχει,
πᾶσα δ᾽ ἀτιμίη καὶ κακότης ἕπεται. 10

εἰ δ' οὕτως ἀνδρός τοι ἀλωμένου οὐδεμί' ὥρη
γίγνεται οὐδ' αἰδώς, οὔτ' ὀπίσω γένεος,
θυμῷ γῆς περὶ τῆσδε μαχώμεθα, καὶ περὶ παίδων
θνήσκωμεν ψυχέων μηκέτι φειδόμενοι.
ὦ νέοι, ἀλλὰ μάχεσθε παρ' ἀλλήλοισι μένοντες, 15
μηδὲ φυγῆς αἰσχρῆς ἄρχετε μηδὲ φόβου,
ἀλλὰ μέγαν ποιεῖσθε καὶ ἄλκιμον ἐν φρεσὶ θυμόν,
μηδὲ φιλοψυχεῖτ' ἀνδράσι μαρνάμενοι·
τοὺς δὲ παλαιοτέρους, ὧν οὐκέτι γούνατ' ἐλαφρά,
μὴ καταλείποντες φεύγετε, τοὺς γεραιούς. 20
αἰσχρὸν γὰρ δὴ τοῦτο, μετὰ προμάχοισι πεσόντα
κεῖσθαι πρόσθε νέων ἄνδρα παλαιότερον,
ἤδη λευκὸν ἔχοντα κάρη πολιόν τε γένειον,
θυμὸν ἀποπνείοντ' ἄλκιμον ἐν κονίῃ,
αἱματόεντ' αἰδοῖα φίλῃσ' ἐν χερσὶν ἔχοντα 25
(αἰσχρὰ τά γ' ὀφθαλμοῖς καὶ νεμεσητὸν ἰδεῖν)
καὶ χρόα γυμνωθέντα. νέοισι δὲ πάντ' ἐπέοικεν,
ὄφρ' ἐρατῆς ἥβης ἀγλαὸν ἄνθος ἔχῃ·
ἀνδράσι μὲν θηητὸς ἰδεῖν, ἐρατὸς δὲ γυναιξὶν
ζωὸς ἐών, καλὸς δ' ἐν προμάχοισι πεσών. 30
ἀλλά τις εὖ διαβὰς μενέτω ποσὶν ἀμφοτέροισιν
στηριχθεὶς ἐπὶ γῆς, χεῖλος ὀδοῦσι δακών.

Καλά γ', ὦ ἄνδρες, καὶ χρήσιμα τοῖς βουλομένοις 108
προσέχειν. οὕτω τοίνυν εἶχον πρὸς ἀνδρείαν οἱ
τούτων ἀκούοντες, ὥστε πρὸς τὴν πόλιν ἡμῶν
περὶ τῆς ἡγεμονίας ἀμφισβητεῖν, εἰκότως· τὰ γὰρ
κάλλιστα τῶν ἔργων ἀμφοτέροις ἦν κατειργα-

σμένα. οἱ μὲν γὰρ ⟨ἡμέτεροι⟩ πρόγονοι τοὺς βαρβάρους ἐνίκησαν, οἳ πρῶτοι τῆς Ἀττικῆς ἐπέβησαν, καὶ καταφανῆ ἐποίησαν τὴν ἀνδρείαν τοῦ πλούτου καὶ τὴν ἀρετὴν τοῦ πλήθους περιγιγνομένην· Λακεδαιμόνιοι δ' ἐν Θερμοπύλαις παραταξάμενοι, ταῖς μὲν τύχαις οὐχ ὁμοίαις ἐχρήσαντο, τῇ δ' ἀνδρείᾳ πολὺ πάντων διήνεγκαν.
109 τοιγαροῦν ἑκατέροις ἐπιτύμβια μαρτύρια ἔστιν ἰδεῖν τῆς ἀρετῆς αὐτῶν ἀναγεγραμμένα ἀληθῆ πρὸς ἅπαντας τοὺς Ἕλληνας, ἐκείνοις μέν·

ὦ ξεῖν', ἄγγειλον Λακεδαιμονίοις, ὅτι τῇδε
κείμεθα τοῖς κείνων πειθόμενοι νομίμοις,

τοῖς δ' ὑμετέροις προγόνοις·

Ἑλλήνων προμαχοῦντες Ἀθηναῖοι Μαραθῶνι
χρυσοφόρων Μήδων ἐστόρεσαν δύναμιν.

110 Ταῦτα, ὦ Ἀθηναῖοι, καὶ μνημονεύεσθαι καλὰ καὶ 29 τοῖς πράξασιν ἔπαινος καὶ τῇ πόλει δόξα ἀείμνηστος. ἀλλ' οὐχ ὁ Λεωκράτης πεποίηκεν, ἀλλ' ἑκὼν τὴν ἐξ ἅπαντος τοῦ αἰῶνος συνηθροισμένην τῇ πόλει δόξαν κατῄσχυνεν. ἐὰν μὲν οὖν αὐτὸν ἀποκτείνητε, δόξετε πᾶσι τοῖς Ἕλλησι καὶ ὑμεῖς τὰ τοιαῦτα τῶν ἔργων μισεῖν· εἰ δὲ μή, καὶ τοὺς προγόνους τῆς παλαιᾶς δόξης ἀποστερήσετε καὶ τοὺς ἄλλους πολίτας μεγάλα βλάψετε. οἱ γὰρ ἐκείνους μὴ θαυμάζοντες τοῦτον πειράσονται μιμεῖσθαι, νομίζοντες ἐκεῖνα μὲν παρὰ τοῖς παλαιοῖς

ΚΑΤΑ ΛΕΩΚΡΑΤΟΥΣ 43

εὐδοκιμεῖν, παρ' ὑμῖν δ' ἀναίδειαν καὶ προδοσίαν καὶ δειλίαν κεκρίσθαι κάλλιστον.

30 Εἰ ⟨δὲ⟩ μὴ δύνασθε ὑπ' ἐμοῦ διδαχθῆναι, ὃν τρόπον δεῖ πρὸς τοὺς τοιούτους ἔχειν, σκέψασθε ἐκείνους τίνα τρόπον ἐλάμβανον παρ' αὐτῶν τὴν τιμωρίαν· ὥσπερ γὰρ τὰ καλὰ τῶν ἔργων ἠπίσταντο ἐπιτηδεύειν, οὕτω καὶ τὰ πονηρὰ προῃροῦντο κολάζειν. ἐκεῖνοι γάρ, ὦ ἄνδρες, θεωρήσατε ὡς ὠργίζοντο τοῖς προδόταις καὶ κοινοὺς ἐχθροὺς ἐνόμιζον εἶναι τῆς πόλεως. Φρυνίχου γὰρ ἀποσφαγέντος νύκτωρ παρὰ τὴν κρήνην τὴν ἐν τοῖς οἰσύοις ὑπὸ Ἀπολλοδώρου καὶ Θρασυβούλου, καὶ τούτων ληφθέντων καὶ εἰς τὸ δεσμωτήριον ἀποτεθέντων ὑπὸ τῶν τοῦ Φρυνίχου φίλων, αἰσθόμενος ὁ δῆμος τὸ γεγονὸς τούς τε εἰρχθέντας ἐξήγαγε καὶ βασάνων γενομένων ἀνέκρινε, καὶ ζητῶν τὸ πρᾶγμα εὗρε, τὸν μὲν Φρύνιχον προδιδόντα τὴν πόλιν, τοὺς δ' ἀποκτείναντας αὐτὸν ἀδίκως εἰρχθέντας· καὶ ψηφίζεται ὁ δῆμος Κριτίου εἰπόντος, τὸν μὲν νεκρὸν κρίνειν προδοσίας, κἂν δόξῃ προδότης ὢν ἐν τῇ χώρᾳ τεθάφθαι, τά γε ὀστᾶ αὐτοῦ ἀνορύξαι καὶ ἐξορίσαι ἔξω τῆς Ἀττικῆς, ὅπως ἂν μὴ κέηται ἐν τῇ χώρᾳ μηδὲ τὰ ὀστᾶ τοῦ τὴν χώραν καὶ τὴν πόλιν προδιδόντος. ἐψηφίσαντο δὲ καὶ ἐὰν ἀπολογῶνταί τινες ὑπὲρ τοῦ τετελευτηκότος, ἐὰν ἁλῷ ὁ τεθνηκώς, ἐνόχους εἶναι καὶ τούτους τοῖς αὐτοῖς ἐπιτιμίοις· οὕτως οὐδὲ βοηθεῖν τοῖς τοὺς ἄλλους ἐγκαταλείπουσιν

ἡγοῦντο δίκαιον εἶναι, ἀλλ' ὁμοίως ἂν προδοῦναι τὴν πόλιν καὶ τὸν διασῴζοντα τὸν προδότην. τοιγαροῦν οὕτω μισοῦντες τοὺς ἀδικοῦντας καὶ τὰ τοιαῦτα κατ' αὐτῶν ψηφιζόμενοι, ἀσφαλῶς ἐκ τῶν κινδύνων ἀπηλλάττοντο. Λαβὲ δ' αὐτοῖς τὸ ψήφισμα, γραμματεῦ, καὶ ἀνάγνωθι.

ΨΗΦΙΣΜΑ

115 Ἀκούετε, ὦ ἄνδρες, τούτου τοῦ ψηφίσματος. ἔπειτα ἐκεῖνοι μὲν τὰ τοῦ προδότου ὀστᾶ ἀνορύξαντες ἐκ τῆς Ἀττικῆς ἐξώρισαν, καὶ τοὺς ἀπολογουμένους ὑπὲρ αὐτοῦ Ἀρίσταρχον καὶ Ἀλεξικλέα ἀπέκτειναν καὶ οὐδ' ἐν τῇ χώρᾳ ταφῆναι ἐπέτρεψαν, ὑμεῖς δ' αὐτὸ τὸ σῶμα τὸ προδεδωκὸς τὴν πόλιν ζῶν καὶ ὑποχείριον ἔχοντες τῇ ψήφῳ, 116 ἀτιμώρητον ἐάσετε; καὶ τοσοῦτόν γ' ἔσεσθε τῶν προγόνων χείρους, ὅσον ἐκεῖνοι μὲν τοὺς λόγῳ μόνον τῷ προδότῃ βοηθήσαντας ταῖς ἐσχάταις τιμωρίαις μετῆλθον, ὑμεῖς δὲ αὐτὸν τὸν ἔργῳ καὶ οὐ λόγῳ τὸν δῆμον ἐγκαταλιπόντα ὡς οὐδὲν ἀδικοῦντα ἀφήσετε; μὴ δῆτα, ὦ ἄνδρες δικασταί· ⟨οὔτε γὰρ ὅσιον⟩ ὑμῖν οὔτε πάτριον, ἀναξίως ὑμῶν αὐτῶν ψηφίζεσθαι. καὶ γὰρ εἰ μὲν ἕν τι τοιοῦτον γεγονὸς ἦν ψήφισμα, εἶχεν ἄν τις εἰπεῖν ὡς δι' ὀργὴν μᾶλλον ἢ δι' ἀλήθειαν ἐποιήσαντο· ὅταν δὲ παρὰ πάντων ὁμοίως εἰληφότες ὦσι τὴν αὐτὴν τιμωρίαν, πῶς οὐκ εὔδηλον ὅτι φύσει πᾶσι 117 τοῖς τοιούτοις ἔργοις ἐπολέμουν; Ἵππαρχον γὰρ

τὸν Χάρμου, οὐχ ὑπομείναντα τὴν περὶ τῆς προδοσίας ἐν τῷ δήμῳ κρίσιν, ἀλλ' ἔρημον τὸν ἀγῶνα ἐάσαντα, θανάτῳ τοῦτον ζημιώσαντες, ἐπειδὴ τῆς ἀδικίας οὐκ ἔλαβον τὸ σῶμα ὅμηρον, τὴν εἰκόνα αὐτοῦ ἐξ ἀκροπόλεως καθελόντες καὶ συγχωνεύσαντες καὶ ποιήσαντες στήλην, ἐψηφίσαντο εἰς ταύτην ἀναγράφειν τοὺς ἀλιτηρίους καὶ τοὺς προδότας· καὶ αὐτὸς ὁ Ἵππαρχος ἐν ταύτῃ τῇ στήλῃ ἀναγέγραπται, καὶ οἱ ἄλλοι δὲ προδόται. Καί μοι λαβὲ πρῶτον μὲν τὸ ψήφισμα, καθ' ὃ ἡ 118 εἰκὼν τοῦ Ἱππάρχου τοῦ προδότου ἐξ ἀκροπόλεως καθῃρέθη, ἔπειτα τῆς στήλης τὸ ὑπόγραμμα, καὶ τοὺς ὕστερον προσαναγραφέντας προδότας εἰς ταύτην τὴν στήλην, καὶ ἀναγίγνωσκε, γραμματεῦ.

ΨΗΦΙΣΜΑ ΚΑΙ ΥΠΟΓΡΑΜΜΑ ΤΗΣ ΣΤΗΛΗΣ

Τί δοκοῦσιν ὑμῖν, ὦ ἄνδρες; ἀρά γ' ὁμοίως 119 ὑμῖν περὶ τῶν ἀδικούντων γιγνώσκειν, καὶ οὐκ, ἐπειδὴ καὶ τὸ σῶμα οὐκ ἐδύναντο ὑποχείριον τοῦ προδότου λαβεῖν, τὸ μνημεῖον τοῦ προδότου ἀνελόντες ταῖς ἐνδεχομέναις τιμωρίαις ἐκόλασαν; οὐχ ὅπως τὸν χαλκοῦν ἀνδριάντα συγχωνεύσειαν, ἀλλ' ἵνα τοῖς ἐπιγιγνομένοις παράδειγμα εἰς τὸν λοιπὸν χρόνον ὡς εἶχον πρὸς τοὺς προδότας καταλίποιεν.

Λαβὲ δ' αὐτοῖς καὶ τὸ ἕτερον ψήφισμα ⟨τὸ⟩ 120 περὶ τῶν εἰς Δεκέλειαν μεταστάντων, ὅτε ὁ δῆμος ὑπὸ Λακεδαιμονίων ἐπολιορκεῖτο, ὅπως εἰδῶσιν ὅτι περὶ τῶν προδοτῶν οἱ πρόγονοι ὁμοίας καὶ

ΛΥΚΟΥΡΓΟΥ

ἀκολούθους ἀλλήλαις τὰς τιμωρίας ἐποιοῦντο.
ἀναγίγνωσκε, γραμματεῦ.

ΨΗΦΙΣΜΑ

121 Ἀκούετε, ὦ ἄνδρες, καὶ τούτου τοῦ ψηφίσματος, ὅτι τῶν ἐν τῷ πολέμῳ μεταστάντων εἰς Δεκέλειαν κατέγνωσαν, καὶ ἐψηφίσαντο, ἐάν τις αὐτῶν ἐπανιὼν ἁλίσκηται, ἀπαγαγεῖν Ἀθηναίων τὸν βουλόμενον πρὸς τοὺς θεσμοθέτας, παραλαβόντας δὲ παραδοῦναι τῷ ἐπὶ τοῦ ὀρύγματος. ἔπειτα ἐκεῖνοι μὲν τοὺς ἐν αὐτῇ τῇ χώρᾳ μεταστάντας οὕτως ἐκόλαζον, ὑμεῖς δὲ τὸν ἐκ τῆς πόλεως καὶ τῆς χώρας ἐν τῷ πολέμῳ φυγόντα εἰς Ῥόδον καὶ προδόντα τὸν δῆμον οὐκ ἀποκτενεῖτε; πῶς οὖν δόξετε ἀπόγονοι εἶναι ἐκείνων τῶν ἀνδρῶν;

122 Ἄξιον τοίνυν ἀκοῦσαι καὶ ⟨τοῦ⟩ περὶ τοῦ ἐν Σαλαμῖνι τελευτήσαντος γενομένου ψηφίσματος, ὃν ἡ βουλή, ὅτι λόγῳ μόνον ἐνεχείρει προδιδόναι τὴν πόλιν, περιελομένη τοὺς στεφάνους αὐτοχειρὶ ἀπέκτεινεν. γενναῖον δ', ὦ ἄνδρες, τὸ ψήφισμα καὶ ἄξιον τῶν ὑμετέρων προγόνων, δικαίως· εὐγενεῖς γὰρ οὐ μόνον τὰς ψυχάς, ἀλλὰ καὶ τὰς τῶν ἀδικούντων τιμωρίας ἐκέκτηντο.

ΨΗΦΙΣΜΑ

123 Τί οὖν, ὦ ἄνδρες; ἆρά γ' ὑμῖν δοκεῖ βουλομένοις μιμεῖσθαι τοὺς προγόνους πάτριον εἶναι Λεωκρά-

ΚΑΤΑ ΛΕΩΚΡΑΤΟΥΣ

την μὴ ἀποκτεῖναι; ὁπότε γὰρ ἐκεῖνοι τὸν ἀνάστατον τὴν πόλιν οὖσαν λόγῳ μόνον προδιδόντα οὕτως ἀπέκτειναν, τί ὑμᾶς προσήκει τὸν ἔργῳ καὶ οὐ λόγῳ τὴν οἰκουμένην ἐκλιπόντα ποιῆσαι; ἆρ' οὐχ ὑπερβαλέσθαι ἐκείνους τῇ τιμωρίᾳ; καὶ ὅτ' ἐκεῖνοι τοὺς ἐπιχειρήσαντας τῆς παρὰ τοῦ δήμου σωτηρίας ἀποστερεῖν οὕτως ἐκόλασαν, τί ὑμᾶς προσήκει τὸν αὐτοῦ τοῦ δήμου τὴν σωτηρίαν προδόντα ποιῆσαι; καὶ ὅτε ὑπὲρ τῆς δόξης ἐκεῖνοι τοὺς αἰτίους οὕτως ἐτιμωροῦντο, τί ὑμᾶς ὑπὲρ τῆς πατρίδος προσήκει ποιεῖν;

Ἱκανὰ μὲν οὖν καὶ ταῦτα τὴν τῶν προγόνων 124 γνῶναι διάνοιαν, ὡς εἶχον πρὸς τοὺς παρανομοῦντας εἰς τὴν πόλιν· οὐ μὴν ἀλλ' ἔτι βούλομαι τῆς στήλης ἀκοῦσαι ὑμᾶς τῆς ἐν τῷ βουλευτηρίῳ περὶ τῶν προδοτῶν καὶ τῶν τὸν δῆμον καταλυόντων· τὸ γὰρ μετὰ πολλῶν παραδειγμάτων διδάσκειν ῥᾳδίαν ὑμῖν τὴν κρίσιν καθίστησι. μετὰ γὰρ τοὺς τριάκοντα οἱ πατέρες ὑμῶν, πεπονθότες ὑπὸ τῶν πολιτῶν, οἷα οὐδεὶς πώποτε τῶν Ἑλλήνων ἠξίωσε, καὶ μόλις εἰς τὴν ἑαυτῶν κατεληλυθότες, ἀπάσας τὰς ὁδοὺς τῶν ἀδικημάτων ἐνέφραξαν, πεπειραμένοι καὶ εἰδότες τὰς ἀρχὰς καὶ τὰς ἐφόδους τῶν τὸν δῆμον προδιδόντων. ἐψηφίσαντο γὰρ καὶ 125 ὤμοσαν, ἐάν τις τυραννίδι ἐπιτιθῆται ἢ τὴν πόλιν προδιδῷ ἢ τὸν δῆμον καταλύῃ, τὸν αἰσθανόμενον καθαρὸν εἶναι ἀποκτείναντα, καὶ κρεῖττον ἔδοξεν αὐτοῖς τοὺς τὴν αἰτίαν ἔχοντας τεθνάναι μᾶλλον ἢ πειραθέντας μετὰ ἀληθείας αὐτοὺς δουλεύειν· ἀρχὴν γὰρ οὕτως ᾤοντο δεῖν ζῆν τοὺς πολίτας, ὥστε μηδ' εἰς ὑποψίαν ἐλθεῖν μηδένα τούτων τῶν ἀδικημάτων. Καί μοι λαβὲ τὸ ψήφισμα.

ΨΗΦΙΣΜΑ

Ταῦτα, ὦ ἄνδρες, ἔγραψαν εἰς τὴν στήλην, καὶ ταύτην ἔστησαν εἰς τὸ βουλευτήριον, ὑπόμνημα τοῖς καθ' ἑκάστην ἡμέραν συνιοῦσι καὶ βουλευομένοις ὑπὲρ τῆς πατρίδος, ὡς δεῖ πρὸς τοὺς τοιούτους ἔχειν. καὶ διὰ τοῦτο ἄν τις αἴσθηται μόνον μέλλοντας αὐτοὺς τούτων τι ποιεῖν, ἀποκτείνειν συνώμοσαν, εἰκότως· τῶν μὲν γὰρ ἄλλων ἀδικημάτων ὑστέρας δεῖ τετάχθαι τὰς τιμωρίας, προδοσίας δὲ καὶ δήμου καταλύσεως προτέρας. εἰ γὰρ προήσεσθε τοῦτον τὸν καιρόν, ἐν ᾧ μέλλουσιν ἐκεῖνοι κατὰ τῆς πατρίδος φαῦλόν τι πράττειν, οὐκ ἔστιν ὑμῖν μετὰ ταῦτα δίκην παρ' αὐτῶν ἀδικούντων λαβεῖν· κρείττους γὰρ ἤδη γίγνονται τῆς παρὰ τῶν ἀδικουμένων τιμωρίας.

Ἐνθυμεῖσθε τοίνυν, ὦ ἄνδρες, τῆς προνοίας ταύτης καὶ τῶν ἔργων ἀξίως, καὶ μὴ ἐπιλανθάνεσθε ἐν τῇ ψήφῳ, οἵων ἀνδρῶν ἔκγονοί ἐστε, ἀλλὰ παρακελεύεσθε ὑμῖν αὐτοῖς, ὅπως ὅμοια ἐκείνοις καὶ ἀκόλουθα ἐν τῇ τήμερον ἡμέρᾳ ἐψηφισμένοι ἐκ τοῦ δικαστηρίου ἐξίητε. ὑπομνήματα δ' ἔχετε καὶ παραδείγματα τῆς ἐκείνων τιμωρίας τὰ ἐν τοῖς περὶ τῶν ἀδικούντων ψηφίσμασιν ὡρισμένα·

ΚΑΤΑ ΛΕΩΚΡΑΤΟΥΣ

διομωμόκατε δ' ἐν τῷ ψηφίσματι τῷ Δημοφάντου, κτείνειν τὸν τὴν πατρίδα προδιδόντα καὶ λόγῳ καὶ ἔργῳ καὶ χειρὶ καὶ ψήφῳ. μὴ γὰρ οἴεσθε τῶν μὲν οὐσιῶν, ἃς ἂν οἱ πρόγονοι καταλίπωσι, κληρονόμοι εἶναι, τῶν δ' ὅρκων καὶ τῆς πίστεως, ἣν δόντες οἱ πατέρες ὑμῶν ὅμηρον τοῖς θεοῖς τῆς κοινῆς εὐδαιμονίας τῆς πόλεως μετεῖχον, ταύτης δὲ μὴ κληρονομεῖν.

32 Οὐ μόνον τοίνυν ἡ πόλις ὑμῶν οὕτως ἔσχε πρὸς τοὺς προδιδόντας, ἀλλὰ καὶ Λακεδαιμόνιοι. καὶ μή μοι ἀχθεσθῆτε, ὦ ἄνδρες, εἰ πολλάκις μέμνημαι τῶν ἀνδρῶν τούτων· καλὸν γάρ ἐστ' ἐκ πόλεως εὐνομουμένης περὶ τῶν δικαίων παραδείγματα λαμβάνειν, ⟨ἵν'⟩ ἀσφαλέστερον ἕκαστος ὑμῶν τὴν δικαίαν καὶ τὴν εὔορκον ψῆφον θῆται. Παυσανίαν γὰρ τὸν βασιλέα αὐτῶν προδιδόντα τῷ Πέρσῃ τὴν Ἑλλάδα λαβόντες, ἐπειδὴ ἔφθασε καταφυγὼν εἰς τὸ τῆς Χαλκιοίκου ἱερόν, τὴν θύραν ἀποικοδομήσαντες καὶ τὴν ὀροφὴν ἀποσκευάσαντες καὶ κύκλῳ περιστρατοπεδεύσαντες, οὐ πρότερον ἀπῆλθον πρὶν ἢ τῷ λιμῷ ἀπέκτειναν, καὶ πᾶσιν ἐπίσημον ἐποίησαν τὴν τιμωρίαν ὅτι οὐδ' αἱ παρὰ τῶν θεῶν ἐπικουρίαι τοῖς προδόταις βοηθοῦσιν, εἰκότως· οὐδὲν γὰρ πρότερον ἀδικοῦσιν ἢ περὶ τοὺς θεοὺς ἀσεβοῦσι, τῶν πατρίων νομίμων αὐτοὺς ἀποστεροῦντες. μέγιστον δὲ τῶν ἐκεῖ γεγενημένων τεκμήριόν ἐστιν ὃ μέλλω λέγειν· νόμον γὰρ ἔθεντο περὶ ἁπάντων τῶν μὴ 'θελόντων ὑπὲρ

τῆς πατρίδος κινδυνεύειν, διαρρήδην λέγοντα ἀποθνήσκειν, εἰς αὐτὸ τοῦτο τὴν τιμωρίαν τάξαντες, εἰς ὃ μάλιστα φοβούμενοι τυγχάνουσι, καὶ τὴν ἐκ τοῦ πολέμου σωτηρίαν ὑπεύθυνον ἐποίησαν κινδύνῳ μετ' αἰσχύνης. ἵνα δ' εἰδῆτε ὅτι οὐ λόγον ἀναπόδεικτον εἴρηκα, ἀλλὰ μετ' ἀληθείας παραδείγματα, φέρε αὐτοῖς τὸν νόμον.

ΝΟΜΟΣ ΛΑΚΕΔΑΙΜΟΝΙΩΝ

130 Ἐνθυμεῖσθε δή, ὡς καλὸς ὁ νόμος, ὦ ἄνδρες, καὶ σύμφορος οὐ μόνον ἐκείνοις, ἀλλὰ καὶ τοῖς ἄλλοις ἀνθρώποις. ὁ γὰρ παρὰ τῶν πολιτῶν φόβος ἰσχυρὸς ὢν ἀναγκάσει τοὺς πρὸς τοὺς πολεμίους κινδύνους ὑπομένειν· τίς γὰρ ὁρῶν θανάτῳ ζημιούμενον τὸν προδότην, ἐν τοῖς κινδύνοις ἐκλείψει τὴν πατρίδα; ἢ τίς παρὰ τὸ συμφέρον τῆς πόλεως φιλοψυχήσει, εἰδὼς ὑποκειμένην αὐτῷ ⟨ταύτην⟩ τιμωρίαν; οὐδεμίαν γὰρ ἄλλην δεῖ ζημίαν εἶναι τῆς δειλίας ἢ θάνατον· εἰδότες γὰρ ὅτι δυοῖν κινδύνοιν ὑποκειμένοιν ἀναγκαῖον ἔσται θατέρου μετασχεῖν, πολὺ μᾶλλον αἱρήσονται τὸν πρὸς τοὺς πολεμίους ἢ τὸν πρὸς τοὺς νόμους καὶ τοὺς πολίτας.

131 Τοσούτῳ δ' ἂν δικαιότερον οὗτος ἀποθάνοι τῶν ἐκ τῶν στρατοπέδων φευγόντων, ὅσον οἱ μὲν εἰς τὴν πόλιν ἥκουσιν, ὡς ὑπὲρ ταύτης μαχούμενοι ἢ κοινῇ μετὰ τῶν ἄλλων πολιτῶν συνατυχήσοντες, οὑτοσὶ δ' ἐκ τῆς πατρίδος ἔφυγεν, ἰδίᾳ τὴν σωτη-

ΚΑΤΑ ΛΕΩΚΡΑΤΟΥΣ

ρίαν ποριζόμενος, οὐδ' ὑπὲρ τῆς ἰδίας ἑστίας ἀμύνεσθαι τολμήσας, ἀλλὰ μόνος οὗτος τῶν πάντων ἀνθρώπων καὶ τὰ τῆς φύσεως οἰκεῖα καὶ ἀναγκαῖα προδέδωκεν, ἃ καὶ τοῖς ἀλόγοις ζῴοις μέγιστα καὶ σπουδαιότατα διείληπται. τὰ γοῦν πετεινὰ ἃ 132 μάλιστα πέφυκε πρὸς τάχος, ἔστιν ἰδεῖν ὑπὲρ τῆς αὑτῶν νεοττιᾶς ἐθέλοντα ἀποθνήσκειν· ὅθεν καὶ τῶν ποιητῶν τινες εἰρήκασιν·

οὐδ' ἀγρία γὰρ ὄρνις, ἣν πλάσῃ δόμον,
ἄλλην νεοσσοὺς ἠξίωσεν ἐντεκεῖν.

34 ἀλλὰ Λεωκράτης τοσοῦτον ὑπερβέβληκε δειλίᾳ, ὥστε τὴν πατρίδα τοῖς πολεμίοις ἐγκατέλιπε. τοιγαροῦν οὐδεμία πόλις αὐτὸν εἴασε παρ' αὑτῇ 133 μετοικεῖν, ἀλλὰ μᾶλλον τῶν ἀνδροφόνων ἤλαυνεν, εἰκότως· οἱ μὲν γὰρ φόνου φεύγοντες εἰς ἑτέραν πόλιν μεταστάντες οὐκ ἔχουσιν ἐχθροὺς τοὺς ὑποδεξαμένους, τοῦτον δὲ τίς ἂν ὑποδέξαιτο πόλις; ὃς γὰρ ὑπὲρ τῆς αὑτοῦ πατρίδος οὐκ ἐβοήθησε, ταχύ γ' ἂν ὑπὲρ τῆς ἀλλοτρίας κίνδυνόν τιν' ὑπομείνειε. κακοὶ γὰρ καὶ πολῖται καὶ ξένοι καὶ ἰδίᾳ φίλοι οἱ τοιοῦτοι τῶν ἀνθρώπων εἰσίν, οἳ τῶν μὲν ἀγαθῶν τῶν τῆς πόλεως μεθέξουσιν, ἐν δὲ ταῖς ἀτυχίαις οὐδὲ βοηθείας ἀξιώσουσι. καίτοι 134 τὸν ὑπὸ τῶν μηδὲν ἀδικουμένων μισούμενον καὶ ἐξελαυνόμενον, τί δεῖ παθεῖν ὑφ' ὑμῶν τῶν τὰ δεινότατα πεπονθότων; ἆρ' οὐ τῆς ἐσχάτης τιμωρίας τυγχάνειν; καὶ μήν, ὦ ἄνδρες, τῶν πώποτε

προδοτῶν δικαιότατ᾽ ἂν Λεωκράτης, εἴ τις μείζων εἴη τιμωρία θανάτου, ταύτην ὑπόσχοι. οἱ μὲν γὰρ ἄλλοι προδόται, μέλλοντες ἀδικεῖν ὅταν ληφθῶσι, τιμωρίαν ὑπέχουσιν· οὗτος δὲ μόνος διαπεπραγμένος ὅπερ ἐπεχείρησε, τὴν πόλιν ἐγκαταλιπὼν κρίνεται.

135 Θαυμάζω δὲ καὶ τῶν συνηγορεῖν αὐτῷ μελλόν- 35 των, διὰ τί ποτε τοῦτον ἀξιώσουσιν ἀποφυγεῖν. πότερον διὰ τὴν πρὸς αὐτοὺς φιλίαν; ἀλλ᾽ ἔμοιγε δοκοῦσι δικαίως οὐκ ἂν χάριτος τυχεῖν, ἀλλ᾽ ἀποθανεῖν, ὅτι χρῆσθαι τούτῳ τολμῶσι. πρὶν μὲν γὰρ τοῦτο πρᾶξαι Λεωκράτην, ἄδηλον ἦν ὁποῖοί τινες ὄντες ἐτύγχανον, νῦν δὲ πᾶσι φανερὸν ὅτι τοῖς αὐτοῖς ἤθεσι χρώμενοι τὴν πρὸς τοῦτον φιλίαν διαφυλάττουσιν, ὥστε πολὺ πρότερον ὑπὲρ αὐτῶν αὐτοῖς ἐστιν ἀπολογητέον ἢ τοῦτον παρ᾽ ὑμῶν ἐξαιτητέον.

136 Ἡγοῦμαι δ᾽ ἔγωγε καὶ τὸν πατέρα αὐτῷ τὸν τετελευτηκότα, εἴ τις ἄρ᾽ ἔστιν αἴσθησις τοῖς ἐκεῖ περὶ τῶν ἐνθάδε γιγνομένων, ἁπάντων ἂν χαλεπώτατον γενέσθαι δικαστήν, οὗ τὴν χαλκῆν εἰκόνα ἔκδοτον κατέλιπε τοῖς πολεμίοις ἐν τῷ τοῦ Διὸς ⟨τοῦ⟩ σωτῆρος ἱεροσυλῆσαι καὶ αἰκίσασθαι, καὶ ἣν ἐκεῖνος ἔστησε μνημεῖον τῆς αὑτοῦ μετριότητος, ταύτην αὐτὸς ἐπονείδιστον ἐποίησε· τοιού- 137 του γὰρ υἱοῦ πατὴρ προσαγορεύεται. διὸ καὶ πολλοί μοι προσεληλύθασιν, ὦ ἄνδρες, ἐρωτῶντες, διὰ τί οὐκ ἐνέγραψα τοῦτο εἰς τὴν εἰσαγγελίαν,

ΚΑΤΑ ΛΕΩΚΡΑΤΟΥΣ

προδεδωκέναι τὴν εἰκόνα τὴν τοῦ πατρός, τὴν ἐν τῷ τοῦ Διὸς τοῦ σωτῆρος ἀνακειμένην. ἐγὼ δ', ὦ ἄνδρες, οὐκ ἠγνόουν τοῦτο τἀδίκημ' ἄξιον ⟨ὂν⟩ τῆς μεγίστης τιμωρίας, ἀλλ' οὐχ ἡγούμην δεῖν περὶ προδοσίας τοῦτον κρίνων ὄνομα Διὸς σωτῆρος ἐπιγράψαι πρὸς τὴν εἰσαγγελίαν.

Ἐκπέπληγμαι δὲ μάλιστα ἐπὶ τοῖς μήτε γένει 138 μήτε φιλίᾳ μηδὲν προσήκουσι, μισθοῦ δὲ συναπολογουμένοις ἀεὶ τοῖς κρινομένοις, εἰ λελήθασιν ὑμᾶς τῆς ἐσχάτης ὀργῆς δικαίως ἂν τυγχάνοντες. τὸ γὰρ ὑπὲρ τῶν ἀδικησάντων ἀπολογεῖσθαι τεκμήριόν ἐστιν ὅτι καὶ τῶν πεπραγμένων τοῖς τοιούτοις ἂν μετάσχοιεν. οὐ γὰρ δεῖ καθ' ὑμῶν γεγενῆσθαι δεινόν, ἀλλ' ὑπὲρ ὑμῶν καὶ τῶν νόμων καὶ τῆς δημοκρατίας.

Καίτοι τινὲς αὐτῶν οὐκέτι τοῖς λόγοις ὑμᾶς 139 παρακρούσασθαι ζητοῦσιν, ἀλλ' ἤδη ταῖς αὑτῶν λῃτουργίαις ἐξαιτεῖσθαι τοὺς κρινομένους ἀξιώσουσιν· ἐφ' οἷς ἔγωγε καὶ μάλιστ' ἀγανακτῶ. εἰς γὰρ τὸν ἴδιον οἶκον αὐτὰς περιποιησάμενοι, κοινὰς χάριτας ὑμᾶς ἀπαιτοῦσιν. οὐ γὰρ εἴ τις ἱπποτρόφηκεν ἢ κεχορήγηκε λαμπρῶς ἢ τῶν ἄλλων τῶν τοιούτων τι δεδαπάνηκεν, ἄξιός ἐστι παρ' ὑμῶν τοιαύτης χάριτος (ἐπὶ τούτοις γὰρ αὐτὸς μόνος στεφανοῦται, τοὺς ἄλλους οὐδὲν ὠφελῶν), ἀλλ' εἴ τις τετριηράρχηκε λαμπρῶς ἢ τείχη τῇ πατρίδι περιέβαλεν ἢ πρὸς τὴν κοινὴν σωτηρίαν ἐκ τῶν ἰδίων συνευπόρησε· ταῦτα γάρ ἐστι κοινῶς 140

ΛΥΚΟΥΡΓΟΥ

ὑπὲρ ὑμῶν ἁπάντων, καὶ ἐν μὲν τούτοις ἔστιν ἰδεῖν τὴν ἀρετὴν τῶν ἐπιδεδωκότων, ἐν ἐκείνοις δὲ τὴν εὐπορίαν μόνον τῶν δεδαπανηκότων. ἡγοῦμαι δ' ἔγωγε οὐδέν' οὕτω μεγάλα τὴν πόλιν εὐεργετηκέναι, ὥστ' ἐξαίρετον ἀξιοῦν λαμβάνειν χάριν τὴν κατὰ τῶν προδιδόντων τιμωρίαν, οὐδ' οὕτως ἀνόητον ὥστε φιλοτιμεῖσθαι μὲν πρὸς τὴν πόλιν, τούτῳ δὲ βοηθεῖν ὃς αὐτοῦ πρώτου τὰς φιλοτιμίας ἠφάνισεν· εἰ μὴ νὴ Δία μὴ ταὐτὰ τῇ πατρίδι καὶ τούτοις ἐστὶ συμφέροντα.

141 Ἐχρῆν μὲν οὖν, ὦ ἄνδρες, εἰ καὶ περὶ οὐδενὸς 36 ἄλλου νόμιμόν ἐστι παῖδας καὶ γυναῖκας παρακαθισαμένους ἑαυτοῖς τοὺς δικαστὰς δικάζειν, ἀλλ' οὖν γε περὶ προδοσίας κρίνοντας οὕτως ὅσιον εἶναι τοῦτο πράττειν, ὅπως ὁπόσοι τοῦ κινδύνου μετεῖχον ἐν ὀφθαλμοῖς ὄντες καὶ ὁρώμενοι καὶ ἀναμιμνήσκοντες ὅτι τοῦ κοινοῦ παρὰ πᾶσιν ἐλέου οὐκ ἠξιώθησαν, πικροτέρας τὰς γνώσεις κατὰ τοῦ ἀδικοῦντος παρεσκεύαζον. ἐπειδὴ δ' οὐ νόμιμον οὐδ' εἰθισμένον ἐστίν, ἀλλ' ἀναγκαῖον ὑμᾶς ὑπὲρ ἐκείνων δικάζειν, τιμωρησάμενοι γοῦν Λεωκράτη καὶ ἀποκτείναντες αὐτόν, ἀπαγγείλατε τοῖς ὑμετέροις αὐτῶν παισὶ καὶ γυναιξίν, ὅτι ὑποχείριον λαβόντες τὸν προδότην αὐτῶν ἐτιμωρήσασθε.

142 καὶ γὰρ δεινὸν καὶ σχέτλιον, ὅταν νομίζῃ δεῖν Λεωκράτης ἴσον ἔχειν ὁ φυγὼν ἐν τῇ τῶν μεινάντων πόλει, καὶ ὁ μὴ κινδυνεύσας ἐν τῇ τῶν παραταξαμένων, καὶ ὁ μὴ διαφυλάξας ἐν τῇ τῶν

ΚΑΤΑ ΛΕΩΚΡΑΤΟΥΣ 55

σωσάντων, ἀλλ' ἥκῃ ἱερῶν θυσιῶν ἀγορᾶς νόμων πολιτείας μεθέξων, ὑπὲρ ὧν τοῦ μὴ καταλυθῆναι χίλιοι τῶν ὑμετέρων πολιτῶν ἐν Χαιρωνείᾳ ἐτελεύτησαν καὶ δημοσίᾳ αὐτοὺς ἡ πόλις ἔθαψαν· ὧν οὗτος οὐδὲ τὰ ἐλεγεῖα τὰ ἐπιγεγραμμένα τοῖς μνημείοις ἐπανιὼν εἰς τὴν πόλιν ᾐδέσθη, ἀλλ' οὕτως ἀναιδῶς ἐν τοῖς ὀφθαλμοῖς τῶν πενθησάντων τὰς ἐκείνων συμφορὰς ἡγεῖται δεῖν ἀναστρέφεσθαι. καὶ αὐτίκα μάλ' ὑμᾶς ἀξιώσει ἀκούειν 143 αὐτοῦ ἀπολογουμένου κατὰ τοὺς νόμους· ὑμεῖς δ' ἐρωτᾶτε αὐτὸν ποίους; οὓς ἐγκαταλιπὼν ᾤχετο. καὶ ἐᾶσαι αὐτὸν οἰκεῖν ἐν τοῖς τείχεσι τῆς πατρίδος· ποίοις; ἃ μόνος τῶν πολιτῶν οὐ συνδιεφύλαξε. καὶ ἐπικαλέσεται τοὺς θεοὺς σώσοντας αὐτὸν ἐκ τῶν κινδύνων· τίνας; οὐχ ὧν τοὺς νεὼς καὶ τὰ ἕδη καὶ τὰ τεμένη προὔδωκε; καὶ δεήσεται καὶ ἱκετεύσει ἐλεῆσαι αὐτόν· τίνων; οὐχ οἷς τὸν αὐτὸν ἔρανον εἰς τὴν σωτηρίαν εἰσενεγκεῖν οὐκ ἐτόλμησε; Ῥοδίους ἱκετευέτω· τὴν γὰρ ἀσφάλειαν ἐν τῇ ἐκείνων πόλει μᾶλλον ἢ ἐν τῇ ἑαυτοῦ πατρίδι ἐνόμισεν εἶναι. Ποία δ' ἡλικία δικαίως 144 ἂν τοῦτον ἐλεήσειε; πότερον ἡ τῶν πρεσβυτέρων; ἀλλ' οὐδὲ γηροτροφηθῆναι, οὐδ' ἐν ἐλευθέρῳ ⟨τῷ⟩ ἐδάφει τῆς πατρίδος αὐτοῖς ταφῆναι τὸ καθ' αὑτὸν μέρος παρέδωκεν. ἀλλ' ἡ τῶν νεωτέρων; καὶ τίς ⟨ἂν⟩ ἀναμνησθεὶς τῶν ἡλικιωτῶν τῶν ἐν Χαιρωνείᾳ ἑαυτῷ συμπαραταξαμένων καὶ τῶν κινδύνων τῶν αὐτῶν μετασχόντων, σώσειε τὸν τὰς ἐκείνων θήκας προδεδωκότα, καὶ τῇ αὐτῇ ψήφῳ τῶν μὲν ὑπὲρ τῆς ἐλευθερίας τελευτησάντων παράνοιαν καταγνοίη, τὸν δ᾽ ἐγκαταλιπόντα τὴν πατρίδα ὡς εὖ φρονοῦντα ἀθῷον ἀφείη; ἐξουσίαν ἄρα δώσετε ⟨τῷ⟩ βουλομένῳ, καὶ λόγῳ καὶ ἔργῳ τὸν δῆμον καὶ ὑμᾶς κακῶς ποιεῖν. οὐ γὰρ μόνον νῦν οἱ φεύγοντες κατέρχονται, ὅταν ὁ ἐγκαταλιπὼν τὴν πόλιν καὶ φυγὴν αὐτὸς ἑαυτοῦ καταγνοὺς καὶ οἰκήσας ἐν Μεγάροις ἐπὶ προστάτου πλείω πέντ᾽ ἢ ἓξ ἔτη, ἐν τῇ χώρᾳ καὶ ἐν τῇ πόλει ἀναστρέφηται, ἀλλὰ καὶ ὁ μηλόβοτον τὴν Ἀττικὴν ἀνεῖναι φανερᾷ τῇ ψήφῳ καταψηφισάμενος, οὗτος ἐν ταύτῃ τῇ χώρᾳ σύνοικος ὑμῶν γίγνεται.

Βούλομαι δ᾽ ἔτι βραχέα πρὸς ὑμᾶς εἰπὼν καταβῆναι, καὶ τὸ ψήφισμα τοῦ δήμου παρασχόμενος, ὃ περὶ εὐσεβείας ἐποιήσατο· χρήσιμον γὰρ ὑμῖν ἐστι τοῖς μέλλουσι τὴν ψῆφον φέρειν. Καί μοι λέγε αὐτό.

ΨΗΦΙΣΜΑ

Ἐγὼ τοίνυν μηνύω τὸν ἀφανίζοντα ταῦτα πάντα πρὸς ὑμᾶς τοὺς κυρίους ὄντας κολάσαι, ὑμέτερον δ᾽ ἐστὶ καὶ ὑπὲρ ὑμῶν καὶ ὑπὲρ τῶν θεῶν τιμωρήσασθαι Λεωκράτην. τὰ γὰρ ἀδικήματα, ἕως μὲν ἂν ᾖ ἄκριτα, παρὰ τοῖς πράξασίν ἐστιν, ἐπειδὰν δὲ κρίσις γένηται, παρὰ τοῖς μὴ δικαίως ἐπεξελθοῦσιν. εὖ δ᾽ ἴστε, ὦ ἄνδρες, ὅτι νῦν κρύβδην ψηφιζόμενος ἕκαστος ὑμῶν φανερὰν ποιήσει τὴν αὑτοῦ διάνοιαν τοῖς θεοῖς. ἡγοῦμαι δ᾽, ὦ ἄνδρες,

ΚΑΤΑ ΛΕΩΚΡΑΤΟΥΣ 57

ὑπὲρ ἁπάντων τῶν μεγίστων καὶ δεινοτάτων ἀδικημάτων μίαν ὑμᾶς ψῆφον ἐν τῇ τήμερον ἡμέρᾳ φέρειν, οἷς ἅπασιν ἔνοχον ὄντα Λεωκράτην ἔστιν ἰδεῖν, προδοσίας μὲν ὅτι τὴν πόλιν ἐγκαταλιπὼν τοῖς πολεμίοις ὑποχείριον ἐποίησε, δήμου δὲ καταλύσεως ὅτι οὐχ ὑπέμεινε τὸν ὑπὲρ τῆς ἐλευθερίας κίνδυνον, ἀσεβείας δ' ὅτι τοῦ τὰ τεμένη τέμνεσθαι καὶ τοὺς νεὼς κατασκάπτεσθαι τὸ καθ' ἑαυτὸν γέγονεν αἴτιος, τοκέων δὲ κακώσεως τὰ μνημεῖα αὐτῶν ἀφανίζων καὶ τῶν νομίμων ἀποστερῶν, λιποταξίου δὲ καὶ ἀστρατείας οὐ παρασχὼν τὸ σῶμα τάξαι τοῖς στρατηγοῖς. ἔπειτα τούτου τις 148 ἀποψηφιεῖται καὶ συγγνώμην ἕξει τῶν κατὰ προαίρεσιν ἀδικημάτων; καὶ τίς οὕτως ἐστὶν ἀνόητος, ὥστε τοῦτον σῴζων τὴν ἑαυτοῦ σωτηρίαν προέσθαι τοῖς ἐγκαταλιπεῖν βουλομένοις, καὶ τοῦτον ἐλεήσας αὐτὸς ἀνηλέητος ὑπὸ τῶν πολεμίων ἀπολέσθαι προαιρήσεται, καὶ τῷ προδότῃ τῆς πατρίδος χάριν θέμενος ὑπεύθυνος εἶναι τῇ παρὰ τῶν θεῶν τιμωρίᾳ;

Ἐγὼ μὲν οὖν καὶ τῇ πατρίδι βοηθῶν καὶ τοῖς 149 ἱεροῖς καὶ τοῖς νόμοις, ἀποδέδωκα τὸν ἀγῶνα ὀρθῶς καὶ δικαίως, οὔτε τὸν ἄλλον τούτου βίον διαβαλών, οὔτ' ἔξω τοῦ πράγματος οὐδὲν κατηγορήσας· ὑμῶν δ' ἕκαστον χρὴ νομίζειν τὸν Λεωκράτους ἀποψηφιζόμενον θάνατον τῆς πατρίδος καὶ ἀνδραποδισμὸν καταψηφίζεσθαι, καὶ δυοῖν καδίσκοιν κειμένοιν τὸν μὲν προδοσίας, τὸν δὲ σωτηρίας είναι, και τας ψήφους φέρεσθαι τας μεν υπέρ αναστάσεως της πατρίδος, τας δ' υπέρ ασφαλείας και της εν τη πόλει ευδαιμονίας. εάν μεν Λεωκράτην απολύσητε, προδιδόναι την πόλιν και τα ιερά και τας ναῦς ψηφιεῖσθε· εάν δε τούτον αποκτείνητε, διαφυλάττειν και σώζειν την πατρίδα και τας προσόδους και την ευδαιμονίαν παρακελεύσεσθε. νομίζοντες οὖν, ὦ Ἀθηναῖοι, ικετεύειν υμών την χώραν και τα δένδρα, δεῖσθαι τους λιμένας ⟨και⟩ τα νεώρια και τα τείχη της πόλεως, αξιοῦν δε και τους νεώς και τα ιερά βοηθεῖν αυτοῖς, παράδειγμα ποιήσατε Λεωκράτη, αναμνησθέντες των κατηγορημένων, ότι ου πλέον ισχύει παρ' υμῖν έλεος ουδέ δάκρυα της υπέρ των νόμων και του δήμου σωτηρίας.

NOTES

ARGUMENT

τὰ ἐν X. δεινά] 'The disaster at Chaeronea,' 338 B.C.

ψήφισμα ποιεῖ] ποιεῖν for ποιεῖσθαι, in this phrase (though the active is also used in classical Greek in similar cases, where it is not always easily distinguishable in sense from the middle), is to be set down here as a trace of late Greek (cf. *ἐν infra*).

ὥστε] For ὥστε introducing the substance of the ψήφισμα (a classical usage), cf. e.g. Thuc. V. 17 ψηφισαμένων...ὥστε καταλύεσθαι, etc.

ἐκθέσθαι] i.q. ὑπεκθέσθαι, which is technical in this sense: cf. *infra* §§ 25, 53.

ἐν Ῥόδῳ] The use of the prep. to express 'motion to' (cf. Paus. VII. 4. 3 διαβάντες ἐν τῇ Σάμῳ) is late: so also *in* c. abl. in late Latin: *missus est in exilio*, etc.

παρρησιαζομένου] The expression is probably inspired by § 5 of the speech (τοῦτον περιορᾶν εἰς τὴν ἀγορὰν ἐμβάλλοντα), and the context would almost suggest that, if L. had kept quiet, Lycurgus would have left him alone.

ἡ δὲ στάσις ὅρος ἀντονομάζων] στάσις (*status* s. *constitutio causae*) is the determination of the point at issue; ὅρος (a subdivision of στάσις—*status definitivus*) is used of a case in which a fact is admitted, and the question is how it is to be defined (ἀντονομάζων: *controversia nominis*)—in L.'s case, *departure* or *desertion*?

στοχασμὸν ἀπὸ γνώμης] στοχ. ἀπὸ γνώμης, *status coniecturalis ex sententia*, signifies a case where, there being no doubt about the deed or the doer, the intention of the doer at the moment of the deed is to be determined (ποίᾳ γνώμῃ ἐξῆλθεν, εἴτε...εἴτε).

ἀντίστασιν] ἀντίστασις is a subdivision of the *status qualitatis*, in which the defendant, while admitting that his action was wrong, places against it some counterbalancing advantage (ἀντίστασις, *compensatio, comparatio*).

[For the explanation of the technical terms, I am indebted to Wyse on Isaeus, I and II, after Volkmann's *Rhetorik*², pp. 70 *sqq.*]

ὑπόθεσις] 'subject.'

Αὐτολύκου] See *infra* § 53 *n.*

c. 1. §§ 1, 2. *I pray the gods and heroes to make me a worthy prosecutor of Leocrates, and you exemplary judges, as my impeachment is just.*

§ 1. δικαίαν...εὐσεβῆ] these two adjectives, emphatic alike from their position and their predicative force, may be said to strike the key-note of the speech : 'Justice and Piety...shall characterize the prosecution,' etc.—ὦ 'Αθηναῖοι: this, and not the more usual ὦ ἄνδρες 'Α., appears to be the regular formula in Lycurgus. [Blass <ἄνδρες> everywhere.]

τὴν ἀρχὴν...ποιήσομαι] more stately than ἄρξομαι. ποιεῖσθαι with a noun is a common periphrasis for the simple verb: cf. πλοῦν ποιεῖσθαι=πλεῖν, λήθην π.=λανθάνεσθαι, καταφυγὴν π.= καταφεύγειν, etc. Cf. *infra* §§ 5, 11, etc.

εὔχομαι...τῇ 'Αθηνᾷ] Athena is given prominence as the tutelary goddess of Athens (cf. *infra* § 26). Only Demosthenes, besides Lycurgus, prefaces a speech with a prayer to the gods, and that only once—in his *De Corona*, delivered shortly after the prosecution of Leocrates.

τοῖς ἥρωσι...ἱδρυμένοις] 'the heroes whose statues stand throughout our city and country.' The 'heroes' may be described as inferior local deities, patrons of tribes, guilds, etc. The ἥρωες ἐπώνυμοι, at Athens, were the heroes after whom the φυλαί were named. Founders of a race or city (ἀρχηγέται, κτίσται) were worshipped under this name, having small temples or chapels (ἡρῷα) dedicated to them by the state, but always distinct from the *national* gods (θεοί), with whom, however, they are regularly coupled. Cf. Thuc. IV. 87 μάρτυρας μὲν θεοὺς καὶ ἥρωας τοὺς ἐγχωρίους ποιήσομαι, Dem. *De Cor.* § 184 [ΨΗΦ.] εὐξαμένους... τοῖς θεοῖς καὶ ἥρωσι τοῖς κατέχουσι τὴν πόλιν καὶ τὴν χώραν τῶν Ἀθηναίων.

εἰ μὲν εἰσήγγελκα Δ.] At Athens, the εἰσαγγελία was a *state prosecution* or *impeachment*, applicable, acc. to the νόμος εἰσαγγελτικὸς quoted by Hyperides, *Eux.* §§ 7, 8, to three main offences: (*a*) treason against the democracy; (*b*) betrayal of a town or any military or naval force; (*c*) corrupt misleading of the people by an orator. The case of Leocrates would fall under (*a*). But it is certain that the list of Hyper. is not exhaustive; and we must at any rate distinguish from 'political' denunciations (1) εἰσαγγελίαι κακώσεως (maltreatment of parents, heiresses, etc.), laid before the First Archon; (2) εἰσ. διαιτητῶν (against unjust arbitrators). A political εἰσαγγελία was usually brought before the Council (εἰσαγγέλλειν τινὰ τῇ βουλῇ, εἰς τὴν βουλήν), sometimes before the Assembly at the meeting in each Prytany which was known as ἡ κυρία (εἰσ. τινὰ εἰς τὸν δῆμον, ἐν τῷ δήμῳ). In the former case, the Council might hand the matter over to an ordinary jury court, if it was considered too serious for the maximum penalty (a fine of 500 drachmae) which the Council was competent to inflict (cf. Ar. *Vesp.* 590, [Dem.] XLVII. § 43); the Assembly might do the same, or it might undertake the trial itself, as in the historic case of the generals after Arginusae, Xen. *Hell.* I. 7. 9.

κρίνω] 'put on his trial': Dem. *De Cor.* § 15 κατηγορεῖ μὲν ἐμοῦ, κρίνει δὲ τουτονί.

νεώς...ἕδη...τεμένη] 'temples'...'shrines'...'sanctuaries,' but English has no sufficiently distinctive equivalents for the Greek terms: (*a*) νεώς is 'the inmost part of a temple, in which the image of the god was placed, like σηκός, ἄδυτον, the sense of ἱερὸν being more general' (L.S.); (*b*) ἕδος, which signifies primarily 'a seated statue,' means either 'temple-statue' or 'temple' (Timaei *lex.* ἕδος· τὸ ἄγαλμα καὶ ὁ τόπος ἐν ᾧ ἵδρυται); (*c*) τέμενος is the space of land 'cut off' (τέμνω) from common uses and dedicated to a god (cf. *templum*): in it stood the 'temple' proper or shrine.

τὰς ἐν τοῖς νόμοις θυσίας] 'the sacrifices prescribed by the laws,' especially the laws of Solon. Cf. *infra* § 4 τοῖς ἐκ τῶν νόμων ἐπιτιμίοις, § 34 τῆς ἐκ τῶν νόμων τιμωρίας.

§ 2. ἐν τῇ τήμερον ἡμέρᾳ.] The phrase is more stately than the simple τήμερον. "The Latin *hodiernus dies* and the German 'der heutige Tag' exactly correspond" (Shilleto, Dem. *De Falsa Leg.* § 339 *n.*).

ὑπό] 'at the mercy of': so *infra* § 27.

τοιαῦτα...τηλικαῦτα] 'such'...'so great': *talia...tanta*. The adjs. are often coupled. So also τοσοῦτος and τηλικοῦτος, where the distinction is between *number* and *size*, the adjs. being frequently further defined by the addition, respectively, of τὸ πλῆθος (τὸν ἀριθμόν) and τὸ μέγεθος: cf. Isocr. *Paneg.* § 136 τοσαύτας τὸ πλῆθος πόλεις καὶ τηλικαύτας τὸ μέγεθος δυνάμεις, *Antid.* § 257.

c. 2. §§ 3–6. *The prosecutor on behalf of the state has come, undeservedly, to be regarded as a busybody rather than as a patriot. The truth is, the accuser constitutes, with the law and the judge, the third great pillar of the public weal. I am not actuated by any personal spite against Leocrates, except in so far as public offenders should justly be reckoned private enemies.*

§ 3. ἐβουλόμην δ' ἂν κ.τ.λ.] 'I could have wished that the presence among us of persons who prosecute offenders were conceived of by the multitude as an arrangement as humane as it is beneficial to the state.'—For the general structure of the sentence, a favourite one with the orators, cf. e.g. Antiph. *De Caed. Herod. init.*; Isaeus, or. x. *init.*; Isocr. *Antid.* § 114, *De Pace* § 36. In such cases, ἐβουλόμην ἄν (as here and in the two Isocr. passages quoted) is the common idiom = *vellem*, expressing what someone wishes were now true (but which is not true): Goodwin, *M. T.* § 426. ἐβουλόμην alone, however, occurs occasionally with no appreciable difference of meaning, as in the first two passages quoted: also in Aeschin. *Ctes.* § 2 and Ar. *Ran.* 866 ἐβουλόμην μὲν οὐκ ἐρίζειν ἐνθάδε. Editors would change the μέν which follows ἐβουλόμην in these exx. to ἄν for the sake of uniformity, but without good reason: ἐβουλόμην was no doubt helped by the

§ 3] NOTES 63

analogy of ἔδει, ἐχρῆν, etc.: cf. Wyse's n. on Isaeus, *l.c.*—**τοὺς κρίνοντας**: the pres. ptcp. indicates a standing class = *accusatores*, as Cicero says *Pro S. Roscio Amer.* 20 *accusatores multos esse in civitate utile est*.—**ταύτῃ**: stronger and more pointed than αὐτῇ, and in Lycurgus' manner: cf. *infra* § 117 ποιήσαντες στήλην... εἰς ταύτην ἀναγράφειν, § 126.—**αὐτὸ** = τὸ εἶναι τοὺς κρίνοντας.— **ὑπειλῆφθαι**: the perf. infin. denotes the permanent attitude: Goodwin, *M.T.* § 110.

νῦν δὲ περιέστηκεν...ὥστε] 'as it is, matters have come to such a pass, that' etc.

τὸν ἰδίᾳ κινδυνεύοντα] the 'personal risk' consisted in the fact that the prosecutor, in a public action, was himself liable to a fine of 1000 drachmae in case he failed to obtain one-fifth of the judges' votes. Cf. *infra* § 7 τοὺς δημοσίους ἀγῶνας *n.*

ὥστε...οὐ...δοκεῖν] Examples of ὥστε οὐ with infin. may be grouped under two main heads:

(*a*) in *oratio obliqua* (or after a verb of *thinking* or *hearing*), where the consecutive clause represents an indic. with οὐ in the *or. recta*, e.g. Xen. *Hell.* VI. 2. 6 ἔφασαν τοὺς στρατιώτας εἰς τοῦτο τρυφῆς ἐλθεῖν ὥστ' οὐκ ἐθέλειν πίνειν (*recta*: εἰς τοῦτο...ἦλθον ὥστε οὐκ ἤθελον), Dem. *De Cor.* § 283 ἢ τοσοῦτον ὕπνον καὶ λήθην (sc. ἡγεῖ) ἅπαντας ἔχειν, ὥστ' οὐ μεμνῆσθαι (where, omitting ἡγεῖ, we have ἅπαντες ἔχουσιν, ὥστε οὐ μέμνηνται—note that the infin. in these cases corresponds to the tense of the *recta*). So also Aeschin. *Ctes.* § 96; Lysias, or. X. § 15; Dem. *F.L.* §§ 167, 351;

(*b*) where the negative belongs to a single word: cf. Isocr. *De Pace* § 107 οὕτω κακῶς προύστησαν τῶν πραγμάτων ὥσθ' ἡμᾶς οὐ πολλοῖς (= ὀλίγοις) ἔτεσιν ὕστερον...ἐπιπολάσαι. So Isaeus, IX. § 17. Goodwin, §§ 594 *sqq.*—The example in the text cannot very well be assigned to either, and should probably be explained, along with some others where, as here, ὥστε with a finite verb would be equally appropriate, as arising from a mixture of the constructions ὥστε οὐ δοκεῖ and ὥστε μὴ δοκεῖν, 'this occasional confusion' being 'made easier by familiarity with ὥστε οὐ c. infin. in indirect discourse.' Goodwin, § 599. See also Shilleto's ed.

of Dem. *De Falsa Legatione*, App. B. The οὐ...οὐδὲ in the last clause requires no explanation, this clause being virtually equivalent to ὅπερ οὐ δίκαιόν ἐστιν οὐδὲ συμφέρον κ.τ.λ.

§ 4. τρία] 'three elements,' 'factors': a didactic opening: cf. *infra* §§ 10, 79.

ἡ τῶν νόμων τάξις] 'the ordinance of the laws'=ἃ οἱ νόμοι τάττουσιν (subj. gen.). Cf. Plat. *Legg.* 925 B κατὰ τὴν τάξιν τοῦ νόμου.

ἡ τούτοις...κρίσις] The κρίσις ('prosecution'), which would logically come *second* in order, bulks largest in the speaker's mind and is placed *third* and last: it acquires additional emphasis as being also the last word of the sentence.—**τἀδικήματα** is almost concrete = τοὺς ἀδικοῦντας.

ὁ...νόμος πέφυκε προλέγειν] 'The essential function of the law is to prescribe,' etc. πέφυκα, of that for which a thing is fitted or disposed 'by nature' (φύσις), either in an active or a passive sense: cf. Thuc. III. 45 πεφύκασι δ' ἅπαντες...ἁμαρτάνειν ('*humanum est errare*'), II. 64 πάντα γὰρ πέφυκε καὶ ἐλασσοῦσθαι.

τοὺς ἐνόχους...ἐπιτιμίοις] 'those who have rendered themselves liable to the penalties prescribed by the laws.'—ἔνοχος (=ἐνεχόμενος) usually (*a*) c. dat., as here, 'subject to,' occasionally c. gen., e.g. ἐν. βιαίων, λιποταξίου (where either δίκῃ, γραφῇ are to be supplied, or the genitive is the ordinary gen. with *verba accusandi*); (*b*) absol. = 'guilty,' Antiph. *Tetr.* Γ. a. § 1 μήτε τοὺς ἐν. ἀφιέντας μήτε τοὺς καθαροὺς εἰς ἀγῶνα καθίσταντας, *De Chor.* § 17 ἀποφαίνω ὅτι οὐκ ἔνοχός εἰμι. But the meaning of (*a*) naturally shades off into (*b*).—Distinguish ἐπιτίμια='penalties,' the word in the text, which is 'of poetical cast, like many which the older prose writers used' [Jebb, *A.O.* (Selections), p. 207: Soph. *El.* 1382 τἀπιτίμια τῆς δυσσεβείας] from ἐπιτιμία, 'enjoyment of civil rights')(ἀτιμία.—**ὑπ' ἀμφοτέρων τούτων**: sc. ὁ νόμος and ὁ κατήγορος.

τοῦ παραδώσοντος] 'some one to hand them over': Goodwin, § 840. Cf. Xen. *Anab.* II. 4. 5 ὁ ἡγησόμενος οὐδεὶς ἔσται, Soph. *Ant.* 261 οὐδ' ὁ κωλύσων παρῆν.

§ 5] NOTES 65

§ 5. ἅπασι...τοῖς γεγραμμένοις] 'all the articles of the indictment' (*capita accusationis*): cf. Dem. *De Cor.* § 56 τὴν αὐτὴν... ποιησάμενος τῶν γεγραμμένων τάξιν.

εἰσαγγελίαν ἐποιησάμην] Cf. *supra* § 1 τὴν ἀρχὴν...ποιήσομαι π.

φιλονεικίαν] The meaning of the word required here is the usual unfavourable one of 'love of strife,' 'contentiousness': cf. Dem. *De Cor.* § 141 εἰ δὲ πρὸς ἐχθρὰν ἢ φ. ἰδίας ἕνεκ' αἰτίαν ἐπάγω: for the use of the word in the good sense, cf. Plat. *Legg.* 834 C ἔστω τούτων...κατὰ νόμον ἅμιλλά τε καὶ φ., Xen. *Anab.* IV. 8. 27 πολλὴ φ. ἐγίγνετο (quoted by L.S. *s.v.* φιλονεικία).—The orthography of the word (φιλονικία *v.* φιλονεικία), and whether we should distinguish two separate words, φιλονικία = 'love of victory' and φιλονεικία = 'love of strife,' are old subjects of dispute. The two words are constantly interchanged in MSS. Sandys on Isocr. *Ad Dem.* § 31 *s.v.* φιλόνικος remarks: 'Derived from φίλος and νίκη,' and quotes in his support Arist. *Rhet.* II. 12. 6, which is the *locus classicus* for the νίκη derivation. He adds that φιλόνεικος (Plat. *Protag.* 336 E, etc.) is really a separate word, derived from νεῖκος. Adam, however, on *Protag. l.c.* (reading φιλόνικος) contends that 'the word comes from φιλο- and νίκη, not from φιλο- and νεῖκος (in which case the form would be φιλονεικής: cf. φιλοκερδής, φιλοκυδής, but φιλότιμος, φιλόδοξος, φιλόθηρος and the like), and adds that 'Schanz declares himself, after a full discussion, for φιλόνικος.'

εἰς τὴν ἀγορὰν ἐμβάλλοντα...μετέχοντα] The speaker implies that the accused, by his conduct, was legally 'debarred from the market-place and the public rites' (εἴργεσθαι τῆς ἀγορᾶς, τῶν ἱερῶν): cf. *infra* § 65 εἴργον τῶν νομίμων.—ἐμβάλλειν and μετέχειν are technical: the former suggests boldness and confidence: cf. Aeschin. I. § 164 ἔπειτα ἐμβάλλεις εἰς τὴν ἀγοράν, Dem. *c. Timocr.* § 103 κἄν τις ἁλοὺς κακώσεως...εἰς τὴν ἀγ. ἐμβάλλῃ. For μετέχειν (the opp. of εἴργεσθαι), cf. *infra* § 142 ἀλλ' ἤκῃ ἱερῶν θυσιῶν ἀγορᾶς...μεθέξων.

πατρίδος ὄνειδος] 'a reproach *to* his country': cf. Soph. *O.C.* 984 αὑτῆς ὄνειδος παῖδας ἐξέφυσέ μοι. With the whole

P. L. 5

passage may be compared the forcible fragment of Lycurgus' speech *Against Lysicles* (Blass 77): τολμᾷς ζῆν...καὶ εἰς τὴν ἀγορὰν ἐμβάλλειν, ὑπόμνημα γεγονὼς αἰσχύνης καὶ ὀνείδους τῇ πατρίδι.

§ 6. πολίτου γάρ ἐστι δικαίου, μὴ κ.τ.λ.] Some editors see in this a side-thrust at Aeschines, whose prosecution of Ctesiphon (Demosthenes was the real object of attack) was pending at the time when the speech against Leocrates was delivered; but the allusion to Aeschines seems less certain than that to Demosthenes, *infra* § 139.

κοινάς] i.e. affecting the state, 'public.'

καὶ τὰ κοινὰ τῶν ἀδικημάτων κ.τ.λ.] 'and that public offences [τῶν ἀδικ.—partitive gen.] involve [ἔχειν] also public grounds of quarrel with them [sc. τοὺς παρανομοῦντας].' For the sentiment and language, cf. Dem. *Mid.* § 225 δεῖ τοίνυν τούτοις βοηθεῖν ὁμοίως ὥσπερ ἂν αὐτῷ τις ἀδικουμένῳ, καὶ τὰ τῶν νόμων ἀδικήματα κοινὰ νομίζειν.—**ἔχειν**, 'involve,' 'carry with them,' as often: Isocr. *Philip.* § 68 τὰ τοιαῦτα τῶν ἔργων φθόνον ἔχει καὶ δυσμένειαν καὶ πολλὰς βλασφημίας.—**προφάσεις**: not necessarily 'pretexts' (i.e. false causes), but often, as here, 'grounds,' 'occasions.' For a discussion of the significance of the word as used by Thuc., who couples it with αἰτία (III. 13 τοιαύτας ἔχοντες προφάσεις καὶ αἰτίας), see Cornford, *Thuc. Mythist.*, pp. 56–9.

c. 3. §§ 7–10. *The enormity of Leocrates' offence makes the case before you unique among state prosecutions. I am at a loss how to characterize my charge, and the laws provide no adequate penalty. Death, the extreme penalty of the laws, is not sufficient. The failure to devise a punishment suitable to L.'s crimes is due, not to the indolence of former legislators, but to the circumstance that no case of equal heinousness was on record nor was expected to occur in future. And so in this case you must be not merely iudges, but legislators. Your decision will be an example to posterity, and will also have a wholesome influence on the youth, whose character is moulded by two factors: (a) the punishment meted out to transgressors, (b) the prizes awarded to virtue.*

§ 7] NOTES 67

§ 7. μὲν...μάλιστα δέ] '*cum...tum maxime.*'—**μεγάλους**: 'important.'

τοὺς δημοσίους ἀγῶνας] ἀγῶνες δημόσιοι, δίκαι δημόσιαι, or more specially γραφαί, were 'public' actions, which might be instituted by any one in possession of his full civic rights (ἐπίτιμος), in name of the state)(ἀγῶνες ἴδιοι, δίκαι ἴδιαι, or simply δίκαι, 'private' suits, in which the plaintiff was the person whose rights were immediately affected. The εἰσαγγελία was a special form of γραφή.

Public actions, with the exception of such εἰσαγγελίαι as were decided in the Council or the Assembly (see note on § 1 *supra*), were tried before a jury court; private suits were often brought before arbitrators (διαιτηταί), a practice which aimed at securing a compromise which should be acceptable to both parties, without the necessity of facing a trial in court. In a public action, the prosecutor, as a rule, did not benefit pecuniarily by the conviction of the accused; and if he either dropped proceedings before the trial or failed to obtain one-fifth of the judges' votes at the trial, he incurred a fine of 1000 drachmae (τὰς χιλίας ὀφλεῖν): cf. *supra* § 3 τὸν ἰδίᾳ κινδυνεύοντα *n.* In nearly all private suits the object in dispute or the damages went to the plaintiff, who similarly in certain cases was penalized for non-success by having to pay to his successful opponent one obol for every drachma of the sum at issue, i.e. one-sixth of the whole (ἡ ἐπωβελία).

ὑπὲρ οὗ] The use of ὑπέρ as an equivalent for περί is characteristic of Lyc.'s Greek (cf. *infra* § 9 τὴν ὑπὲρ τῶν τοιούτων τιμωρίαν, § 147 ὑπὲρ τῶν μεγίστων...ἀδικημάτων...ψῆφον φέρειν), and is fairly frequent also in Lysias and Demosthenes.

τὴν ψῆφον φέρειν] *suffragium ferre*, 'give your vote.'

ὅταν μὲν γὰρ κ.τ.λ.] 'For whenever you give judgment in indictments for unconstitutional proposals, you merely rectify a detail and prohibit the operation of a particular measure in so far as it is calculated to injure the state; whereas the present case has a far-reaching constitutional significance and is of no transient interest: on the contrary, it affects your country

5—2

as a whole, and the verdict you pronounce will be bequeathed to, and held in everlasting remembrance by, your posterity for all succeeding time.'—τὰς τῶν παρανόμων γραφάς: at Athens, the γραφὴ παρανόμων was a safeguard against hasty or inconsistent legislation. A new legislative proposal, after certain formalities had been observed, was first discussed by the Council who, if they approved of it, submitted it as a προβούλευμα for ratification by the Assembly: if so ratified, it became properly ψήφισμα or 'decree.' Such a psephism might be intended merely to serve a temporary purpose, or to become a permanent part of the constitution, i.e. a νόμος, in which latter case it was referred for consideration to the court of the νομοθέται, a committee of dicasts appointed for the purpose. The measure, if pronounced upon favourably by the νομοθέται, was then registered as a law. At any time between the date of its passing the Council, however, and the expiration of a year after its becoming νόμος (if it were raised to this status), it was competent for any citizen to prosecute the proposer of such a measure on the ground of its being in conflict with an existing law, or perhaps even on the general ground of inexpediency. Notice of such intention to prosecute was given by a ὑπωμοσία or affidavit, which had the effect of suspending all further action in respect of the contemplated measure till the suit should be decided. If the proposer thought fit to withdraw his measure in the face of the threatened attack, he was said ἐᾶν (τὸν νόμον) ἐν ὑπωμοσίᾳ: if he decided to contest the point, the matter proceeded in due course to trial, in the ordinary way, before a jury court, on whose verdict the subsequent fate of the measure depended.—δικάζητε: δικάζειν = 'sit in judgment on')(δικάζεσθαι = 'go to law.'—τοῦτο μόνον κ.τ.λ. : lit. 'you merely correct this point and prohibit this action (i.e. prevent the new proposal from becoming operative), in so far as,' etc. τοῦτο and ταύτην τὴν πρᾶξιν both look forward to, and are defined by, the clause καθ' ὅσον...βλάπτειν τὴν πόλιν.—ὁ...ἐνεστηκὼς ἀγών: 'the action which has now begun,' 'the present case': cf. Dem. c. Androt. § 24 ὁ νῦν ἐνεστηκὼς ἀγών ἐστι παρα-

νόμων, *Ep. apud* Dem. *De Cor.* § 157 τοῦ ἐνεστῶτος μηνός.—
συνέχει: 'embraces,' 'concerns.'—τῶν τῆς πόλεως: 'the interests
of the state.'—κατὰ παντὸς τοῦ αἰῶνος: *in sempiternum* (opp. to
ἐπ' ὀλίγον χρόνον): rather a rare use of the prep., but paralleled
by Dem. *c. Androt.* § 72 κατὰ παντὸς τοῦ χρόνου. αἰών is poetic
and suitable to Lyc.'s δείνωσις: it occurs other three times in the
speech (*infra* §§ 62, 106, 110), and, among the other orators,
only in Isocrates.

§ 8. ὥστε μήτε κατηγορίαν κ.τ.λ.] See Crit. App.

(τὸν) μὴ βοηθήσαντα] 'a man who did not defend': generic.

τοῖς πατρῴοις ἱεροῖς] Cf. *infra* § 25 τὰ ἱερὰ τὰ πατρῷα n.

τὸ μὲν γὰρ μέγιστον κ.τ.λ.] 'For the greatest and most extreme
penalty, death, though a punishment that the laws require us to
be content with, is yet inadequate to L.'s offences': a common
complaint with the orators: cf. Lysias, XXVIII. § 1 ὥστε οὐκ ἄν
μοι δοκεῖ δύνασθαι Ἐργοκλῆς...πολλάκις ἀποθανὼν δοῦναι δίκην
ἀξίαν.—**μὲν...δέ**: 'though...yet,' often so best rendered, like
sicut...ita in Latin.—**καθέστηκε**: a stronger ἐστί: so *supra* § 4
τοὺς ἐνόχους...καθεστῶτας.

§ 9. παρεῖσθαι] Emphatic by position and introducing the
main thought of the paragraph, with which may be compared
Lysias, or. XXXI. § 27 οὐ γὰρ οἴεται ὑμᾶς γνώσεσθαι ὅτι διὰ τὸ
μέγεθος τοῦ ἀδικήματος οὐδεὶς περὶ αὐτοῦ ἐγράφη νόμος. τίς γὰρ ἄν
ποτε ῥήτωρ ἐνεθυμήθη ἢ νομοθέτης ἤλπισεν ('expected') ἁμαρτή-
σεσθαί τινα τῶν πολιτῶν τοσαύτην ἁμαρτίαν;

τὴν ὑπὲρ τῶν τοιούτων τιμωρίαν] 'punishment *for* such
offences': cf. *supra* § 7 ὑπὲρ οὗ n., Soph. *Ant.* 932 κλαύματα
βραδυτῆτος ὕπερ, 'tears for (= on account of) tardiness.'

τῶν τότε νομοθετούντων] 'of previous legislators,' we should
say: τότε refers to the period in the speaker's mind when the
main code of laws was framed.

μηδ'...ἐπίδοξον εἶναι γενήσεσθαι] 'nor was it expected to
occur in the future': ἐπίδοξος has regularly this *passive* significa-
tion: cf. Aeschin. *Ctes.* § 165 ἐπίδοξος ἦν ἁλῶναι (sc. Μεγάλη
πόλις), 'was expected to be captured,' Isocr. *Areop.* § 48 τοὺς

ἐπιδόξους ἁμαρτήσεσθαι, 'those on whose part an offence was apprehended' (Jebb). Cf. the passive use of προσδοκᾶν, Dem. *F.L.* § 170 τῶν ἄλλων...προσδοκωμένων ἀφεθήσεσθαι, 'when it was expected that the others would be released.'

μὴ μόνον...δικαστάς...νομοθέτας] 'you must show yourselves not merely judges in the case of the present offence, but legislators as well,' i.e. your decision in a case not adequately covered by the existing laws (as explained in the next sentence) will set up a precedent which will be virtually equivalent to a law (νόμος). For an exact commentary on this passage, cf. Lysias, or. XIV. § 4 εἰκὸς τοίνυν ἐστίν, ὦ ἄνδρες δικασταί,...πρῶτον περὶ τούτων νυνὶ δικάζοντας μὴ μόνον δικαστὰς ἀλλὰ καὶ νομοθέτας αὐτοὺς γενέσθαι, εὖ εἰδότας ὅτι, ὅπως ἂν ὑμεῖς νυνὶ περὶ αὐτῶν γνῶτε, οὕτω καὶ τὸν ἄλλον χρόνον ἡ πόλις αὐτοῖς χρήσεται. Conversely, we have or. XV. § 9 μεμνῆσθαι χρὴ ὅτι οὐ νομοθετήσοντες περὶ αὐτῶν ἥκετε, ἀλλὰ κατὰ τοὺς κειμένους νόμους ψηφιούμενοι.—**νομοθέτας**: here, and in the Lysias passages quoted, in the general sense of 'legislators,' 'law-makers': technically, the νομοθέται, at Athens, were a select committee of the jurors (δικασταί) for the year, appointed normally at the third κυρία ἐκκλησία in each year, and charged both with the revision of existing laws and the scrutiny and ratification of new ones: cf. *n.* on γραφὴ παρανόμων, *supra* § 7. The dicasts in this capacity were thus the ultimate source of Athenian legislation.

ὅσα μὲν γὰρ κ.τ.λ.] 'For in the case of such offences as are clearly defined by a particular law, it is easy to employ this as your standard and punish transgressors; but in the case of such as are not expressly specified by the law, through its including them in a single designation, and when a person has committed greater enormities than these and is chargeable with them all alike, your verdict must necessarily be bequeathed to posterity as an example.'—**τούτῳ κανόνι**: 'this as your standard' (predicative). κανών, (*a*) in the literal sense, the carpenter's or mason's rule (Lat. *amussis*), (*b*) met., 'rule,' 'standard' (Lat. *norma, regula*). Both uses are illustrated in Aeschin. *Ctes.* §§ 199, 200

§ 10] NOTES 71

ὥσπερ γὰρ ἐν τῇ τεκτονικῇ, ὅταν εἰδέναι βουλώμεθα τὸ ὀρθὸν καὶ τὸ μή, τὸν κανόνα προσφέρομεν, ᾧ διαγιγνώσκεται, οὕτω καὶ ἐν ταῖς γραφαῖς τῶν παρανόμων παράκειται κανὼν τοῦ δικαίου τουτὶ τὸ σανίδιον, τὸ ψήφισμα καὶ οἱ παραγεγραμμένοι νόμοι.—**ὅσα δὲ μὴ σφόδρα περιείληφεν...προσαγορεύσας**: περιείληφεν (sc. ὁ νόμος) is here practically equivalent in sense to the διώρικε preceding, and ἑνὶ ὀνόματι goes closely with προσαγορεύσας. The argument is that the law, in providing penalties for an offence to which it gives a specific designation (e.g. murder, treason), implies the inclusion in that designation of kindred offences which it does not, or cannot, expressly label : it 'calls them by a single name' (ἑνὶ ὀνόματι προσαγορεύει). Cf. Lysias, or. X. (c. *Theomnest.*) § 7 πολὺ γὰρ <ἂν> ἔργον ἦν τῷ νομοθέτῃ ἅπαντα τὰ ὀνόματα γράφειν, ὅσα τὴν αὐτὴν δύναμιν ἔχει· ἀλλὰ περὶ ἑνὸς εἰπὼν περὶ πάντων ἐδήλωσεν. Thus Lycurgus would make the crime of 'treason' (προδοσία), of which he accuses L., include several others, such as 'impiety,' 'desertion,' 'maltreatment of parents,' etc. (*infra* § 147). The inadequacy of the law to provide for every conceivable offence is a common topic with prosecutors, who frequently appeal to the jurors to judge according to the spirit of the law where the letter is deficient: this was known in Latin as *dilatare legem* or *extensio legis* (Rehd. *ad loc.*). To defendants, on the other hand, the same circumstance naturally afforded opportunities for quibbling and evasion : see especially Lysias, or. X (quoted above), §§ 6-14, also XIII and XIV; Dem.'s speech *Against Midias*, and particularly the argument prefixed thereto. —**κρίσιν** : 'decision,' 'verdict.'

§ **10. κατεψηφισμένοι**]= *si damnaveritis.*

δύο γάρ ἐστι...τοὺς νέους] The editors compare the didactic and moralising tone of Aeschines, *c. Ctes.* § 246 εὖ γὰρ ἴστε, ὦ ἄνδρες Ἀ., ὅτι οὐχ αἱ παλαῖστραι οὐδὲ τὰ διδασκαλεῖα οὐδ' ἡ μουσικὴ μόνον παιδεύει τοὺς νέους, ἀλλὰ πολὺ μᾶλλον τὰ δημόσια κηρύγματα. Cf. also *supra* § 4, *infra* § 79.

ἡ...τοῖς ἀγαθοῖς διδομένη δωρεά] 'the bounties awarded to good men': these would include ἀτέλεια, exemption from some or all of the state burdens (λητουργίαι); σίτησις ἐν πρυτανείῳ, public maintenance in the state-hall, etc.

πρὸς ἑκάτερον...ἀποβλέποντες] 'with an eye on each of these,' i.e. having regard to the terrors of the one and the encouragement of the other. ἀποβλέπειν is regularly so used of a pattern or authority which sanctions or influences one's conduct: εἰς interchanges with πρὸς as the accompanying preposition.

προσέχειν τούτῳ τῷ ἀγῶνι] 'give your attention to the case before you': τὸν νοῦν, which often accompanies προσέχειν, is frequently omitted, as here, and at Her. IX. 33, Thuc. I. 15, etc.

τοῦ δικαίου] 'than justice': this is gen. of τὸ δίκαιον (neut. adj. with article = abstract noun), and depends upon the comp. in περὶ πλείονος ποιήσασθαι.

c. 4. §§ 11–13. *Unlike the great bulk of the prosecutors who appear before you, I shall confine myself strictly to the matter at issue. It is outrageous to conduct a prosecution unjustly, and still ask you to give a just verdict. For this state of things you yourselves are to blame, in spite of the example of the court of Areopagus. You should insist on relevancy and so secure the best interests of prosecutors, defendants, and judges alike.*

§ 11. ποιήσομαι δὲ κἀγώ] 'I, too, on my part, shall conduct the prosecution fairly': δικαίαν echoes τοῦ δικαίου of the previous clause. For ποιήσομαι...τὴν κατηγορίαν, cf. *supra* § 1 τὴν ἀρχὴν...ποιήσομαι *n*.

ἔξω τοῦ πράγματος] 'extraneous to the point at issue,' *extra causam dicere* (Cicero). πρᾶγμα = *res de qua agitur*, is very frequent in this phrase in the orators.

τῶν εἰς ὑμᾶς εἰσιόντων] regularly, of the parties to a suit, 'those who appear before you in court.' So οἱ παριόντες, of the speakers in the Assembly.

πάντων ἀτοπ. ποιοῦσιν] 'do the most absurd thing imaginable': πάντων is neut.

ἢ γὰρ συμβουλεύουσιν κ.τ.λ.] 'either they offer you advice on public affairs, or they connect their accusations and misrepresentations with anything rather than the matter on which you are

§ 12] NOTES 73

going to vote': cf. Lysias, *Pro Mil.* [or. IX] § 1 ἢ τόδε μὲν (sc. ὅτι περὶ τοῦ πράγματος προσήκει λέγειν) ἐπίστανται (sc. οἱ ἀντίδικοι), ἡγούμενοι δὲ λήσειν περὶ παντὸς πλείω λόγον ἢ τοῦ προσήκοντος ποιοῦνται;—The frequent complaints in the orators about irrelevant pleading in the courts no doubt point to a real abuse in the judicial system of Athens; but the precepts of the orators in this matter were better than their own practice. The very character of the dicasteries, composed as they were of average citizens with no special legal knowledge, must have been such as to encourage irrelevant argument and enable it to achieve its ends. 'We can have no better evidence as to the working of the popular courts than the speeches by which the pleaders hoped to influence the decisions of the judges.... The judges heard each party interpreting the law in its own sense; but they had themselves no knowledge of the law, and therefore, however impartial they sought to be, their decision was unduly influenced by the dexterity of an eloquent pleader, and affected by considerations which had nothing to do with the matter at issue.' Bury, *History of Greece* (1900), p. 350.—**συμβουλεύουσιν**, absol. 'give advice': συμβουλεύειν τινί, σ. τινί τι = *suadere alicui*, *s. aliquid alicui*; συμβουλεύεσθαί τινι = *consulere aliquem*. Cf. Her. II. 107 τὸν δὲ ὡς μαθεῖν τοῦτο, αὐτίκα συμβουλεύεσθαι τῇ γυναικί...τὴν δέ οἱ συμβουλεῦσαι, κ.τ.λ. —**πάντα**: accusative of the 'extent' or 'compass' of the action of the verb: Madvig, § 27.—ἢ περὶ οὗ = ἢ ἐκεῖνο περὶ οὗ.

γνώμην ἀποφήνασθαι] 'declare one's opinion': γνώμην without the article in this phrase is the regular idiom: see exx. from Dem. cited by Sandys on *First Philippic*, § 1.

§ 12. ὑμᾶς μὲν ἀξιοῦν...αὐτοὺς δὲ μή] '*while* they ask you... they themselves should not': cf. *supra* § 8 *n.*—The speaker in Antiph. *De Caed. Herod.* § 89 reminds the court that 'a wrong prosecution is less serious than a wrong judgment': οὐκ ἴσον ἐστὶ τόν τε διώκοντα μὴ ὀρθῶς αἰτιάσασθαι καὶ ὑμᾶς τοὺς δικαστὰς μὴ ὀρθῶς γνῶναι.

ὑμεῖς] emphatic, 'you yourselves.'

τὴν γὰρ ἐξουσίαν ταύτην] Cf. Dem. *De Cor.* § 138 ἀλλὰ

δεδώκατε ἔθει τινὶ φαύλῳ πολλὴν ἐξουσίαν τῷ βουλομένῳ τὸν λέγοντα...ὑποσκελίζειν καὶ συκοφαντεῖν, *De Chers.* § 23 οἱ...τοσαύτην ἐξουσίαν τοῖς αἰτιᾶσθαι καὶ διαβάλλειν βουλομένοις διδόντες. —τοῖς ἐνθάδ' εἰσιοῦσι: cf. τῶν εἰς ὑμᾶς εἰσιόντων in previous § *n.*

καὶ ταῦτα κάλλιστον ἔχοντες κ.τ.λ.] 'and that although you possess the noblest example among the Greeks in the council of the Areopagus, which so far excels other courts that it is acknowledged even by those whom it convicts to conduct its trials fairly.' —κάλλιστον τῶν ῾Ε. π.: i.e. 'a *nobler* example *than any others* of the Greeks possess,' a common idiomatic use of the superlative: cf. Antiph. *De Caed. Herod.* § 17 ἐδέθην...παρανομώτατα ἁπάντων ἀνθρώπων, 'in a far more unconstitutional way than ever man was.'—τὸ ἐν Ἀρείῳ πάγῳ συνέδριον: the venerable Council of Areopagus (otherwise styled ἡ βουλὴ ἡ ἐξ Ἀρείου πάγου, ἡ ἐξ Ἀ. π. β., ἡ ἐν Ἀ. π. β., or simply Ἄρειος πάγος), the mythical origin of which (Aesch. *Eum.*, Dem. *contra Aristocr.* § 66, Paus. I. 28. 5) points, at any rate, to its extreme antiquity, was now, as indeed it had been for more than a century past (since the reforms of Ephialtes, *c.* 462 B.C.), but a shadow of its former self, in respect of the large and undefined powers which it had originally exercised. These included (*a*) a general supervision of all magistrates and law-courts, (*b*) a general guardianship of the laws, (*c*) a general control of education and censorship of public morals, (*d*) power to assume dictatorial authority in grave public emergencies, as in the stress of the Persian wars (e.g. before Salamis, Plut. *Themist.* 10). These indefinite powers were almost entirely abolished by the reforms of Ephialtes, and transferred either to the Council of Five Hundred, the Assembly, or the popular law-courts. But the Areopagus still retained one of its traditional definite powers—jurisdiction in certain criminal cases—wilful homicide, poisoning, and arson: cf. the emphatic language of Dem. *C. Aristocr.* § 66 τοῦτο μόνον τὸ δικαστήριον οὐχὶ τύραννος, οὐκ ὀλιγαρχία, οὐ δημοκρατία τὰς φονικὰς δίκας ἀφελέσθαι τετόλμηκεν. But while the Areopagus had thus been shorn of its political

§ 13] NOTES 75

significance, its time-honoured associations as the guardian of religion and morals secured for it a considerable amount of prestige and explain the extreme respect with which the court is mentioned down to the latest orators. For the justice of its judgments, as asserted in this passage, cf. Dem. *l.c.* ἐνταυθοῖ μόνον οὐδεὶς πώποτ' οὔτε φεύγων ἁλοὺς οὔτε διώκων ἡττηθεὶς ἐξήλεγξεν ὡς ἀδίκως ἐδικάσθη τὰ κριθέντα.—**παρ' αὐτοῖς ὁμολογεῖσθαι**: sc. αὐτό (i.e. τὸ ἐν 'A. π. συνέδριον) as subject of ὁμολογεῖσθαι, which is used personally (τὸ...συνέδριον ὁμολογεῖται δικαίαν ποιεῖσθαι τὴν κρίσιν). For the const., cf. Xen. *Anab.* I. 9. I ὁμολογεῖται παρὰ πάντων, *Ib.* 20 ὁμολ. πρὸς πάντων.— **τοῖς ἁλισκομένοις**: 'those who are convicted': the frequent legal sense of the vb., often with the gen. of the charge (κλοπῆς, ἀσεβείας, etc.).

§ 13. πρὸς ὅ...ἀποβλέποντας] ὅ: sc. τὸ ἐν 'A. π. συν.—**ἀποβλέποντας**: cf. *supra* § 10 *n*.

ἐπιτρέπειν τοῖς...λέγουσιν] For this absolute use of ἐπιτρέπειν c. dat. = 'give way to,' 'indulge,' cf. Her. II. 120 ἀδικέοντι τῷ ἀδελφεῷ ἐπιτρέπειν, Plat. *Euthyph.* 5 E.—**ἔξω τοῦ πράγματος**: cf. *supra* § 11. Rehdantz aptly cites Lucian, *Anach.* 19 in connexion with the traditional strictness of the Areopagus: ἔστ' ἂν μὲν περὶ τοῦ πράγματος λέγωσιν, ἀνέχεται ἡ βουλὴ [the Areopagus] καθ' ἡσυχίαν ἀκούουσα· ἢν δέ τις ἢ φροίμια εἴπῃ πρὸ τοῦ λόγου...ἢ οἶκτον ἢ δείνωσιν ἔξωθεν ἐπάγῃ τῷ πράγματι, παρελθὼν ὁ κῆρυξ κατεσιώπησεν εὐθύς, οὐκ ἐῶν ληρεῖν πρὸς τὴν βουλήν.

οὕτω γὰρ ἔσται κ.τ.λ.] 'For by this means cases will be conducted so as to shield defendants from false accusations, prosecutors will have least chance of bringing vexatious charges, and you will be in a position to give your vote in a way most in keeping with your oath.'—The mixture of subjects to ἔσται (subst. followed by two infins.) is due to ἔσται passing over into the meaning of ἐξέσται with the infins.—**συκοφαντεῖν**: regularly, in the orators, of malicious or vexatious prosecution, as Lysias says, or. XXV. § 3 τούτων (sc. τῶν συκοφαντῶν) ἔργον ἐστὶ καὶ τοὺς μηδὲν ἡμαρτηκότας εἰς αἰτίαν καθιστάναι, often with the added implication that the object is personal gain. There seems no justification for the meaning 'inform' or 'informer,' as pointed out by L.S. *s.v.* συκοφάντης.—**εὐορκοτάτην**: a clause in the dicastic oath ran: ἀκροάσομαι τοῦ τε κατηγόρου καὶ τοῦ ἀπολογουμένου ὁμοίως ἀμφοῖν.

ἀδύνατον γάρ ἐστιν κ.τ.λ.] 'For it is impossible for you, without such a speech (i.e. such as I have described, a speech which keeps to the point), and unless you have been rightly instructed, to pass a right verdict.'—**μὴ δικαίως δεδιδαγμένους** is explanatory of ἄνευ τοῦ <τοιούτου> λόγου: the two might almost be combined into 'unless you have been properly instructed by a proper speech.' [<τοιούτου> is due to Nicolai: see Crit. App.]

c. 5. §§ 14, 15. *The notoriety of the accused and of his conduct must make your verdict of more than merely local interest. In dealing with him, you must remember your hereditary reputation for piety and patriotism.*

§ 14. δεῖ...μηδὲ ταῦτα λαθεῖν ὑμᾶς] A common formula of transition to a new point: ταῦτα (τοῦτο) [like ἐκεῖνο, *illud*] is prospective: cf. Dem. *Ol.* I. § 25 μηδὲ τοῦθ' ὑμᾶς λανθανέτω, Isocr. *Antid.* § 295 χρὴ γὰρ μηδὲ τοῦτο λανθάνειν ὑμᾶς.

οὐχ ὅμοιος] 'the case of L. is *quite different* from,' etc.: a very common *litotes* with this adj.

περὶ μὲν γὰρ ἀγνῶτος κ.τ.λ.] 'Were it a case of an individual who was unknown to the Greeks, the reputation of the verdict passed by you, be it good or be it bad, would be confined to your own community': the protasis of the sentence is contained in the prepositional clause, which is = εἰ ἀγνὼς ἦν ἄνθ. τοῖς Ἕ., 'if the individual was unknown' (but he is not): Goodwin, *M.T.* § 472. For the thought, cf. Lysias, *In Alcib.* I. [or. XIV]. § 12 ἐὰν μὲν τοίνυν τοὺς ἀγνῶτας κολάζητε, οὐδεὶς ἔσται τῶν ἄλλων βελτίων· οὐδεὶς γὰρ εἴσεται τὰ ὑφ' ὑμῶν καταψηφισθέντα· ἐὰν δὲ τοὺς ἐπιφανεστάτους τῶν ἐξαμαρτανόντων τιμωρῆσθε, πάντες πεύσονται, or. VI. § 6, Gorgias, *Palam.* § 36.

ἔσται λόγος] 'will be talked about.'

οἵ ἴσασι...ὄντα] See Crit. App.—**τοῖς τούτῳ διαπεπραγμένοις**:

§ 15] NOTES 77

'the defendant's conduct': so τὰ ἐμοὶ πεπολιτευμένα, 'my political acts, career': Madvig, § 38. g.

ἐπιφανής] 'a marked man,' 'notorious.'

τὴν ἀπαγγελίαν...καθ' ὑμῶν] 'the report...*about* you,' not necessarily '*against* you,' 'to your detriment,' though, in point of fact, L.'s report was so: cf. Arist. *Pol.* V. 7. 11 τοῦτο εἴρηται κατὰ πασῶν τῶν πολιτειῶν (*de omnibus civitatibus*).

πρός τε τὴν πόλιν...τοῖς ἐπιδημοῦσιν] the first, of the official announcement to the Rhodian authorities; the second, of information conveyed conversationally.

τῶν ἐμπόρων τοῖς ἐπιδημοῦσιν ἐκεῖ] 'the merchants who were in town at the time': ἐπιδημεῖν (*a*) 'to be *or* live at home')(ἀποδημεῖν, 'to be away from home'; (*b*) of foreigners, as here, 'to come to a city,' 'stay at' a place: cf. Lysias *c. Eratosth.* § 35 ὅσοι δὲ ξένοι ἐπιδημοῦσιν, Dem. 1357. 17 ἐπιδ. εἰς Μέγαρα (with 'pregnant' prep.).

§ 15. πᾶσαν τὴν οἰκουμένην] 'the whole inhabited (Greek) world': Dem. *De Cor.* § 48 ἐλαυνομένων καὶ ὑβριζομένων...πᾶσ' ἡ οἰκουμένη μεστὴ γέγονεν. In Roman times, the phrase was similarly used of the Roman world. [At Her. II. 32 ἰέναι τὰ πρῶτα διὰ τῆς οἰκεομένης, also IV. 110 ἀποβᾶσαι ἀπὸ τῶν πλοίων αἱ Ἀμαζόνες ὡδοιπόρεον ἐς τὴν οἰκεομένην, the expression is used in the narrower sense of 'the inhabited country' as opp. to 'desert': the citation of the latter passage by L.S. *s.v.* οἰκουμένη (= 'the inhabited world') is therefore hardly accurate.]

δι' ἐργασίαν] 'in pursuit of their calling,' lit. 'for the purpose of trade': of this use of διὰ c. acc. = 'for the sake of,' 'in order to,' four exx. are quoted from Thuc.: II. 89 διὰ τὴν σφετέραν δόξαν, *suae gloriae causa*, IV. 40 δι' ἀχθηδόνα, 'in order to vex,' *Ibid.* 102 διὰ τὸ περιέχειν (τὴν πόλιν) (?), V. 53 διὰ τοῦ θύματος τὴν ἔσπραξιν.

ἃ Λ. ἠκηκόεσαν] 'what they had heard *from* L.': for the simple gen. of source, cf. Plat. *Apol.* 17 B ὑμεῖς ἐμοῦ ἀκούσεσθε πᾶσαν τὴν ἀλήθειαν, Soph. *El.* 424 τοιαῦτα τοῦ παρόντος...ἔκλυον. So also πυνθάνομαι, Ar. *Av.* 1120.

78 NOTES [§ 15

πρός τε τοὺς θεούς...γονεῖς...πατρίδα] The speaker has probably in his mind concrete historical examples: we may compare generally the compliments of the banished Oedipus in Soph. *O.C.* 260 εἰ τάς γ' Ἀθήνας φασὶ θεοσεβεστάτας | εἶναι, 1006 εἴ τις γῆ θεοὺς ἐπίσταται | τιμαῖς σεβίζειν, ἥδε τοῦθ' ὑπερφέρει, 1125 ἐπεὶ τό γ' εὐσεβὲς | μόνοις παρ' ὑμῖν εὗρον ἀνθρώπων ἐγὼ | καὶ τοὐπιεικὲς καὶ τὸ μὴ ψευδοστομεῖν, etc.; Isocr. *Paneg. passim*; Dem. *Ol.* III. § 26.—**γονεῖς**: so the MSS. here, and also *infra* §§ 96, 97, but γονέας *infra* § 94: Blass (with Es) changes everywhere to γονέας.— **τὴν παρ' ὑμῶν...τιμωρίαν**: "the substitution of the more closely defining preposition for the simple case made steady progress" (Rehd., App. 2, p. 127): cf. *infra* § 26 τὴν παρὰ τῶν θεῶν βοήθειαν, §§ 82, 97, 123, 129.

c. 6. §§ 16–19. *I must begin with a brief recital of the circumstances of the case. After Chaeronea, the people passed a decree, directing the women and children to be conveyed into the city, and the generals to provide for the defence of Athens, as they should see fit. But Leocrates, with a supreme contempt for these regulations, and in utter heartlessness, packed up his belongings and sailed away to Rhodes, where he noised abroad the discomfiture of his native city. The Rhodians believed his tale, and stopped shipments of corn and other supplies for Athens—all which I can prove by witnesses.*

§ 16. διὰ τέλους] 'throughout,' 'to the end,' a common idiom both in poetry and prose, the root idea being the 'between' (cf. διατελεῖν) that extends right to the end. Sometimes the idea of 'time' is prominent; sometimes rather that of 'thoroughness,' 'completeness,' as Soph. *Ai.* 685 διὰ τέλους...εὔχου τελεῖσθαι τοὐμὸν ὧν ἐρᾷ κέαρ, 'pray that my desires may be fulfilled *in all fulness*' (Jebb): cf. Wunder *ad loc.*: '*Lobeckius, διὰ τέλους, inquit, ab Hippocrate semper pro διὰ παντὸς τοῦ χρόνου dici affirmat Galenus...sed Sophocles hoc loco pro τελέως posuit, ut* Aesch. *Prom.* 275 (ὡς μάθητε διὰ τέλους τὸ πᾶν).' But the two ideas often seem to merge into one.

τοῖς αἰτίοις...καὶ δι' οὕς] The persons intended in each case

§ 17]   NOTES   79

are identical; but the const. is varied by the substitution of a relative clause for a second adj. or a ptcp. (τοῖς αἰτίοις καὶ ἀναγκάζουσί με π. τ. μ.): cf. Dem. *De Cor.* § 35 τίνες ἦσαν οἱ παρὰ τούτου λόγοι τότε ῥηθέντες καὶ δι' οὓς ἅπαντ' ἀπώλετο, *F. L.* § 132 τὸν ἁπάντων τῶν κακῶν αἴτιον καὶ ὃν εἰλήφατ'...τοῦτον ἀφεῖναι.

γάρ] *narrativum* (introducing the story): do not translate.

ἐψηφίσατο...κατακομίζειν] 'passed a resolution...that they should be brought in,' is the Eng. idiom, but Gk. in these cases prefers the infin. active (or middle), the subject being understood: cf. e.g. Dem. *c. Timocr.* § 11 ψήφισμ' εἶπεν...Ἀριστοφῶν ἑλέσθαι ζητητάς, 'that commissioners should be appointed.' The proposer of the decree was Hyperides: cf. *infra* §§ 36, 37.

τοὺς δὲ στρατηγοὺς κ.τ.λ.] 'and that the generals should appoint to the duties of the defence Athenians and others resident at Athens, as they should see fit.'—**φυλακάς** (acc. plu. of φυλακή), 'defence duties' rather than 'defence forces,' 'garrisons,' though the word is capable of the concrete meaning (cf. *custodia*): cf. Thuc. VII. 17 ἡ ἐν τῇ Ναυπάκτῳ φυλακή (of a squadron of ships), followed immediately by τὴν φ. ποιούμενοι (abstract); also III. 114.—**τῶν Ἀθηναίων**, with **τάττειν**: partitive gen.— **καθ' ὅ τι...δοκῇ**: the usual language where 'discretionary powers' are concerned: cf. the familiar παρέδοσαν σφᾶς αὐτούς...χρῆσθαι ὅ τι ἂν βούλωνται. The phrase looks like a quotation from the actual decree.

§ 17. Λ. δὲ τούτων κ.τ.λ.] For a similar dereliction of duty, described in similar language, cf. Lysias, XXXI. §§ 8 *sqq.* (of Philo after Aegospotami) τὰ ἐναντία ἅπασι τοῖς ἄλλοις πολίταις ἐποίησε· συσκευασάμενος γὰρ τὰ ἑαυτοῦ ἐνθένδε εἰς τὴν ὑπερορίαν ἐξῴκησε κ.τ.λ.

μετὰ τῶν οἰκετῶν] with κατεκόμισε, 'with the help of his slaves': they do not embark with him.

λέμβον...νεώς] The λέμβος is the small 'cock-boat' (τὸ μικρὸν πλοιάριον, τὸ ἐφόλκιον Hesych.), which L. used to convey his belongings to the larger ναῦς which was 'already lying off the shore.' This arrangement would be dictated either by the undesirability of bringing his vessel close in, and so attracting notice, or by the impracticability of doing so, as his point of departure is ἐκ τῆς ἀκτῆς and not εἴσω τοῦ λιμένος, 'inside the (regular) harbour,' *infra* § 55. ἡ ἀκτή meant specifically the southern peninsula of the Piraeus: ἐπιθαλαττίδιός τις μοῖρα τῆς Ἀττικῆς, Harpocr.

μετὰ τῆς ἑταίρας] unimportant, but 'showing the man' (Rehd. *ad loc.*).

διὰ τῆς πυλίδος] 'through the postern gate': the walls of Athens, as of other cities, included a number of such 'posterns,' as distinct from the main gates (πύλαι): it would be clear to Lycurgus' hearers, from his narrative, which particular one he meant. So at Torone some of Brasidas' troops are admitted κατὰ τὴν πυλίδα (Thuc. IV. 111), Xen. *Hell.* II. 4. 8 (of Eleusis).

ᾤχετο φεύγων] the *impf.* ptcp. (instead of aorist) with ᾤχετο suits the highly descriptive passage, and agrees with the impfs. ἀνήγετο...κατέλειπεν following.

τὰ τείχη...αἰσχυνόμενος] 'feeling shame before the walls of his native city': so *infra* § 45 οὐδὲ τὰς θήκας παριὼν ᾐσχύνθη. The whole passage is a good example of δείνωσις.

ὧν τὴν φυλακὴν ἔρημον...κατέλειπεν] 'which, for his part, he was leaving defenceless,' another way of expressing ἃ ἔρημα φυλακῆς...κατέλειπεν, perhaps with a suggestion of the legal use of the adj., 'let it go by default.'—**τὸ καθ' αὐτὸν μέρος**: 'for his part,' *quantum in eo erat*. It is interesting to note Lycurgus' variety of phrase:—(*a*) here, and *infra* § 144, τὸ καθ' αὐτὸν μέρος, (*b*) § 97 κατὰ τὸ ἑαυτοῦ μέρος, (*c*) §§ 26, 147 τὸ καθ' ἑαυτόν, (*d*) § 78 τὸ τούτου μέρος, (*e*) § 45 τὸ ἐπὶ τούτῳ μέρος. Es, among others, lays it down that the three forms recognized by the classicists are (*a*) τὸ ἐκείνου μέρος, (*b*) τὸ ἐπὶ τούτῳ, (*c*) τὸ καθ' αὐτόν, and would make variants such as τὸ καθ' αὐτὸν μέρος, κατὰ τὸ ἑαυτοῦ μέρος, etc. (which he regards as the work of copyists) conform to one or other of the types, by the omission of the prep. or of μέρος, as the case may be. This method, however, does not take sufficient account of the elasticity and constant change of language; and Rehdantz, in an exhaustive note (App. 2, pp. 128-9), suggests, with more reason, that Lycurgus (like Dinarchus), either for variety or expressiveness, strengthened the more general τὸ κατὰ by the addition of the more definite μέρος.

Δ. τοῦ σωτῆρος...Ἀ. τῆς σωτείρας] The attributes are emphatic and are intended by the speaker to be in telling contrast with L.'s conduct: he could not trust the gods who save to save *him*.—σωτήρ...σώτειρα, of 'protecting' gods and goddesses respectively, but the masc. form is coupled also with fem. nouns: cf. Aesch. *Agam.* 664 τύχη σωτήρ, *S.C.T.* 826 (conj. Dindorf), Soph. *O.T.* 81.

ἀφορῶν καὶ προδιδούς] 'as he viewed from afar [the acropolis, etc.], which he was forsaking,' we should probably say, instead of the co-ordinate const. in the Gk. Rehd. remarks that the order in which the various objects are mentioned (λιμένας, τείχη, etc.) corresponds with that in which they would present themselves to the view of L. as he put out to sea: the last three [Acropolis, Temple of Z. Soter (in the Piraeus), Temple of A. Soteira (near the sea, in the deme Corydallus)] he would 'behold from afar' (ἀφορᾶν).

σώσοντας] σώσοντας echoes, of course, τοῦ σωτῆρος...τῆς σωτείρας, and is a somewhat harsh extension of the final use of the future ptcp.: 'to save him.' Cf. *infra* § 143 ἐπικαλέσεται τοὺς θεοὺς σώσοντας αὐτὸν ἐκ τῶν κινδύνων.

§ 18. ὥσπερ...εὐαγγελιζόμενος] 'as though he were bringing glad tidings of great good fortune for his country': τῇ πατρίδι depends upon εὐτυχίας. Cf. Ar. *Eq.* 643 λόγους ἀγαθοὺς εὐαγγελίσασθαι, Dem. *De Cor.* § 323 τὴν δεξιὰν προτείνων καὶ εὐαγγελιζόμενος, 'offering my congratulations.'

τὸ ἄστυ τῆς πόλεως] 'the city proper,' πόλεως being a partitive gen. and πόλις including both the ἄστυ or 'upper city' and the Piraeus. The distinction τὸ ἄστυ)(ὁ Πειραιεύς is familiar: cf. οἱ ἐξ ἄστεος)(οἱ ἐκ Πειραιῶς, of the parties in the time of the Thirty.

ἑαλωκός...πολιορκούμενον] 'captured'...'in a state of blockade.' καὶ οὐκ ᾐσχύνθη κ.τ.λ.] Cf. Lysias XXXI. § 17 (of Philo) ἑτέροις...οἷς τὰ ὑμέτερα δυστυχήματα εὐτυχήματα ἐγεγόνει, Dem. *De Cor.* § 323 (of Aeschines).

ὥστε τριήρεις πληρώσαντες...κατῆγον] 'that they manned triremes and proceeded to bring merchantmen into port': note the tenses, for which see Goodwin, §§ 36, 143.—κατάγειν τὰ πλοῖα was said of *forcing vessels to land* (*naves vi coactas abducere, quo velimus*, Es), either for the purpose of discharging part of their cargo or of extorting dues. This practice on the part of Philip in respect of Athenian corn-ships from the Propontis was a standing grievance against him at Athens, to which we find reference in Dem. (cf. *De Cor.* § 73). Cf. also Dem. *De Pace* § 25 καὶ Βυζαντίους (sc. ἐῶμεν) κατάγειν τὰ πλοῖα, *De Chers.* § 9 Διοπείθης ἀδικεῖ κατάγων τὰ πλοῖα, *Adv. Polycl.* [or. L] § 17 Βυζάντιοι...κατάγουσι τὰ π. καὶ ἀναγκάζουσι τὸν σῖτον ἐξαιρεῖσθαι. The alleged conduct of the Rhodians on this occasion, resting, as it did, on the supposed impotence of Athens to prevent it, would no doubt be expected by the speaker to raise considerable *invidia* on the part of his hearers against L. [Jebb in his rendering of this passage (*Attic Orators*, vol. II. p. 378) gives: 'that they told off crews for their triremes, and set about *launching the vessels*,' apparently identifying τριήρεις and τὰ πλοῖα, and taking κατῆγον as = καθεῖλκον. This is clearly wrong.]

αὐτοῦ τὸν σῖτον ἐξείλοντο...διὰ τοῦτον] 'discharged their corn and other cargo on the spot (αὐτοῦ—adv.), all through L.,' i.e. either they were compelled to do so (cf. previous note), or they did so voluntarily on the assumption (presuming L.'s tale to be true) that they would be unable to make the Piraeus.—διὰ τοῦτον: note the emphatic position of these words, which would be preceded by a slight pause on the part of the speaker.

§ 19. καὶ ὅτι ταῦτ' ἀληθῆ λέγω] 'and in proof of the truth of my statement': for this initial use of ὅτι, 'to prove that,' 'as evidence that,' looking forward to, but not depending directly upon, a following predicate (here ἀναγνώσεται...τὰς μαρτυρίας), see the elaborate excursus of Rehd., App. 2, pp. 129-133.

ἀναγνώσεται] sc. ὁ γραμματεύς, 'the clerk of court.'

Φυρκίνου] probably the farmer-in-chief of the πεντηκοστή: see note below.

ὅν...κατηγοροῦντα ἐν τῷ δήμῳ τούτῳ] 'whom most of you know as the accuser of L. before the Assembly': the pres. ptcp. expresses the standing relation, being equivalent to κατήγορον ὄντα or γεγενημένον, in which case κατηγορεῖν = 'to be (have been) some one's prosecutor,' may be compared with ἀδικεῖν, 'to be guilty,' τίκτειν, 'be the mother of' (Eur. *Ion* 1560 ἥδε᾽τίκτει σε): Goodwin, § 27.

ὡς καὶ μεγάλα...μετέχων αὐτῆς] 'on the charge that he had also seriously damaged the 2 per cent. tax, in which he had an interest.'—The πεντηκοστή, at Athens, was a duty of one-fiftieth or 2 per cent. on all imports and exports, imported corn, manufactured commodities, etc. These duties were collected by the πεντηκοστολόγοι (Böckh, *Publ. Econ. Ath.*, pp. 314 *sqq.*). From an important passage of Andocides, *De Myst.* §§ 133, 134, it appears that it was customary for a company to lease the tax: at the head of such company was a chief farmer (ἀρχώνης), by whose name it was called. The lease was sold to the highest bidder by the πωληταὶ near the White Poplar (ἡ λεύκη), and is mentioned by Andoc. *l.c.* as twice realizing 30 talents and once 36 talents. A member of such a company was said μετέχειν τῆς π. (Andoc. *l.c.* Ἀγύρριος γὰρ οὑτοσί...ἀρχώνης ἐγένετο τῆς π.... καὶ ἐπρίατο τριάκοντα ταλάντων, μετέσχον δ᾽ αὐτῷ οὗτοι πάντες κ.τ.λ.). L. had evidently been a member of such a company of farmers as is here described. The 'damage' to the tax would result from his action in holding up, by his alarming news, merchantmen bound for Athens, as described in the previous paragraph.—**καὶ μεγάλα**: καί, 'also,' 'further,' i.e. in addition to the fact of his desertion, which Lyc. is specially concerned with, though it may also be taken as intensive in force = 'very seriously.'—For the text, see Crit. App.

c. 7. § 20. *You are familiar with the various influences which are brought to bear on witnesses to prevent them doing their duty. Request them, therefore, either to give their evidence without fear or favour, or else excuse themselves in the prescribed form.*

§ 20. ἀναβαίνειν] Said of a witness who at the trial 'mounts the tribune' (βῆμα) to acknowledge his evidence as put in at the ἀνάκρισις or preliminary investigation before the archon: see note on ἢ λαβόντας τὰ ἱερὰ...ἐξομόσασθαι *infra*.

τὰς παρασκευὰς τῶν κρινομένων] 'the tricks of defendants': παρασκευή is so used constantly by the orators of corrupt practices in getting up or conducting a case: cf. Lysias, XXVIII. § 11 οὐκ ἄξιον ὑμῖν τῆς τούτων παρασκευῆς ἡττᾶσθαι, Isaeus, VIII. § 5 παρασκευὰς λόγων, 'fabricated statements,' Dem. XXX. § 3, Aeschin. *Ctes.* § 1, etc. So also παρασκευάζειν and παρασκευάζεσθαι: Lysias *c. Agorat.* [or. XIII] § 12 δικαστήριον παρασκευάσαντες, 'having packed a court for his trial,' Dem. XXIX. § 28 μάρτυρας ψευδεῖς παρεσκεύασται, etc.

τὰς δεήσεις τῶν ἐξ.] 'the entreaties of those who seek to beg them off': cf. Aeschin. *Ctes.* § 1 τὰς κατὰ τὴν ἀγορὰν δεήσεις, Dem. *F.L.* § 1 αἱ τῶν παρακλήτων (*advocatorum*) δεήσεις.—For ἐξαιτεῖσθαι, *exorare*, cf. *infra* § 139, Lysias, XIV. § 20 ἐὰν μέν τινες τῶν συγγενῶν αὐτὸν ἐξαιτῶνται, Dem. *Mid.* § 99, etc.

χρημάτων...χάριτος] 'for a fee or as a favour,' i.e. from a desire to oblige. So τὰς χάριτας below. For the various shades of meaning of which χάρις is susceptible, see L.S. *s.v.*

ὑμῶν καὶ τῆς πόλεως] gens. of comparison after περὶ πλείονος ποιεῖσθαι, not with τὰς χάριτας: this would be made clear in speaking by a short pause after χάριτας.

ἀποδιδόναι] *reddere*, 'duly render.'

τάξιν] 'duty', 'rôle,' a favourite word with Dem. in this sense: *De Cor.* § 138 τὴν ὑπὲρ ὑμῶν τάξιν, *Ibid.* § 173 τὴν τῆς εὐνοίας τάξιν ἐν τοῖς δεινοῖς οὐκ ἔλιπον.

ἢ λαβόντας τὰ ἱερά...ἐξομόσασθαι] 'or else to take the oath of disclaimer with their hands on the sacrifice.'—All depositions relative to a case, at Athens, were required to be put in at the preliminary investigation (ἀνάκρισις), and no fresh evidence could be admitted at the actual trial. A person, however, who refused to appear as a witness at the ἀνάκρισις might be required by either of the parties to attend in court on the day of hearing, when he might be called upon to mount the platform (ἀναβαίνειν) and either depose to the truth of a written statement drawn up by the litigant and read out by the clerk, or swear that he had no knowledge of the facts as set forth in the document. In case of his refusal to obey, he was liable to a fine of 1000 drachmae. (See Wyse on Isaeus, or. IX. 18. 8, 9.)—A witness who in such cases affirmed his ignorance on oath was said ἐξομόσασθαι, and his disclaimer was ἐξωμοσία: Dem. XLV. § 60 ἢ μαρτυρεῖτ' ἢ ἐξομόσασθε, *F.L.* § 176, Isaeus, *l.c.* The middle, as appears from these exx., is regular in this sense, but the active also occurs: Dem. XXIX. § 20 μαρτυρεῖν ἢ ἐξομνύειν, *F.L.* § 176, where ἐξομνύωσιν immediately follows ἐξόμνυσθαι. [Distinguish from this use ἐξομόσασθαι πρεσβείαν, *eiurare legationem*, 'to decline an embassy on a sworn plea that one has not the means, health, etc. to perform it,' Dem. *F.L.* §§ 122, 172, and ἐξομνύναι, 'to put in such a plea *on behalf of another*,' *Ibid.* § 124 ἐξώμοσεν ἀρρωστεῖν τουτονί.—**λαβόντας τὰ ἱερά**: a solemn formality accompanying the oath, such as is described e.g. in Antiph. *De Caed. Herod.* § 12 ἁπτομένους τῶν σφαγίων καταμαρτυρεῖν, 'with hand laid upon the sacrifice' (Jebb), Dem. *c. Aristocr.* §§ 67, 68 (of the accuser before the Areopagus) διομεῖται...στὰς ἐπὶ τῶν τομίων κάπρου καὶ κριοῦ καὶ ταύρου, XLIII. § 14.

κλητεύσομεν αὐτούς] In respect of the preliminaries to the actual trial, κλητεύειν is said (*a*) of summoning in the presence of κλητῆρες, i.e. witnesses to the proper service of the summons, Dem. *De Cor.* § 150 τίς ἐκλήτευσεν ἡμᾶς; (*b*) to act as κλητήρ. In what sense is it said (as here) of recalcitrant witnesses at the actual trial (see previous note)? It seems to be generally understood as 'to formally summon to depose,' in other words, to require a witness μαρτυρεῖν ἢ ἐξομόσασθαι. But in the present passage, and also in [Dem.] LIX. 28 ἀναγκάσω μαρτυρεῖν ἢ ἐξόμνυσθαι κατὰ τὸν νόμον ἢ κλητεύσομεν αὐτόν, κλητεύειν is clearly said of witnesses who refuse to do either. The definitions of κλητεύειν in this connexion, and its precise relation to ἐκκλητεύειν, are unfortunately not clear enough to remove all doubt about the procedure. Pollux (8. 37) says: τὸν δ' οὐ βουλόμενον μαρτυρεῖν ἐκλήτευον ἀνάγκην τοῦ μαρτυρεῖν προστιθέντες· ἔδει δὲ αὐτὸν ἢ μαρτυρεῖν ἢ ἐξομόσασθαι ὡς οὐκ εἰδείη ἢ μὴ παρείη ἢ χιλίας ἀποτίνειν. κλητεύεσθαι μὲν οὖν ἐστὶ τὸ καλεῖσθαι εἰς μαρτυρίαν, ἐκκλητεύεσθαι δὲ τὸ δίκην ὀφείλειν ἐπὶ τῷ τὰς χιλίας καταβαλεῖν. Harpocr.: λέγεται δὲ κλητεύεσθαι καὶ ἐκκλητεύεσθαι ἐπὶ τῶν μαρτύρων, ὅταν μὴ ὑπακούωσι πρὸς τὴν μαρτυρίαν ἐν τοῖς δικαστηρίοις, καὶ ἔστιν ἐπιτίμιον κατ' αὐτῶν δραχμαὶ χίλιαι, ὡς Ἰσαῖος ἐν τῷ ὑπὲρ Πύθωνος ἀποστασίου. From Aeschin. I. 47 it would appear that ἐκκλητεύεσθαι was equivalent to τὸ χιλίας ἀποτίνειν (ἐὰν δὲ προαιρῆται ἐκκλητευθῆναι, προαιρήσεται χιλίας δραχμὰς ἀποτῖσαι τῷ δημοσίῳ). If then we are justified in inferring from Harpocr. that κλητεύειν and ἐκκλητεύειν were said indifferently of the same thing, κλητεύσομεν here will mean: 'we shall set in motion against them the recognized machinery for punishing contumacy,' i.e. compel them to pay the prescribed fine of 1000 drachmae. Otherwise it seems necessary to read ἐκκλητεύσομεν, with Dobree. [So, in substance, van Es, who says: *testes κλητεύονται*, i.e. *citantur ad testimonium dicendum aut eierandum...cum Lycurgus autem iudices oraverat testes iubere dicere aut eierare, nihil reliquum erat, si horum neutrum facerent, nisi eos* ἐκκλητεύειν, *quare omnino probanda est Dobraei emendatio* ἐκκλητεύσομεν.]

c. 8. §§ 21–27. *When the falsity of his tale was exposed, Leocrates in alarm quitted Rhodes for Megara, and lived there for more than five years under a Megarian patron. How completely he had condemned himself to perpetual exile is shown by the arrangements he made for the disposal of his property and slaves at Athens, for which I shall produce evidence. Worst of all, however, he transported the sacred things of his country* *from their consecrated soil and made them to share his exile. All this he aggravated by engaging in the export of corn to foreign places, an act forbidden an Athenian under the most severe penalties. Will you not then condemn him?*

§ 21. ἐγένετο...ἀφικνεῖτο] 'when an interval had elapsed... and vessels were keeping arriving': note the tenses.

φοβηθείς] 'taking fright': Goodwin, § 55.

προστάτην ἔχων Μεγαρέα] 'with a Megarian as his patron': the practice at Athens whereby a resident alien (μέτοικος) was required to choose a citizen as his προστάτης (cf. *patronus*), who represented him in the courts and otherwise looked after his interests, appears to have been customary in other states. The μέτοικος was technically said νέμειν προστάτην (whence Es would read νέμων here, but πρ. ἔχειν was also said, Rehd., p. 134): his state was also described as ἐπὶ προστάτου οἰκεῖν: cf. *infra* § 145, Lysias, XXXI. § 9 ἐν Ὠρωπῷ μετοίκιον κατατιθεὶς ἐπὶ πρ. ᾤκει.

αἰσχυνόμενος] Cf. *supra* § 17 οὔτε τὰ τείχη τῆς πατρίδος αἰσχυνόμενος.

ἐν γειτόνων...μετοικῶν] 'living as a stranger next door to the country that brought him up': ἐν γειτόνων, sc. χώρᾳ or οἴκοις, but the phrase, like ἐκ γειτόνων, which some read here, has come to be virtually equivalent to πέλας or πλησίον. Cf. Luc. *Philops*. 25.

§ 22. καὶ οὕτως...φυγήν] Cf. Lysias, *In Alcib.* I. [or. XIV] § 38 ἀλλὰ φυγὴν αὐτοῦ καταγνούς, καὶ Θρᾴκης καὶ πάσης πόλεως ἐβούλετο πολίτης γενέσθαι μᾶλλον ἢ τῆς πατρίδος εἶναι τῆς ἑαυτοῦ.

ἐντεῦθεν] in relation to L., from Megara; in relation to the speaker, from Athens. ἐντεῦθεν might mean either, the first being the more likely.

τὸν...ἔχοντα] 'him who had to wife,' a common idiomatic meaning of ἔχω: cf. Thuc. II. 29 Νυμφόδωρον τὸν Πύθεω...οὗ εἶχε τὴν ἀδελφὴν Σιτάλκης.

τῶν φίλων] partitive gen.

88 NOTES [§ 22

Ξυπεταιόνα] 'of Xypete,' a deme of the tribe Cecropis, W. of Athens.

τοῦ κηδεστοῦ] 'his brother-in-law': the word means 'a connexion by marriage' (Lat. *affinis*) and takes its colour from the context.

ἀποδόσθαι ταλάντου] 'he sold them for a talent': πωλεῖν, 'have for sale')(ἀποδόσθαι, 'sell.'

ἀπὸ τούτου] 'from' or 'with' this money, sc. ταλάντου.

προσέταξε...ὀφειλόμενα] The const. is: προσέταξεν (αὐτῷ) ἀποδοῦναι τὰ ὀφ. τοῖς χρήσταις, 'commissioned him to pay his creditors what was owing to them.'

τοὺς ἐράνους διενεγκεῖν] 'to pay off his loans,' i.q. διαλύσασθαι (L.S. *s.v.* διαφέρω).—ἔρανος seems capable of the following meanings: (*a*) 'a meal to which each contributes his share,' 'a pic-nic' (*cena collaticia*), opp. to εἰλαπίνη, *Od*. I. 226; (*b*) 'a subscription,' for whatever purpose, and especially (*c*) 'a contribution' made by friends to assist a person in difficulties, 'a friendly loan' (Antiph. *Tetr*. A. β. § 9 ἔρανον παρὰ τῶν φίλων συλλέξας), which was, however, recoverable at law (Wyse, Isaeus XI. 43): this seems to be the meaning here; (*d*) figuratively, a 'contribution' or 'offering' to a cause: Thuc. II. 43 κάλλιστον... ἔρανον αὐτῇ προιέμενοι, 'lavishing on the city the tribute of their lives' (Jebb); (*e*) a 'society' or 'club' for social purposes or for mutual relief: such associations gradually acquired a political character and influence, somewhat like the Roman *sodalicia* and *collegia*.

τὸ λοιπόν] 'the balance.'

§ 23. Ἀχαρνεῖ] 'of Acharnae,' one of the best-known Attic demes.

ἀργύριον δὲ...δοῦναι] 'not being able to pay cash.'

συνθήκας...Λυσικλεῖ] 'having arranged a bond and deposited it with L.,' who presumably was a banker (τραπεζίτης): cf. [Dem.] or. XLVIII. § 11 Ἀνδροκλείδην Ἀχαρνέα, παρ' ᾧ κατεθέμεθα τὰς συνθήκας.

μίαν μνᾶν τόκον ἔφερεν] 'he paid A. one mina as interest':

this, if calculated in the ordinary way as so much *per mina per month*, works out at 2⅔ per cent. per month or 34⅔ per cent. per annum, which strikes us as an extraordinarily high rate, especially in a transaction between relatives. The text is generally suspected, and Mätzner's (Rehd.) ἡμιμναῖον for μίαν μνᾶν seems most attractive: ἡμιμναῖος ('half-mina') τόκος would accordingly represent about 17 per cent. Other suggestions are: μίαν δραχμὴν ἀνὰ μνᾶν Meier, δραχμὴν τῆς μνᾶς Es, μίαν τῆς μνᾶς? Blass. [Common rates of interest among the Greeks were 12 p.c. and 18 p.c. per annum (ἐπὶ δραχμῇ, ἐπ' ἐννέα ὀβολοῖς, respectively, on the *per mina per month* basis), and the former was considered low].

λόγον] 'an idle tale': Dem. *Lept.* § 92 ἵν' οὖν μὴ λόγον λέγω μόνον, *Ibid.* § 101 ἐκεῖνό γ' οὐ λόγος.

ἀναγνώσεται] Cf. *supra* § 19 *n*.

παρειχόμην] sc. μάρτυρα, as a witness.—**νυνί** = ἐπειδήπερ τέθνηκε.—**ὑμῖν**: ethic dative, or dative of the person interested in the action, common in calling upon witnesses or asking for documents to be read: cf. the familiar καί μοι λέγε (λαβέ, ἀνάγνωθι) τὴν μαρτυρίαν, and *infra* § 114 λαβὲ δ' αὐτοῖς τὸ ψήφισμα, etc.—**καλῶ**: future.

§ 24. ἀπέλαβε] 'duly received,' of payment to which a person is entitled, as ἀποδοῦναι is 'duly pay' (cf. *supra* § 20 *n*.): Xen. *Anab.* VII. 7. 14 ἀπολ. τὸν ὀφειλόμενον μισθόν, Isaeus, V. § 40 οὐκ ἀπέλαβον ἃ ἐδάνεισαν.

Φιλόμηλος...Μενέλαος] two of L.'s creditors.—**Χολαργεύς**: 'of Cholargus,' a deme of the Acamantid tribe.—**ὁ πρεσβεύσας ὡς βασιλέα**: the occasion of the embassy is uncertain: some refer to Dem. *Phil.* III. § 71 ἐκπέμπωμεν πρέσβεις πανταχοῖ...ὡς βασιλέα λέγω κ.τ.λ., but this is merely a recommendation.

τὴν Τ.] sc. μαρτυρίαν.

§ 25. ἀγανακτῆσαι...μισῆσαι] 'to get indignant'...'to conceive a hatred of': for the force of the aorists, cf. Goodwin, § 55.—**τουτονὶ Λ.**: οὑτοσὶ usually follows its subst., but sometimes precedes it, as here.

οὐ γὰρ ἐξήρκεσε...μόνον ὑπεκθ.] 'he was not content...merely with removing,' etc.: Baiter and Sauppe point out that even where μόνον precedes ἀρκεῖ (ἐξαρκεῖ), it is to be joined with the infin. rather than with the impers. verb (Rehd., App. 2, p. 134).—
ὑπεκθέσθαι: technical of removal from the 'danger zone' in the case of hostile invasion: cf. *infra* § 53 ἔχοντος δ' αἰτίαν τοὺς υἱεῖς καὶ τὴν γυναῖκα ὑπεκθέσθαι)(ὑπεκκεῖσθαι, to be so removed: Her. VIII. 41 ὡς δέ σφι πάντα ὑπεξέκειτο, etc.

ἀλλὰ καὶ τὰ ἱερὰ...ἱδρυσάμενοι] 'but even the sacred things of his family, which, in accordance with your settled practice and hereditary usage, his forefathers bequeathed to him as a permanent trust' (ἱδρυσάμενοι, lit. 'having established,' 'set up,' with the intention that they should remain there in perpetuity— that they should not be 'moved' from their place (κινήσας *infra*).—ἱερά (with μετεπέμψατο and ἐξήγαγεν) must mean something concrete, 'sacred images': cf. *supra* § 20 λαβόντας τὰ ἱερά.—πατρῷα...πατρίοις: the adjs. are usually distinguished as 'belonging to' or 'derived from' one's *father*)(one's *fathers*: *paternus*)(*patrius*, v. L.S. *s.v.* πατρῷος; and the distinction seems applicable here, where τὰ πατρῷα has reference to L.'s own family)(τοῖς πατρίοις, 'ancestral,' 'hereditary,' in a general sense. But it is doubtful whether any of the canons which have been laid down regarding πατρῷος, πάτριος, πατρικός is of universal application: the first two especially are sometimes hard to separate. Bekker, *Anec.* I. p. 297 (quoted by Sandys on Isocr. *Ad Dem.* § 2) lays it down: πατρῷα λέγουσιν οἱ ῥήτορες χρήματα καὶ κτήματα καὶ τόπους, πάτρια δὲ τὰ ἔθη καὶ τὰ νόμιμα καὶ τὰ μυστήρια καὶ τὰς ἑορτάς, πατρικὸν δὲ φίλον ἢ ἐχθρόν.

μετεπέμψατο εἰς M.] 'sent for them (and had them brought) to M.': a 'pregnant' const.

οὐδὲ τὴν ἐπωνυμίαν...φοβηθείς] "'not dreading even the appellation of 'family images,'"' i.e. the sanctity implied in their very name: τῶν πατρῴων ἱερῶν is a gen. defining ἐπωνυμίαν.—
ὅτι introduces the motive for his fear: 'in that,' etc.

κινήσας] The verb is specially said of 'removing from its

place,' 'tampering with,' anything sacred: cf. Her. VI. 134 (of Miltiades at Paros) ὑπερθορόντα δὲ ἰέναι ἐπὶ τὸ μέγαρον...εἴτε κινήσοντά τι τῶν ἀκινήτων εἴτε κ.τ.λ., Thuc. IV. 98 (of the Athenians using the sacred water at Delium), II. 24 (of applying a special reserve of money to other than the original purpose).

ἱδρῦσθαι] Bekker (Blass, Thalh.), for ἱδρύσασθαι of the MSS. (Rehd.), brings the three infins. into line (all passive), though ἱδρύσασθαι is quite defensible.—**ἐπὶ ξένης**: sc. γῆς, 'on foreign soil.'

ὀθνεῖα τῇ χώρᾳ κ.τ.λ.] 'alien to the country and to the rites sanctioned by custom in the Megarian community.' ὀθνεῖος, rather a rare word)(οἰκεῖος: cf. Harpocr. *s.v.*: Ἰσαῖος ἐν τῷ κατὰ Στρατοκλέους [or. IV. 18] ἀντὶ τοῦ ἀλλοτρίους ὡς καὶ παρὰ Πλάτωνι ἐν α΄ Νόμων, Plat. *Protag.* 316 C τὰς τῶν ἄλλων συνουσίας καὶ οἰκείων καὶ ὀθνείων, *Rep.* V. 470 B τὸ μὲν οἰκεῖον καὶ συγγενές, τὸ δὲ ἀλλότριον καὶ ὀθνεῖον.

§ 26. τῇ Ἀθηνᾷ] depending upon ὁμώνυμον following. For the reading, see Crit. App.

ὡς τὴν χώραν εἰληχυίᾳ] 'on the ground of her having received the country as her portion': λαγχάνω is thus used, esp. in the perf., of the tutelary deity of a place: cf. Her. VII. 53 θεοῖσι τοὶ Περσίδα γῆν λελόγχασι, Plat. *Tim.* 23 D ᾗ τὴν ὑμετέραν πόλιν ἔλαχε (of Athena). Here, and in other passages relating to Athena, there may also be a suggestion of the traditional contest between the goddess and Poseidon for the possession of the Acropolis (Her. VIII. 55).

ὁμώνυμον] From another point of view, A. was the 'eponymous' goddess of Athens: cf. the 'eponymous heroes' and *supra* § 1 τοῖς ἥρωσι...ἱδρυμένοις *n.*

ἐγκαταλίπωσι] The 'vivid' subj. is especially appropriate here, of a purpose that was to hold good for all time: Goodwin, § 318.

τὸ καθ' ἑαυτόν] Cf. *supra* § 17 τὸ καθ' αὐτὸν μέρος *n.*

ἐξαγώγιμον ὑμῖν...ἐποίησε] 'made the very help of heaven one of your articles of export': ὑμῖν, which it is difficult to give force to in translating, may be described either as an ethic dat. or as a *dativus incommodi.*—**τὴν παρὰ τῶν θεῶν β.**: cf. *supra* § 15 τὴν παρ' ὑμῶν...τιμωρίαν *n.*

τοσαῦτα καὶ τηλικαῦτα] cf. *supra* § 2 *n.*

ἀφορμῇ] 'as his working capital': cf. Dem. *Pro Phorm.* [or. XXXVI] § 11 εἰ ἦν ἰδία τις ἀφορμὴ τουτῳὶ πρὸς τῇ τραπέζῃ, 'any private capital at the bank.'

Κλεοπάτρας] Sister of Alexander the Great, and wife of Alexander of Epirus, who was also her maternal uncle. It was at her marriage that Philip was murdered (336 B.C.). During the absence of her husband on his campaigns in Italy, she apparently acted as regent.

Λευκάδα] Leucas was an island (since the time of the Cypselids, *c.* 625 B.C.), originally a peninsula, off Acarnania in N.W. Greece (now *S. Maura*).

§ 27. τούτων]neut., and referring to the clause ἐάν τις...ὡς ὑμᾶς.

τὰς ἐσχάτας τιμωρίας...σιτηγήσῃ] As Athens, acc. to Böckh, *Public Economy of Athens*, p. 81, was dependent upon sea-borne corn to the extent of at least a third of her consumption, it was natural not only that the exportation of corn from Attica should be forbidden, but that stringent supervision should be exercised over the sale and distribution of what was imported. This was managed by a board of fifteen σιτοφύλακες, five of whom seem to have been charged with the duty of keeping a register of the imports of corn at the Piraeus (Dem. *Lept.* § 32 ἐκ τῆς παρὰ τοῖς σιτοφ. ἀπογραφῆς): cf. also *Ibid.* § 31 πλείστῳ τῶν πάντων ἀνθρώπων ἡμεῖς ἐπεισάκτῳ σίτῳ χρώμεθα (where it is remarked that half the amount came from the coasts of the Pontus), *De Cor.* § 87. Rehdantz remarks that jurists must decide whether these corn-laws, the breach of which was subject to the special process known as φάσις, held good for L. *at Megara.*

ἔπειτα] 'then,' 'after all this,' characteristically (cf. εἶτα) introducing a question at the end of an argument which is thought to make the answer self-evident: cf. *infra* §§ 115, 121, 148.

ὑπὸ τῇ ὑμετέρᾳ ψήφῳ] cf. *supra* § 2.

§ 28]   NOTES   93

ἄρ'] ἄρα denotes 'subjective consequence' (Madvig, § 257. c):
'it follows that,' 'well then.'

c. 9. §§ 28–30. *To show you the fairness of my procedure, I challenged the defendant to allow his slaves to be tortured— one of the fairest and most reliable means of ascertaining the truth in a case of this kind. Leocrates, however, convicted by his own conscience, declined the challenge, and stands self-condemned by his refusal.*

§ 28. καὶ ταῦτα δέ...ἐμοῦ] '*and* this action *too* on my part,' etc.: for καὶ...δέ used for emphasis and enclosing, as here, the emphatic word, cf. Dem. *Ol.* III. § 15 καὶ πρᾶξαι δὲ δυνήσεσθε, 'and you will be able to *act* too,' *Phil.* III. § 70 ἐγὼ νὴ Δί' ἐρῶ, καὶ γράψω δέ, 'and, what is more, I'll *move*': Madvig, § 229. *a*, 'καί being both *and* and *also*, the Greek was obliged to have recourse to δέ to express *and also*....In Attic, the word that has the emphasis comes between.'—ταῦτα: here prospective, referring to the account of the challenge which follows (so often ἐκεῖνο).—
ἐμοῦ, with ταῦτα: this use of the gen.= 'in me (you, etc.),' 'on my (your, etc.) part,' is very idiomatic of something that one *praises*, *blames* or *wonders at* on the part of another: cf. Thuc. I. 84 τὸ βραδύ, ὃ μέμφονται μάλιστα ἡμῶν, Plat. *Apol.* 17 A μάλιστα αὐτῶν (sc. τῶν κατηγόρων) ἐν ἐθαύμασα, *Ibid.* 17 B τοῦτό μοι ἔδοξεν αὐτῶν ἀναισχυντότατον εἶναι. Sometimes the pronominal subject or object is replaced by a sentence, as in Xen. *Mem.* I. 1. 12 καὶ πρῶτον μὲν Σωκράτης αὐτῶν (sc. τῶν τὰ μετέωρα ἐρευνώντων) ἐσκόπει, πότερά ποτε νομίσαντες κ.τ.λ., 'the first thing he considered in (about) them was, whether' etc.

καὶ τοὺς μάρτυρας κ.τ.λ.] 'and that the witnesses should submit to a test of veracity before, and not after, they give their evidence in court. Now I made them (αὐτούς, 'the opposite side') a challenge, in writing, referring to all these points, and claiming to put the defendant's slaves to the torture.'—The evidence of slaves under torture was considered to be (or rather, perhaps, was made out to be—see *infra*) of great value in Greek law-courts; and it was customary for a litigant to challenge the other side to allow his slaves to be tortured, or to offer his own slaves. Such challenge was made in the presence of witnesses, and frequently in writing (γράψας). The challenger was said προκαλεῖσθαι εἰς βάσανον; to accept the challenge was δέχεσθαι τὴν πρόκλησιν, τὴν βάσανον; to decline it was φεύγειν τὴν π., τὴν β., τὸν ἔλεγχον; to offer one's slaves for torture, διδόναι, παραδιδόναι, εἰς β.; to call for the other's slaves, ἐξαιτεῖν; to comply with the demand, ἐκδιδόναι; to have slaves so given up, παραλαμβάνειν. When the speaker says that 'the witnesses should submit to a test of veracity *before*, and not *after*, giving evidence,' he means that they should come into court with their evidence supported by that of slaves previously obtained under torture. In that case they might be regarded as having already passed the test of veracity (δεδωκότας): otherwise such test would be merely prospective (δώσοντας)—in the shape of a possible trial for perjury (ψευδομαρτυριῶν). For a close parallel to the whole passage, cf. Isaeus, VIII. § 10 βουλόμενος οὖν πρὸς τοῖς ὑπάρχουσι μάρτυσιν ἔλεγχον ἐκ βασάνων ποιήσασθαι περὶ αὐτῶν [the facts in dispute], ἵνα μᾶλλον αὐτοῖς [the witnesses] πιστεύητε μὴ μέλλουσι δώσειν ἔλεγχον ἀλλ' ἤδη δεδωκόσι περὶ ὧν μαρτυροῦσι, τούτους [my opponents] ἠξίουν ἐκδοῦναι τὰς θεραπαίνας καὶ τοὺς οἰκέτας περί τε τούτων καὶ περὶ τῶν ἄλλων ἁπάντων ὅσα τυγχάνουσι συνειδότες, and the whole section §§ 10–13 of Isaeus with §§ 28–30 of Lycurgus.—**προὐκαλεσάμην...πρόκλησιν**: πρόκλησιν is an internal acc. with προύκ., though partly also with γράψας: cf. [Dem.] LIII. § 22 περὶ τῆς προκλήσεως...ἣν οὗτοί τ' ἐμὲ προὐκαλέσαντο καὶ ἐγὼ τούτους.—**αὐτούς**, which in its context would most naturally be referred to τοὺς μάρτυρας preceding (but προκαλεῖσθαι is not said of *witnesses*), must mean generally 'the defence,' 'the opposite side' (L. and his slaves—Rehd., Sofer). [Dobree's αὐτόν, which is attractive and would seem to mend matters, is difficult with τούτου following.]

ἧς ἀκοῦσαι ἄξιόν ἐστιν] See Crit. App.

καί μοι λέγε ταύτην] Cf. *supra* § 23 νυνὶ δ' ὑμῖν καλῶ τοὺς συνειδότας n.

§ 29. ἀκούετε] The pres. is so used, in reference to a document, decree, etc. which has just been read, with the force of a perf., as we too may say, 'Gentlemen, you hear (have heard) the evidence': so *infra* §§ 37, 115, 121.

ἅμα...οὐκ ἐδέχετο...καὶ κατεμαρτύρει] lit. 'no sooner did L. decline...than he bore witness against himself,' i.e. *by* declining... he bore witness, etc.: *cum noluit, se damnavit.* Cf. *infra* § 50, Isocr. *Paneg.* § 119 ἅμα γὰρ ἡμεῖς τε τῆς ἀρχῆς ἀπεστερούμεθα καὶ τοῖς Ἕλλησιν ἀρχὴ τῶν κακῶν ἐγίγνετο, 'the loss of our ἀρχή ('dominion') was the ἀρχή ('beginning') of troubles for the Greeks.'

ὁ γὰρ...ἔλεγχον φυγὼν κ.τ.λ.] 'for he who has declined the test afforded by the examination of his accomplices has admitted the truth of the articles of impeachment': ἔλεγχον φεύγειν is technical in this connexion: cf. *supra* § 28 *n.*, Antiph. *De Chor.* § 27 ἐπεὶ δ' ἐμοῦ προκαλουμένου οὗτοι ἦσαν οἱ φεύγοντες τὸν ἔλεγχον, Dem. *Adv. Aphob.* [or. XXIX] § 5 ἐπιδείξω...πεφευγότα τοῦτον τοὺς ἀκριβεστάτους ἐλέγχους.—**τὸν παρὰ τῶν συνειδότων**: see Crit. App.

δημοτικώτατον] rather a hard word to translate: the root idea is no doubt 'most in keeping with the spirit of democracy,' which to the Athenian was the ideal government: δημοτικός· χαίρων τῇ δημοκρατίᾳ, says schol. on Aeschin. *Ctes.* § 169. Thuc. (VI. 28) (of Alcibiades) speaks of τὴν ἄλλην αὐτοῦ...οὐ δημοτικὴν παρανομίαν, 'his general contempt for the law, so opposed to the spirit of democracy' (Dale), and Dem. (*De Cor.* § 6) describes Solon as εὔνους ὢν ὑμῖν καὶ δημοτικός, where Drake suggests 'a friend of the democracy,' 'a lover of equality.'

ὅταν οἰκέται ἢ θεράπαιναι...πιστεύειν] συνειδῶσιν ἃ δεῖ, sc. εἰδέναι, 'are in possession of the requisite knowledge' (for establishing the facts in dispute).—**ἐλέγχειν καὶ βασανίζειν**: hendiadys, 'to examine them by torture.'—**τοῖς ἔργοις...τοῖς λόγοις**: a somewhat harsh extension of the familiar λόγῳ...ἔργῳ antithesis, τοῖς ἔργοις again referring to the evidence of slaves as something that has been established 'by deeds' (i.e. by the physical test of torture), whereas that of free witnesses is substantiated only 'by words' (τοῖς λόγοις).—For similar commonplaces on the value of torture, cf. esp. Isaeus, VIII. § 12 (already referred to), where the speaker asserts that, while free witnesses have been known to give false evidence, τῶν δὲ βασανισθέντων οὐδένες πώποτε ἐξηλέγχθησαν ὡς οὐκ ἀληθῆ <τὰ> ἐκ τῶν βασάνων εἰπόντες, Dem. XXX. § 37 (practically a repetition of the Isaeus passage), Isocr. *Trapez.* § 54. Against these appraisements of the orators must be set the following practical considerations:— (*a*) The evidence of a slave so obtained was not necessarily good, as the slave, in such circumstances, unless unusually obstinate and unless the fear of what might happen to himself afterwards at the hands of his master outweighed the physical pain of the moment, would give the answers which he saw his torturers desired (cf. the instructive passage in Antiph. *De Caed. Herod.* §§ 31, 32); (*b*) the cases where we hear of the torture being actually applied are negligible compared with the challenges: this would seem to argue a mistrust, on the part of Athenian juries, of evidence obtained by the rack; (*c*) slaves could not be tortured except with their owner's consent and on the conditions which he chose to prescribe, a circumstance which no doubt suggested to a litigant as his proper cue the formulating of such conditions as would almost certainly be refused, and then quoting such refusal as an *a priori* weakening of his opponent's case at the actual trial. We may therefore conclude that 'challenges were not serious attempts to reach a settlement, but were designed to influence the dicasts. The aim of a challenger was to construct such a proposal as would be refused, in order to be able to denounce his opponent in court for concealing the truth from fear of revelations; the opponent sought to turn the tables by an inconvenient counter-challenge, and both sides recited to the judges commonplaces on the use of torture as an instrument to elicit truth.' (Wyse, *Companion to Greek Studies*, § 421.)

§ 30] NOTES

§ 30. τοσοῦτον ἀφέστηκα τοῦ...ποιήσασθαι, ὅσον] '*tantum abest, ut faciam, ut*' (Sofer).

τοῖς ἰδίοις κινδύνοις] 'at my own personal risk,' because the challenger, apparently, had to indemnify the owner of the slaves for any injury they might sustain through the torture: cf. [Dem.] LIX. 124 ἤθελον...εἴ τι ἐκ τῶν βασάνων βλαφθείησαν οἱ ἄνθρωποι, ἀποτίνειν ὅ τι βλαβείησαν.

ἐν τοῖς...οἰκέταις...τὸν ἔλεγχον γενέσθαι] 'that the test (i.e. the means of discovering the truth) should consist in (should be furnished by) the torture of L.'s slaves': they were to be the *instruments* by which the truth was to be ascertained: for this use of ἐν, cf. [Dem.] XLVII. § 16 ἐθέλεις ἐν τῇ ἀνθρώπῳ τὸν ἔλεγχον γίγνεσθαι, XLIX. 55 ἠξίουν αὐτὸν ἐν τῷ αὑτοῦ δέρματι τὸν ἔλεγχον διδόναι. So more generally Thuc. VII. 11 τὰ πραχθέντα... ἐν ἐπιστολαῖς ἴστε, 'ye know...*by* letters,' etc.—τοῖς...βασανισθεῖσι: the slaves, though of different genders, are grouped together in the masc. as a single idea: cf. τούτους of the preceding section.

διὰ τὸ συνειδέναι ἑαυτῷ] practically 'because of his guilty conscience': usually σύνοιδα has a supplementary participle either in nom. or dat.: Plat. *Apol.* 21 B σ. ἐμαυτῷ σοφὸς ὤν, *Ib.* 22 C οὐδὲν ἐπισταμένῳ, or an acc.: Ar. *Thesm.* 477 σύνοιδ' ἐμαυτῇ πολλὰ δεινά, Dem. 1472. 16 εἰς τὴν πατρίδα εὔνοιαν ἐμαυτῷ σ.

ἔφυγε] sc. τὴν βάσανον or τὸν ἔλεγχον, as above.

τῶν γενομένων...κατεψεύσαντο] 'would far more readily have denied some of the facts than invented a false tale to the prejudice of their own master,' and so he should have had all the less reason for refusing the challenge. The slaves would be deterred from the latter course by the damage it would do to their prospects of freedom: cf. Antiph. *De Caed. Herod.* §§ 31, 32.

c. 10. §§ 31–35. *Leocrates will exclaim that he is an amateur who is being swept off his feet by the cleverness of the professional speaker; yet with strange inconsistency he has elected to come before a court which is liable to be influenced by the* *tricks of rhetoric rather than give up his slaves, who would have been proof against such devices. His reason can only be that he is afraid lest the convicters and the convicted be forthcoming from the same house. If he admits the truth of the indictment, he must be punished; if he denies it, why does he refuse to surrender his slaves? His rejection of a fair offer is tantamount to a confession of guilt.*

§ 31. χωρὶς τοίνυν τούτων] "now 'apart from' or 'besides' all this": cf. *infra* § 56.

Δ. ἀναβοήσεται κ.τ.λ.] 'L. will be immediately crying out that he is a mere layman, and that he is being swept off his feet by the cleverness of the professional speaker and vexatious prosecutor.'—ἰδιώτης: here, as often, of one *who has no professional knowledge*, 'a layman' as we say)(ῥήτωρ, a 'professional' speaker: cf. Isocr. *Paneg.* § 11 τῶν λόγων τοῖς ὑπὲρ τοὺς ἰδιώτας ἔχουσι καὶ λίαν ἀπηκριβωμένοις, 'speeches which are too highly elaborated and beyond the range of ordinary hearers,' Thuc. II. 48 καὶ ἰατρὸς καὶ ἰδιώτης, VI. 72 ἰδιώτας, ὡς εἰπεῖν, χειροτέχναις ἀνταγωνισαμένους (of the Syracusan seamen as opp. to the Athenians).—τοῦ ῥήτορος: the article marks the class—'the professional speaker'—and the word has perhaps the slightly unfavourable sense which is attached to it at the three places where it occurs in Thuc. (III. 40, VI. 29, VIII. 1), and freq. in Isocr., e.g. *Panath.* § 12, *De Pace* § 129, though in these passages the reference is mainly to the regular speakers in the Assembly.—συκοφάντου: cf. *supra* § 13 *n.*—δεινότητος: esp. of 'cleverness' in an orator, 'rhetorical skill': Thuc. III. 37 δεινότητι καὶ ξυνέσεως ἀγῶνι ἐπαιρομένους, Dem. *De Cor.* §§ 242, 277, Isocr. *Ad Dem.* § 4 τὴν δ. τὴν ἐν τοῖς λόγοις, 'oratorical power.'—ἀναρπαζόμενος: the vb. occurs several times in Dem. [*Mid.* §§ 120, 124; [Dem.] *Phil.* IV. § 18] in the sense of being 'carried off by force' (before a magistrate, to prison, etc., *rapi in ius*), and it may possibly partake of this meaning here: probably, however, the sense is more general, 'that he is being annihilated': cf. Aeschin. *Ctes.* § 133 (of Thebes) ἐκ μέσης τῆς

Ἑλλάδος ἀνήρπασται, 'has been extirpated,' 'blotted out,' *de medio sublata*.

συκοφαντεῖν] Cf. *supra* § 13 καὶ τοῖς διώκουσιν ἥκιστα συκοφαντεῖν n.

ἅμα...προαιρεῖσθαι καὶ ζητεῖν] 'in choosing this rôle (i.e. that of the συκοφάντης), to seek,' etc.

χωρία] in the rhetorical sense, 'themes,' 'topics,' i.q. τόποι, Lat. *loci*, somewhat as at Thuc. I. 97 τοῖς πρὸ ἐμοῦ ἅπασιν ἐκλιπὲς τοῦτο ἦν τὸ χωρίον, 'this subject,' 'department.'

ἐν οἷς...ποιήσονται] final, 'in which they can practise.'—
παραλογισμούς: 'false reasonings,' 'quibbles,' divided by Aristotle into οἱ παρὰ τὴν λέξιν (verbal) and οἱ ἔξω τῆς λέξεως (material): *Soph. Elench.* 4. 9 *sqq.*

τῶν...τὰς κρίσεις ἐνισταμένων] Cf. Dem. *De Cor.* § 4 ὁ τοιοῦτον ἀγῶν' ἐνστησάμενος, and, passively, ὁ νῦν ἐνεστηκὼς ἀγών, *supra* § 7.

ταῖς ἀραῖς] 'the curses,' such as the herald recited against traitors and corrupt advisers before sittings of the Assembly: cf. Dem. *F.L.* §§ 70, 201, etc.

τούτοις] neuter, acc. to Rehd., but the masc. (sc. τοῖς δεινοῖς καὶ συκοφ. ἐπιχειροῦσι) is certainly defensible.

ὥσπερ ἡμεῖς] sc. ποιοῦμεν.

§ 32. παρ' ὑμῖν αὐτοῖς] apud vosmet ipsos: *iudicantis*.

τίνας ἀδύνατον ἦν] The impf. is probably potential in force: 'whom would it have been impossible?,' 'who might have been expected to be proof against being misled?': Goodwin, § 416.

ταῖς παρασκευαῖς ταῖς τοῦ λόγου] 'the tricks of speech': cf. *supra* § 20 τὰς παρασκευὰς τῶν κρινομένων n., Dem. *Mid.* § 191 ἴσως καὶ τὰ τοιαῦτ' ἐρεῖ, ὡς ἐσκεμμένα καὶ παρεσκευασμένα πάντα λέγω νῦν.

κατὰ φύσιν] with ἔμελλον φράσειν, 'they would naturally have told the truth.'

παραδοῦναι ἔφυγε] 'shrank from surrendering': cf. Antiph. I. § 13 ἔφευγον τῶν πραχθέντων τὴν σαφήνειαν πυθέσθαι, Plat. *Apol.* 26 A συγγενέσθαι...καὶ διδάξαι ἔφυγες: with μή, Soph.

Ant. 263 ἔφευγε μὴ εἰδέναι, 'denied knowledge of the deed.'—
καὶ ταῦτα οὐκ ἀλλοτρίους: 'and that although they were not
another's': concessive. Cf. *supra* § 12 καὶ ταῦτα κάλλιστον
ἔχοντες...παράδειγμα.

§ 33. ψυχαγωγῆσαι] 'inveigle,' 'mystify': cf. Isocr. *Evag.*
§ 10 αὐταῖς ταῖς εὐρυθμίαις καὶ ταῖς συμμετρίαις ψυχαγωγοῦσι τοὺς
ἀκούοντας, *Ad Nicoc.* § 49 τοὺς ἀκροωμένους ψ., [Dem.] *Adv.
Leoch.* [or. XLIV] § 63 ταῖς κολακείαις οἱ πλεῖστοι ψυχαγωγού-
μενοι...ποιητοὺς υἱεῖς ποιοῦνται. In a rather different application,
rhetoric is defined by Plato (*Phaedr.* 261 A, 271 C) as a
ψυχαγωγία, 'a winning of men's souls,' 'persuasion.'

τὴν ὑγρότητα...τοῦ ἤθους] 'their pliability of temper': so
also ὑγ. ἕξεως, Plut. 2. 680 D. For ὑγρὸς in the metaph. sense =
mollis, facilis, cf. Plut. *Mar.* 28. 1 ὑγρός τις εἶναι βουλόμενος καὶ
δημοτικός, *Sull.* 30. 5 πρὸς οἶκτον ὑγρός, *Peric.* 5. 3 τὸ Κίμωνος
ὑγρόν, 'his good humour,' 'complaisance.'

εἰς ἔλεον προαγαγέσθαι] So Her. II. 121. 24 ἐς γέλωτα
προαγαγέσθαι, 'to move to laughter.'

ἐνταῦθα] with ἐλήλυθεν, 'here,' 'to this court,' εἰς τοὺς δικαστάς.
For ἐνταῦθα used where motion is implied, cf. Her. V. 72 οὐ
θεμιτὸν παριέναι ἐνθαῦτα, Aesch. *Pers.* 450 ἐνταῦθα πέμπει,
Plat. *Theaet.* 187 B ἐνταῦθα προελήλυθας.

οὐδὲν ἕτερον ἤ] an unusual variant for the commoner οὐδὲν
ἄλλο ἤ, from which it does not appear to differ in meaning:
'simply and solely because he feared.' Lyc. seems to affect
variations of the οὐδὲν ἄλλο ἤ idiom: cf. *infra* § 92 οὐδὲν πρότερον
ποιοῦσιν ἤ, § 129 οὐδὲν πρότερον ἀδικοῦσιν ἤ, which the editors
usually emend.

ἐκ τῆς αὐτῆς οἰκίας] sc. from his own.

οἱ ἐξελέγχοντες τῷ ἔργῳ] sc. οἱ οἰκέται.

προφάσεων...λόγων...σκήψεως] 'pretexts...pleas...excuses.'
For πρόφασις, cf. *supra* § 6 *n*. The first and the third are
conjoined by Dem.: *F.L.* § 100 σκήψεις καὶ προφάσεις ἐρεῖ;
Mid. § 41 ποία πρόφασις, τίς ἀνθρωπίνη καὶ μετρία σκῆψις φανεῖται
τῶν πεπραγμένων αὐτῷ; The combination of the three, as Rehd.

remarks, is probably intended to lead up to the triple-headed asyndeton immediately following.

ἁπλοῦν τὸ δίκαιον, κ.τ.λ.] The asyndeton belongs to the elevated style, and its 'gnomic' character (γνώμη, 'maxim,' *sententia*) imparts a touch of ἦθος (ἠθικὸν ποιεῖ τὸν λόγον, indicates the character of the speaker) (Rehd. *ad loc.*). We may compare generally the famous passage of Eur. *Phoen.* ll. 469 *sqq*.

ἁπλοῦς ὁ μῦθος τῆς ἀληθείας ἔφυ,
κοὐ ποικίλων δεῖ τἄνδιχ' ἑρμηνευμάτων·

and Cicero, *De Off.* 1. 13 *quod verum est, idem simplex est.*

§ **34.** ὅσια] stronger than δίκαια: Lyc. applies the standard of *fas*, he is not content merely with *ius*.

τῆς ἐκ τῶν νόμων τιμωρίας] cf. *supra* § 4 τοῖς ἐκ τῶν νόμων ἐπιτιμίοις.

προσήκει] a general statement: προσῆκεν (Blass) would refer to the particular case of L.

τὸν ὑπὲρ πρ. κινδυνεύοντα] 'a man who is on his trial for treason': κινδυνεύω here of the peril connected with a judicial sentence, cf. *periculum*, O.E. *danger*.—For ὑπὲρ προδοσίας, cf. *supra* § 7 ὑπὲρ οὗ...μέλλετε τὴν ψῆφον φέρειν *n*.

παραδιδόναι] sc. τοὺς οἰκέτας as obj.—βασανίζειν: 'to be tortured': Goodwin, § 770.

§ **35.** καταμεμαρτυρηκώς] concessive.

καὶ πῶς] introducing an objection, with a suggestion of incredulity or absurdity: cf. Soph. *O.T.* 1019 καὶ πῶς ὁ φύσας ἐξ ἴσου τῷ μηδένι;

τὸν τὴν ἐξουσίαν...περιηρημένον] 'a man who has robbed himself of the privilege of defence by declining a fair offer, as well as by many other means': cf. Dem. *F.L.* § 220 καὶ μόνον οὐ τὴν Ἀττικὴν ὑμῶν περιήρηνται, 'have all but robbed you of A.'—τοῦτον: for the resumptive pronoun, rather a favourite const. with Lyc., cf. *infra* §§ 46, 82, 93, etc.—ὑπέρ: cf. *supra* §§ 7, 9.

c. 11. §§ 36–45. *The desertion of Leocrates was aggravated by the pitiable plight of Athens after Chaeronea—Athens, once the arbitress of Greece, 'now none so poor to do her reverence.' But the defendant shirked personal service at a crisis when even the dead might be said to be contributing to the defence of the city: did not even help to bury the men who fell at Chaeronea. Who then would acquit him?*

§ 36. μὲν οὖν] μὲν οὖν (like μὲν δή, and often μὲν alone, cf. Thuc. VII. *ad fin.* ταῦτα μὲν τὰ περὶ Σικελίαν γενόμενα) indicates that a definite stage in the argument has been concluded, and that fresh ground is to be broken. The speaker assumes the fact of L.'s offence to have been established: he now proceeds, with a good deal of αὔξησις ('amplification') and δείνωσις ('rhetorical heightening'), and by numerous digressions (παρεκβάσεις) covering a wide field (ancient history, ancestral usage, legend, the poets, Sparta, etc.), to emphasise the seriousness of the offence and to marshal an array of precedents for its condign punishment.

ὅτι ὁμολογούμενόν ἐστιν] lit. 'that it is an admitted thing': stronger than ὁμολογεῖται.

μεμαθηκέναι] 'that you have been instructed': μανθάνω acts as pass. of διδάσκω.

ἐν οἷς δὲ καιροῖς...οὖσαν...προδέδωκεν] '(I wish to remind you) of the gravity of the crisis and the magnitude of the perils which beset the city when L. deserted it': the stress, as often, falls on the ptcp., which is impf. in tense. The trans. offered does not fully represent προδέδωκεν, which combines both past and present elements: ἐν οἷς καιροῖς ἡ πόλις ἦν (*a*) ὅτε Λ. προὔδωκε, (*b*) ἧς προδότης ἐστίν.

λαβὲ...ἀναγίγνωσκε] '*λαβὲ statim et celeriter peragendum, ἀναγίγνωσκε aliquid temporis postulat*,' Schoemann (Isaeus, p. 236).

Ὑπερείδου] Hyperides, 'the Sheridan of Athens' (Jebb), was a contemporary of Lycurgus and Demosthenes, and a vigorous supporter of the latter's anti-Macedonian policy both before and after Chaeronea. After the death of Alexander, he was closely concerned with the so-called Lamian War, and pronounced the funeral oration (of which considerable fragments survive) on the general Leosthenes and the Athenians who fell with him. When Antipater (after the battle of Crannon) demanded the surrender of the leaders of the war party, Hyperides fled, but was captured and put to death, 322 B.C. Six of his speeches (including the Funeral Speech above mentioned), mostly in fragments (that *For Euxenippus* entire and that *Against Athenogenes* nearly so), have been discovered among Egyptian papyri at various times from 1847 onwards.

§ 37. ἀκούετε] cf. *supra* § 29 ἀκούετε...τῆς προκλήσεως *n*.

τὴν βουλὴν τοὺς π.] the language is official, and also distinctive: 'the council of the 500')(ἡ βουλὴ ἡ ἐξ Ἀρείου πάγου, *supra* § 12. A still fuller designation was ἡ β. οἱ π. οἱ λαχόντες τῷ κυάμῳ. For the apposition, cf. Lysias *c. Agorat.* § 35 ἐν τῷ δικαστηρίῳ ἐν δισχιλίοις, etc.

καταβαίνειν] i.e. from ἡ ἄνω πόλις (ἄστυ): cf. *supra* § 18 τὸ ἄστυ τῆς πόλεως *n*.

χρηματιοῦσαν] 'to consult about,' *agere*, a technical word of official bodies, ἐκκλησία, πρυτάνεις, στρατηγοί, etc.)(χρηματίζεσθαι, 'transact business to one's profit,' 'make money.'

πράττειν...ὅ τι ἂν δοκῇ] 'take such measures...as should be deemed advantageous,' etc. : the editors compare with this (no doubt a quotation from the actual ψήφισμα), the terms of the Roman *senatus consultum ultimum*, '*videant consules, ne quid res publica detrimenti capiat*.'—**διεσκευασμένην**: ἠτοιμασμένην Hesych., *habitu militari*, practically = ἐν τοῖς ὅπλοις: Aeschines indeed combines the two (*Ctes.* § 140) ἐν τοῖς ὅπλοις διεσκευασμένοι.

οἱ ἀφειμένοι τοῦ στρ.] Senators, and probably other officials, were excused from military service during their term of office.

μικροὶ καὶ οἱ τυχόντες] 'slight *or* ordinary' is our idiom: for the Gk. usage, cf. χθὲς καὶ πρώην, 'yesterday or the day before,' Plat. *Apol.* 23 ὀλίγου ἄξια καὶ οὐδενός, 'worth little or nothing.'— For οἱ τυχόντες, 'ordinary,' 'such as may happen to any one,' cf. *infra* § 62 ἐκ τῶν τυχόντων ἀνθρώπων, Aeschin. *Ctes.* § 250 οὐ παρὰ τῶν τυχόντων ἀνθρώπων ἀλλὰ παρὰ τῶν πρωτευόντων κ.τ.λ.

§ 38. ἐν οἷς] sc. φόβοις, '*Yet* it was then,' we should say.

ἐξεκόμισε...μετεπέμψατο] 'fetched out' (with his own hands)... 'had them brought.'—<τὰ> ἱερὰ τὰ πατρῷα, cf. *supra* § 25 *n*.

κατὰ τὴν τούτου προαίρεσιν] 'if L. had had his way,' lit. 'according to his deliberate purpose': ἡ προαίρεσις is the characteristic of moral action in Aristotle's *Ethics*.

ναοί] so the MSS. here, but οἱ νεῴ, τοὺς νεὼς elsewhere (cf. *supra* §§ 1, 25; *infra* §§ 43, 143, 147): cf. the interchange of γονεῖς and γονέας, *supra* § 15 *n*. The more archaic form heightens the effect of a passage marked by δείνωσις: see also Crit. App.

ἔρημοι δ' αἱ φ. τῶν τειχῶν] 'the walls would have been left defenceless' we may render, but the Gk. really is, 'the defence (or rather 'defence forces') of the walls would have been *left unprovided for*': cf. *supra* § 16 τάττειν εἰς τὰς φυλακὰς τῶν Ἀθηναίων *n*.

ἐξελέλειπτο] The plupf. denotes the state resulting from L.'s action: 'would have been abandoned' (and so remained).

§ 39. τίς οὐκ ἄν...ἐπιδεδημηκώς] For ἐπιδημεῖν, cf. *supra* § 14 τῶν ἐμπόρων τοῖς ἐπιδημοῦσιν ἐκεῖ *n*. For the sentiment, cf. [Lysias] *Epitaph*. § 40 (of Athens before Salamis) τίς οὐκ ἂν θεῶν ἠλέησεν αὐτοὺς ὑπὲρ τοῦ μεγέθους τοῦ κινδύνου; ἢ τίς ἀνθρώπων οὐκ ἂν ἐδάκρυσεν;

ἐδυνήθη ἄν...ὑπομεῖναι] Const. ὅστις ἐδυνήθη ἂν ὑπομεῖναι ἰδεῖν αὐτὸν ἄτακτον (ὄντα). The expression is no doubt redundant, but the text is probably sound: Blass (with Corais) reads ὅστις ἂν ἄτ. αὐτὸν ὑπέμεινε ἰδεῖν.

τῷ <στρατῷ>] with τὸ γεγονὸς πάθος. For the arrangement of the words, probably due to a desire to avoid the cacophony τὸ τῷ <σ.> γ. π., see Kühner, *Gr. Gram.* § 464. 8.—See Crit. App.

ὀρθὴ δ' ἦν...ἐπὶ τοῖς συμβ.] 'and the city was in a state of tension in view of what had happened': for ὀρθή=*spe* or *metu erecta*, cf. Isocr. *Philip*. § 70 τὴν Ἑλλάδα πᾶσαν ὀρθὴν οὖσαν (of hope), *De Big*. § 7 ὀρθῆς τῆς πόλεως γενομένης διὰ τὸ μέγεθος τῶν αἰτιῶν (of alarm): so Livy, I. 25 *erecti suspensique in minime gratum spectaculum animo incenduntur*.

τοῖς ὑπὲρ πεντήκοντ' ἔτη] Technically, the age for military service at Athens extended from 18-60, the first two years (18-20) of which period were spent in service in Attica: from 20-50 a citizen was liable to service outside it. Men above 50 would be a last line of reserves, charged with the defence of the walls in cases of extreme emergency.

§ 40. ὁρᾶν δ' ἦν] *licuit videre*, 'one might have seen.'

περιφόβους κατεπτηχυίας κ.τ.λ.] 'crouching in terror and asking, Is he alive?—one for a husband,' etc.: the edd. compare Hom. *Il.* VI. 237 Ἕκτωρ δ' ὡς Σκαιάς τε πύλας καὶ φηγὸν ἵκανεν, | ἀμφ' ἄρα μιν Τρώων ἄλοχοι θέον ἠδὲ θύγατρες | εἰρόμεναι παῖδάς τε κασιγνήτους τε ἔτας τε | καὶ πόσιας, and Livy, XXII. 7. 7 (of Rome after Trasimene) *matronae vagae per vias, quae repente clades allata quaeve fortuna exercitus esset, obvios percunctantur*, etc.

ὁρωμένας] This, the MSS. reading, seems pointed enough, because it was unusual for Athenian women to be seen in public, esp. in such a plight: among the substitutes suggested are ὀδυρομένας Orelli, ῥωομένας? Scheibe, ὠρυομένας Rehdantz.

ταῖς ἡλικίαις] a defining dative, cf. *maiores natu*. αἱ ἡλικίαι signified the years embraced by the 'military age' at Athens (Harpocr.). [ταῖς ἡλικίαις is due to Suidas (Sch., Bl., Thalh.) and goes well with τοῖς σώμασιν : τὰς ἡλικίας codd. (Rehd.).]

ἐπὶ γήρως ὁδῷ περιφθ.] 'hurrying about helplessly, on the threshold that leads from age to death' (Jebb).—ἐπὶ γήραος οὐδῷ is a Homeric phrase (*Il.* XXII. 60, XXIV. 487, *Od.* XV. 348), which is variously interpreted as 'on the *path* of old age' (οὐδός = ὁδός, so Leaf on *Il.* XXIV. 487), 'on the *threshold* of old age,' i.e. either (*a*) 'at the beginning' or (*b*) 'at the end' of old age (cf. schol. on *Il.* XXII. 60: ἐπὶ τῇ τοῦ γήρως ἐξόδῳ, ἐπὶ τῷ τέρματι, Eustath. ὑπεξιὼν καὶ πρὸς τῷ θανάτῳ ὤν), which last is undoubtedly the meaning here, as we say 'with one foot in the grave.'—**περιφθειρομένους**: cf. Isocr. *Ep.* IX. § 10 ἐν ῥάκεσι περιφθειρομένας δι' ἔνδειαν τῶν ἀναγκαίων.

διπλᾶ θαἰμάτια [i.e. τὰ ἱμάτια] **ἐμπεπορπημένους**] 'with their cloaks pinned about them double' (predicative adj.).—The ἱμάτιον, which was the loose outer garment worn above the χιτών or tunic, was ordinarily held together by the pressure of the arms (esp. the left upper arm) against the body; but it might also be *fastened* on one shoulder by a fibula (πόρπη)—the method of wearing which we might expect in old age. The pinning of it 'double,' and the consequent shortening of it, would permit a freer use of the limbs (cf. *succinctus*). [From an interesting passage of Polyaenus, *Strategemata*, IV. 14, it would seem that the expression was used contemptuously of poor, or poorly equipped, fighters. The passage runs: "Polysperchon, when the Peloponnesians were guarding the frontiers, encouraged his men thus. Donning an Arcadian cap (πῖλον) and *pinning a cloak about him double* (τρίβωνα διπλοῦν ἐμπορπησάμενος) and taking a stick in his hand, he said: 'Fellow-soldiers, this is what the men who are going to fight us are like.' Then discarding these things and assuming his full armour, he said: 'But those who are going to fight them are like this....' Whereupon the soldiers asked him to lead them to battle without delay."]—θαιμάτια ἐμπεπ.: for the acc. *induendi et exuendi*, cf. Her. VII. 77 Μιλύαι...εἵματα ἐνεπεπορπέατο.

§ 41. πολλῶν δὲ...γιγνομένων...ἠτυχηκότων] concessive.

τοὺς μὲν δούλους ἐλευθέρους κ.τ.λ.] sc. εἶναι. Cf. [Dem.] XXVI. § 11 ὅτε Ὑπερείδης ἔγραψε, τῶν περὶ Χαιρώνειαν ἀτυχημάτων... γενομένων...εἶναι τοὺς ἀτίμους ἐπιτίμους. The 'enfranchising of the disfranchised,' like the other measures, showed the gravity of the crisis: two other such occasions, at least, in Athenian history are cited by Andocides, *De Myst*. § 107 (before Marathon), § 80 (after Aegospotami).

ὅς] emphatic, 'that people which.'

αὐτόχθων] The special boast of the Athenians: no eulogy of Athens is complete without the word: cf. the Eur. frag. quoted *infra* § 100, also Thuc. I. 2 τὴν γοῦν Ἀττικήν...ἄνθρωποι ᾤκουν οἱ αὐτοὶ ἀεί, *Ibid*. 6; Isocr. *Panath*. § 124, *Paneg*. § 24, etc. So also παλαίχθων, Aeschin. *Ctes*. § 190 (epigram).

§ 43] NOTES 107

§ 42. ἐκέχρητο] 'had experienced,' of good or ill fortune: cf. *utor*.

ὥστε πρότερον μὲν...ἐν δὲ τοῖς] 'that *whereas* she had formerly ...she was now content,' etc. So also *infra* § 115, etc.

αὐτῶν] referring to the collective πόλις preceding. [αὐτῆς standing where it would is almost ruled out of court.]

ὑπὲρ τῆς ἰδίας] Philip, acc. to Dem. *De Chers.* § 39, was ἐχθρὸς ὅλῃ τῇ πόλει καὶ τῷ τῆς πόλεως ἐδάφει, 'the very ground on which it stood': cf. also XXVI. § 11 (quoted above) καὶ τῆς πόλεως ὑπὲρ αὐτῶν τῶν ἐδαφῶν εἰς κίνδυνον μέγιστον κατακεκλειμένης.

Λ. καὶ Π....βοηθὸν ἐπεκαλοῦντο] The language is no doubt general: specific occasions on which Athenian help was either asked or received were the traditional summoning of Tyrtaeus (cf. *infra* § 106) during the Second Messenian War, the Helot revolt of 464 B.C. (expedition of Cimon), and the latter part of the Theban hegemony (campaign of Mantinea, 362 B.C.).—**οἱ τὴν Ἀσίαν...Ἕλληνες**: after the Persian invasions, when Athens took the Asiatic Greeks under her protection, and gradually built up the Confederacy of Delos.

τοῦτον ἔδει] For the redundant pronoun, enforcing a preceding subst. (τὸν δῆμον), 'which is separated by a parenthetic clause from the rest of the sentence' (Madvig, § 100. *e.*), cf. *supra* § 35 *n.*, *infra* §§ 46, 82, 93.—Note that the ὥστε const., which at first sight would appear to be continued in τὸν δῆμον κ.τ.λ., is replaced by a finite clause: τοῦτον ἔδει τότ' is due to Reiske (Bl., Sofer): οὗτος ἐδεῖτο τῶν codd. (Sch., Rehd., Thalh.).

ἐξ Ἄνδρου καὶ Κέω κ.τ.λ.] The comparative insignificance of the places cited would emphasise the necessity which led to their being called upon. Andros and Ceos were islands of the Cyclades, Troezen (Attic, Trozen) and Epidaurus towns of Argolis.

§ 43. τοιούτοις...τηλικούτοις] Cf. *supra* § 2 *n.*

μήτε...μήτε] generic: 'a man who neither...nor.' For the form of the sentence and the negatives, cf. e.g. [Dem.] or. XLII. § 30 ἔπειτα...τὸν οὕτω καταφανῶς ἐν ἅπασιν ἀδίκως πεποιημένον τὴν ἀπόφασιν, καὶ μήτε τῶν νόμων φροντίσαντα...μήτε τῶν ἰδίων ὁμολογιῶν...τοῦτον δικαίως ψηφιεῖσθε πεποιῆσθαι τὴν ἀπόφασιν;

<τὰ> ὅπλα θέμενον] '*took up* arms' is the Eng. equivalent of the phrase here: for its various meanings, see L.S. *s.v.* τίθημι, A. II. 10. The article is rightly supplied in view of the almost universal practice of Greek authors in respect of this phrase: cf. e.g. Her. IX. 52, Thuc. IV. 44, Lysias, or. XXXI. § 14 οὔτ' ἐν τῷ Πειραιεῖ οὔτ' ἐν τῷ ἄστει ἔθετο τὰ ὅπλα (of Philo).

τὸ σῶμα παρασχόντα τάξαι τοῖς σ.] 'offered himself to the generals for enrolment in the ranks,' the regular phrase of a person reporting himself for service: cf. Isocr. *Adv. Callimach.* § 47 οὐδὲ μίαν παρέσχεν αὑτὸν ἡμέραν τάξαι τοῖς στρατηγοῖς, Lysias, *In Alcib.* I. § 7 μόνος οὐ παρέσχε μετὰ τῶν ἄλλων ἑαυτὸν τάξαι, *In Philon.* § 9.—For the act. infin. with παρέχω, cf. Ar. *Nub.* 441 π. τὸ σῶμα τύπτειν, Plat. *Apol.* 33 B πλουσίῳ καὶ πένητι παρέχω ἐμαυτὸν ἐρωτᾶν.

φιλόπολις καὶ εὐσεβεῖν β.] a moral and religious, not a judicial, point of view, as Rehd. well remarks.

κληθείς] i.e. as συνήγορος: 'what advocate would hold a brief for him?' would be our equivalent: cf. Aeschin. II. 14 ἐκάλεσεν αὐτῷ συνήγορον τὸν Δημοσθένην, and the still commoner παρακαλεῖν.

τὸν...τολμήσαντα] Note that the const. is carried on as though ἢ ῥήτωρ...βοηθήσειε did not intervene. The explanation no doubt is that the main emphasis of the question falls upon ἀπολύσειεν, the influence of which overrides the following clause and makes it practically a parenthesis.—τὸν οὐδὲ...οὐδέ: 'the man who did not even...no, nor yet,' a particular case: contrast τὸν μήτε...μήτε above. For οὐδὲ...οὐδέ, which marks a stronger opposition than οὔτε...οὔτε, the second negation being usually the stronger of the two ('not even...no, nor yet'), see L.S. *s.v.* οὐδέ, A. III.—**τολμήσαντα**: 'had the grace to': τολμᾶν is regularly used (cf. ἔτλην in poetry) of overcoming some strong natural inclination towards a course of action opposed to that indicated by the accompanying infin.: Lat. *sustineo*.

§ 45] NOTES 109

ὅθ' ἡ μὲν χώρα] see Crit. App.—τὰ δένδρα...τὰς θήκας...τὰ ὅπλα.—The first would be used for palisades (τῆς χαρακώσεως below), though in ordinary times the olive trees (of which the speaker is probably thinking) were protected by law; the second for the walls (τῆς τῶν τειχῶν κατασκευῆς), as Thuc. I. 93 speaks of gravestones being freely used for the hastily built wall of Themistocles; the third would be 'dedications' (ἀναθήματα), which would be used only under great pressure.

§ 44. οὐκ ἔστιν ἥτις] i.q. οὐδεμία. For a discussion of this idiom, see Rehd., App. 2, pp. 137–8.

τειχῶν...τάφρων...χαρακώσεως] Cf. last note on previous §.

ἐφ' ὧν οὐδενός] 'in none of which departments': ἐπὶ c. gen. is said of that which one is 'engaged in' or 'set over,' frequent in the designation of officials: cf. οἱ ἐπὶ τῶν πραγμάτων, '*chargés d'affaires*,' ὁ ἐπὶ τῶν ὅπλων, ὁ ἐπὶ τῆς διοικήσεως, etc. Cf. *infra* § 58 ἐγένετο ἐπὶ ταύτης τῆς ἐργασίας.

τὸ σῶμα...παρέσχε τάξαι] 'offered himself for personal service': cf. *supra* § 43 n.—Λεωκράτης: note the bitter emphasis, conveyed more fully by (no doubt) a short pause before the word in speaking, which falls upon the name by its position at the end.

§ 45. τὸν μηδὲ συνενεγκεῖν...ἀξιώσαντα] 'a man who did not deign so much as to help in collecting the bodies, or even to attend the funeral, of those who,' etc. The first of the two infins. depending upon ἀξιώσαντα seems most naturally to refer, like the second, to 'the men who died at Ch.' In that case, συνενεγκεῖν Z [or ξυν—LP (Rehd.)] would have reference (as Rehd. suggests) to the work of bringing the urns together in the market-place, from which the public procession would take place to the Ceramicus (ἐπ' ἐκφορὰν ἐλθεῖν). συμφέρειν and ἐκφέρειν thus denote two distinct moments in the process of burial, whereas Dobree's (Bl., Sof.) συνεξενεγκεῖν (which is attractive in the light of Thuc. II. 34 ἐπειδὰν δὲ ἡ ἐκφορὰ ᾖ...ξυνεκφέρει δὲ ὁ βουλόμενος καὶ ἀστῶν καὶ ξένων) coincides with ἐπ' ἐκφορὰν ἐλθεῖν (Rehd., App. 1, p. 108).—See Crit. App.

ὡς τὸ ἐπὶ τούτῳ...γεγενημένων] This would be one of the

speaker's strong cards, when we remember that the burying of those who fell in battle was a most sacred duty to a Greek, and that neglect of it was viewed with peculiar abhorrence: cf. generally Thuc. II. 34, Xen. *Hell.* I. 7, Soph. *Ant.*—For τὸ ἐπὶ τούτῳ μέρος, cf. *supra* § 17 τὸ καθ' αὐτὸν μέρος *n.*

ὧν οὗτος...προσαγορεύων] 'whose very tombs the defendant passed by with never a qualm, when he greeted their country eight years afterwards.' Cf. *infra* § 142 ὧν οὗτος οὐδὲ τὰ ἐλεγεῖα...ἐπανιών...ᾐδέσθη.—ὀγδόῳ ἔτει: a piece of internal evidence (assuming L. to have been impeached immediately, or shortly, after his return) for the date of the speech (330 B.C.). —προσαγορεύων : here = *salutare* (προσαγορεύει· ἀσπάζεται Hesych.): cf. Aesch. *Agam.* 514, Ar. *Ach.* 264.

c. 12. §§ 46—51. *The praises of brave men are a condemnation of men of the opposite character, and should not be neglected at public trials. The heroes of Chaeronea, trusting in their valour rather than in walls of stone, laid down their lives for the freedom of Greece: they were victorious in death and their glory survives them. Those men carried the liberty of Greece in their persons: the liberty of Greece is buried with their bodies. You alone among the Greeks, Athenians, know how to honour the brave, as witness the statues you erect to brave generals and slayers of tyrants rather than to victorious athletes. The signal honours you pay to public benefactors should imply equally signal penalties for public traitors.*

[The section summarised above is 'nothing but a condensed funeral speech on those who died at Chaeronea,' the relevancy of which, such as it is, serves merely 'to point the contrast between the patriot and the traitor' (J. F. Dobson, *The Greek Orators*, p. 278).]

§ 46. περὶ ὧν] sc. τῶν ἐν X. τελευτησάντων.

μικρῷ πλείω...διελθεῖν] 'I wish to speak at a little greater length.'

ἀλλοτρίους εἶναι...ἀγώνων] 'that such topics (as I am going to deal with) are alien to public trials.'—For ἀλλότριος c. gen., *alienus ab*, cf. Lysias, XXXI. *ad fin. ἐπιτηδεύματα...πάσης δημοκρατίας ἀλλότρια*, 'practices...alien to every democratic principle.'

—**τοὺς τοιούτους < λόγους >** looks forward generally to the 'eulogies' following: τοιοῦτος will then be, as sometimes, *prospective* in force: cf. Thuc. IV. 58 τοιούτους λόγους εἶπεν, 'spoke as follows.'—**τῶν δημοσίων ἀγώνων**: cf. *supra* § 7 τοὺς δημοσίους ἀγῶνας *n*.—For the text, see Crit. App.

αἱ γὰρ εὐλογίαι...ποιοῦσιν] 'for the eulogies of (i.e. 'bestowed upon': obj. gen.) brave men constitute a clear condemnation of those who practise the opposite principles': lit. 'make the ground of conviction (ἔλεγχον) clear against (κατὰ) them.'

ἔπαινον, ὃς μόνος ἆθλον] For the sentiment, cf. Dem. *F.L.* § 313 καὶ μὴν τῶν μὲν ἄλλων ἀγαθῶν οὐ μέτεστι τοῖς τεθνεῶσιν, οἱ δ' ἐπὶ τοῖς καλῶς πραχθεῖσιν ἔπαινοι τῶν οὕτω τετελευτηκότων ἴδιον κτῆμ' εἰσίν· οὐδὲ γὰρ ὁ φθόνος αὐτοῖς ἔτι τηνικαῦτ' ἐναντιοῦται.

τοῦτον] resuming and reinforcing τὸν ἔπαινον: cf. *supra* § 42 τὸν δῆμον...τοῦτον ἔδει *n*.

ἐπειδὴ καὶ ἐκεῖνοι] The connexion of thought is: '*as* they gave their lives for the safety of the state...*so* their praise should not be neglected at trials affecting the state.' The state aspect of the matter is strengthened by the addition of δημοσίοις to κοινοῖς, the latter of which in itself would be a sufficient balance to κοινὴν preceding.

§ 47. ἐπὶ τοῖς ὁρίοις τῆς B.] i.e. at Chaeronea: Thuc. IV. 76 ἔστι δὲ ἡ Χαιρώνεια ἔσχατον τῆς Βοιωτίας πρὸς τῇ Φανοτίδι τῆς Φωκίδος.

μαχούμενοι] *fut.* ptcp., 'to fight.'

κακῶς ποιεῖν προέμενοι] *terram devastandam relinquentes* (Sofer). Cf. *supra* § 43 τὸ σῶμα παρασχόντα τάξαι, etc.

φυλακήν] 'means of defence,' 'safeguard': cf. Lysias, XXV. § 28 ἡγούμενοι ταύτην δημοκρατίας εἶναι φυλακήν, Isocr. *Bus.* § 13.

τῶν λιθίνων περιβόλων] We may compare the language of Demosthenes in vindicating his policy, *De Cor.* § 299 οὐ λίθοις ἐτείχισα τὴν πόλιν οὐδὲ πλίνθοις ἐγώ, also Nicias' address to his army at Syracuse, Thuc. VII. 77 ἄνδρες γὰρ πόλις, καὶ οὐ τείχη οὐδὲ νῆες ἀνδρῶν κεναί, and Soph. *O.T.* 56, 57 ὡς οὐδέν ἐστιν οὔτε πύργος οὔτε ναῦς | ἔρημος ἀνδρῶν. The earliest occurrence of the sentiment in Gk. is perhaps Alcaeus, fr. 23 ἄνδρες πόλιος πύργος ἀρεύιοι.

τὴν δὲ θρέψασαν] sc. γῆν or χώραν. *Infra* § 85 we have τὴν θρεψαμένην without any apparent difference of meaning.

εἰκότως] 'and rightly so,' 'and with good reason,' regularly (nine times) so used by Lyc. at the *end* of its clause (as occasionally by Isocr., Dem., and Aeschin., once by Lysias, not by Antiphon and Andocides: Rehd., App. 2, pp. 138–9), with γάρ immediately introducing the supporting argument.

§ 48. ὥσπερ γὰρ...διάκεινται] 'For just as people universally (ἅπαντες) do not entertain feelings of equal affection towards natural and towards adopted fathers, so they lie looser (are less well disposed) to countries to which they do not belong by birth but which they acquire later.' The sentiment was no doubt (as Rehd. and Sofer remark) a commonplace of the rhetorical schools, and appropriated especially in praise of Athenian 'autochthony.' Cf. Isocr. *Panath.* § 125 καὶ στέργοντας αὐτὴν (sc. τὴν χώραν) ὁμοίως ὥσπερ οἱ βέλτιστοι τοὺς πατέρας καὶ τὰς μητέρας τὰς αὐτῶν, [Dem.] XL. § 47.—**τῶν πατέρων**: partitive gen.—**ταῖς εὐνοίαις**: 'feelings of affection,' if we are to press the plural) ('benevolences,' in the concrete sense, of presents offered to Athenian commanders by subject states, Dem. *De Chers.* § 25. Lyc. has a partiality for the plural of abstract nouns: cf. *supra* § 6 τὰς ἔχθρας, § 18 εὐτυχίας, § 20 τὰς χάριτας, *infra* § 64 τὰς διανοίας, § 140 τὰς φιλοτιμίας, etc.—**ἐπικτήτους**: lit. 'acquired besides' or 'in addition,' as of land added to one's hereditary property, Plat. *Legg.* 924 A; ἐπίκτ. φίλοι, 'newly acquired')(ἀρχαῖοι, Xen. *Ages.* I. 36; τὰ ἐπίκτ.)(τὰ φύσει ὄντα, Plat. *Rep.* 618 D. Our 'adopted country' is the idea here, and we may correlate the terms as follows:—

πατήρ		χώρα	
φύσει γεννήσας : ποιητός	. .	φύσει προσήκουσα : ἐπίκτητος	
natural : adopted	. .	native : adopted.	

§ 49]   NOTES   113

τοιαύταις δὲ γνώμαις...ἐκοινώνησαν] In plain language, they were less fortunate than brave.—τοῖς ἀρίστοις ἀνδράσιν: with ἐξ ἴσου, but partly also with μετασχόντες (μετέχειν τινός τινι, 'to share a thing with another').—This and the two following paragraphs are fair specimens, in form and substance, of the commonplaces in praise of the dead which were the stock-in-trade of the rhetorical schools and were highly elaborated by 'epideictic orators' (the oratory of 'display'), even though they did not rise to the heights of their master in this field, Gorgias of Leontini (in Sicily, born *c*. 485 B.C., visited Athens on an embassy, 427), with whose dead 'though they died, loving sorrow died not with them, but immortal in bodies bodiless it lives though they live not': τοιγαροῦν αὐτῶν ἀποθανόντων ὁ πόθος οὐ συναπέθανεν, ἀλλ' ἀθάνατος ἐν ἀσωμάτοις σώμασι ζῇ οὐ ζώντων (from a fragment of Gorgias' *Epitaphius*). Reference may be made generally to the Funeral Speeches of [Lysias] and Hyperides. The closest parallel to Lyc. here is perhaps Isocr. *Paneg.* § 92 (of the Spartans who fell at Thermopylae) ἴσας δὲ τὰς τόλμας παρασχόντες οὐχ ὁμοίαις ἐχρήσαντο ταῖς τύχαις, ἀλλ' οἱ μὲν διεφθάρησαν καὶ ταῖς ψυχαῖς νικῶντες τοῖς σώμασιν ἀπεῖπον (οὐ γὰρ δὴ τοῦτό γε θέμις εἰπεῖν, ὡς ἡττήθησαν· οὐδεὶς γὰρ αὐτῶν φυγεῖν ἠξίωσεν).

τῆς...ἀρετῆς] 'the fruits of their valour.'

ἀμύνοντες] unusual for ἀμυνόμενοι, though the active is quoted also from Plat. *Legg.* 692 D ἀμ. ὑπὲρ τῆς Ἑλλάδος, Polyb. VI. 6. 8 ἀμ. πρὸ πάντων.

§ 49. εἰ δὲ δεῖ...νικῶντες ἀπέθανον] 'and if I may use an expression which is highly paradoxical indeed, but nevertheless true, those men were victorious in death': εἰ δεῖ is apologetic in tone, cf. Isocr. *Nicoc.* § 26 εἰ δὲ δεῖ τι καὶ τῶν ἀρχαίων εἰπεῖν, 'if I may be allowed to quote examples from antiquity,' Dem. *Ol.* II. § 28 εἰ δεῖ τι τῶν ὄντων καὶ περὶ τῶν στρατηγῶν εἰπεῖν, 'if one may say a word of truth about the generals as well.'

ἃ γὰρ ἆθλα] see Crit. App.—ἆθλα, honourable prizes of war)(λήμματα, personal and selfish gains: the two are con-

P. L.   8

trasted by Dem. *Ol.* II. § 28.—ἀρετή: 'reputation for valour' (ἀρετή· ἀντὶ τοῦ εὐδοξία Harpocrat.). Cf. Hyper. *Epitaph.* § 41 μεμνῆσθαι μὴ μόνον τοῦ θανάτου τῶν τετελευτηκότων, ἀλλὰ καὶ τῆς ἀρετῆς ἧς καταλελοίπασι.

οὐδ' οἷόν τ' ἐστὶν...ἡττῆσθαι] Cf. Isocr. *Paneg.* § 92, quoted *supra* § 48.

τοὺς...μὴ πτήξαντας...φόβον] 'men who did not quail in spirit under the terror of their assailants.' L.S. *s.v.* πτήσσω say that 'in the strange passage ταῖς διανοίαις μὴ πτήξαντες φόβον [giving reference], φόβον must be taken as a cognate acc.' [like φόβον φοβεῖσθαι, φ. δεδοικέναι, φ. ταρβεῖν, in which case τῶν ἐπιόντων will be *objective* gen., 'the fear which they felt of their assailants']. This, if possible, is certainly somewhat strained; and the syntax of the passage is simplified by taking τῶν ἐπιόντων as *subjective*, 'the fear which their assailants inspired': cf. the use of φόβος with preps. denoting the source of the fear, φ. ἀπό τινος, ἔκ τινος, as *infra* § 130 ὁ παρὰ τῶν πολιτῶν φόβος, and Xen. *Anab.* I. 2. 18 Κῦρος δ' ἥσθη τὸν ἐκ τῶν Ἑλλήνων ἐς τοὺς βαρβάρους φόβον ἰδών. In the latter case, φόβον is an ordinary external acc., as in πτήσσειν ἀπειλάς, Aesch. *P.V.* 175, which Rehd. also quotes in the same sense (App. 2, p. 139); but his interpretation of τῶν ἐπιόντων as = 'the future' seems, in this context, improbable: cf. *infra* § 57 τοὺς ἐπιόντας ἀμύνασθαι.

μόνους] See Crit. App.

οὐδ' ἂν εἷς] οὐδὲ εἷς (which is never elided unless a particle, as often, intervenes) is a more emphatic οὐδείς, 'no one whatever.'

φεύγοντες] 'in seeking to shun': Goodwin, *M.T.* § 25.

§ 50. ἐδήλωσε] 'was proof of' the truth of my statements, rather than = δήλη ἦν, though the latter is possible [and approved by Rehd.].

ἅμα γὰρ οὗτοι...μετέπεσεν] 'for no sooner did these men die than the fortunes of Greece changed to slavery': the two events were coincident. For ἅμα...καὶ = *simul ac* (except that the latter is never separated, the former always), combining two clauses in what is virtually a cause and effect relationship, cf. *supra* § 29

§ 51] NOTES 115

ἅμα τοίνυν...οὐκ ἐδέχετο, καὶ κατεμαρτύρει n.—**τὸν βίον μεταλλάσσειν**, 'to exchange life' (for death), with the notion of 'quitting' it, hence 'to die': so also μεταλλ. χώραν, 'to go to another country,' cf. *infra* § 86.—**τὰ τῆς Ἑλλάδος**: practically = 'Greece.'—**εἰς δουλείαν μετέπεσεν**: μεταπίπτειν generally, as here, *in deterius*, but also *in melius*: cf. *infra* § 60 ἐκ τοῦ κακῶς πρᾶξαι μεταπεσεῖν.

συνετάφη γὰρ...ἐλευθερία] Cf. the famous sentence, [Lysias], *Epitaph.* § 60 ὥστ' ἄξιον ἦν ἐπὶ τῷδε τῷ τάφῳ τότε κείρασθαι τῇ Ἑλλάδι...ὡς συγκαταθαπτομένης τῆς αὐτῶν ἐλευθερίας τῇ τούτων ἀρετῇ (of those who fell in the Corinthian War, 394 B.C.), and with the whole passage [Dem.] LX. § 23.

φανερὸν πᾶσιν ἐποίησαν...πολεμοῦντες] 'they made it clear to all that they were not warring,' etc.: φ. ἐποίησαν is constructed with a ptcp. like φανεροὶ ἦσαν (ἐγένοντο) πολεμοῦντες, or ἐδήλωσαν πολεμοῦντες. Cf. Her. VI. 21 δῆλον ἐποίησαν ὑπεραχθεσθέντες, Thuc. III. 64 δῆλον ἐποιήσατε...μόνοι οὐ μηδίσαντες.

οὐκ <ἂν> αἰσχυνθείην...ψυχάς] 'I would not be abashed at declaring that those men's lives are a crown of glory to their country': for στέφανος in the met. sense, *decus*, cf. Her. IV. 88 (of Mandrocles) αὐτῷ μὲν στέφανον περιθείς, Σαμίοισι δὲ κῦδος, Hyper. *Epitaph.* § 19 τὴν εὐδοξίαν ἀπὸ τῶν πράξεων ἴδιον στέφανον τῇ πατρίδι περιέθηκαν.

§ 51. καὶ δι' ἃ οὐκ ἀλόγως κ.τ.λ.] 'and *why* they showed reason in the exercise of their valour is, that you, Athenians, alone among the Greeks know how to honour brave men': according to this interpretation, which makes ἐπίστασθε...τιμᾶν the *cause* and not the *effect* of ἐπετήδευον ('*because* they showed reason...you know how to, etc.'), δι' ἃ is to be taken as looking forward to, and in apposition with, ἐπίστασθε...τιμᾶν, as though we had: δι' ἃ οὐκ ἀλόγως...ἐπετήδευον, ταῦτ' ἐστίν, ὅτι ἐπίστασθε κ.τ.λ. For the position of δι' ἃ at the beginning of the sentence, Rehd. cites the somewhat similar use of ὅθεν in Lys. XII. § 43, Isaeus, VI. § 8, etc. But the text is suspect: see Crit. App.—For the claim made by the speaker, we may compare Dem. *Lept.*

8—2

§ 141 πρῶτον μὲν μόνοι τῶν πάντων ἀνθρώπων ἐπὶ τοῖς τελευτήσασι δημοσίᾳ ποιεῖτε λόγους ἐπιταφίους, ἐν οἷς κοσμεῖτε τὰ τῶν ἀγαθῶν ἀνδρῶν ἔργα. καίτοι τοῦτ' ἐστὶ τὸ ἐπιτήδευμα ζηλούντων ἀρετήν.

ἀνακειμένους] 'set up,' i.e. statues of them. ἀνακεῖσθαι in this connexion acts as pass. of ἱστάναι: ἱστάναι τινὰ χαλκοῦν)(χαλκοῦς ἀνακεῖσθαι: cf. Theocr. X. 33 χρύσεοι ἀνεκείμεθα. In Dem. *F.L.* § 251 we have both the person and the statue as subject: ἔφη τὸν Σόλων' ἀνακεῖσθαι...καίτοι τὸν μὲν ἀνδριάντα τοῦτον...φάσ' ἀνακεῖσθαι Σαλαμίνιοι.

παρ' ὑμῖν...στρατηγούς] After Solon, and Harmodius and Aristogiton (see *infra*), the only generals so honoured, as far as we know, were Conon, Iphicrates, and Timotheus (Rehd. *ad loc.*).

τοὺς τὸν τύραννον ἀποκτείναντας] Harmodius and Aristogiton, who slew Hipparchus, son of the tyrant Pisistratus (Thuc. I. 20, VI. 54–57), and were consecrated for all time in the Athenian mind as the doyens of tyrannicides: their descendants were voted special privileges: cf. Dem. *Lept. passim*, *F.L.* § 280; Andoc. *De Myst.* § 98 [ΝΟΜΟΣ]; *infra* § 87 ἐν πρυτανείῳ...σίτησιν ἔδοσαν *n*.—**τὸν τύραννον** : the speaker implies that the τύραννος was a phenomenon that was well known or might be taken for granted in the past history of most Greek cities.

καὶ τοιούτους μὲν...εὑρεῖν ῥᾴδιον] 'of such men it would not be easy to find a few even from the whole of Greece': the form of the clause might lead us to expect οὐδ' ἐξ ἁπάσης...πολλούς, but ὀλίγους is to be taken in a positive sense.

τοὺς στεφανίτας ἀγῶνας] lit. 'games in which the prize is a wreath (στέφανος),' esp. the four great athletic festivals of Greece, the winners at which were considered to confer great honour on their native cities and received high honours from them: cf. generally the *Odes* of Pindar, and Dem. *Lept.* § 141 εἶτα μεγίστας δίδοτ' ἐκ παντὸς τοῦ χρόνου δωρεὰς τοῖς τοὺς γυμνικοὺς νικῶσιν ἀγῶνας τοὺς στεφανίτας.

πολλαχόθεν] with γεγονότας.—Polle (*N. Jahrb. f. Philol.*,

1869, quoted by Rehd., App. 2, p. 140) states that, up to the year 330 B.C., we have knowledge of as many as 104 statues of Olympic victors in the whole of Greece; at Athens of one at most, and that not absolutely certain. Lyc.'s disparaging reference to the athletic games here may have been inspired by the circumstance that Athens, two years before the date of this speech, had been temporarily debarred from participation in the Olympic games owing to quarrels with Elis. Euripides, before Lyc.'s time, had had some severe things to say about athletes, cf. fr. 284 (Dind.).

εὐεργέταις] the word is technical of state benefactors, and occurs frequently in inscrr.

μεγίστας] without article, absol. 'very great.' [<τὰς> μεγ., however, which would balance ταῖς ἐσχάταις τιμωρίαις, is read by Reiske and Heinrich.]

δίκαιον] Blass's δίκαιοι is attractive, but δίκαιον without ἐστὶ seems easier than δίκαιοι without ἐστέ.

c. 13. §§ 52–54. *You have no choice but condemn Leocrates, if you do your duty. His case has already been decided (a) by the action of the Areopagus in similar cases, (b) by your own sentence on Autolycus, (c) by the decree of the people prescribing the extreme penalty for public defaulters. Will you reverse all these?*

§ 52. οὐδ' ἐν ὑμῖν ἐστιν] 'it is not even in your power,' 'it does not even rest with you': cf. Dem. *De Cor.* § 193 ἐν γὰρ τῷ θεῷ τὸ τούτου τέλος ἦν, οὐκ ἐμοί. [ἐφ' ὑμῖν ci. Bk. (Bl.).]

τὰ δίκαια ποιοῦσι] conditional, 'if you do your duty.'

κεκριμένον ἐστὶ καὶ κατεγνωσμένον] 'has been tried and has had sentence passed on it,' long ago: there is a standing verdict against it. The perf. ptcps. passive with the subst. verb are forcible and emphasise the abiding result: Goodwin, *M. T.* § 45. Cf. [Dem.] *c. Aristogit.* I. § 2 ὑπολαμβάνω τὴν μὲν κατηγορίαν... ἔθους εἵνεκα...δεῖν ποιήσασθαι, κεκρίσθαι δὲ τοῦτο τὸ πρᾶγμα πάλαι ὑπὸ τῆς ἑκάστου φύσεως οἴκοθεν.

μηδείς μοι θορυβήσῃ] a common appeal in the orators, 'let no one interrupt me,' i.e. with expressions of disapproval (Lat.

acclamare, in Ciceronian usage): the vb., however, is also used of applause: cf. Isocr. *Panath.* § 264 οὐκ ἐθορύβησαν, ὃ ποιεῖν εἰώθασιν ἐπὶ τοῖς χαριέντως διειλεγμένοις, *Ibid.* § 233 λόγος τεθορυβημένος, 'a loudly-applauded speech' (cf. *acclamare* post-Aug.). Lyc. here evidently desires to correct what may have been a prevalent notion among his hearers, that the action of the Areopagus which he is about to mention was an unwarranted and anti-democratic usurpation of power: cf. the similar case of Cicero in the matter of the Catilinarian conspirators.

ταύτην] sc. τὴν ἐν 'Α. π. βουλήν, rather than a case of 'predicative attraction' of the pronoun.

τότε] i.e. immediately after Chaeronea. For the dictatorial powers exercised by the Areopagus in grave public crises, cf. Plut. *Themist.* § 10 (before Salamis), Lysias, *c. Eratosth.* § 69 (after Aegospotami), Dem. *De Cor.* § 134 (intervention in the case of the traitor Antiphon), also *supra* § 12 *n.*

λαβοῦσα] i.q. συλλαβοῦσα [Naber (Bl.)]: cf. *infra* § 112 καὶ τούτων ληφθέντων.

φονικὰ ἀδικήματα] the special sphere of the Areopagus under the full democracy: cf. *supra* § 12 *n.*

ὁσιώτατα] is of course adv., with δικάζοντας.

§ 53. ἀλλὰ μὴν 'Α. γε ὑμεῖς] ἀλλὰ μήν, *verum enimvero*, 'alleging what is not disputed' (L.S. *s.v.* μήν, 3), introduces a fresh and emphatic point.—Αὐτολύκου and ὑμεῖς are both emphatic: A.)(other offenders: ὑμεῖς, the Heliaea)(ἡ ἐν 'Α. π. βουλή. Lyc. tactfully says nothing of his having been himself the prosecutor of A., who was an Areopagite (Harpocr. *s.v.* Αὐτόλυκος, quoting the present passage): cf. also the *Argument* to the speech, *ad fin.* A. has been supposed to be the person alluded to (in conjunction with Leocrates) by Aeschin. *Ctes.* § 252, but the account of him given there does not tally with the present passage: ἐγένετό τις...ἀνὴρ ἰδιώτης, ὃς ἐκπλεῖν εἰς Σάμον ἐπιχειρήσας ὡς προδότης τῆς πατρίδος αὐθημερὸν ὑπὸ τῆς ἐξ 'Α. πάγου βουλῆς θανάτῳ ἐζημιώθη.

μείναντος μὲν αὐτοῦ...ἔχοντος δ' αἰτίαν] 'who, though he remained himself...was charged with having,' etc. For αἰτίαν ἔχειν c. infin.=*crimen habere*, cf. *infra* § 125 τοὺς τὴν αἰτίαν ἔχοντας, Ar. *Vesp.* 506 αἰτίαν ἔχω ταῦτα δρᾶν ξυνωμότης ὤν. But Plat. *Gorg.* 503 B δι' ὅντινα αἰτίαν ἔχουσιν Ἀθηναῖοι βελτίους γεγονέναι, 'are reputed, 'are credited with.'—For **ὑπεκθέσθαι**, cf. *supra* § 25 τὰ χρήματα...ὑπεκθέσθαι n.

τί δεῖ πάσχειν] sc. ἐκεῖνον as subject.

οὐκ ἀπέδωκε τὰ τροφεῖα τῇ π.] 'failed in duly rendering to his country the price of his nurture,' to which his country, as ἡ θρέψασα (§§ 21, 47, 85), was morally entitled, even as aged parents were legally entitled γηροτροφηθῆναι (*infra* § 144). Cf. [Lys.], *Epitaph*. § 70 τῇ πατρίδι τὰ τροφεῖα ἀποδόντες, Lys. *c. Andoc.* § 49 ποῖα τροφεῖα ἀνταποδούς; So also τρ. ἐκτίνειν, Plat. *Rep.* 520 B.—For **ἀποδοῦναι**=*reddere*, cf. *supra* § 20.

τὸ γιγνόμενον] 'what was happening,' 'the state of things,' as revealed by the case of A. and those condemned by the Areopagus.

ἐψηφίσατο] on the motion of Hyperides: *supra* § 36.

ἐνόχους...τῇ προδοσίᾳ] 'amenable to the charge of treason': cf. *supra* § 4 τοὺς ἐνόχους τοῖς...ἐπιτιμίοις n.

τοὺς φεύγοντας] 'those who sought to shirk': cf. *supra* § 49 τὴν δουλείαν φεύγοντες n.

§ 54. **δή**] *igitur*, concluding and summing up.

παρὰ τῷ...συνεδρίῳ] παρὰ c. dat. *iudicantis*: cf. Her. III. 160 παρὰ Δαρείῳ κριτῇ, παρ' ἐμοί=*me iudice*, etc. So also παρὰ τῷ δήμῳ immediately following, for which cf. *supra* § 12 παρ' αὐτοῖς ὁμολ. τοῖς ἁλισκομένοις n.

τῶν δικάζειν λαχόντων] 'the duly appointed judges.' The designation is common of officers or official bodies *appointed by lot* (λαγχάνω): cf. Her. VI. 109 ὁ τῷ κυάμῳ λαχὼν Ἀθηναίων πολεμαρχέειν, οἱ λαχόντες βουλεύειν, etc.: cf. *supra* § 37 τὴν βουλὴν τοὺς πεντακοσίους n. The dicasts were chosen by lot from the body of the citizens who were over 30 years of age and in possession of their full civic rights (ἐπίτιμοι), Arist. 'Αθ. Πολ. c. 63.

τούτοις] referring formally to ἅ ('offences which'), but in substance to the content of the three preceding clauses, and so = 'these decisions.'

ἄρ'] cf. *supra* § 27 πάντων ἄρ' ἀνθρώπων ῥᾳθυμότατοι ἔσεσθε *n*.

ἀγνωμονέστατοι] 'most unscionable.'

ἐλαχίστους ἕξετε...κινδυνεύοντας] 'and shall find very few who will be disposed to run risks on your behalf': cf. Antiph. *Tetr.* A. γ. *ad fin.* ἐλάσσους μὲν τοὺς ἐπιβουλεύοντας καταστήσετε, πλείους δὲ τοὺς τὴν εὐσέβειαν ἐπιτηδεύοντας, Dem. *Lept.* § 166 οὐκ ἀπορήσετε τῶν ἐθελησόντων ὑπὲρ ὑμῶν κινδυνεύειν.

c. 14. §§ 55–58. *Leocrates is clearly guilty on all the counts of the indictment; but perhaps he will plead that he sailed to Rhodes as an ordinary merchant. To this I reply, that merchants do not embark stealthily, but in open harbour. Again, what object had a merchant in sojourning five years in Megara, unless he was conscious of having deeply wronged his country? But even admitting his plea, I would ask him, (a) why he started on a voyage then, when all other merchants were hastening home to their country's defence, (b) what possible import could have been more useful than personal service at that crisis? As a matter of fact, Leocrates was never a merchant at all, but an owner of coppersmiths. His interest in the fiftieth, moreover, disproves his statement.*

§ 55. τοῖς εἰσ. ἅπασιν] cf. *supra* § 5 ἅπασι τοῖς γεγραμμένοις ἔνοχον ὄντα.

πυνθάνομαι] a formula of προκατάληψις, *anteoccupatio*, 'anticipation of an adversary's arguments,' with a view to weakening or defeating them. πυνθάνομαι introduces the first of a series of such 'anticipations,' e.g. *infra* §§ 59, 63, 68, 90.

ἔμπορος] '*as* a merchant.' [<ὅτι> ὡς ἔμπ. Es.]

κατὰ ταύτην τὴν ἐργασίαν] 'on this business,' a use of the prep. as old as Homer: *Od.* III. 72 ἤ τι κατὰ πρῆξιν ('on a trading enterprise') ἦ μαψιδίως ἀλάλησθε; cf. *infra* § 57, but δι' ἐργασίαν, *supra* § 15.

ᾧ] 'how,' 'by what means.' [ὡς Bk., Bl.]

§ 56]   NOTES   121

πρῶτον μέν...ἔπειτα] 'in the first place'...'in the second place,' 'then again': the ἔπειτα may, or may not (as here), have a δέ answering the preceding μέν: cf. Thuc. I. 33 πρῶτον μὲν ὅτι ἀδικουμένοις...ἔπειτα περὶ τῶν μεγίστων κ.τ.λ.

ἐκ τῆς ἀκτῆς κατὰ τὴν πυλίδα] cf. *supra* § 17.

ὁρώμενοι καὶ ἀποστελλόμενοι] 'being seen off,' in popular language; but ὁρ. is emphatic, 'in full view of all their friends,' as contrasted with the furtive flight of L.

μετὰ τῆς ἑταίρας] cf. *supra* § 17.

μόνος] sc. ἐμβαίνει ὁ ἔμπορος. [μόνος, which the Aldine (Bl.) corrects to μόνοι, seems somewhat harsh after οἱ κατ' ἐμ. πλέοντες, but the change to the sing. serves all the better to point the contrast to L. Also τῆς ἑταίρας...παιδὸς τοῦ διακ. are difficult with μόνοι.]

§ 56. τὸν 'A. ἔμπορον] Acc. to this reading [Bk., Bl.; τὸν 'A. ὡς ἔμπ. codd. (Rehd., Thalh.)], τὸν 'A. seems best taken as attributive, the article adding a touch of sarcasm: 'our Athenian merchant.'

ἐν Μ....τὰ ἱερά...τὴν οἰκίαν] cf. *supra* §§ 21-25.

πωλεῖν] 'advertise for sale ')(ἀποδόσθαι ταλάντου: *supra* § 22.

κατεγνώκει τε αὐτοῦ προδεδωκέναι] 'had pronounced himself guilty of having betrayed': cf. Lys. xx. § 6 καταγνόντες σφῶν αὐτῶν ἀδικεῖν with Andoc. *De Myst.* § 3 καταγνόντες αὐτῶν ἀδικίαν.—κατεγνώκει τε...καί: on the principle that τε...καί should connect corresponding elements, we might have expected προδ. τε τὴν π. καὶ κ.τ.λ. But exceptions are frequent: cf. in consecutive chaps. of Thuc. (IV. 9, 10), ἀσπίσι τε φαύλαις καὶ οἰσυΐναις and ἦν ἐθέλωμέν τε μεῖναι καὶ μὴ...καταπροδοῦναι.

ὃ καὶ πάντων...εἰ] 'and so it would be the most absurd thing imaginable, if' etc. For this use of the neut. relative, referring generally to what has preceded and explained more particularly by a clause which follows, introduced often by εἰ (as here), see Madvig, § 195. *d.*, and esp. Rehd. (App. 2, pp. 141-3), who distinguishes three separate uses, (*a*) ὅ, (*b*) ὃ δέ, (*c*) ὃ καί. The first, he contends, is retrospective in force; the second, prospective; the third, half retrospective, half prospective: see the numerous exx. quoted by him, *l.c.* We may compare the somewhat similar use of *quod* in Latin, in adjurations: Virg. *Aen.* II. 141 *quod te per superos...oro,* VI. 363; and for the present passage *infra* § 82 ὃ καὶ πάντων ἂν εἴη δεινότατον, τοὺς μὲν προγόνους κ.τ.λ.

ἀπολύσαιτε] with ταῦτα, must have the meaning of 'dismissing,' 'quashing' a charge, in which sense ἀπολύεσθαι is very frequently said of a defendant, cf. *diluere*: ἀπολύεσθαι τὴν αἰτίαν, τὰ κατηγορημένα, etc. The use of ἀπολύειν in the present passage is illustrated by Hyper. *Eux.* § 38 (εἰσαγγελία)...ὑπ' αὐτοῦ τοῦ κατηγόρου τρόπον τινὰ ἀπολελυμένη. But there is no doubt a suggestion of 'if you should *acquit him* on these charges.'

κύριοι γενόμενοι τῆς ψήφου] 'now that the verdict rests with you,' somewhat like *supra* § 2 ἔχοντας ὑπὸ τῇ ψήφῳ. For κύριος, cf. *infra* § 59 οὔτε γὰρ νεωρίων κύριος n.

χωρὶς δὲ τούτων] cf. *supra* § 31.

§ **57.** τοὺς μὲν...τοῦτον δέ] The regular *paratactic* (co-ordinate) arrangement in Greek, where we use the *hypotactic* (subordinate): cf. *supra* §§ 8, 42, notes.

ἐν τοῖς τότε καιροῖς καὶ κατ' ἐργασίαν] καί, which at first sight might seem to go intensively with κατ' ἐργ. ἐκπλεῖν, 'should *actually* leave on a trading voyage,' is probably rightly taken as simply connecting ἐν...καιροῖς and κατ' ἐργασίαν, at the same time throwing considerable emphasis on the latter: L.'s crime consisted in (*a*) sailing (at all) at such a time—*and* (*b*) on a trading voyage (of all things), i.e. with a view to private gain, this aspect of his ἐργασία being made more explicit by ἡνίκα... προσκτήσασθαι κ.τ.λ. We may compare generally the charge against Andocides in Lys. VI. § 49 ἐπιστάμενος ἐν πολλῷ σάλῳ καὶ κινδύνῳ τὴν πόλιν γενομένην, ναυκληρῶν οὐκ ἐτόλμησεν...σῖτον εἰσάγων ὠφελῆσαι τὴν πατρίδα. ἀλλὰ μέτοικοι μὲν καὶ ξένοι... ὠφέλουν τὴν πόλιν εἰσάγοντες.

οὐδ' ἂν εἷς...ἂν ἐζήτησεν] For οὐδ' ἂν εἷς, cf. *supra* § 49 n.— For the repeated ἄν, which is especially common when a negative or interrogative opens the sentence, see Goodwin, *M. T.* §§ 223 ff.

—**προσκτήσασθαι**: 'acquire *in addition*' (πρός).—**τὰ ὑπάρχοντα**, 'what they had.'

ἡδέως δ' ἂν αὐτοῦ πυθοίμην κ.τ.λ.] 'I should like to ask him, by importing what merchandise he could have served the state better than by submitting himself for enrolment in the ranks.' This rendering, it may be said, suggests rather ἢ παρασχὼν as the natural Greek: τοῦ παρασχεῖν, on the other hand, suggests that the question should be, 'What *merchandise* that he could have imported *would have been more useful* than personal service?' There is thus probably a mixture of the constructions τίν' ἐμπ. εἰσάγων χρησιμώτερος ἐγένετο ἂν ἢ παρασχὼν and τίν' ἐμπ. εἰσ. ἠδύνατο χρησιμωτέραν τοῦ παρασχεῖν: in other words, the comparison of two *actions* is confused with the comparison of two *things*.

ἐγὼ μὲν οὐδεμίαν] The 'isolated' μέν is common in the orators at the end of an argument, emphasising the speaker's own conviction and implying opposition to others: '*I* don't see' (whatever may be true of you): cf. Madvig, § 188, R. 5. So Dem. *Ol.* III. § 8 ἐγὼ μὲν οὐχ ὁρῶ, c. *Timocr.* § 157 ἐγὼ μὲν οὐδέν' ἂν οἶμαι, Xen. *Cyr.* I. 4. 12 ἐγὼ μὲν οὐκ οἶδα.

§ 58. αὐτῷ] The unusual position of the unemphatic αὐτῷ is probably due to a desire partly to avoid the hiatus αὐτῷ ὀργίζεσθαι, partly to make the antithesis διὰ τὴν πρᾶξιν ταύτην...διὰ τὸν λόγον τοῦτον more strongly marked: cf. Rehd., *ad loc.*, who quotes Dem. *Lept.* § 33 οὐ μόνον ὑμῖν ἱκανὸν σῖτον ἀπέστειλεν, ἀλλὰ τοσοῦτον κ.τ.λ., *Ib.* § 70 διόπερ οὐ μόνον αὐτῷ τὴν ἀτέλειαν ἔδωκαν οἱ τότε, ἀλλὰ καὶ χαλκῆν εἰκόνα...ἔστησαν.

οὐδὲ πώποτε] "'οὔποτε, οὐδέποτε cum verbo *futuri* temporis; οὐπώποτε, οὐδεπώποτε cum verbo temporis *praeteriti* construuntur,' Brunck's *Index Aristoph.* Lobeck, *Phryn.* pp. 457, 458. But the rule is neglected by late writers' (Hickie on Andoc. *De Myst.* § 22).

ἐγένετο ἐπὶ...ἐργασίας] 'he was engaged in this business': cf. *supra* § 44 ἐφ' ὧν οὐδενὸς n.

ἐκέκτητο χαλκοτύπους] 'he was a master smith,' i.e. owned a number of slaves who were so employed, as Lysias and his brother owned a shield factory, Demosthenes' father a cutlery factory, etc. The verb is almost technical in this sense.— χαλκοτύπος probably signifies a 'smith' generally, cf. χαλκεύς (χαλκέας (sc. καλοῦσι) τοὺς τὸν σίδηρον ἐργαζομένους, Arist. *Poet.* 25. 14), though the two are distinguished in Xen. *Hell.* III. 4. 17 οἵ τε χαλκοτύποι καὶ οἱ τέκτονες καὶ οἱ χαλκεῖς (v. L.S. *s.v.* χαλκοτύπος).

ἀποδημήσας] concessive, 'though he was away.'

<τῆς> πεντηκοστῆς μετέχων] cf. *supra* § 19 τὴν π., μετέχων αὐτῆς n.

ἣν οὐκ ἂν καταλιπών...ἀπεδήμει] The impf. in the apodosis denotes the action as extending over a considerable time (in the past): 'he would not have abandoned it (act) and *engaged in trade* abroad': ἀπεδήμησε would have referred rather to the act of his departure: cf. generally Goodwin, § 410.

ἂν μέν τι] The μέν here is probably not 'isolated' (cf. *supra* § 57 ἐγὼ μὲν οὐδεμίαν ὁρῶ n.), but is balanced by the δέ of the next paragraph.

λέγῃ] *conative*, 'attempts to say.'

οὐδ' ὑμᾶς ἐπιτρέψειν] = ὑμᾶς οὐδ' ἐπιτρέψειν, 'I think you will simply not allow him': the subj. is inserted between οὐδέ and ἐπιτρέψειν, which last the negative really qualifies: cf. Soph. *Ant.* 280 παῦσαι, πρὶν ὀργῆς καί με μεστῶσαι λέγων, 'ere thou dost utterly fill me with wrath,' where κἀμέ (C. and A.) is pointless: see Jebb *ad loc.*

c. 15. §§ 59–62. *He will perhaps advance a plea suggested to him by some of his counsel—that he is not amenable to the charge of treason because he had no specific duty assigned him. If he had not, this only makes his case worse: he betrayed the whole state and not merely one department of it. Treachery on the part of particular officials would have meant, at worst, the enslavement of the state, from which it might have recovered; Leocrates' desertion involved its desolation, and there is no* *recovery from that. For proof of my statement, I have only to refer you to the history of Athens, Troy, and Messene.*

§ 59. ἥξει δ' ἴσως...φερόμενος] 'But perhaps he will come in his impetuous course to the plea which,' etc. Both φέρων and φερόμενος are thus used idiomatically along with another verb of motion, and seem to convey the notion of *haste and recklessness*. The const. occurs at least four times in Aeschin. *Ctes.* : § 89 Καλλίας ὁ Χαλκιδεὺς...πάλιν ἦκε φερόμενος εἰς τὴν ἑαυτοῦ φύσιν, 'returned headlong to his old practices' (of bad faith), § 82 εἰς τοῦτο φέρων περιέστησε τὰ πράγματα, 'speedily gave such an evil turn to events': so also §§ 90, 146 (φέρων in both cases): Goodwin, *M.T.* § 837. A more literal use of the ptcp. can be seen (I think) in such as Her. VIII. 91 φερόμενοι ἐσέπιπτον ἐς τοὺς Αἰγινήτας, 'fell upon them *at full speed*,' *Ibid.* 87 φέρουσα ἐνέβαλε νηὶ φιλίῃ (of Artemisia at Salamis).

ὃν αὐτῷ συμβεβ.] cf. *supra* § 11 ἦ γὰρ συμβουλεύουσιν...περὶ τῶν κοινῶν πραγμάτων *n.*

τῶν συνηγόρων] These were not professional advocates, in our sense, but (usually) personal friends of the parties in a case, who were allowed to speak on either side after the case had been opened by the parties themselves. Athenian theory presumed that every citizen was capable of conducting his own prosecution or defence. Some would distinguish συνήγορος = plaintiff's counsel)(σύνδικος = defendant's, but both terms seem to have come to be of general application (cf. Drake on Dem. *De Cor.* § 134).

τῇ προδοσίᾳ] 'the charge of treason.'

οὔτε γὰρ νεωρίων κύριος] sc. ἦν (the mood and tense of the *recta*: the speaker imagines L. to say ' I *was* not responsible,' οὐ κύριος ἦν), 'for he was not in charge either of arsenals,' etc.— κύριος, of that of which one has the disposing or control: cf. Dem. *F.L.* § 183 εἰσὶ γὰρ οἱ πρέσβεις οὐ τριήρων οὐδὲ τόπων οὐδ' ὁπλιτῶν οὐδ' ἀκροπόλεων κύριοι...ἀλλὰ λόγων καὶ χρόνων.—The enumeration νεωρίων...πυλῶν...στρατοπέδων has specific reference to the scope of the νόμος εἰσαγγελτικός (*supra* § 1 *n.*): cf. Poll.

8. 52 ἐγένοντο εἰσαγγελίαι...κατὰ τῶν προδόντων φρούριον ἢ στρατιὰν ἢ ναῦς, and the Lysias passage quoted hereunder.

οὔθ' ὅλως...οὐδενός] 'nor in short of any state department whatever': ὅλως marks a climax, as often, *nec denique, neque omnino*: cf. Dem. *Mid.* § 101 οὔτ' ἐλεῶν οὔθ' ὅλως ἄνθρωπον ἡγούμενος.

ἐγὼ δ' ἡγοῦμαι...τὴν πόλιν] For the sentiment, cf. Lysias, *In Phil.* [or. XXXI] § 26 ἄξιον δὲ καὶ τόδε ἐνθυμηθῆναι, ὅτι εἰ μέν τις φρουρίον τι προὔδωκεν ἢ ναῦς ἢ στρατόπεδόν τι...ταῖς ἐσχάταις ἂν ζημίαις ἐζημιοῦτο, οὗτος δὲ προδοὺς ὅλην τὴν πόλιν κ.τ.λ.—**ἔκδοτον ποιῆσαι**: a stronger προδοῦναι, cf. Aeschin. *Ctes.* § 142 ἔκδοτον τὴν Βοιωτίαν πᾶσαν ἐποίησε Θηβαίοις, 'abandoned,' 'betrayed,' *Ibid.* § 61 : *infra* § 85 ἔκδοτον...παρέδοσαν.

τοὺς τετελευτηκότας] I have followed Herw. (Bl.) in omitting καὶ τὰ ἐν τῇ χώρᾳ ἱερά, which the MSS. give after τετελευτηκότας.

τῶν πατρίων νομίμων ἀποστερῶν] 'by robbing them of their ancestral rites': cf. Thuc. III. 58 (the Plataeans are speaking) οὓς...ταφέντας ἐν τῇ ἡμετέρᾳ ἐτιμῶμεν...ἐσθήμασί τε καὶ τοῖς ἄλλοις νομίμοις. [πατρίων Schoem. (Rehd.) : πατρῴων codd.: cf. *supra* § 25 *n.*]

§ 60. καὶ ὑπὸ μὲν ἐκείνων κ.τ.λ.] 'Moreover, had the city been betrayed by them (τῶν τινος κυρίων—'heads of departments'), the result would have been that, though enslaved, it would still be inhabited; but in the way that L. abandoned it, it would have been made desolate': the protasis of the sentence is contained in προδοθεῖσαν = εἰ προὐδόθη, a supposed past *act*: συνέβαινεν ἄν represents the abiding result of the act in the present, *si urbs prodita esset, tamen incoleretur* : cf. Goodwin, §§ 410, 411. So οἰκεῖσθαι = 'would *still* be inhabited' (present state): ἀοίκητον ἂν γενέσθαι = 'would have been desolated' (act). For οἰκεῖσθαι, cf. [Dem.] *c. Aristog.* I. [or. XXV] § 26 εἰ ταῦτα ποιοῖμεν, ἔστ' ἔτι τὴν πόλιν οἰκεῖσθαι;—**ὃν δὲ τρόπον**: the *modal accusative* is generally preferred to the dative by Greek prose writers in these phrases with τρόπος (τοῦτον τὸν τρόπον, τίνα τρόπον; τὸν αὐτὸν τρόπον, etc.), though τούτῳ τῷ τρόπῳ in

§ 61] NOTES 127

Andoc. *De Myst.* § 41, *De Pace* § 20, *De Redit.* § 18 ὁτῳοῦν τρόπῳ, and always μηδενὶ τρόπῳ. (Hickie on Andoc. *De Myst. l.c.*)

τυχεῖν...εἰκός ἐστιν...στερηθῆναι] For the aor. infins. with εἰκός (where we might expect the *fut.*), cf. Thuc. IV. 24 ἤλπιζον ...ῥᾳδίως χειρώσασθαι, Xen. *Hell.* V. 4. 7 ἠπείλησαν ἀποκτεῖναι, and other exx. quoted by Goodwin, *M. T.* § 136. But the use of the aorist in these and similar cases is sufficiently explained by the cardinal idea of *an act done once for all* as opp. to a continuous process.—**ἀναστάτους**: ἀνάστατος, of towns and countries, 'depopulated,' 'destroyed,' 'laid waste': of a population, 'homeless': cf. Antiph. *De Caed. Herod.* § 79 ἐπεῖδον τὴν ἑαυτῶν πατρίδα ἀνάστατον γενομένην, Her. I. 76 Συρίους...ἀναστάτους ἐποίησε, etc. [ἀναστάτους Reiske (Bl.) : ἀνάστατον codd., which some editors retain, agrees with πόλιν understood.]

καὶ τῶν κοινῶν ἐλπίδων] 'even of ordinary hopes,' i.e. hopes that are common to all men alike.

ἐλπὶς...μεταπεσεῖν] For aor. infin. with ἐλπίς, cf. τυχεῖν... εἰκός ἐστιν and note above: for μεταπεσεῖν *in melius*, cf. *supra* § 50 *n.*

οὕτω καὶ περὶ τὰς πόλεις κ.τ.λ.] 'so too it is true of cities that their misfortune reaches its climax when they become desolate': i.e. there is no longer so much as a chance of δυστυχία changing to εὐτυχία. For πέρας ἔχειν, of a limit which may not be passed, cf. Lysias *c. Eratosth.* § 88 ἐκεῖνοι δὲ... τελευτήσαντες τὸν βίον πέρας ἔχουσι τῆς τῶν ἐχθρῶν (subj. gen.) τιμωρίας, Isocr. *Paneg.* § 5, *Philip.* § 141, Dem. *Lept.* § 91.

§ 61. εἰ γὰρ δεῖ] cf. *supra* § 49 εἰ δὲ δεῖ καὶ παραδοξότατον μὲν εἰπεῖν, ἀληθὲς δέ, *n.*

πόλεώς ἐστι θάνατος...γενέσθαι] 'it is death for a city to be laid waste': for ἀνάστατον in acc. agreeing with the implied subject of the infin. (αὐτὴν, τὴν πόλιν), cf. Goodwin, *M. T.* § 744.

τεκμήριον δὲ μέγιστον] sc. ἐστίν, which seems to be regularly omitted in this formula.

ἡμῶν γάρ] γάρ introduces, as regularly, the matter of the τεκμήριον: do not translate.

τὸ μὲν παλαιὸν...τὸ δ' ὕστερον] 'of old'...'later': accusatives, like τὸ πρῶτον, τοὐναντίον, etc.

ὑπὸ τῶν τυράννων] Pisistratus and his sons, especially Hippias, who between them ruled Athens for fifty years, 560–510 B.C.

ὑπὸ τῶν τριάκοντα] The Thirty were installed in the summer of 404, and held office till May, 403 B.C.

τὰ τείχη καθῃρέθη] 404 B.C. (April).

ἐκ τούτων...ἀμφοτέρων] neuter, 'from both of these plights.' The liberation from the first was effected by the Alcmaeonids, headed by Cleisthenes, who procured the help of Sparta; from the second, also through the intervention of Sparta, following on the defeat of the Thirty and their adherents by the exiles under Thrasybulus (May, 403 B.C.).

τῆς τῶν 'Ε. εὐδαιμονίας] The term εὐδαιμονία, which Dem. (*Mid.* § 143) and Isocr. (*Paneg.* § 103) had used of the Greece of the fifth cent. B.C., was hardly applicable (as Rehd. observes *ad loc.*) to the Greece of the fourth, even though the speaker may have had in view the period following the victory of Cnidus (394), and the building up of the Second Athenian Confederacy. Nothing is to be gained, however, by substituting ἐλευθερίας or ἡγεμονίας (Es), as neither the one nor the other holds good for *both* centuries.

§ 62. ἀλλ' οὐχ ὅσαι...γεγόνασι] 'But not so with such as have ever become desolate': sc. as predicate something like τοῦτο πεπόνθασι, 'have had this (fortunate) experience,' out of the general sense of the preceding argument. Hyper. takes an opposite view to that of Lyc.: or. II. [*In Philip.*] § 8 πόλεις δὲ πολλαὶ ἄρδην ἀναιρεθεῖσαι πάλιν ἴσχυσαν.

τοῦτο μὲν...τοῦτο δέ] 'on the one hand'...'on the other,' a common formula in introducing examples: frequent in Herodotus.

εἰ καὶ παλαιότερον εἰπεῖν ἐστι] 'though I may be quoting somewhat ancient history,' lit. 'even if (as I grant) it is rather ancient to mention' (παλ. goes with εἰπεῖν: Goodwin, *M.T.*

§ 763): cf. *infra* § 95 εἰ γὰρ καὶ μυθωδέστερόν ἐστιν, ἀλλ' ἁρμόσει κ.τ.λ.—For the distinction between εἰ καί and καὶ εἰ, the former allowing, but minimising, the affirmation of the condition, the latter rather asserting its improbability, see L.S. *s.v.* καί, B. II. 3; Madvig, § 194. *d.*

τὴν Τροίαν] a good example of 'anticipation,' but due also to its balancing Μεσσήνην, which naturally comes first in the participial clause to which the const. changes. Cf. Xen. *Anab.* I. 8. 21 (Κῦρος) ᾔδει αὐτὸν (sc. βασιλέα) ὅτι μέσον ἔχοι τοῦ Περσικοῦ στρατεύματος, 'knew that the king held,' etc. So in Latin, *nosti Marcellum, quam tardus sit*: Madvig, § 191.

πάσης ἐπάρξασα τῆς 'Α.] 'after acquiring dominion over the whole of Asia': a rhetorical exaggeration, designed to heighten the merit of the Greek achievement: cf. Isocr. *Panath.* § 83 (of Agamemnon) λόγῳ μὲν πρὸς μίαν πόλιν πολεμήσας, ἔργῳ δὲ... πρὸς ἅπαντας τοὺς τὴν 'Ασίαν κατοικοῦντας κ.τ.λ.

τὸν αἰῶνα ἀοίκητός ἐστι] 'is uninhabited for all time,' i.e. has been (since the time of its sack) and will so remain.—τὸν αἰῶνα, *in sempiternum*, is noteworthy for the omission of πᾶς (ἅπας, σύμπας) which accompanies αἰών in the sense of 'time without end' e.g. in Isocr. (I. I ὁ πᾶς αἰών, VI. 109 πάντα τὸν αἰῶνα, IV. 46 ἅπαντα τὸν αἰῶνα, VIII. 34 τοῦ σύμπαντος *al.*) and Plato, *Tim.* 38 C πάντα *al.* (δι' αἰῶνος in Trag.): so also Lyc. himself, *supra* § 7, *infra* §§ 106, 110.

τοῦτο δὲ Μεσσήνην...συνοικισθεῖσαν] 'and how, on the other hand, Messene, five hundred years later, was restored by a casual population,' which may pass as a rendering, but the Greek requires some explanation.—Messene, the later capital of Messenia (which name is not used by Homer), in W. Peloponnesus, was founded in 369 B.C. by Epaminondas, the Theban general and statesman, who gathered together for the purpose the dispersed remnants of the Messenian exiles, the inveterate enemies of Sparta. The citadel of the new town was the historic Mt. Ithome, and the town itself was formed by 'synoecising' (i.e. combining into one for political purposes) the neighbouring districts, the effect of which was to make Messene the Messenian state, as Athens was to Attica (cf. Thuc. III. 2 ξυνοικίζουσι τὴν Λέσβον ἐς τὴν Μυτιλήνην). The speaker's contention is that the 'synoecism' was effected so easily (ἐκ τῶν τ. ἀνθ.) because Messenia had never become ἀνάστατος, the inhabitants who had survived the early traditional wars with Sparta and any remnant that remained after the settlement by the Athenians at Naupactus in 459 B.C. remaining on the land in the condition of Helots, so that Messenia ᾠκεῖτο δούλη οὖσα.—**πεντακοσίοις ἔτεσιν ὕστερον**: 500 years after—the fall of Troy? or the Spartan conquest of Messenia? If the first, the fall of Troy is much too late; if the second (which we presume is what Lyc. intends), the conquest of Messenia is much too early, even if we suppose him to be reckoning from the 'First Messenian War,' the central date of which is placed *c.* 725 B.C., whereas Lyc. would bring it forward to about 870 B.C. Dinarchus, who speaks of 400 years (I. 73 Μεσσήνην τετρακοσιοστῷ ἔτει κατῴκισαν), apparently reckons from the first war; Ephorus, with whom Pausanias practically agrees, gives 300 years; Plutarch (*Apophth. Epam.* 23) and Aelian, only 230 years. The last four authorities evidently refer the conquest of Messenia to the 'Second Messenian War,' with which tradition connected the names of Aristomenes and Tyrtaeus (for the latter, see more particularly *infra* § 106 *n.*), and which may accordingly be dated to *c.* 640 B.C.—**ἐκ τῶν τυχόντων ἀνθ.**: ἐκ is hardly to be explained as a somewhat rare equivalent of ὑπό with a passive verb, but has reference rather to the *composition* of the inhabitants (cf. *constare ex*): cf. Xen. *Symp.* 8. 32 στράτευμα ἐξ ἐραστῶν, 'composed of lovers.'—τῶν τυχόντων: cf. *supra* § 37 μικροὶ καὶ οἱ τυχόντες φόβοι *n.*

c. 16. §§ 63–67. *Perhaps some of his advocates will have the face to plead that none of the results I have foreshadowed could have depended on the action of a single individual. But the safety of the state depends upon each individual doing his particular duty: 'he that offends in one point is guilty of all.' The truth of this principle is attested by the spirit of ancient legislators, who in* *assigning penalties did not discriminate between greater and lesser offences, but had regard to the principle underlying them. You would not tolerate the erasing of a single law on the ground that it made no difference to the state. In the same way, you cannot consider Leocrates apart from the rest of the citizens: you must have regard not to the individual, but to the principle.*

§ 63. τῶν συνηγόρων αὐτῷ] = τῶν αὐτῷ συνηγορούντων: for the const., cf. (in a slightly different sense) Soph. *Trach.* 1165 μαντεῖα καινά, τοῖς πάλαι ξυνήγορα, 'agreeing with,' 'supporting,' [Dem.] LIX. § 14.

μικρὸν τὸ πρᾶγμα ποιῶν] 'seeking to represent the matter as trivial')(μικρὸν ποιούμενος, 'regarding it as trivial,' in the subjective sense. The distinction seems good here, though not perhaps universally: cf. Isocr. *Paneg.* § 59 οὐ γὰρ παρὰ μικρὸν ἐποίησαν (of the Athenian protection of the Heraclidae), which seems equally subjective in sense with παρὰ μικρὸν ἡγεῖσθαι Id. *Philip.* § 79, or ἐν σμικρῷ ποιεῖσθαι Soph. *Phil.* 498. With the present passage, cf. Isocr. XX. § 5 ἴσως οὖν Λοχίτης ἐπιχειρήσει μικρὸν ποιεῖν τὸ πρᾶγμα, διασύρων τὴν κατηγορίαν κ.τ.λ.

ὡς οὐδὲν ἂν παρ' ἕνα...ἐγένετο τούτων] 'that none of those calamities could have been brought about by the action of a single individual': for παρὰ c. acc. 'of that which turns the scale, and on which the result critically depends' (Madvig, § 75), cf. Dem. *Phil.* III. § 2 οὐ παρ' ἓν οὐδὲ δύο εἰς τοῦτο τὰ πράγματα ἀφῖκται, Isocr. *Archid.* § 52 ὑπὸ πάντων ἂν ὡμολογεῖτο παρὰ τοῦτον γενέσθαι τὴν σωτηρίαν αὐτοῖς, Dinarch. I. § 72. The use of the prep. in this sense with *persons* appears to be somewhat rare and late, v. Rehd., App. 2, p. 144.

τὴν πατρίδα αὐτὸν ἐκλιπεῖν] The strictly correct order in a case of this kind appears to be τὴν πατρίδα (obj.) ἐκλιπεῖν αὐτόν (subj.): Hickie on Andoc. *De Myst.* § 16, where he quotes as a type Antiph. V. 39 ἐγὼ δέ φημι ταῦτα οὐ λέγειν αὐτόν, and adds 'and so the *prose* writers *passim.*' But the precise relationship of the accs. is usually easily determined from the context.

τοῦτο...τοῦ μεγέθους] 'the point of fact'...'its importance.'—

9—2

ἐάτωσαν: 'the usual form of the imper. from the Macedonian period,' Rehd. In inscrr. not before 300 B.C. [ἐώντων Es (Blass).]

εἰ δ' ὅλως μηδέν] 'but if they roundly assert his innocence,' we might say: for ὅλως, cf. *supra* § 59 οὔθ' ὅλως τῶν τῆς πόλεως οὐδενός *n.*

§ 64. τούτοις] personal, sc. τοῖς συνηγόροις αὐτῷ.

παρὰ τοῦτον εἶναι...τὴν σωτηρίαν] 'that the very safety of the state depended on him': for παρά, cf. previous §: εἶναι is imperf. infin. The main antithesis is between οὐδέν of the preceding sentence and τῇ πόλει τὴν σωτηρίαν.

ἡ γὰρ πόλις οἰκεῖται κ.τ.λ.] 'For the life of the state depends upon the protection afforded it by each man doing his particular part; and so whenever a man neglects his duty (ταύτην=τὴν ἰδίαν μοῖραν) in one point, he unwittingly neglects it in all' (τοῦτο πεποιηκώς=παρεωρακώς). For the sentiment, cf. Isocr. *Nicoc.* § 48 μηδενὸς ὀλιγωρεῖτε μηδὲ καταφρονεῖτε τῶν προστεταγμένων, ὑπολαμβάνοντες ὡς οὐ παρὰ τοῦτ' ἐστίν, ἀλλ' ὡς παρ' ἕκαστον τῶν μερῶν ἢ καλῶς ἢ κακῶς τὸ σύμπαν ἕξον, οὕτω σπουδάζετε περὶ αὐτῶν, i.e. 'neglect no duty, however trivial, *under the impression that nothing depends upon it*, but perform your duties with zeal, *remembering that, as the parts are, so will the whole be good or bad.*'—**ἐφ' ἑνός...ἐφ' ἁπάντων**: ἐπί='in the case' or 'matter' of: cf. Dem. *Mid.* § 38 οὐκ ἐπὶ τούτου μόνον, ἀλλ' ἐπὶ πάντων φαίνεται προῃρημένος μ' ὑβρίζειν, *Ibid.* § 44.

τῶν ἀρχαίων νομοθετῶν] Esp. Draco and Solon, to one or other of whom, especially the latter, the Athenians were inclined to attribute the bulk of their ancient statutes: cf. Aeschin. *Ctes.* § 175 ὁ γὰρ Σόλων ὁ παλαιὸς νομοθέτης, Dem. *De Cor.* § 6 οἱ νόμοι...οὓς ὁ τιθεὶς ἐξ ἀρχῆς Σόλων, κ.τ.λ. 'Draco's laws were specially called θεσμοί, as distinguished from Solon's νόμοι' (Pape, quoted by Hickie, Andoc. *De Myst.* § 81 τέως δὲ χρῆσθαι τοῖς Σόλωνος νόμοις καὶ τοῖς Δράκοντος θεσμοῖς. But Solon himself spoke of his laws as θεσμοί: v. Sandys on Arist. Ἀθ. Πολ. c. 4 *init.*)—νομοθετῶν...ἀποβλέψαντας: cf. *supra* §§ 9, 10, respectively.

§ 65. ἐκεῖνοι γὰρ οὐ κ.τ.λ.] The code of Draco especially was proverbial for its severity: Demādes the orator said of him ὅτι δι' αἵματος, οὐ διὰ μέλανος τοὺς νόμους ἔγραψεν, 'wrote his laws not in ink but in blood' (Plut. *Sol.* 17). It probably got this character as a whole from the severity of the punishment meted out to certain minor offences: we know only that part of it which dealt with murder and homicide. Cf. with the whole §, Dem. *c. Timocr.* §§ 113 *sqq.*, *Mid.* §§ 44 *sqq.*—Note that the force of οὐ extends to the second clause τῷ δὲ δέκα κ.τ.λ. as well: so also the οὐδέ's following.

τῷ μὲν ἑκατὸν...τῷ δὲ δέκα δραχμάς] Cf. Dem. *c. Timocr.* § 114 (of Solon) καὶ εἴ τίς γ' ἐκ Λυκείου...ἱμάτιον ἢ ληκύθιον ἢ ἄλλο τι φαυλότατον, ἢ εἰ τῶν σκευῶν τι τῶν ἐκ τῶν γυμνασίων ὑφέλοιτο ἢ ἐκ τῶν λιμένων, ὑπὲρ δέκα δραχμάς, καὶ τούτοις θάνατον ἐνομοθέτησεν εἶναι τὴν ζημίαν.—**ἐπιτίμιον**, 'penalty': cf. *supra* § 4 τοῖς ἐκ τῶν νόμων ἐπιτιμίοις *n.*, and Aeschin. *Ctes.* § 175 ὁ Σόλων ...ἐν τοῖς αὐτοῖς ἐπιτιμίοις ᾤετο δεῖν ἐνέχεσθαι τὸν ἀστράτευτον καὶ τὸν λελοιπότα τὴν τάξιν καὶ τὸν δειλὸν ὁμοίως.

τὸν μεγάλα ἱεροσυλήσαντα] 'a man who had committed great sacrilege': Madvig, § 27.

τιμωρίᾳ ἐκόλαζον...ὥρισαν] For τιμωρεῖσθαι)(κολάζειν, see *infra* §§ 123, 146, *nn.*—Note the impfs. ἀπέκτεινον, ἐκόλαζον, ἐζημίουν, 'nor was it their practice to,' etc.)(ἔταξαν, ὥρισαν, of the fixing of the penalty as a definite legislative act.

οὐδὲ τὸν μὲν οἰκέτην...εἶργον τῶν νομίμων] 'nor did they impose a money fine on him who had killed a slave, while they excluded him who had killed a freeman from the public rites': οἰκέτην is obj. of ἀποκτείναντα, which is to be supplied after τὸν δὲ ἐλεύθερον.—εἶργον τῶν νομίμων: cf. Antiph. *De Chor.* § 36 ὁ γὰρ νόμος οὕτως ἔχει, ἐπειδάν τις ἀπογραφῇ φόνου δίκην, εἴργεσθαι τῶν νομίμων, Dem. *Lept.* § 158 ὁ Δράκων...γράφων... εἴργεσθαι τὸν ἀνδροφόνον σπονδῶν, κρατήρων, ἱερῶν, ἀγορᾶς. Cf. also *supra* § 5 εἰς τὴν ἀγορὰν ἐμβάλλοντα καὶ τῶν κοινῶν ἱερῶν μετέχοντα *n.*, *infra* § 142.

ἀλλ' ὁμοίως ἐπὶ πᾶσι...τὴν ζημίαν] 'but for all offences alike, even the smallest, they defined death as the penalty.'—For ἐπί

c. dat. 'in the case of,' cf. the common νόμον τιθέναι ἐπί τινι, 'to make a law in the case of a person' (*for* or *against* him): so νόμος κεῖται ἐπί τινι.—**καὶ τοῖς ἐλ.**: the καί is intensive= *etiam*: rather different is the 'corrective' use of the conj. in e.g. Dem. *De Cor.* § 12 μεγάλας καὶ τὰς ἐσχάτας τιμωρίας, 'great, or rather the greatest.'—**θάνατον**: so regularly, without the article, in similar phrases (θάνατον τάττειν, ἐπιτιθέναι, γράφειν, etc.) where it stands in predicative apposition to τὴν ζημίαν, 'the (legal) penalty,' which latter, however, is often anarthrous: cf. Thuc. III. 44 θάνατον ζημίαν προθεῖσι, and other exx. cited by Rehd., App. 2, p. 145.

§ 66. οὐ γὰρ πρὸς τὸ ἴδιον κ.τ.λ.] 'For they did not severally have an eye to the individual aspect of the deed that had been done, nor did they gauge the enormity of a crime by that standard (ἐντεῦθεν = ἀπὸ τοῦ ἰδίου τοῦ γ. π.): what they considered rather was just this, whether the particular offence was calculated, if it acquired a wider scope, to inflict serious injury on the community': τὸ ἴδιον represents what we may term the *material* aspect of the crime (e.g. whether it was a sacrilege or a petty theft, etc.), as opposed to the *moral* aspect and the motive behind it. For ἀπέβλεπε, cf. *supra* § 10 πρὸς ἑκάτερον...ἀποβλέποντες *n.*—**ἐλάμβανον**: 'judged,' 'estimated': cf. Thuc. II. 42 τὴν τῶν ἐναντίων τιμωρίαν ποθεινοτέραν λαβόντες, 'holding it more dear to them,' III. 20 (of the Plataean besieged) τὴν ξυμμέτρησιν τῶν κλιμάκων οὕτως ἔλαβον, Lys. X. § 13 εἰ οὕτω τοὺς νόμους λαμβάνεις.—**εἰ πέφυκε**: the tense of the *recta*: they asked themselves ἆρα πέφυκε, 'is the crime calculated?' etc.: for πέφυκε, cf. *supra* § 4 ὁ νόμος πεφ. προλέγειν *n.*—**ἐπὶ πλεῖον ἐλθόν**: conditional, 'if it went to greater lengths,' 'by acquiring a wider scope.'

καὶ γὰρ ἄτοπον...ἐξετάζειν] 'and indeed it would be absurd to review this matter on any other principle': τούτου refers to the general thought of the previous sentence, i.e. the proper method of appraising crimes. For ἐξετάζειν περί, cf. Isaeus IV. § 2 περὶ τῆς...ἐπιγραφῆς ἄξιόν ἐστιν ἐξετάσαι, *Ib.* § 11.

φέρε γάρ, κ.τ.λ.] 'For supposing, gentlemen, a person were to enter the Metroum and erase one law, and then plead that its erasure made no difference to the state—would you not have condemned him to death? Yes, and rightly, to my mind, if you were to guarantee the preservation of the rest' (τοὺς ἄλλους sc. νόμους).—For φέρε 'before a question which usually serves to refute another,' v. L.S. *s.v.* φέρω, IX. 3 and reff.—**τὸ Μητρῷον**: the Metroum, the temple of Cybele, mother of the gods, stood in the marketplace near the council chamber (βουλευτήριον): it was the work of Phidias, and in it the state archives were kept: cf. Dem. *F.L.* § 129 ἐν τοῖς κοινοῖς τοῖς ὑμετέροις γράμμασιν ἐν τῷ μητρῴῳ, Aeschin. *Ctes.* § 187, etc.—**εἰ...ἐξαλείψειεν...ἀπολογοῖτο ...οὐκ ἂν ἀπεκτείνατε**; We have here a mixed conditional sentence, which it is quite easy to make conform to type by reading ἐξήλειψεν...ἀπελογεῖτο (Dobree) or ἀποκτείναιτ' (Es). But there is no reason for suspecting the text, the indic. in the apodosis being explained by a sudden change in the point of view of the speaker, who concludes as though he had put (more vividly) a supposed case in the past (indic.) rather than one of remote future contingency (opt.): Goodwin, *M. T.* § 508. ἐξαλείψειεν, of the act)(ἀπολογοῖτο, of the attempt (conative), 'should seek to put forward the plea.'—**εἶτα**: so regularly (without καί) in conditional clauses, 'marking continuation and further consequence' (Madvig, § 185, R. 6): cf. Dem. *Ol.* I. § 12 εἰ δὲ προησόμεθα τούτους τοὺς ἀνθρώπους, εἶτ' Ὄλυνθον ἐκεῖνος καταστρέψεται.—**οὐδὲν παρὰ τοῦτον**: cf. *supra* §§ 63, 64.—**ἐγὼ μὲν οἶμαι δικαίως**: sc. ὑμᾶς ἂν ἀποκτεῖναι αὐτόν. For μέν, cf. *supra* § 57 ἐγὼ μὲν οὐδεμίαν ὁρῶ *n.*—**εἴπερ**, 'that is to say, if,' etc., assuming the fact of the condition: Madvig, § 194.—**ἐμέλλετε... σῴζειν**, but just immediately **μέλλετε...ποιήσειν**: acc. to the usual rule, μέλλω is constructed (*a*) mostly with *fut.* infin., (*b*) less frequently with *pres.* infin., (*c*) more rarely still with *aor.* infin. The precise difference of meaning between (*a*) and (*b*) is difficult to define, and (*c*) has been emended practically out of existence by the editors (following, apparently, the lead of some of the older grammarians, esp. Phrynichus, who condemned this const.) in *prose* passages; but certain places in the poets (e.g. Aesch. *P.V.* 625, Eur. *Or.* 292, *Med.* 393) refuse to yield to treatment. The governing consideration in the constructions of μέλλω is no doubt (as with verbs of hoping, cf. *supra* §60 *n.*) the nature of the action contemplated—whether a definite act (aor.) or a continuous process (pres.): the fut. may represent either.

§ 67. τὸν αὐτὸν...τρόπον] Cf. *supra* §60 ὃν δὲ τρόπον οὗτος ἐξέλιπεν *n.*

κολαστέον ἐστὶ τοῦτον] Note that this (the gerund) const. of the verbal is commoner in Gk. than the personal or gerundive (κολαστέος ἐστὶν οὗτος): contrast the Latin usage in the case of verbs that take an object acc. So *infra* § 135 τοῦτον...ἐξαιτητέον.

ἀλλ' εἰς τὸ πρᾶγμα] sc. λογιεῖσθε, 'but you will have an eye to the fact,' and the principle which it involves. εἰς τὸ πρ. seems capable of being joined with λογιεῖσθε on the analogy of λέγειν εἰς αὐτὸ τὸ πρᾶγμα, κατηγορεῖν εἰς˙αὐτὸ τὸ π. (cf. Dem. LVII. § 7, Antiph. VI. § 9, etc.) and other exx. cited by Rehd., App. 2, *ad loc.* The text, however, has been freely emended: see Crit. App.

τὸ μὴ πολλοὺς...ἡμέτερον εὐτύχημα εἶναι] 'that it is a piece of good fortune for us not to have had many such (citizens),' i.e. such as L.: the clause τὸ μὴ...γενέσθαι is subj. of ἡμέτερον...εἶναι.

μόνος τῶν ἄλλων] Rather a curious, but frequent, expression (cf. *infra* § 102 μόνου τῶν ἄλλων ποιητῶν) for the more logical μόνος τῶν πάντων (cf. *supra* § 50, *infra* § 131). *Infra* § 143 we have μόνος τῶν πολιτῶν simply.

c. 17. §§ 68–74. *But I am most indignant of all at the plea that Leocrates' departure did not constitute desertion: did not our forefathers abandon the city and cross over to Salamis in the war with Xerxes? As if the two cases had anything in common! Who would not envy the record of those 'deserters'—who forced on the fight at Salamis and saved the rest of the Greeks in spite of themselves, and nearly stoned to death Alexander, Xerxes'*

*envoy? who championed Greece for ninety years, won by sea
and land at the Eurymedon, fixed limits for the barbarian, and
gave the Greeks of Asia autonomy? Where in all this do we
trace the spirit of Leocrates?*

§ 68. ὡς οὐκ ἔστι τοῦτο...εἴ τις ᾤχετο] 'that departure from
the city does not constitute desertion,' is our idiom: for the
form of the sentence, cf. Lysias *c. Andoc.* § 41 οὐ γὰρ τοῦτο
λύειν ἐστὶ τὰ συγκείμενα, εἰ 'Ανδοκίδης...δίδωσι δίκην, *c. Theomnest.*
§ 6.—ᾤχετο must be translated as a plupf. (cf. Goodwin, § 37),
as its action must be referred strictly to the case of L., 'that
departure from the city (on that occasion—after Chaeronea)
cannot be construed as treason.'

ὅτε πρὸς Ἁ. ἐπολέμουν...διέβησαν] 480 B.C. Cf. Her. VIII.
41, Isocr. *Paneg.* § 96, etc.

ἐστὶν...καταπεφρονηκώς] The periphrastic perf. 'expresses
more fully the continuance of the *result* of the action of the
perfect to the *present* time': Goodwin, § 45.

ὥστε τὸ κάλλιστον...ἠξίωσε] For a similar perversion of a
noble historical episode, cf. Lys. *In Alcib.* I [or. XIV] §§ 32, 33
τολμᾷ γὰρ λέγειν ὡς 'Αλκιβιάδης οὐδὲν δεινὸν εἴργασται...καὶ γὰρ
ὑμᾶς φεύγοντας Φυλὴν καταλαβεῖν καὶ δένδρα τεμεῖν καὶ πρὸς τὰ
τείχη προσβαλεῖν, καὶ ταῦτα ποιήσαντας οὐκ ὄνειδος τοῖς παισὶ
καταλιπεῖν, ἀλλὰ τιμὴν...κτήσασθαι.—ἠξίωσε: '*has* presumed':
Goodwin, § 58.

§ 69. τὸν τόπον μετήλλαξαν] Cf. *supra* § 50 τὸν βίον μετήλλαξαν *n.*

§ 70. Ἐτεόνικος μὲν γὰρ κ.τ.λ.] For the preliminaries to
Salamis, cf. generally Her. VIII. cc. 49–82, and esp. cc. 56, 70,
74 for the attitude of the Peloponnesians: also Isocr. *Paneg.*
§ 93 ἀθύμως γὰρ ἁπάντων τῶν συμμάχων διακειμένων, καὶ Πελοποννησίων μὲν διατειχιζόντων τὸν Ἰσθμὸν καὶ ζητούντων ἰδίαν
αὑτοῖς σωτηρίαν, κ.τ.λ. Note, however, that in Herod.'s account
(*a*) the Lacedaemonian commander, who was also commander
of the confederate fleet, is Eurybiadas, not Eteonicus. Lyc. is apparently thinking of the Spartan general of the latter name who

appears towards the close of the Peloponnesian War, and in the Corinthian War, and is mentioned several times by Xen. (*Hell.* I. 6, II. 1, v. 1); (*b*) the Aeginetans support the Athenians and Megarians in urging the expediency of fighting at Salamis (c. 74). The Peloponnesian scheme of falling back on the Isthmus would of course have meant the sacrifice of Aegina. The part which Lyc. makes them play here (as Rehd. well remarks, App. 3, p. 170) would no doubt appear quite plausible to his hearers in view of the traditional enmity between Athens and Aegina, which was bitterly intensified by the subsequent expulsion of the Aeginetans from their island about the beginning of the Peloponnesian War (431 B.C.).—**τὸ Α. ναυτικόν**: Aegina was represented by a contingent of thirty ships at Salamis, Her. VIII. 46.—**αὑτοῖς...πορίζεσθαι**: for the fulness of expression, cf. Isocr. *Nicoc.* § 37 αὑτοῖς ἐπορίσαντο τὰς ἡδονάς, *infra* § 141 παρακαθισαμένους ἑαυτοῖς.

ἐγκαταλειπόμενοι] 'finding themselves threatened with abandonment': cf. *infra* § 95 ἐγκαταλαμβανόμενον, 'like to be caught': Goodwin, § 25.

βίᾳ...ἠλευθέρωσαν] *ceteros quoque etiam invitos liberaverunt*: βίᾳ, 'in spite of themselves,' here without the gen. which often accompanies it: Thuc. I. 43 βίᾳ ἡμῶν, Soph. *Ant.* 79 βίᾳ πολιτῶν.

ἀναγκάσαντες] The 'compulsion,' according to the wellknown story, came from Themistocles, who sent Sicinnus to Xerxes with a message that the Greeks intended to sail away in the night. Xerxes thereupon proceeded to block up the straits to prevent their escape (Aesch. *Pers.* 353 *sqq.*, Her. VIII. 75, 76). Cf. Isocr. *Paneg.* § 97 ἠναγκάσθησαν (sc. οἱ Πελοποννήσιοι) μετασχεῖν τῶν κινδύνων, but he assigns prudential motives: καταισχυνθέντες τὴν ἀρετὴν αὐτῶν (sc. τῶν Ἀθηναίων), καὶ νομίσαντες προδιαφθαρέντων τῶν ἡμετέρων οὐδ' αὐτοὶ σωθήσεσθαι.

ὡς ἑκατέρων προσῆκε] sc. περιγενέσθαι. Cf. Isocr. *Paneg.* § 72 ἀμφοτέρων (sc. τῶν πολεμίων...τῶν συμμάχων) κρατήσαντες ὡς ἑκατέρων προσῆκεν.

τοὺς μὲν εὐεργετοῦντες, τοὺς δὲ μαχόμενοι νικῶντες] Either (a) εὐεργετοῦντες and μαχόμενοι νικῶντες ('conquering in battle') go with περιγεγόνασι, or (b) εὐεργ. and μαχ. are both subordinate to νικῶντες. Rehd. and Sofer both explain as (b), but νικᾶν μαχόμενοι is so frequent in Gk. that it is impossible to decide between the two: cf. Rehd., App. 2, ad loc.

ἆρά γ' ὅμοιοι] 'A good match, forsooth, for the man who fled his country on a four days' voyage to Rhodes!' ἆρά γε introduces a question which constitutes a *reductio ad absurdum* in the light of previous argument: cf. Dem. *c. Aristocr.* § 43 ἆρά γε μικρὸν ἢ τὸ τυχόν ἐστιν ὑπὲρ οὗ δεῖ λῦσαι τὸ ψήφισμ' ἡμᾶς; *infra* §§ 119, 123.—τῷ φεύγοντι: perhaps, though not necessarily, *impf.* ptcp.: Goodwin, § 140.—τεττάρων ἡμερῶν πλοῦν: a secondary acc. of 'the extent of the action' denoted by the verb: 'he fled his country—a four days' voyage': Madvig, § 26.

§ 71. ἦ που ταχέως κ.τ.λ.] 'One of those men, I suppose, would readily have brooked such conduct (as L.'s), instead of stoning to death the man who sought to sully their valour': the slight inconsistency ('one...their') in the rendering offered may be said to reflect the change of subject in ἠνέσχετό τις...κατέλευσαν.—ἦ που, *sane, opinor, scilicet*, of ironical conjecture: see further below.—ταχέως: cf. the corresponding use of σχολῇ, lit. 'at one's leisure,' which comes to have the meaning 'scarcely,' 'hardly': freq. in Plato.—τοιοῦτον: this is the regular form of the neut. in Homer, and the best MSS. of Plato give τοιοῦτον, τηλικοῦτον, τοσοῦτον, ταὐτόν, rarely the -ο forms: Meyer, *Griech. Gr.*[3] p. 519.—ἀλλ' οὐκ ἂν κατέλευσαν: the οὐκ is not redundant or contradictory, as may appear at first sight, if we remember that the whole sentence is under the influence of ἦ που and that the Greeks said ἀλλ' οὐ where we say more naturally '*and* not': the sense therefore is, 'I suppose they would have tolerated it...and not have stoned (or, instead of stoning) to death.'—τὸν καταισχύνοντα: conative: cf. *supra* § 53 τοὺς φεύγοντας τὸν ὑπὲρ τῆς πατρίδος κίνδυνον n.

γοῦν] γοῦν indicates the transition from conjecture to historical fact: 'they would have stoned L.: at all events they stoned A.'

τὸν παρὰ Ξ. πρεσβευτὴν 'Α.] Alexander of Macedon, son of Amyntas I, had been obliged to submit to Persia as early as the expedition of Mardonius in 492 B.C., and accompanied Xerxes in his invasion of Greece in 480 B.C. On the latter occasion, he dissuaded the Greeks from attempting to defend the pass of Tempe (Her. VII. 173), and Herodotus makes him appear again at Plataea to warn the Athenians of Mardonius' intention to attack on the morrow (IX. 44, 45). He is described by Herod. as πρόξεινος καὶ εὐεργέτης (VIII. 136) and again as πρόξεινός τε καὶ φίλος (sc. τῶν 'Αθηναίων) (*Ibid.* 143). The only mission that we hear of his having undertaken to Athens is that described by Herod. VIII. 136 ff., in the interval between Salamis and Plataea, when he came as the immediate representative of Mardonius, not 'to demand earth and water,' but as the bearer of most honourable terms for Athens on condition of her accepting the status of a free ally of Persia. The offer was rejected, but we hear nothing of Alexander being 'almost stoned to death'—a treatment indeed which would be strangely inconsistent with the uniformly friendly relations between Athens and the Macedonian king to which other sources testify. Herodotus, however, goes on to relate (IX. 4, 5) the episode of the stoning of *Lycidas* (cf. *infra* § 122) for proposing that a similar offer of Mardonius, conveyed this time by one Murychides, should be accepted; and we can hardly help concluding that Lycurgus has simply confused Alexander's mission with the Lycidas incident. (Cf. Macan, *Herod.* Bks. VII–IX, vol. II, p. 41.)—**γῆν καὶ ὕδωρ**: 'earth and water,' the Persian tokens of submission.—**μικροῦ δεῖν**: infin. absol., 'almost': Goodwin, § 779.

ὅπου δὲ...ἦ που κ.τ.λ.] 'When therefore they thought fit to exact vengeance for mere words, they would have refrained, I imagine, from visiting with severe penalties a man who had in deed given over their city to the mercy of their enemies': for this type of sentence, in which ὅπου (in a causal sense) introduces a case just established, or not disputed, with ἤ που introducing an *à fortiori* argument based upon it ('much more' or 'much less,' as the sense requires), cf. Andoc. *De Myst.* § 86 ὅπου οὖν ἀγράφῳ νόμῳ οὐκ ἔξεστι χρήσασθαι, ἦ που ἀγράφῳ γε ψηφίσματι παντάπασιν οὐ δεῖ χρήσασθαι, *Ib.* § 90, Isocr. *De Pace* § 24, etc. The main clause with ἤ που appears in such cases either as a *statement* or as a *question* (both sarcastic), and some passages (like the present one) seem capable of being taken as either. [Rehd. and Thalh. place a point of interrogation after ἐκόλασαν: I follow Mätzner (Sch., Bl.) in omitting it.]—**τοῦ λόγου...ἔργῳ**: a somewhat forced example of the favourite antithesis. τοῦ λόγου refers more specifically to A.'s message: A. offended only in *words*, L. in *deeds*.—**οὐ μεγάλαις...ἐκόλασαν**: οὐ by position belongs to μεγάλαις perhaps rather than to ἐκόλασαν, but the sense is the same: 'I presume they would have visited with *light* (οὐ μεγάλαις) penalties'...'I presume they would have *refrained-from-visiting* (οὐκ ἐκόλασαν) with heavy penalties.'

§ 72. ἐνενήκοντα μὲν ἔτη] ἑβδομήκοντα [to which Taylor (Bl.) corrected ἔνεν. of the MSS., and which Lyc. may really have written, for numerals are notoriously liable to confusion] would certainly agree better with the figures of other writers; but there is nothing intrinsically improbable in ἐνενήκοντα, for Lyc., whom we have already detected in an error of 200 years in regard to Messene (*supra* § 62 *n.*), might quite well be 20 years out in his reckoning here. The *terminus ad quem* of the first Athenian empire was no doubt Aegospotami (405 B.C.): the *terminus a quo* seems to have been less certain. [Lysias] (II. § 55) speaks of 70 years; Isocr. *Paneg.* § 106, 70 years, *Panath.* § 56, 65 years; Dem. *Phil.* III. § 23, 73 years. If we take in conjunction with Dem. *l.c.*, [Dem.] *De Syntax.* [or. XIII] § 26 πέντε μὲν καὶ τετταράκοντ' ἔτη τῶν Ἑλλήνων ἦρξαν ἑκόντων ἐκεῖνοι (sc. οἱ πρόγονοι), where ἑκόντων means 'up to the Peloponnesian War,' 432–431 B.C., Dem.'s 73 years will be as nearly as possible 477–405 B.C., giving as the (usually accepted) *terminus a quo* the capture of Sestus.

Φοινίκην δὲ καὶ Κ. ἐπόρθησαν] Perhaps a rhetorical exaggeration of the victory gained by the Athenians off Salamis in Cyprus over a combined Phoenician and Cilician fleet, after raising the siege of Citium, in the course of which Cimon had died (*c.* 449 B.C.): Thuc. I. 112 Κίμωνος δὲ ἀποθανόντος... ἀπεχώρησαν ἀπὸ Κιτίου, καὶ πλεύσαντες ὑπὲρ Σαλαμῖνος τῆς ἐν Κύπρῳ Φοίνιξι καὶ Κίλιξιν ἐναυμάχησαν καὶ ἐπεζομάχησαν ἅμα, καὶ νικήσαντες ἀμφότερα ἀπεχώρησαν ἐπ᾿ οἴκου. The objection that this victory was some 18 years later than that at the Eurymedon, and would naturally have been referred to *after* and not *before* the latter, need not be regarded as serious in an orator whose strong point is not historical accuracy (see notes on the two preceding §§), and who at best is summing up in a few graphic touches the main features of Graeco-Asiatic relations over an extended period.

ἐπ᾿ Εὐρυμέδοντι] 'at the Eurymedon,' a river in Pamphylia, where the Greeks under Cimon won a brilliant double victory by sea and land over the Persian fleet and army (*c.* 467): Thuc. I. 100; Diod. XI. 60–62; Plut. *Vit. Cim.* 12, 13.

ἑκατὸν δὲ τριήρεις...ἔλαβον] Thuc. *l.c.* καὶ εἶλον τριήρεις Φοινίκων καὶ διέφθειραν τὰς πάσας ἐς διακοσίας, which seems to mean, as we say, 'they took *or* destroyed 200 in all.' Plut. *Cim.* 12 *ad fin.* makes them *capture* 200. If Lycurgus' figures are to be pressed, we may suppose (*a*) that he is giving the number of vessels *captured* at the Eurymedon, as opp. to those *destroyed* (cf. Diod. XI. 60 and inscr. *ibid.* 62, which, however, may not be relevant); (*b*) that he is confusing the victory at the Eurymedon with a later victory (itself a confusion with that won at Salamis, *supra*?) off Cyprus, attributed to Cimon by Diod. and Plut., in which the former (XII. 3) makes him capture '100 vessels with their crews'; (*c*) that he is not referring to the immediate results of the Eurymedon victory at all, but to the results of operations extending over a considerable period.

§ 73. τὸ κεφάλαιον τῆς νίκης] 'to crown their victory,' an expression roughly in apposition with the thought of the sentence,

§ 73]   NOTES   143

like πᾶν τοὐναντίον, etc.: cf. *infra* § 92 τοῦτ' αὐτὸ πρῶτον, κ.τ.λ.: Madvig, § 19, R. 3, § 31, *c*.

ἀγαπήσαντες [ἔστησαν]] See Crit. App.

ὅρους τοῖς βαρβάροις πήξαντες κ.τ.λ.] 'having fixed for the barbarian bounds which were to guarantee the freedom of Greece, and forbidden him to overstep these, they made a covenant that he should not sail with a ship of war inside the Cyanean islands and Phaselis.'—This 'bridling of the barbarian' is a favourite topic with the Greek orators, and with the present passage should be compared the substantially similar statements and language of Isocr. *Paneg.* § 118, *Areop.* § 80, *Panath.* § 59; Dem. *F.L.* § 273; Plut. *Vit. Cim.* 13; Diod. XII. 4. All the passages cited agree with Lycurgus in respect of the sea-limit prescribed, except that Dem. and Plut. substitute 'the Chelidonian islands' [S.W. of Phaselis] for Phaselis; the land-limit (which Lycurgus omits) is specified by Isocr. (*Areop.*, *Panath.*, *ll.cc.*) as 'this side the river Halys' (ἐντὸς Ἅλυος ποταμοῦ), by Dem. and Plut., *ll.cc.*, as 'within a day's ride of the sea,' and by Diod., *l.c.*, as 'within a three days' march of the sea.' The last-mentioned further makes 'the independence of all the Greek cities in Asia' one of the articles subscribed to by the Persian.

From a comparison of Lycurgus and the other authorities quoted, it further appears that Lycurgus, Plutarch and Diodorus expressly, and Isocrates and Demosthenes presumably, connect this circumscription of Persian power with the victory at the Eurymedon: sometimes it is represented as an *ipso facto* result of that victory (Isocr. *Paneg.* § 118, *Areop.* § 80), but Isocr. at another place (*Paneg.* § 120), and Dem., Plut. and Diod., *ll.cc.*, as Lycurgus here, speak of a definite 'peace' (εἰρήνη) or 'convention' (συνθῆκαι) concluded between Athens and Persia. Dem., Plut. and Diod. all name Callias as the Athenian ambassador to Persia, though the first two are sharply at variance as to the treatment accorded him on his return (Dem. *l.c.* Καλλίαν τὸν Ἱππονίκου...ὅτι δῶρα λαβεῖν ἔδοξε πρεσβεύσας, μικροῦ ἀπέκτειναν, Plut. *l.c.* φασὶ δὲ καὶ βωμὸν εἰρήνης διὰ ταῦτα τοὺς Ἀθηναίους ἱδρύσασθαι, καὶ Κ. τὸν πρεσβεύσαντα τιμῆσαι διαφερόντως). Plut. further mentions that a copy of the convention was to be found 'in the collection of Craterus' (flor. *c.* 250 B.C.—*ἐν τοῖς ψηφίσμασιν ἃ συνήγαγε Κρατερός*), but Theopompus (historian and pupil of Isocr.) maintained that the convention was a fabrication. (See Sandys on Isocr. *Paneg.* §§ 118, 120.)

The whole subject of the so-called 'Peace of Callias' (or Cimon), which is now generally dated (by those who accept it) to *c.* 448 B.C., or some twenty years later than the victory at the Eurymedon, is evidently wrapt in an obscurity of long standing, and modern historians are divided in opinion as to its historicity. We may perhaps safely assume that a definite understanding resulting in peace was come to between Athens and Persia about the date mentioned, but that the conditions subscribed to by the latter were in course of time much exaggerated by Athenian vanity, which required, at a later date, a plausible off-set to the discreditable Peace of Antalcidas (386 B.C.). In particular, the limit prescribed for the operations of the Persian land forces (the river Halys) is ridiculous, and the Great King 'certainly did not stoop to the humiliation of formally acknowledging the independence of the Greek cities of Asia.' Bury, *H.G.* (1900), p. 360. See also Grote, *H.G.* (1904), vol. IV. pp. 422–8; Holm, *H.G.* vol. II. pp. 176–8.—**μακρῷ πλοίῳ**: 'i.q. *navis longa*, the long and narrow ship-of-war)(στρογγύλη ναῦς, ὁλκάς, γαῦλος, *navis oneraria*, the rounded and roomy merchant-vessel' (Sandys on Isocr. *Paneg.* § 118, *s.vv.* μακρὸν πλοῖον).—**Κυανέων ...Φασηλίδος**: the Cyanean islands (or rocks—otherwise the Symplegades) were situated at the entrance to the Euxine (Black Sea): Phaselis was a sea-coast town of Lycia, standing on a headland overlooking the Pamphylian gulf. 'The light sailing-boat called the *phaselus* is supposed to have been invented there, and was commonly represented on the coins of the place.' Sandys, *l.c.* [The dictt., however, derive from φάσηλος, *phaselus*, = 'kidney-bean,' from the likeness of the ship in question to a bean-pod.]

§ 76] NOTES 145

§ 74. οἴεσθ' ἄν...τούτων ἄν τι γενέσθαι] 'ἄν is sometimes used twice, or even three times, with *the same verb*...to make the conditional force felt through the whole, especially when the connexion is broken by intermediate clauses': Goodwin, § 223.

γενέσθαι...κατοικεῖν] 'would have been achieved'...'would still be inhabiting.'—ὑμᾶς is necessary to distinguish the subject of κατοικεῖν from that of γενέσθαι, and is also intended to balance the ὑμᾶς which follows ᾐσχύνθη as obj. below.

c. 18. §§ 75–78. *Your attitude towards such cases as Leocrates' is attested by your ancient laws and by the oath which all the citizens swear when they come to man's estate. If Leocrates took that oath, he has palpably perjured himself; if he did not, he has manifestly made up his mind to shirk his duty from the first. The oath you shall now hear. Leocrates has flouted every clause of it. Will you reserve your vengeance for those who have violated but one clause, and so put a premium upon great crimes?*

§ 75. τίνα τρόπον νενομίκατε] 'what your standing attitude is to cases like these,' lit. 'what manner you have adopted (made customary).'—περὶ τούτων: τούτων may be either masc. referring to τοὺς κακοὺς of the previous sentence, or neut. referring to L.'s actions, the latter being the more probable.

πῶς ἔχετε ταῖς διανοίαις] Cf. *supra* § 48 οὐχ ὁμοίως ἔχουσιν... ταῖς εὐνοίαις *n.*

ὅμως καίπερ πρὸς εἰδότας διελθεῖν] i.q. καίπερ πρὸς εἰδότας, ὅμως διελθεῖν. For the position of ὅμως close to the protasis, though really belonging to the verb of the apodosis, cf. Thuc. VIII. 93 οἱ τετρακόσιοι...ὅμως καὶ τεθορυβημένοι ξυνελέγοντο = καίπερ τεθορυβημένοι, ὅμως ξ., and other exx. quoted by L.S. *s.v.* ὅμως, II.—πρὸς εἰδότας διελθεῖν: so Thuc. II. 36 μακρηγορεῖν ἐν εἰδόσιν.

ταῦτα] i.e. the laws and similar institutions.

οἷς ἂν προσέχητε] cf. *supra* § 10 προσέχειν τούτῳ τῷ ἀγῶνι *n.*

§ 76. ἐπειδὰν...ἐγγραφῶσι καὶ ἔφηβοι γένωνται] 'whenever they are enrolled in the public register and rank as *ephebi*.'—

P. L. 10

The institution of ἐφηβεία at Athens comes into prominence in the second half of the 4th cent. B.C. and appears to have been an elaboration of a system of training for the Athenian youth, mainly military in character, which was in vogue as early, at least, as the time of Thucydides. On attaining the age of 18, the youth passed a scrutiny (δοκιμασία) and was enrolled in the register of his deme (τὸ ληξιαρχικὸν γραμματεῖον). For the next two years he ranked as an ἔφηβος and underwent a course of training at the public expense, under the supervision of a chief officer (κοσμητής) who was assisted by ten σωφρονισταί. For the first year the ephebi were charged with police duty at Munychia and along the coast; in the second year, after receiving a shield and spear from the state, they patrolled the frontiers or garrisoned the forts (cf. the older περίπολοι). On the occasion of receiving his arms, or perhaps when he entered upon his course of discipline, the ephebus took an oath of loyalty to his country at the temple of Aglaurus (see *infra*). The ephebi of each tribe messed together, somewhat after the Spartan manner, and there was a uniform ephebic dress, consisting of a dark mantle and a broad-brimmed hat. Much of our information regarding the 'epheby' is derived from a body of 'ephebic' inscriptions, the earliest dating from *c.* 334 B.C., embodying lists of ephebi or complimentary decrees respecting them. In the course of the third and following cents. B.C. the military and gymnastic training was supplemented, and to some extent replaced, by courses in philosophy, rhetoric and science, and the whole system corresponded more or less to a modern university education. See Aristotle, 'Αθ. Πολ. c. 42, with Sandys' notes; A. Dumont, *L'Éphébie attique*; P. Girard in Darem. and Sag. III. pp. 621 ff. (1891).

τὰ ἱερὰ ὅπλα] i.e. the shield and spear given by the state.—καταισχυνεῖν, etc.: the *fut.* infins. refer of course to ὅρκος, ὃν ὀμνύουσι πάντες οἱ πολῖται, the substance of which they embody.

ὃν εἰ μὲν ὀμώμοκε] an artificial *dilemma*: the speaker does not doubt that L., as a matter of fact, took the oath in his time.

§ 77] NOTES 147

εὐθὺς δηλός ἐστι παρασκευασάμενος] 'he has plainly made up his mind to evade his duty from the first.'—For παρασκευάζεσθαι, of deliberate intention, cf. Dem. *Lept.* § 143 εἴ τις μεγάλας τὰς τιμωρίας τῶν ἀδικημάτων τάττοι, οὐκ ἂν αὐτός γ' ἀδικεῖν παρεσκευάσθαι δόξαι.—<ὡς> **οὐδὲν ποιήσων**: see Crit. App.—
ἀνθ' ὧν: i.q. ὥστε, 'wherefore,' drawing the inference from the argument preceding.

§ 77. <ΟΡΚΟΣ> The 'ephebic' oath which follows is preserved in Poll. VIII. 105, Stobae. *Floril.* XLIII. 48.

τὸν παραστάτην ὅτῳ ἂν στοιχήσω] 'the comrade by whose side I shall be ranged' in battle: παραστάτης is one's *comrade-on-the-flank*, as προστάτης is one's *front-rank-man*, and ἐπιστάτης one's *rear-rank-man*: Arist. *Eth. Nic.* v. 2. 5 εἰ ἐγκατέλιπε τὸν παραστάτην, ἐπὶ δειλίαν (sc. γίνεται ἡ ἐπαναφορά, 'the act is referred to cowardice'), Soph. *Ant.* 671.—στοιχήσω: of arrangement in 'rows' or 'ranks' (στοῖχοι).

ἱερῶν...ὁσίων] *sacra et profana*: Thuc. II. 52 (of the plague-stricken Athenians) ἐς ὀλιγωρίαν ἐτράποντο καὶ ἱερῶν καὶ ὁσίων ὁμοίως, etc.

ἀρείω] 'better' (√AR, *ἄρω, ἀραρίσκω) is the comp. corresponding roughly to ἄριστος: epic and tragic, rare in prose.—
ὅσης ἂν π.: = τοσαύτης ὅσην ἂν π.

εὐηκοήσω τῶν ἀεὶ κραινόντων] εὐηκοήσω = *dicto audiens ero*: apparently a ἅπαξ λεγόμενον, though εὐήκοος is found, and δυσήκοος and δυσηκοεῖν in later Gk.—τῶν ἀεὶ κραινόντων: 'the rulers for the time being': the verb is poetical. [I have adopted κραινόντων (Blass) for κρινόντων of the MSS.]

τοῖς θεσμοῖς τοῖς ἱδρυμένοις] 'the established ordinances': θεσμὸς was a word of more archaic and solemn flavour than νόμος: cf. *supra* § 64 τῶν ἀρχαίων νομοθετῶν *n.*

ὁμοφρόνως] with πείσομαι.

ἀναιρῇ] conative, 'seek to subvert,' *de medio tollere*.

οὐκ ἐπιτρέψω] Cf. *supra* § 13 *n.*

ἱερὰ τὰ πάτρια] Cf. *supra* § 25 τὰ ἱερὰ τὰ πατρῷα *n.*

ἵστορες θεοί] 'as witness the gods,' etc. ἵστωρ occurs twice in

Homer (*Il.* XVIII. 501 ἐπὶ ἴστορι πεῖραρ ἐλέσθαι, XXIII. 486 ἴστορα δ' Ἀτρείδην Ἀγαμέμνονα θείομεν ἄμφω), clearly in the sense of 'judge,' 'umpire.' θεοὺς πάντας ἴστορας ποιεύμενος is quoted from an oath in Hippocrates (L.S. *s.v.*). The word no doubt comes from the rt. ϝιδ (seen in εἶδον, οἶδα, etc.), as is shown by the first Homeric example and also by the occurrence of ϝίστορες (= 'arbitrators') in inscrr.

Ἄγλαυρος] It was 'in the temple of Aglaurus' that the *ephebi* took the oath: cf. Dem. *F.L.* § 303 τὸν ἐν τῷ τῆς Ἀγλαύρου τῶν ἐφήβων ὅρκον. Herod. (VIII. 53) makes the Persians scale the Acropolis at the point where this shrine was situated (on the north side, near the cave of Pan), and describes Aglaurus as the daughter of Cecrops (κατὰ τὸ ἱρὸν τῆς Κέκροπος θυγατρὸς Ἀγλαύρου). She and her two sisters, Pandrosos and Herse, were charged by Athena (according to the legend) with the keeping of the chest in which was the child Erichthonius: Aglaurus and Herse, who proved false to their trust, were driven mad and threw themselves from the rocks of the Acropolis (Paus. I. 18; Eur. *Ion*, 270 *sqq.*). Another legend, however, preserved in Ulpian (quoted by Shilleto on Dem. *F.L. l.c.*) connected the shrine with the self-immolation of 'Aglaurus' on behalf of the state; and the occasion, further, was represented as the war of Erechtheus and Eumolpus (*infra* §§ 98, 99). 'Aglaurus' was thus apparently identified with the daughter whom the oracle required Erechtheus to sacrifice, but whom Lycurgus does not name (τὴν θυγατέρα εἰ θύσειε, § 99). Ulpian says simply ἐάν τις ἀνέλῃ ἑαυτὸν ὑπὲρ τῆς πόλεως, but he follows immediately with: ἡ τοίνυν Ἄγραυλος ἑκοῦσα αὑτὴν ἐξέδωκεν εἰς θάνατον. ἔρριψε γὰρ ἑαυτὴν ἐκ τοῦ τείχους—which last statement looks like a return to Aglaurus, daughter of Cecrops. He concludes: εἶτα ἀπαλλαγέντες τοῦ πολέμου, ἱερὸν ὑπὲρ τούτου ἐστήσαντο αὐτῇ περὶ τὰ προπύλαια τῆς πόλεως, καὶ ἐκεῖσε ὤμνυον ('went there to take the oath') οἱ ἔφηβοι μέλλοντες ἐξιέναι εἰς πόλεμον. On the whole, the statement of Ulpian seems to point to a very general confusion between Aglaurus, daughter of Cecrops, and (a namesake?) the daughter of Erechtheus and Praxithea, who sacrificed herself for her country. What seems to be certain is that Aglaurus (as well as Pandrosos and Herse) was originally a title of Athena herself, and we may suppose that the legends connected with 'Aglaurus,' which probably have reference to an ancient human sacrifice, were only evolved long after the goddess and these titles had parted company. Aglaurus (Agraulus), in fact, to adapt Prof. Bury's dictum on Lycurgus (the Spartan lawgiver), 'was not a woman; she was only a goddess.'

Ἐνυάλιος Ἄρης] These words probably denote one deity, not two; for Ἐνυάλιος is an epithet of Ares in his special character as war-god (Hom. *Il.* XVII. 210 Ἄρης δεινὸς ἐνυάλιος), or occurs absol. as his name (*Ib.* XX. 69 ἄντα δ' Ἐνυαλίοιο θεὰ γλαυκῶπις Ἀθήνη: cf. Soph. *Ai.* 179, Eur. *Andr.* 1016), while the two are distinguished by Ar. *Pax* 457 and later writers. The names are used of one deity in an oath on an Arcadian inscr. published in 1906. There was a shrine of Enyalius in Salamis, founded by Solon to commemorate the recovery of the island from the Megarians. (See Jebb on *Ai. l.c.* and App.)

Θαλλώ, Αὐξώ, Ἡγεμόνη] 'Growth,' 'Increase,' 'Guidance': the first, one of the Horae; the second and third, two of the Charites (Graces).

καλός γ'...ὁ ὅρκος] 'An honourable and holy oath!' we may say, though the adjs. are, of course, predicative.

τίνα δ' ἂν τρόπον] Cf. *supra* § 60 ὃν δὲ τρόπον n.

§ 78. ποῦ] 'how?,' perhaps, rather than 'where?,' as frequently: cf. Soph. *O. T.* 390 ποῦ σὺ μάντις εἶ σαφής; Dem. *c. Aristocr.* § 58 ποῦ δὲ γένοιτ' ἂν ταῦτα;

τίνι δ' ἂν...παρέδωκε μείζονα—προδοσίᾳ;] 'to whom would he have handed over his country in an enhanced condition—by treason?': the question has specific reference to the fourth clause of the oath above quoted (τὴν πατρίδα δὲ οὐκ ἐλάττω παραδώσω), which the orator does not systematically pursue further, but rounds off with the sarcastic προδοσίᾳ; which paves the way for the concluding τὸ γὰρ...ὑποχείριός ἐστιν. It seems an open question whether τίνι should be taken as neut. ('by what?'), in app. with προδοσίᾳ (so Sofer), or personally ('to whom?'): the latter is favoured, I think, by τοῖς πολεμίοις following, and has perhaps some support from Lys. XIII. § 62 οἱ στρατηγήσαντες ὑμῖν πολλάκις μείζω τὴν πόλιν τοῖς διαδεχομένοις στρατηγοῖς παρεδίδοσαν (so Rehd., *ad loc.*).

τὸ γὰρ τούτου μέρος] Cf. *supra* § 17 τὸ καθ' αὑτὸν μέρος *n.*

ὑπ. ἐστιν] The vivid present represents the state of things that might have resulted from L.'s desertion as actually existing.

εἶτα] Cf. *supra* § 27 ἔπειτα τὸν προδόντα...οὐκ ἀποκτενεῖτε; *n.*

τίνας οὖν τιμωρήσεσθε;] 'whom then *will* you punish?'

ἆρα] 'one must conclude': cf. *supra* § 27 *n.*

μεγάλα ἀδικεῖν] 'to commit great offences': Madvig, § 27.

εἰ φανεῖσθε...ὀργιζόμενοι] 'if you shall show that you keep your anger rather for small offences': μᾶλλον perhaps with ἐπὶ τοῖς μικροῖς, *potius de parvis*, rather than with ὀργιζόμενοι, *magis irati*, though the sense is practically the same.

c. 19. §§ 79–82. *Let me remind you that it is an oath that keeps the democracy together. The constitution consists of three elements—magistrate, judge, private individual—and all three give this pledge, the breaking of which exposes them to the wrath of the gods even if they escape punishment at the hands of men. The oath taken by the Greeks at Plataea, modelled on that which is customary among you, is instructive as an indication of the spirit which inspired it. This oath they scrupulously observed. It would be outrageous to allow the glory of Athens, won by your ancestors at such cost, to be tarnished by such conduct as the defendant's.*

§ 79. καὶ μήν] introducing a new argument, as regularly in the orators: in tragedy, to mark the entrance of a new character on the stage.

καὶ τοῦθ'] so often κἀκεῖνο (cf. *illud*), referring to, and explained by, the ὅτι clause following: cf. *supra* § 14 *n.*

τὸ συνέχον τὴν δημοκρατίαν] cf. Andoc. *De Myst.* § 9 ὅπερ καὶ συνέχει μόνον τὴν πόλιν (sc. τὸ ψηφίζεσθαι κατὰ τοὺς ὅρκους), Dem. *c. Timocr.* § 2 ἃ δοκεῖ συνέχειν τὴν πολιτείαν, τὰ δικαστήρια.

§ 79] NOTES

τρία γάρ ἐστιν] For the didactic tone, cf. *supra* § 4 τρία γάρ ἐστι τὰ μέγιστα, κ.τ.λ., § 10 δύο γάρ ἐστι τὰ παιδεύοντα τοὺς νέους, κ.τ.λ.

ὁ ἰδιώτης] the term here means simply 'one who takes no part in public affairs,' 'private individual': as such it is contrasted with βασιλεύς, ἄρχων, στρατηγός, δικαστής, πολιτευόμενος (v. L.S. *s.v.* II). Rather different is the meaning at *supra* § 31 ἀναβοήσεται αὐτίκα ὡς ἰδιώτης ὤν, where the contrast is with 'the professional speaker': see note.

ταύτην πίστιν δίδωσιν] 'gives *this as a pledge*')(ταύτην τὴν πίστιν = 'this pledge.' ' If there is anything in Greek [prose] more certain than another, it is that τοῦτο πρᾶγμα, *minus* the article, for *this affair*, is a solecism of the grossest kind' (Hickie on Andoc. *De Myst.* § 39, where he enumerates the uses of οὗτος in which the article may be omitted, and cites as parallels to the passage in the text, Aeschin. *Fals. Leg.* § 40 ἐξηγητὴν τοῦτον λαβών, 'him as an instructor,' Isocr. *De Pace*, § 4 ταύτην τέχνην ἔχω, 'I have this as my business' (τὴν τέχνην Blass), Xen. *Oecon.* XI. 14 περιπάτῳ τούτῳ χρῶμαι, 'this as a constitutional exercise').

εἰκότως · τοὺς μὲν γάρ] cf. *supra* § 47 *n*.

πολλοὶ ἤδη...ἀπελύθησαν, ἀλλὰ καὶ κ.τ.λ.] 'many before now ...have not only escaped (i.e. it often happens that people not only escape)...but actually go unpunished for such crimes for the rest of their lives': the aorist is here seen in the stage of transition from the ordinary to the *gnomic* use, a circumstance which makes it more easily coupled with the present (ἀθῷοί εἰσι), though the present also denotes the *state* of impunity as opposed to the *act* of escape (ἀπελύθησαν). Cf. Thuc. II. 89 πολλὰ στρατόπεδα ἤδη ἔπεσεν ὑπ' ἐλασσόνων, i.e. 'it often happens that great armaments are overthrown by small,' and Goodwin, *M. T.* §§ 155–157.—**τὸν ἄλλον χρόνον**: 'for all future time.'—**τῶν ἀδικημάτων**: i.e. from the consequences of them, 'unpunished for' them.

εἰ μὴ αὐτός, οἱ παῖδές γε κ.τ.λ.] The classic example is perhaps Glaucus, the Lacedaemonian, who repudiated a deposit: Her. VI. 86 Γλαύκου νῦν οὔτε τι ἀπόγονόν ἐστι οὐδὲν οὔτ' ἱστίη οὐδεμία νομιζομένη εἶναι Γλαύκου· ἐκτέτριπταί τε πρόρριζος ἐκ Σπάρτης.

Cf. Lys. VI. § 20 οὔτε γὰρ ὁ θεὸς παραχρῆμα κολάζει (ἀλλ' αὕτη μέν ἐστιν ἀνθρωπίνη δίκη)· πολλαχόθεν δὲ ἔχω τεκμαιρόμενος εἰκάζειν, ὁρῶν καὶ ἑτέρους ἠσεβηκότας χρόνῳ δεδωκότας δίκην, καὶ τοὺς ἐξ ἐκείνων διὰ τὰ τῶν προγόνων ἁμαρτήματα, Cic. *De Nat. Deor.* III. c. 38 (§ 90).—For **περιπίπτει**, agreeing with the nearer subject, cf. Madvig, § 2. *d.* R. 1: [Xen.] *Rep. Ath.* I. 2 Ἀθήνησι καὶ οἱ πένητες καὶ ὁ δῆμος πλέον ἔχει...τῶν πλουσίων.

§ 80. ταύτην πίστιν ἔδοσαν αὐτοῖς] 'took' or 'bound themselves by' this pledge (strictly 'this *as* a pledge': cf. ταύτην πίστιν δίδωσιν in previous § and *n.*), i.e. by an oath, ὅρκος, with which πίστις here is evidently interchangeable, although the two appear to be distinguished in Arist. *Rhet.* I. 14. 5 οἷον ὅρκους δεξίας πίστεις κ.τ.λ. διδόναι πίστιν (ὅρκον) is usually said of 'tendering an assurance (oath),' i.e. offering to swear to another party, and δέχεσθαι or λαμβάνειν πίστιν (ὅρκον) of 'accepting such a tender from another': Xen. *Cyr.* VII. 1. 44 π. διδόναι καὶ λαμβάνειν, 'to exchange assurances.' When the oath is 'proposed' or 'administered' to oneself, δοῦναι αὐτῷ πίστιν becomes practically = ὅρκον ὀμόσαι, 'to swear an oath.'

οὐ παρ' αὐτῶν εὑρόντες, ἀλλὰ μιμησάμενοι τὸν...εἰθισμένον ὅρκον] The 'customary oath' is apparently the 'ephebic' oath (*supra* § 77), though the 'Plataean' oath quoted does not resemble it very closely.—The historicity of the oath here recorded by Lycurgus as having been taken by the confederate Greeks before Plataea has been generally doubted, both on intrinsic grounds and especially in view of the silence of Herodotus on the subject. Isocrates (*Paneg.* § 156) attributes to the Ionians (after the capture of Miletus, 494 B.C., and the burning by the Persians of the temple of Apollo at Branchidae?) an imprecation, closely parallel to the 'Plataean' oath of Lycurgus, upon those who should seek to restore the burnt shrines; but here again Herodotus and the historians are silent. It may well be, however, that the loyal Greeks resolved not to rebuild the burnt temples—a resolution, indeed, which is quoted by Pausanias (X. 35. 2) as accounting for the ruinous condition of certain notable temples in his own day.

Finally, Theopompus denounced the 'Plataean' oath as an Athenian fabrication. Herodotus, however, *does* record (VII. 132) a solemn oath taken by the Greeks *before Thermopylae* to the effect that 'they would tithe, for the benefit of the god at Delphi, such as, being Greeks, uncompelled submitted to the Persian,' and we may reasonably suppose that the more elaborate formula of Lycurgus, which is repeated elsewhere (e.g. Diod. XI. 29), is 'a mere subsequent development of the short and sensible resolution' mentioned by Herod. *l.c.* See Sandys on Isocr. *Paneg. l.c.*; Macan's *Herodotus*, VII–IX, vol. II., pp. 40, 41.

παλαιῶν ὄντων] concessive.

ὅμως ὡς ἴχνος] i.e. as though it were 'a sketch in outline' which can be filled in: cf. ἰχνογραφία.—See Crit. App.

§ 81. ἀνάστατον] Cf. *supra* § 60 *n*.

τὰς τὰ τοῦ β. προελομένας] 'such as have espoused the cause of the barbarian.'

δεκατεύσω] 'betithe,' i.e. exact a tenth part from, by way of satisfaction; but the word as used in threats is clearly stronger than its literal meaning, and connotes 'signal punishment,' 'utter destruction,' as in its proverbial application to Thebes before Leuctra (371 B.C.): Xen. *Hell.* VI. 3. 20 οἱ Ἀθηναῖοι εἶχον τὴν γνώμην ὡς Θηβαίους τὸ λεγόμενον δὴ δεκατευθῆναι ἐλπὶς εἴη.

ἀνοικοδομήσω] 'rebuild,' *reficere*.

§ 82. ἐνέμειναν ἐν τούτῳ] sc. τῷ ὅρκῳ. The simple dative with ἐμμένω in the transferred sense, 'abide by' (τοῖς ὅρκοις, ταῖς σπονδαῖς, etc.), is usual, but not universal: cf. Thuc. IV. 118 *ad fin.* ἦ μὴν ἐμμενεῖν ἐν ταῖς σπονδαῖς, and Rehd., App. 2, *ad loc.*

πάντων...γενομένων] concessive.

πρός] of relation, 'in face of.'

ὃ καὶ πάντων] Cf. *supra* § 56 ὃ καὶ πάντων γένοιτ' ἂν ἀτοπώτατον *n*.

τοὺς μὲν προγόνους...ὑμᾶς δέ] '*whereas* your ancestors dared to die...*you* decline to punish': cf. *supra* §§ 8, 42, etc.

εὔκλειαν] a word of poetic flavour, like ἐπιτίμιον, αἰών, etc.

ταύτην] For the resumptive pronoun, cf. *supra* §§ 42, 46 *nn*.

c. 20. §§ 83-89. *You of all the Greeks cannot afford to overlook such offences, because your city has always been an ensample of good works to others. Your ancient kings, like Codrus, elected to die on behalf of their country, and they have found in it honourable graves. But Leocrates has no lot nor part therein, either in life or in death.*

§ 83. οἷς παραδείγμασι] 'which as examples': παραδ. is predicative. Cf. Dem. *F. L.* § 276 οὐ τοίνυν τὰ παλαί' ἄν τις ἔχοι μόνον εἰπεῖν καὶ διὰ τούτων τῶν παραδειγμάτων ὑμᾶς ἐπὶ τιμωρίαν παρακαλέσαι.

ἀρχαιοτάτη] For Athens' claim to antiquity, cf. §§ 41, 100, and notes.

§ 84. ἐπὶ Κόδρου βασιλεύοντος] Codrus, son of Melanthus, was the last king of Athens, according to the popular tradition, which added that the kingship was abolished because no one was thought worthy to succeed him—'a curious reversal of the usual causes of such a revolution' (Bury, *H. G.* (1900), p. 169). He is most probably a fictitious character, and the exploits attributed to him are mainly of late origin. Lyc.'s account here of the circumstances in which he met his death—his disguise and his encounter with enemy soldiers—agrees in the main with that of later authorities: peculiar to Lyc. are (1) the famine, as the motive of the Dorian invasion; (2) the communication of the oracle to the Athenians by Cleomantis. According to other accounts, the oracle was unknown to the Athenians, but Codrus got wind of it. For the literature of the subject, see further Rehd., App. 3, p. 167.

Πελοποννησίοις ... ἔδοξε ... ἐξαναστήσαντας κατανείμασθαι] The change of the participle in a case of this kind to agreement with the *accusatival subject* of the infinitive may be said to be the rule rather than the exception: cf. Thuc. I. 53 ἔδοξεν οὖν αὐτοῖς... ἐμβιβάσαντας...προσπέμψαι, IV. 2 εἶπον δὲ τούτοις...παραπλέοντας ...ἐπιμεληθῆναι, Andoc. *De Myst.* § 9 ὑμῶν δέομαι...ἀκροασαμένους ...ψηφίζεσθαι, *Ibid.* § 37, Dem. *F. L. ad fin.,* ὑμῖν συμφέρει ...τιμωρησαμένους παράδειγμα ποιῆσαι.—Πελοποννησίοις: partly with γενομένης ἀφορίας, partly with ἔδοξε.—**γενομένης ἀφορίας**

§ 85] NOTES 155

(ἀ-priv., φέρω): 'on the occasion of a famine in their country.'—
ἐξαναστήσαντας: ἐξανίστημι (lit. 'make to rise') is said of the wholesale removal of a population: Her. I. 171 τοὺς Κᾶρας... Δωριέες τε καὶ Ἴωνες ἐξανέστησαν ἐκ τῶν νήσων, II. 171 ἐξαναστάσης πάσης Πελοποννήσου ὑπὸ Δωριέων, Soph. *Ant.* 297 τόδ' (sc. ὁ ἄργυρος) ἄνδρας ἐξανίστησιν δόμων. Cf. ἀνάστατος, and *supra* § 60 *n.*

ἀποστείλαντες...ἐπηρώτων] The absol. use of ἀποστέλλω (cf. πέμπω) is exactly the Eng. '*sent* and asked.'—ἐπηρώτων: the verb is technical of consulting an oracle, as ἀνελεῖν (*infra*) is of the answer: cf. Thuc. I. 25, etc.—εἰ λήψονται: their question was ληψόμεθα; 'shall we take?': both mood and tense are preserved in the indirect question in historic sequence: cf. Dem. *F. L.* § 122 ἐβουλεύοντο...τίν' αὐτοῦ καταλείψουσιν (direct: τίνα καταλείψομεν;): Goodwin, § 669. 2.

ἀνελόντος...τοῦ θεοῦ] 'on the god answering them, that,' etc.: v. L.S. *s.v.* ἀναιρέω, III, and cf. Thuc. I. 25 ὁ δὲ (sc. θεὸς) αὐτοῖς ἀνεῖλε παραδοῦναι κ.τ.λ.—ἐστράτευον: 'set about their expedition,' perhaps, if we press the tense.

§ 85. δι' ἀπορρήτων] 'secretly,' 'confidentially': cf. Plat. *Rep.* 378 A δι' ἀπορρ. ἀκούειν ὡς ὀλιγίστους, Aeschin. *Ctes.* § 96. So also ἐν ἀπορρήτῳ: Andoc. *De Myst.* § 45, Plat. *Theaet.* 152 C, etc.

οὕτως...εὔνους ἔχοντες διετέλουν] 'to such an extent, it would appear, did they continue to enjoy the good-will even of foreigners': though οὕτως, *tam*, is frequently separated from its adj. (cf. οὕτως ἦσαν...γενναῖοι a few lines below), the distance between οὕτως and εὔνους here suggests that each should be given a separate force: the distinction, it is true, is rather fine, but may be represented perhaps as that between *usque adeo etiam externis sui studiosis utebantur* and *tam studiosis...utebantur.*—τοὺς ἔξωθεν ἀνθρώπους, 'foreigners': cf. the characteristic οἱ ἐκ τῆς πόλεως, 'the people *in* the city,' etc.

τὴν θρεψαμένην] sc. γῆν or πατρίδα. But *supra* § 47 τὴν θρέψασαν αὐτούς *n.*

διεκαρτέρουν εἰς τὴν π.] 'staunchly stood by their country': so also L.S. *s.v.* διακαρτερέω. [I cannot agree with Rehd. that εἰς τὴν π. is to be joined with κατακλῃσθέντες, if ἐπολιορκοῦντο καὶ is kept: see Crit. App.]

§ 86. ἑτέραν μεταλλάξαι...χώραν] Cf. *supra* § 50 τὸν βίον μετήλλαξαν *n.*

γοῦν] introducing, as often, an actual illustration of a general statement: cf. §§ 71, 95.

προσέχειν ὅταν τελευτήσῃ τὸν βίον] 'to have regard to the moment of his death,' i.e. in relation to the oracle: for προσέχειν, cf. *supra* § 10 *n.*

κατὰ τὰς πύλας ὑποδύντα] There are difficulties about taking these words in the sense which at first sight they seem to require, viz. 'slipping out by the gate,' a statement which (leaving out of account the equation ὑποδῦναι='slip *out*' (from), in the absence of an accompanying gen. as at *Od.* VI. 127 θάμνων ὑπεδύσετο, XX. 53 κακῶν ὑποδύσεαι) must be said to convey a somewhat superfluous piece of information. Nor does ὑπεκδύντα, Ernesti and Schulz (Bl., Sofer), apparently in the sense of ὑπεξελθόντα, mend matters, for ὑπεκδῦναι is properly said of 'stealing unobserved from a place of concealment' (cf. Her. I. 10); but even admitting that the word can mean, absolutely, 'to make one's way out *secretly* or *unobserved*,' this does not go well with κατὰ τὰς πύλας—the last place where one might expect to do so. Rehdantz, in the face of these difficulties, 'sees only the possibility of taking κατὰ τὰς πύλας with συλλέγειν,' and Sofer, reading ὑπεκδύντα, takes κατὰ τὰς π. both with the ptcp. and with συλλέγειν. Rehd. further explains ὑποδύντα as 'stooping so as to conceal his kingly stature,' which I greatly doubt: he would have to stoop to gather his wood, if for nothing else, and in any case we should expect this to be expressed not by ὑποδῦναι but by κύπτω (or ἐγκύπτω—cf. Thuc. IV. 4). Madvig, who corrects to κᾆτα, thereby making τὰς πύλας the direct obj. of ὑποδύντα, makes the words bear the only sense which seems possible in the Greek, viz. 'slipping under,' 'taking cover in' the gate, which I do not understand.

With the text as it stands, and taking ὑποδύντα in the sense which (I think) most naturally suggests itself, viz. 'going into' or 'under' something, for cover or shelter (Lat. *subire*), I understand Lycurgus to say that Codrus 'donning a beggar's garb and *secreting himself opposite* the gate [till the opportune moment came, as presently explained], set to gathering wood before the city,' and I picture the whole episode thus: Codrus [making his way out of the town—it may have been by the gate] concealed himself in a position from which he could watch for the approach of enemy soldiers: the whole narrative, indeed, assumes that he was expecting them. It was essential to his project that he should himself be the first to encounter them, so as to anticipate any information they might gather as to his personal appearance or his whereabouts—information which they would presumably be very eager to obtain. Immediately he saw what he was looking for, he left his place of concealment, made a feint at woodgathering, and indeed did what he could to put himself in the way of the soldiers and pick a quarrel with them without raising any suspicions in them as to his identity or his purpose. For further discussion of the passage, see Crit. App.

συλλέγειν] 'set to gathering': impf. infin.: Goodwin, § 119.

ἀποκτεῖναι τῷ δρεπάνῳ προσπεσόντα] τῷ δρεπάνῳ is ἀπὸ κοινοῦ with ἀποκτ. and προσπ.—προσπεσόντα, for which Blass reads παίσαντα out of Suidas' πλήξαντα, seems well enough supported by Dem. LIV. 8 Φανοστράτῳ προσπίπτει, 'falls upon (attacks) P.,' and other passages.

§ 87. τῷ Κόδρῳ...τὸν Κόδρον] Blass brackets the first, Taylor the second; but probably both should stand (as Rehd. points out, App. I, *ad loc.*): (*a*) τῷ Κόδρῳ is necessary to show that τὸν δὲ περιλελ. is a subject, not a second object corresponding to τὸν ἕτερον preceding; (*b*) τὸν Κόδρον serves to bring out more sharply the whole point of the narrative.

σπασάμενον] The middle seems more frequent than act. in this sense, but Eur. *Or.* 1194 ξίφος σπάσαντα, *I. T.* 322 φάσγανον σπάσας χερί.

θάψαι] 'for burial': cf. *supra* § 43 τὸ σῶμα παρασχόντα τάξαι *n*.

κατασχεῖν] *occupare*, 'get possession of': note the aorist.

ἡ πόλις...ἔδοσαν] for the plural vb. with collective subject, cf. *infra* § 142 ἡ πόλις ἔθαψαν, Thuc. I. 20 Ἀθηναίων τὸ πλῆθος Ἵππαρχον οἴονται...τύραννον ὄντα ἀποθανεῖν.

αὐτῷ τε καὶ ἐκγόνοις] The article is regularly omitted in this formula.

ἐν πρυτανείῳ...σίτησιν ἔδοσαν] 'granted them perpetual maintenance in the state-hall,' a signal honour at Athens. Besides the πρυτάνεις (the fifty representatives of the φυλὴ πρυτανεύουσα, v. L.S. *s.v.* πρύτανις), who had meals provided for them originally in the πρυτανεῖον, but later in the θόλος or 'Round Room' (for the two buildings are to be carefully distinguished, though their uses seem to have been largely similar), a number of other persons were so entertained for special reasons, whom Pollux (IX. 40) classifies as (1) ambassadors, (2) citizens or others who had done good service to the state (οἱ διὰ πρᾶξίν τινα σιτήσεως ἀξιωθέντες), (3) those who had been granted perpetual maintenance (εἴ τις ἐκ τιμῆς ἀείσιτος ἦν), such as the children of Aristides (Plut. *Arist.* 27) and the descendants of Harmodius and Aristogiton. Dem. *Lept. passim, F. L.* §§ 280, 330, etc.

§ 88. ἀρά γ' ὁμοίως] Cf. *supra* § 70 ἀρά γ' ὅμοιοι τῷ φεύγοντι τὴν πατρίδα κ.τ.λ.; *n.*—See Crit. App.

μονώτατοι] a superlative probably of comic origin: cf. Ar. *Eq.* 352, *Plut.* 182: so μονώτατος just below.

ἐπώνυμοι τῆς χώρας] 'have their names associated with the country,' 'have given their names' to it, as the ἥρωες ἐπώνυμοι were the heroes after whom the Athenian tribes were named: cf. *supra* § 1 τοῖς ἥρωσι τοῖς...ἱδρυμένοις *n*.

ἰσοθέων τιμῶν τετυχηκότες] Cf. Dem. *F. L.* § 280 οὓς (sc. public benefactors) νόμῳ διὰ τὰς εὐεργεσίας ἃς ὑπῆρξαν εἰς ὑμᾶς ἐν ἅπασι τοῖς ἱεροῖς ἐπὶ ταῖς θυσίαις σπονδῶν...κοινωνοὺς πεποίησθε, καὶ ᾄδετε καὶ τιμᾶτ' ἐξ ἴσου τοῖς ἥρωσι καὶ τοῖς θεοῖς.

ὑπὲρ ἧς...ἐσπούδαζον] There is an obvious temptation to insert <ζῶντες> somewhere here, to balance τεθνεῶτες, and give more force to οὔτε ζῶν οὔτε τεθνεὼς immediately following: Lobeck (Es) would place it after γάρ, Halm after ἐσπούδαζον.

ἐκληρονόμουν] 'they received a portion in it,' as of an inheritance: cf. *infra* § 127, Isocr. *Ad Demon.* § 2 πρέπει γὰρ τοὺς παῖδας ὥσπερ τῆς οὐσίας οὕτω καὶ τῆς φιλίας τῆς πατρικῆς κληρονομεῖν.

§ 89. ἐξορισθείη τῆς χώρας] ἐξορίζειν, 'to send beyond the borders,' 'banish,' Lat. *exterminare*: so also ὑπερορίζειν. Cf. *infra* § 113 ἐξορίσαι ἔξω τῆς Ἀττικῆς.

οὐδὲ γὰρ καλόν] *neque enim decet*.

τὴν αὐτήν] sc. χώραν or γῆν.

CC. 21–23. §§ 90–97. *He will perhaps tell you that he would never have stood his trial had he been conscious of guilt—a proof appealed to by every thief and perpetrator of sacrilege; but it is a proof, not of their innocence, but of their effrontery. Let him rather disprove the facts of his voyage and of his residence at Megara. The circumstance of his coming here to answer for his deeds among those whom he wronged is the work of Providence.*

'Quem Iuppiter volt perdere, dementat prius.'

You will remember how divine vengeance overtook Callistratus. The gods survey all human actions, especially such as relate to parents, the dead, and piety towards themselves. 'The Place of the Pious' in Sicily has a useful lesson. Leocrates has sinned against all three—gods, parents, and the dead.

§ 90. ὡς οὐκ ἄν ποτε ὑπέμεινε...συνειδώς] 'that he would never have faced this trial, had he been conscious,' etc.: συνειδώς = εἰ συνῄδει. Cf. Antiph. *De Caed. Herod.* § 93 εὖ δ' ἴστε ὅτι οὐκ ἄν ποτ' ἦλθον εἰς τὴν πόλιν, εἴ τι ξυνῄδειν ἐμαυτῷ τοιοῦτον.

ὥσπερ οὐ πάντας...χρωμένους] For this acc. absol. of a *personal* verb, common with ὡς or ὥσπερ, cf. Plat. *Protag.* 342 C βραχείας ἀναβολὰς φοροῦσιν, ὡς δὴ τούτοις κρατοῦντας τῶν Ἑλλήνων τοὺς Λακεδαιμονίους, Dem. *F. L.* § 189 ταῦτα γὰρ τραγῳδεῖ περιιών, ὥσπερ οὐχὶ τοὺς ἀδικοῦντας τούτων ὄντας προδότας, ἀλλὰ τοὺς τὰ δίκαια ποιοῦντας: Madvig, § 182, Goodwin, § 853.—**καὶ τοὺς κλέπτοντας...ἱεροσυλοῦντας**: καὶ is intensive=*etiam*, and two distinct classes are denoted by the ptcps. though they are served by one article: *quasi vero universi, et (etiam) qui fures qui sacrilegi sint*, etc.

τοῦ πράγματος] The 'anticipated' gen. is no doubt meant to give a pointed balance to τῆς ἀναιδείας.

τεκμηρίῳ...σημεῖον] 'proof'...'evidence.' The *locus classicus* for these terms is Arist. *Rhet.* I. 2. 16 ff., where he says: τῶν δὲ σημείων...τὸ μὲν ἀναγκαῖον τεκμήριον, τὸ δὲ μὴ ἀναγκαῖον ἀνώνυμόν ἐστι κατὰ τὴν διαφοράν. ἀναγκαῖα μὲν οὖν λέγω ἐξ ὧν γίνεται συλλογισμός, 'of signs...that which is necessary is a *demonstration*, that which is not necessary has no distinctive name. By "necessary" signs, I mean the propositions of which a syllogism is composed.' From this it appears that to Arist. σημεῖον is 'proof' in general (whether fallible or not), and the *genus* σημεῖον is divided into two *species*, τεκμήριον and σημεῖον, of which the first is a 'demonstrative' or 'certain' proof, and the second a 'sign' or 'probable argument.' Another definition is found in Antiphon, frag. XXII. 72 (Blass): σημεῖον καὶ τεκμήριον διαφέρει. Ἀ. ἐν τῇ τέχνῃ ('handbook of rhetoric') τὰ μὲν παροιχόμενα σημείοις πιστοῦσθαι, τὰ δὲ μέλλοντα τεκμηρίοις, 'where σημεῖα = indications furnished by facts, τεκμήρια = grounds of conjecture: and so Andoc. *De Pace* § 2 περὶ τῶν μελλόντων' (Jebb on Antiph. *De Caed. Herod.* § 81). But cf. Plato, *Laches* 195 E τὰ σημεῖα...τῶν ἐσομένων. On the whole it seems doubtful whether the use of the terms by Greek writers accords strictly with either definition, though the Aristotelian distinction will generally apply. The words occur frequently in close connexion, as here: cf. Isocr. *Ad Demon.* § 2 τεκμήριον μὲν τῆς πρὸς ὑμᾶς εὐνοίας, σημεῖον δὲ τῆς πρὸς Ἱππόνικον συνηθείας, Dem. *Lept.* § 140 ὅτι παντάπασι φύσεως κακίας σημεῖόν ἐστιν ὁ φθόνος...τεκμήρια δ' ἡλίκα τούτου θεωρήσατε.

§ 91. τοῦ πράγματος] 'the fact' (at issue), 'the matter in hand': cf. *supra* § 11 ἔξω τοῦ πράγματος λέγων *n*.

ἐπεί γε τὸ ἐλθεῖν τοῦτον] 'since, as to his coming here,' etc.: the articular infin. here and elsewhere corresponds to the acc. of *respect* or *limitation* (Goodwin, § 795), but the present case differs from others in so far as the simple infin. could not be substituted, as it might be e.g. at Soph. *Ant.* 79 τὸ δὲ | βίᾳ πολιτῶν δρᾶν ἔφυν ἀμήχανος, *O.T.* 1417, Thuc. II. 53 τὸ προσταλαιπωρεῖν...οὐδεὶς πρόθυμος ἦν.

οἶμαι θεόν τινα...τιμωρίαν] 'I fancy some god brought him expressly for punishment': a common sentiment in the orators: cf. Lys. *C. Andoc.* § 27 <τοσαύτην γὰρ ὁ> θεὸς λήθην ἔδωκεν, ὥστε εἰς τοὺς ἠδικημένους αὐτοὺς ἐπεθύμησεν ἀφικέσθαι, *Ibid.* § 32 παραδέδωκεν αὐτὸν ὑμῖν χρῆσθαι ὅ τι ἂν βούλησθε, οὐ τῷ μὴ ἀδικεῖν πιστεύων, ἀλλ' ὑπὸ δαιμονίου τινὸς ἀγόμενος ἀνάγκης, Andoc. *De Myst.* § 137, Dem. *c. Timocr.* § 121.

ἑτέρωθι μὲν γὰρ ἀτυχῶν κ.τ.λ.] 'for had misfortune overtaken him elsewhere, it would not have been clear whether it was for this (the crime of desertion) that he was being punished': the tense of ἀτυχῶν suggests that the sentence should run either εἰ... ἠτύχει, οὐκ ἂν δῆλον ἦν, or εἰ...ἀτυχοίη, οὐκ ἂν...εἴη (Goodwin, § 472): the first, which represents a condition contrary to the existing facts (as emphasised in the following clause ἐνταῦθα δὲ κ.τ.λ.), is the more probable, though it must be observed that the normal form of the condition is somewhat obscured by its presentation as a vivid present.—**οὔπω**: here probably a strengthened form of the negative (L.S. *s.v.* 2), though the temporal sense is admissible ('something would *still* have been wanting to prove,' etc.).—**δῆλον**: sc. ἐστι [δῆλος Frohb. (Es, Bl.)].

ἐνταῦθα δέ] sc. ἀτυχῶν.

αὑτοῦ] Blass reads αὐτοῦ (adv.), 'his offences committed here, but αὑτοῦ, 'his very own,' is quite forcible.

ταύτην τὴν τιμωρίαν] 'this punishment': the retention of the article is supported by τοῦ ἀκλεοῦς...θανάτου above: Bekker (Es) would omit τήν, Blass ταύτην.

§ 92. οἱ γὰρ θεοὶ...παράγουσι] 'for the very first thing the gods do is to warp the understanding of wicked men,' a characteristic Greek doctrine which may be briefly formulated thus: the man who is wealthy or powerful overmuch excites the jealousy (φθόνος) of the gods: he waxes wanton and commits an act of insolence (ὕβρις):

the gods visit him with a blinding influence (ἄτη—ἀάω) which leads him on till the cup of his iniquity is full and he commits the error which causes his own destruction. ἄτη—the influence which 'perverts the understanding'—is related to ὕβρις as child to parent: Aesch. *Pers.* 821 ὕβρις γὰρ ἐξανθοῦσ' ἐκάρπωσε στάχυν | ἄτης, 'insolence when it hath conceived bringeth forth blindness of heart,' as we might say in the language of St James, I. 15. The doctrine here outlined is expounded both by Greek prose writers and poets: the whole career of Xerxes in Herodotus is intended by the historian as a vindication of it, and a similar claim is made by some for the plan of Thucydides' history. For the poets, see more particularly next note.—**οὐδὲν πρότερον ποιοῦσιν**: certain of the editors (Bk., Bl.) inevitably bracket ποιοῦσιν, but Lyc. appears to affect variations of these idiomatic expressions: cf. *infra* § 129 οὐδὲν γὰρ πρότερον ἀδικοῦσιν ἤ, and *supra* § 33 οὐδὲν ἕτερον ἢ φοβούμενος *n*.

τῶν ἀρχαίων τινὲς ποιητῶν] The four lines quoted here are of uncertain authorship (*trag. adesp.* fr. 240), but their form and substance may be illustrated from Homer, Theognis, Aeschylus and Sophocles, the last two of whom would probably have been voted τῶν ἀρχαίων by a man of Lycurgus' temperament: *Il.* XIX. 137 ἀλλ' ἐπεὶ ἀασάμην, καί μευ φρένας ἐξέλετο Ζεύς, Theognis 403 σπεύδει ἀνήρ, κέρδος διζήμενος, ὅν τινα δαίμων | πρόφρων εἰς μεγάλην ἀμπλακίην παράγει, | καί οἱ ἔθηκε δοκεῖν, ἃ μὲν ᾖ κακά, ταῦτ' ἀγάθ' εἶναι, | εὐμαρέως, ἃ δ' ἂν ᾖ χρήσιμα, ταῦτα κακά, Soph. *Ant.* 621 σοφίᾳ γὰρ ἔκ του κλεινὸν ἔπος πέφανται, τὸ κακὸν δοκεῖν ποτ' ἐσθλὸν τῷδ' ἔμμεν ὅτῳ φρένας θεὸς ἄγει πρὸς ἄταν. The schol. on this last quotes two lines by an unknown poet, ὅταν δ' ὁ δαίμων ἀνδρὶ πορσύνῃ κακά, | τὸν νοῦν ἔβλαψε πρῶτον, ᾧ βουλεύεται, which Jebb (Soph. *Ant. l.c.* and App.) thinks were probably the original of the Latin, '*quem Iuppiter volt perdere, dementat prius*,' itself a line of uncertain origin, as far as the wording goes, though close parallels are furnished from various sources, the most familiar being perhaps Publilius Syrus' '*stultum facit fortuna quem volt perdere.*'

§ 93] NOTES 163

ὥσπερ χρησμοὺς γράψαντες] For χρησμούς, cf. Isocr. *Paneg.*
§ 171 (the leading statesmen of Greece should have offered counsel
about an expedition against Persia: even if they had failed) ἀλλ᾽
οὖν τούς γε λόγους ὥσπερ χρησμοὺς εἰς τὸν ἐπιόντα χρόνον ἂν
κατέλιπον, where Sandys renders 'solemn, oracular utterances,'
quoting the present passage and Aeschin. *Ctes.* § 136 οἶμαι ὑμῖν
δόξειν οὐ ποιήματα Ἡσιόδου εἶναι ἀλλὰ χρησμὸν ('solemn warning')
εἰς τὴν Δημοσθένους πολιτείαν.

βλάπτῃ] Cf. *Od.* XIV. 178 τὸν δέ τις ἀθανάτων βλάψε φρένας,
etc. "ἄτη (ἀάω), as the heaven-sent influence that leads men to
sin, is properly 'hurt done to the mind.' Milton, *Samson* 1676
'Among them he a spirit of phrenzy sent, Who hurt their minds.
Cf. βλαψίφρων, φρενοβλαβής." (Jebb on Soph. *Ant.* 622 ff.)

τοῦτ᾽ αὐτὸ πρῶτον] acc. in apposition to the sentence, like
πᾶν τοὐναντίον, etc.: cf. *supra* § 73 τὸ κεφάλαιον τῆς νίκης *n.*

ἐξαφαιρεῖται φρενῶν τὸν νοῦν τὸν ἐσθλόν] 'taketh utterly
from out his breast his good understanding.' The most instructive
parallel to this passage is perhaps Soph. *Ant.* 1090 (ἵνα γνῷ
τρέφειν) τὸν νοῦν τ᾽ ἀμείνω τῶν φρενῶν ἢ νῦν φέρει, where Jebb
points out that τὸν νοῦν τῶν φρενῶν must be taken together as =
'his mind within his breast,' if ἢ is to be retained. After quoting
Il. XVIII. 419 τῆς ἐν μὲν νόος ἐστὶ μετὰ φρεσίν, 'there is understanding in their breasts,' XXII. 475 ἐς φρένα θυμὸς ἀγέρθη, 'the
soul returned to her breast,' he adds: 'The word φρὴν being
thus associated with the physical seat of thought and feeling,
ὁ νοῦς τῶν φρενῶν was a possible phrase.'

τρέπει] sc. αὐτόν, 'him.'

γνώμην] 'judgment,' 'purpose,' the practical manifestation
of the νοῦς, as they may perhaps be distinguished when in
juxtaposition. Cf. Lysias *c. Andoc.* § 22 καίτοι πῶς οὐ θεῶν τις
τὴν τούτου γνώμην διέφθειρεν;

c. 22. § 93. **τῶν πρεσβυτέρων...τῶν νεωτέρων**] These are of
course partitive gens. with τίς, though it is curious that the verb
adjacent to each is a verb which takes its object in the gen.
Note the chiastic arrangement.

Καλλίστρατον] This Callistratus, son of Callicrates, of Aphidna, was a prominent statesman and orator at Athens in the second quarter of the 4th cent. B.C. He was closely identified with the upbuilding of the Second Athenian Confederacy, and his policy generally was marked by a conciliatory attitude towards Sparta and opposition to the aggrandisement of Thebes. As an orator, his speech on the affair of Oropus (366 B.C.) is said to have excited the admiration of Demosthenes and to have given him his first impulse towards oratory. In 361 B.C. the Athenians, in a fit of exasperation at a sudden raid on the Piraeus by Alexander of Pherae, condemned Callistratus to death, whereupon he fled from Athens to Methone, on the Thermaic Gulf. Some years later he ventured to return without authority, and was seized and put to death.

τοῦτον φυγόντα] For the resumptive τοῦτον, cf. Xen. *Anab.* II. 2. 20 Κλέαρχος Τολμίδην Ἠλεῖον, ὃν ἐτύγχανεν ἔχων παρ' ἑαυτῷ...τοῦτον ἀνειπεῖν ἐκέλευσε: cf. *supra* § 42, Madvig § 100. *e.* [Sofer, however, explains τοῦτον as = τὸν θάνατον, which seems less likely.]

τεύξεται τῶν νόμων] 'he would have fair treatment by the laws': cf. [Dem.] or. XLIV. § 3 ἀγαπῶντες, ἄν τις ἡμᾶς ἐᾷ τῶν νόμων τυγχάνειν, *Ibid.* § 28, etc. The ambiguous phrase would be interpreted by C. as the opp. of τῶν νόμων εἴργεσθαι: cf. *supra* § 65.

τὸν βωμὸν τῶν δώδεκα θεῶν] The 'altar of the twelve gods' stood in the new Agora, having been placed there by the younger Pisistratus, son of Hippias, as the central point from which distances were to be measured (cf. the *miliarium aureum* at Rome): Her. II. 7, Thuc. VI. 54. It seems to have been a recognised asylum: cf. Her. VI. 108.

τὸ γὰρ τῶν νόμων...τιμωρίας ἐστίν] 'for to meet with the laws, for the guilty, is to meet with punishment': with the reading in the text, τυχεῖν goes ἀπὸ κοινοῦ with τῶν νόμων and τιμωρίας, i.e. τὸ τῶν νόμων τυχεῖν τοῖς ἠδ. ἐστὶ τὸ τυχεῖν τιμωρίας. Note that τιμωρίας τυχεῖν is itself an ambiguous phrase: (*a*) 'to obtain vengeance' (Thuc. II. 74, Xen. *Cyr.* IV. 6. 7); (*b*) 'to suffer punishment' (Plat. *Gorg.* 472 D). [For this reason, Bursian's (Bl.) τιμωρίας, which I have adopted, seems preferable to τιμωρία of the MSS.]

ὁ δέ γε θεὸς...κολάσαι τὸν αἴτιον] 'yes, but the god too was right in allowing the injured to punish the guilty': the connexion of thought is, 'the state rightly put C. to death. Yes, but the god too rightly allowed it to do so.' The combination δέ γε appears to have two main uses: (1) as a simple adversative, 'on the other hand,' 'on the contrary': Plat. *Protag.* 334 A ἀλλ' ἔγωγε πολλὰ οἶδ' ἃ ἀνθρώποις μὲν ἀνωφελῆ ἐστι, καὶ σιτία καὶ ποτά...τὰ δέ γε ὠφέλιμα·...τὰ δὲ βουσὶν μόνον, τὰ δὲ κυσίν· τὰ δέ γε τούτων μὲν οὐδενί, δένδροις δέ, Dem. *Mid.* § 27 φεύγοντος μὲν γάρ...ἐστί...τὸν οὐκ ὄνθ' ὡς ἔδει γενέσθαι λέγειν, δικαστῶν δέ γε σωφρόνων τούτοις τε μὴ προσέχειν κ.τ.λ., (2) to cap a previous statement with a fresh detail which illustrates or amplifies or corrects it: hence frequent in retorts: Dem. *F.L.* § 279 (quoting a ψήφισμα) 'καὶ ἠλέγχθησάν τινες αὐτῶν ἐν τῇ βουλῇ οὐ τἀληθῆ ἀπαγγέλλοντες.' οὗτοι δέ γε καὶ ἐν τῷ δήμῳ, 'and so were these *too*,' etc., Soph. *Ai.* 1142 ἤδη ποτ' εἶδον ἄνδρα..., 1150 ἐγὼ δέ γ' ἄνδρ' ὄπωπα, 'yes, and I too have seen one,' Eur. *Ion* 1329, 1330 προγόνοις δάμαρτες δυσμενεῖς ἀεί ποτε. ἡμεῖς δὲ μητρυιαῖς γε πάσχοντες κακῶς, 'yes, and we stepsons to our stepdames *too*,' which last is quoted by Shilleto on Dem. *F.L.* § 90.—ἀπέδωκε...κολάσαι τὸν αἴτιον: lit. 'granted it (as their due) to the injured to punish the guilty,' *not* 'delivered up the guilty to punish,' i.e. to be punished, as *supra* § 87 ἠξίουν δοῦναι τὸν βασιλέα θάψαι. Cf. Dem. *c. Aristocr.* § 56 τοὺς ἐχθρὰ ποιοῦντας...κολάζειν ἀπέδωκεν ὁ νόμος, 'the law empowers you.'

δεινὸν γὰρ ἂν εἴη, εἰ...φαίνοιτο] 'for it would be strange if the same signs were shown to the righteous and to evildoers,' i.e. if the same interpretation of divine signs was necessary in each case. σημεῖα, which, in respect of syntax, is perhaps predicative, 'the same things *as* signs,' is here 'signs from the gods,' in which oracular responses would be included: cf. Antiph. *De Caed.*

Herod. § 81 χρὴ δὲ καὶ τοῖς ἀπὸ τῶν θεῶν σημείοις...τεκμηραμένους ψηφίζεσθαι, Soph. *O.C.* 94.—For the reading, see Crit. App.

§ 94. ἔγωγ'] 'I for my part': *equidem existimo.*

τοὺς γονέας...τοὺς τετελευτηκότας...αὑτούς] Lyc. goes on to deal with piety towards the first only, whence Hirschig (Thalh.) brackets καὶ τοὺς τετελ....πρὸς αὑτούς. As Rehd. observes, however, he has already dealt, to some extent, with the second at *supra* § 45, and with the third at *supra* §§ 25, 76 *sqq.*, and elects to elaborate the first here.

μὴ ὅτι ἁμαρτεῖν, ἀλλὰ μὴ κ.τ.λ.] 'it is a monstrous impiety, I will not say to sin against them, but even to decline to lavish our own lives in benefiting them': *non modo (non)...sed ne... quidem.*—**τὸν αὑτῶν βίον**, i.q. τὸν ἡμέτερον αὑτῶν β.

c. 23. **§ 95. λέγεται γοῦν ἐν Σ.**] For γοῦν, cf. *supra* § 86 φασὶ γοῦν τὸν Κόδρον *n.*—The account of 'the Place of the Pious' here given by Lyc. appears to be the earliest version of a story which had a great vogue in the ancient world, and which, while agreeing in substance with Lyc., differs somewhat in detail, in respect that (*a*) *two* brothers carry off their aged parents (i.e. another brother carries the mother); (*b*) the names of the brothers are given mostly as Anapius and Amphinomus, but also as Philonomus and Callias, and differently in different writers. See Rehd., App. 3, p. 166.

εἰ γὰρ καὶ μυθωδέστερόν ἐστιν] It will be, on that account, ἐς ἀκρόασιν εὐτερπέστερον (Thuc. I. 22). For εἰ καί, cf. *supra* § 62 εἰ καὶ παλαιότερον εἰπεῖν ἐστι *n.*

ἁρμόσει] *conveniet*: cf. Dem. *c. Timocr.* § 4 νομίζω κἀμοὶ νῦν ἁρμόττειν εἰπεῖν.

καὶ νῦν] 'even at this time of day': cf. Isocr. *Paneg.* § 28 καὶ γὰρ εἰ μυθώδης ὁ λόγος γέγονεν, ὅμως αὐτῷ καὶ νῦν ῥηθῆναι προσήκει. [καὶ νῦν Frohb. (Bl., Rehd.) for καὶ ὑμῖν of the MSS., which does not seem satisfactory as ὑμῖν...τοῖς νεωτέροις must presumably include the judges, whom the description does not suit.]

ῥύακα πυρός] the regular phrase for 'an eruption,' or more strictly perhaps 'the stream of lava' from a volcano: cf. Thuc.

§ 97] NOTES 167

III. 116 ἐρρύη δὲ περὶ αὐτὸ τὸ ἔαρ τοῦτο ὁ ῥύαξ τοῦ πυρὸς ἐκ τῆς Αἴτνης (where the article seems to imply that it was a familiar occurrence).

ῥεῖν] impf. infin.

ἐπί <τε>...καὶ δὴ καί] <τε> is inserted by Baiter (Es, Bl.): καὶ δή καί introduces an emphatic additional detail: cf. Her. I. 30 (of Solon) ἐς Αἴγυπτον ἀπίκετο...καὶ δὴ καὶ ἐς Σάρδις.

κατοικουμένων] sc. πόλεων, passive: cf. Dem. XII. § 5 τὰς πόλεις τὰς ἐν τῷ Παγασίτῃ κόλπῳ κατοικουμένας, and *supra* § 64 ἡ γὰρ πόλις οἰκεῖται.

πρεσβύτερον ὄντα καί] Es (Bl.) brackets καί so as to bring πρεσβ. ὄντα into direct causal connexion with οὐχὶ δυνάμενον ἀποχ., but unnecessarily: the difference is merely that between 'You are old, and can't escape' and 'You can't escape owing to your age.'

ἐγκαταλαμβανόμενον] 'like to be caught' in the stream (ἐν): cf. *supra* § 70 ἐγκαταλειπόμενοι οἱ πρόγονοι ὑπὸ πάντων τῶν Ἑλλήνων.

§ 96. φορτίον...προσγενομένου] 'by the addition of this load': φορτίου is perhaps suggested by ἀράμενον just preceding, as φορτίον ἄρασθαι seems to have been said proverbially of 'taking a heavy burden upon oneself,' [Dem.] XI. § 14 ὃ νῦν παθεῖν εἰκὸς ἐκεῖνον (sc. τὸν Φίλιππον) μεῖζον φορτίον ἢ καθ' αὐτὸν ἀράμενον (vulg.: αἰρόμενον S), 'bitten off more than he can chew,' to use a colloquialism.

τὸ θεῖον] anticipation: 'how kind Providence is to good men.'

περιρρεῦσαι] later for the classical περιρρυῆναι: cf. Thuc. IV. 12 ἡ ἀσπὶς περιερρύη εἰς τὴν θάλασσαν.

ἀφ' ὧν...προσαγορεύεσθαι] i.q. καὶ ἀπὸ τούτων τὸ χ. προσαγ. The relative clause is simply an additional detail in the story as reported, and the infin. const. is continued accordingly. The same thing is exemplified in Latin; but Greek goes to greater lengths than Latin in extending the acc. and infin. const. to subordinate clauses.

γονεῖς] For the form, here and also in next §, cf. *supra* § 15 *n*.

§ 97. ὥστε καὶ ὑμᾶς δεῖν] The occurrence of 'ὥστε introductory' with the infin. (instead of ὥστε δεῖ, which latter the MSS. give, with the exception of AB) seems to be due, in this case at least, to the indirect form of the preceding paragraph throwing its influence over this as well: the speaker, in fact, forgets for the moment that he has finished his story. Cf. Plat. *Apol.* 22 E (after a stop) ὥστε με ἐμαυτὸν ἀνερωτᾶν (=ὥστε ἀνηρώτων, 'I began to question myself').

τὴν παρὰ <τῶν> θεῶν...μαρτυρίαν] Cf. *supra* § 15 τὴν παρ' ὑμῶν...τιμωρίαν *n.*

κατὰ τὸ ἑαυτοῦ μέρος] Cf. *supra* § 17 τὸ καθ' αὑτὸν μέρος *n.*

cc. **24-29.** §§ 98-110. *The action of Erechtheus on the occasion of the invasion of Eumolpus is a proof of the spirit of his age, and Euripides is to be commended for making it the theme of a noble drama. Listen to the speech which he has put into the mouth of Praxithea. If women set their country before their children, how much more is expected of men? I should like also to quote you some verses of Homer, whom your fathers singled out for special honour. Hear Hector's exhortation. The influence of such verses on your ancestors is reflected in their heroic conduct at Marathon and elsewhere. Their reputation for valour is attested by the fact that even the Lacedaemonians sought from them a general in the person of Tyrtaeus, under whom they conquered their enemies and whose elegies are still recited on the field of battle. The Spartans who faced the barbarian at Thermopylae owned his sway, as may be seen from the epigrams composed in their honour. Your condemnation of Leocrates is due to the fair fame of your forefathers.*

§ 98. οὐ γὰρ ἀποστήσομαι τῶν παλαιῶν] 'for I won't depart from ancient history,' i.e. from seeking examples from it: cf. Dem. *Lept.* § 139 οὐδ' ἐκείνου γ' ἀποστατέον τοῦ λόγου, Isocr. *De Pace* § 81 οὐ μὴν ἀποστήσομαι παντάπασιν ὧν διενοήθην.—τῶν παλαιῶν is probably neut. (so Rehd. and Sofer), cf. *supra* § 83 βούλομαι μικρὰ τῶν παλαιῶν...διελθεῖν, in spite of ἐκεῖνοι following; but ἐκεῖνοι certainly makes the case for masc. arguable: cf. the similar doubt *supra* § 31 τἀναντία φαίνεσθαι τούτοις ποιοῦντας *n.*

ἐφ' οἷς γὰρ ἐκεῖνοι...ἀποδέχοισθε] 'for it is only right that *you* should consent to *hear* what *they* made it their glory to *do*': cf. Dem. *De Cor.* § 160 αἰσχρόν ἐστιν...εἰ ἐγὼ μὲν τὰ ἔργα τῶν ὑπὲρ ὑμῶν πόνων ὑπέμεινα, ὑμεῖς δὲ μηδὲ τοὺς λόγους αὐτῶν ἀνέξεσθε.

γάρ] *narrativum*, introducing the story: 'Well, it is recorded that,' etc.

Εὔμολπον τὸν Π. καὶ X.] 'E., son of P. and Chione,' the daughter of Boreas. According to the story, the Eleusinians, who were at war with Athens, called Eumolpus to their assistance. He came with a numerous band of Thracians, but he was slain by Erechtheus. Eumolpus was regarded as the founder of the Eleusinian mysteries, and as the first priest of Demeter and Dionysus. He was succeeded in the priestly office by his son Ceryx, and his family, the Eumolpidae, continued till the latest times the priests of Demeter at Eleusis (v. Class. Dict.). Acc. to Preller, 'the historical kernel' of the Eleusinian war 'is the fusion of the Eleusinian rites with the Attic, of Eleusis with Athens.' Isocr. *Panath.* § 193 connects the coming of Eumolpus with the vindication of the claims of Poseidon to be the founder of Athens as against Athena: Θρᾷκες μὲν γὰρ μετ' Εὐ. τοῦ Ποσ. εἰσέβαλον εἰς τὴν χώραν ἡμῶν, ὃς ἠμφισβήτησεν Ἐρεχθεῖ τῆς πόλεως, φάσκων Ποσειδῶ πρότερον Ἀθηνᾶς καταλαβεῖν αὐτήν, *Paneg.* § 68 (cf. Eur. frag. *infra*, ll. 46–49).

τῆς χώρας...ἀμφισβ.] For the const., cf. Isocr. *Panath. l.c.*, Dem. xxxix. § 19 τῆς ἀρχῆς ἠμφεσβήτει, ἣν ὑμεῖς ἔμ' ἐχειροτονήσατε.

Ἐρεχθέα] This Erechtheus was the son of Pandion by Zeuxippe, and grandson of Erechtheus (Erichthonius), son of Hephaestus and Atthis (or Gaia) (v. Class. Dict.). The family of the Eteobutadae, to which Lycurgus belonged, traced their descent from his brother Butes.

Κηφισοῦ] no doubt the god of the river of the same name. Class. Dict. makes Praxithea 'daughter of Phrasimus and Diogenia.'

§ 99. αὐτοῖς] dative of 'interest' or of 'the person affected by the action,' and referring here either to the Athenians generally, or to E. and P. as representing them.—**μέλλοντος...εἰσβάλλειν**: cf. *supra* § 66 ἐμέλλετε...σώζειν n.

ἰών] poetic for ἐλθών N, probably betrays as its origin another place of the play from which the ῥῆσις following is quoted: εἰς Δ. ἰών might be the end of an actual iambic trimeter.

τί ποιῶν ἂν νίκην λάβοι] 'what he must do to obtain victory.'

χρήσαντος...τοῦ θεοῦ] Cf. *supra* § 84 ἀνελόντος δ' αὐτοῖς τοῦ θεοῦ.

τὴν θυγατέρα] The emphatic position of these words lays stress on the hardness of the demand.

πρὸ τοῦ συμβαλεῖν τὼ στρ.] *priusquam duo exercitus congrederentur*. But v. Class. Dict. s. Erechtheus II: 'In the war between the Eleusinians and Athenians, Eumolpus was slain; *whereupon Poseidon demanded* the sacrifice of *one of the daughters* of Erechtheus' (contrast τὴν θυγατέρα above, and see further note on δύο θ' ὁμοσπόρω in l. 36 of the iambics, *infra*).

ὁ δέ] The prose uses of δέ *in apodosi* are succinctly set forth by Abbott and Matheson on Dem. *De Chers.* § 3, after Buttmann, *Excurs.* XII ad Dem. *Mid.* To the exx. quoted by A. and M., *l.c.*, may be added Isocr. *Areopag.* §§ 47, 63, *Adv. Callim.* § 58, *De Pace* § 55; Dem. *De Cor.* § 126, *c. Aristocr.* § 126, all of which are worth careful study. Also Andoc. *De Myst.* §§ 27, 149, on which last Hickie observes that 'this usage [δέ *in apod.*] is mostly found in sentences beginning with a participle, or with a hypothetical clause, or with such conjunctions as ὅτε, ἐπεί, ἐπειδή, ὅταν, οὖν, ἕως, etc.' In the present case, the force of δέ is best described as *resumptive*, ὁ δέ at once reinforcing the αὐτῷ at the opening of the sentence and taking up the thread after the intervening parenthesis: 'upon the god answering him that, if he sacrificed his daughter...he would overcome...he then, I say, obeyed,' etc.

§ 100. ὅτι τά τ' ἄλλ' ὧν...καὶ τοῦτον κ.τ.λ.] Note that in this const., where we have τά τε ἄλλα with a ptcp. followed by καί with a finite verb, τά τε ἄλλα belongs entirely to the ptcp.

clause and not at all to the finite verb: so here 'in that, besides being a good poet in other respects, *he also* elected,' etc. Cf. Hickie on Andoc. *De Myst.* § 17, where he quotes the present passage, and corrects Shilleto on Dem. *F. L.* § 139, where φιλανθρωπευόμενος belongs entirely to its own clause, and not at all to that of προύπινεν. [τά τ' ἀλλ' ἦν Bekk. (Bl., Es).]

τοῦτον τὸν μῦθον προείλετο ποιῆσαι] 'he elected to dramatise this story': ποιεῖν of *artistic production*, esp. in poetry (cf. ποιητής, Eng. *maker, makyr*), Plat. *Phaedo* 61 B ἐποίησα μύθους τοὺς Αἰσώπου, 'put them into verse.'—μῦθος, in the technical language of Aristotle, = 'plot,' *Poet.* 6. 6, where it is defined as μίμησις τῆς πράξεως, 'representation of the action.'

πρὸς ἃς ἀποβλέποντας...φιλεῖν] 'by regarding and contemplating which they should become habituated in their souls to a love of their country.'—πρὸς ἅς...συνεθίζεσθαι: the infin. is final in force = ὥστε πρὸς ταύτας κ.τ.λ., *quae intuentes ac contemplantes assuescerent*, and τὸ τὴν π. φιλεῖν is to be taken as an 'acc. of the inner object,' defining the scope of συνεθίζεσθαι, 'to become habituated *in the matter of* patriotism,' somewhat like Soph. *Ant.* 1105 καρδίας ἐξίσταμαι τὸ δρᾶν, 'I withdraw from my resolution—in the matter of doing,' and other exx. quoted by Goodwin, § 791.

ἃ πεποίηκε λέγουσαν] 'which he has put into the mouth' of the mother, lit. 'represented her as saying': cf. *supra* τοῦτον τὸν μῦθον προείλετο ποιῆσαι *n.*, Aeschin. *Ctes.* § 231 εἴ τις τῶν τραγικῶν ποιητῶν...ποιήσειεν ἐν τραγῳδίᾳ τὸν Θερσίτην ὑπὸ τῶν Ἑλλήνων στεφανούμενον.

ἀξίαν...τοῦ γενέσθαι Κ. θυγατέρα] Cf. Shakespeare, *Julius Caesar,* II. 1: 'a woman, but withal
A woman well-reputed—Cato's daughter.
Think you I am no stronger than my sex,
Being so father'd and so husbanded?'

ΡΗΣΙΣ ΕΥΡΙΠΙΔΟΥ] The iambics quoted are from Euripides' *Erechtheus*, Dindorf *P. S. G.* fr. 362.—ῥῆσις was the technical term for the messenger's speech describing the catastrophe in a tragedy: the ῥήσεις of Eur. in particular appear to have been favourite pieces for recitation: cf. Ar. *Nub.* 1371, *Vesp.* 580, *Rān.* 151, etc. So, in prose, 'a long story': Plat. *Phaedr.* 268 C περὶ σμικροῦ πράγματος ῥήσεις παμμήκεις ποιεῖν, *Rep.* 605 D μακρὰν ῥῆσιν ἀποτείνοντα, 'spinning a long tale.'— The practice of quoting the poets in speeches appears to have been introduced by Aeschines, whom Dem. meets with counter quotation, but as though under provocation and in self-defence: cf. Aeschin. I. §§ 128 *sq.*, 144 *sq.*, II. § 158, III. §§ 135, 184; Dem. XVIII. § 267, XIX. §§ 243 *sqq.* In the last quoted speech (*De Fals. Leg.*) Dem. quotes 16 lines from Soph. *Ant.* and some 40 lines from Solon's *Elegies*. Both Aeschin. and Dem., however, may be said to have kept quotation within bounds, whether as regards amount or relevancy: Lycurgus offends against both with this great block of 55 iambics, which he follows up with 32 lines of Tyrtaeus. (Cf. J. F. Dobson, *The Greek Orators*, p. 281.)

1, 2. **τὰς χάριτας ὅστις...ἥδιον**] For χάριτας...χαρίζεται, cf. Isocr. *Ad Dem.* § 31 χάριτας ἀχαρίστως χαριζόμενος, Dem. *De Cor.* § 239 εἶτα κενὰς χαρίζει χάριτας συκοφαντῶν ἐμέ.—ἥδιον: sc. ἐστι. The neut. adj. is really in agreement with the thought of the previous line, as though the const. were τὸ χάριτας εὐγ. χαρίζεσθαι ἥδιον κ.τ.λ., but the substitution of the relative clause for the articular infin. (or εἴ τις) is thoroughly Euripidean: cf. *Hel.* 271 καὶ τοῦτο μεῖζον...κακόν, ὅστις...κέκτηται, *Ib.* 941 παισὶ γὰρ κλέος τόδε...ὅστις κ.τ.λ., *I.T.* 606, *Phoen.* 509, *Med.* 220, etc. So also Thuc. II. 44, 62; III. 45 πολλῆς εὐηθείας ὅστις οἴεται κ.τ.λ., 'it is great folly to imagine,' etc.

2, 3. **οἳ δὲ δρῶσι μέν, χρόνῳ δὲ δρῶσι**] '*bis dat qui cito dat*' is the idea. [For the completion of l. 3 I have adopted Meineke's <λέγω>, which word may have somehow disappeared before the ἐγὼ following. See Crit. App.]

4. **κτανεῖν**] *interficiendam*: cf. *supra* §§ 43, 87, notes. [παῖδα τὴν ἐμὴν Tayl.]

5. **πρῶτα μέν**] answered by ἔπειτα, *infra* l. 14.

6. **λάβοιν**] So Dind. (Sch., Rehd.) = λάβοιμι, on the strength

§ 100. 10]   NOTES   173

of two or three supposed such forms of 1st pers. opt. in trag. (τρέφοιν, ἁμάρτοιν, ἔχοιν). The sense will then be 'I can win no other city,' etc. But λαβεῖν of the MSS. (Bl., Thalh.) gives quite a good point with δώσω: 'I am prepared to *give* my daughter, and I reckon that there is no other city more worthy to *receive* her.'

7, 8. ᾗ πρῶτα μὲν λεὼς οὐκ ἐπακτὸς...αὐτόχθονες] Note that this πρῶτα μὲν has no ἔπειτα (δὲ) answering it.—λεὼς is scanned as one syllable (*synizesis*).—οὐκ ἐπακτὸς...αὐτόχθονες: for the topic, which is a well-worn one both with poets and orators, cf. *supra* § 41 ὃς πρότερον ἐπὶ τῷ αὐτόχθων εἶναι...ἐσεμνύνετο n.; also Isocr. *Paneg.* § 24 ταύτην γὰρ οἰκοῦμεν οὐχ ἑτέρους ἐκβαλόντες... οὐδ' ἐκ πολλῶν ἐθνῶν μιγάδες συλλεγέντες...αὐτόχθονες ὄντες κ.τ.λ., a passage which recurs with little variation in [Lys.] *Epitaph.* § 17.

8-10. αἱ δ' ἄλλαι πόλεις...εἰσαγώγιμοι] 'whereas other cities have been settled as though by the odds of draughts and are imported, one from this, one from that,' i.e. the populations of other cities are as fluctuating and uncertain as though they were determined by the shifting positions in a game of draughts (πεσσοί), and owe their existence to 'importation,' i.e. colonisation from other cities (as opp. to αὐτόχθονες). The general meaning is clear, but the details of the simile cannot be pressed owing to our insufficient knowledge of the rules governing the game of πεσσοί, and its connection with dice (κύβοι), which may have determined the position of the πεσσοὶ on the board. Plutarch, indeed (*Mor.* 604 D), quotes l. 9 as πεσσῶν ὁμοίως διαφορηθεῖσαι βολαῖς, which seems to mean 'tossed to and fro (*ultro citro iactatae*) as by casts of the *dice*,' though διαφορεῖν has usually the stronger sense of 'harry,' 'plunder': cf. Her. III. 53, Dem. XLV. § 64. Also in l. 10 he gives ἀγώγιμοι (*contra metrum*).—**πεσσῶν ὁμ. διαφ. ἐκτισμ.** = διαφοραῖς ὁ. ταῖς πεσσῶν διαφ.: compendious comparison.—εἰσαγώγιμοι: practically = ἐπακτοί, the idea of 'permissibility' suitable to the termination of the adj. (as in εἰσαγώγιμος δίκη) being here quiescent: so τὰ εἰσαγ. = 'imports.'

11—13. ὅστις δ' ἀπ' ἄλλης κ.τ.λ.] 'but whoso leaves a city to settle in another, he, like a bad fastening fitted in wood, is a citizen in word only, and not in deed.'—For πόλεος *metri causa*, cf. Aesch. *S.C.T.* 218, *Supp.* 345; Soph. *Ant.* 162; Eur. *Or.* 897, *El.* 412, *Ion* 595, which acc. to Jebb on Soph. *l.c.* exhaust the instances of this particular form in the trimeters of the three tragedians.—οἰκήσῃ Meineke (Bl., Sof.: ᾤκησεν Dobree) seems distinctly preferable to οἰκίζει of the MSS. (Sch., Rehd., Thalh.), which latter would naturally refer to the *founder* of a city; but the idea is of a new-comer who does not fit into the body of the community he has joined. For the omission of ἂν with the conj., cf. Soph. *O.T.* 1231, *O.C.* 395, *El.* 771, etc.—ἁρμός: here, as παγεὶς shows, a 'fastening' in the concrete sense, 'a peg,' 'bolt,' as Eur. *Med.* 1315 ἐκλύεθ' ἁρμούς, 'undo the fastenings' of the doors; otherwise, 'a chink,' 'aperture' between two things which are joined together: Soph. *Ant.* 1216 ἁρμὸν χώματος λιθοσπαδῆ, 'the opening made by wrenching away the stones.' —λόγῳ...τοῖς δ' ἔργοισιν: for omission of the article with one member, and variation of the number, in this phrase, cf. Soph. *O.C.* 782 λόγῳ μὲν ἐσθλά, τοῖσι δ' ἔργοισιν κακά.

14. ἕκατι] Doric and tragic form of ἕκητι = ἕνεκα.

15. θεῶν...τε ῥυώμεθα] θεῶν is one syllable by *synizesis*: cf. *supra* l. 7 λεώς.—τε ῥυώμεθα: for the lengthening of the short vowel *in arsi* before ρ, due to the strong pronunciation of the letter initially (v. L.S. *s. lit.* III), cf. Soph. *O.T.* 847 τοῦτ' ἐστὶν ἤδη τοὔργον εἰς ἐμὲ ῥέπον.

16. πόλεως δ' ἁπάσης...πολλοὶ δέ νιν] The first part of the line is a purely formal antithesis to the main thought, 'there are many dwellers in the city.'—νιν: tragic acc. form, here = αὐτήν.

18. προπάντων μίαν ὕπερ δοῦναι θανεῖν] προπάντων (Meineke, for πρὸ πάντων) here depends upon ὕπερ (as the accentuation of the prep. shows: ὑπερδοῦναι MSS.): others writing ὑπὲρ δ. θ. make ὑπὲρ...θανεῖν a case of *tmesis* = ὑπερθανεῖν, on which compound προπάντων then depends: cf. Eur. *Phoen.* 998 ψυχήν τε δώσω τῆσδ' ὑπερθανεῖν χθονός.

§ 100. 29]   NOTES   175

19, 20. **εἴπερ γὰρ ἀριθμόν...τὸ μεῖζον**] 'for if I understand number, and what is greater than the less': εἴπερ...ἀριθμὸν οἶδα was probably a proverbial expression: v. L.S. s.v. ἀριθμός.

20, 21. **οὑνὸς οἶκος...οὐδ' ἴσον φέρει**] 'the misadventure of *one* house outweigheth not that of the whole city, nay, nor doth it count as equal.'—οὑνὸς (Emper. et vulg.) = ὁ ἑνός, 'the (house) of one man.'—**σθένει** (στένει Blass) = δύναται, in the sense of 'equivalence': Lat. *valere*.—**πταίσας**, conditional, 'if it come to grief': supply πταισάσης with ἁπάσης πόλεος.—**πόλεος**: cf. *supra* l. 11 *n.*—ἴσον φέρει: cf. the Homeric ἰσοφαρίζειν.

22, 23. **εἰ δ' ἦν ἐν οἴκοις...ἄρσην**] 'now had I in my house male offspring in place of female,' sons instead of daughters: θηλειῶν is used as a subst. The form of the protasis implies 'but I have not a son' (Goodwin, § 410): Class. Dict., however, makes P. the mother of 'Cecrops, Pandorus, Metion, Orneus, Procris, Creusa, Chthonia and Orithyia.'

24, 25. **οὐκ ἄν νιν ἐξέπεμπον...προταρβοῦσ'**;] 'would I shrink from sending him (them) forth...for that I blenched at death?' Some would make this a statement by giving the negative to προταρβοῦσ', 'I would send...without blenching,' but this seems less likely.

25–27. **ἀλλ' ἔμοιγ' ἔστω τέκνα...πεφυκότα**] 'nay, *mine* be children [ἔστω G. Herm. (Turr., Thalh.): εἴη Ald. (Bl.): ἐστὶν Rehd.: ἐστι codd.] who should both fight and be illustrious among men, and not be mere figures in the state.'—**μάχοιτο** and **πρέποι** are best taken as optatives of 'assimilation,' common after an optative expressing a wish in the main clause: see Goodwin, § 531 and exx. there, also §§ 558 ff.—**πρέποι**: cf. Hom. *Od.* VIII. 172 μετὰ δὲ πρέπει ἀγρομένοισιν.—**σχήματ' ἄλλως**: σχῆμα, of the appearance as opp. to the reality: cf. Eur. *Frag.* 25 γέροντες οὐδέν ἐσμεν ἄλλο πλὴν ὄχλος | καὶ σχῆμ', 'nothing but number and *a mere outside*' (L.S.); we may compare the somewhat similar use of ἀριθμός, Eur. *Troad.* 476 οὐκ ἀριθμὸν ἄλλως, ἀλλ' ὑπερτάτους Φρυγῶν, and Horace's *nos numerus sumus*.

28, 29. **τὰ μητέρων δὲ...ὁρμωμένους**] 'but whene'er a mother's tears escort her sons, they unman many as they set forth to the fray': πέμπειν here of 'escorting' perhaps rather than 'sending' (cf. πομπή, πομπαῖος).—ἐθήλυν': gnomic.

30. πρό] 'before,' i.e. 'in preference to' honour (τοῦ καλοῦ).

31. εἵλοντ' ἤ] The MSS. give εἵλοντο καί, for which none of the numerous remedies proposed seems satisfying palaeographically: εἵλοντ' ἤ (Matthiae) at least cuts the knot.

32–35. καὶ μὴν θανόντες γε...δοθήσεται] καὶ μὴν introduces, as regularly, a new line of thought, which is this: 'other mothers' sons by dying in battle win a common grave and glory which is (but) equal (i.e. no greater than that of their fellows), for they share it with many (πολλῶν μέτα): my daughter by dying for the state will win a crown of glory which none shall divide with her': for στέφανος, cf. *supra* § 50 στέφανον τῆς πατρίδος εἶναι τὰς ἐκείνων ψυχάς *n*.—εἷς μιᾷ μόνῃ: the juxtaposition of these words emphasises the oneness of the sacrifice and the oneness of the reward.

36. δύο θ' ὁμοσπόρω] This most naturally means, in Eur.'s context, 'and *her* two *sisters*,' for P. has just implied (ll. 22, 23) that she has no son, while ἀντὶ θηλειῶν (*supra* l. 22) and παίδων τῶν ἐμῶν (*infra* l. 40) imply that she has more than one daughter. Lycurgus' language at § 99 *supra*, τὴν θυγατέρα εἰ θύσειε, would suggest that the maiden to be sacrificed was certainly an only daughter, if not an only child. It seems less likely that the words mean 'and *thy* two sisters' [i.e. the two sisters of Erechtheus (v. Class. Dict.), who is presumably being addressed], though this would square better with Lycurgus, *l.c.*

38. τὴν οὐκ ἐμὴν πλὴν <ἤ> φύσει] 'who is not mine except by nature,' i.e. except so far as the natural claim of parentage goes: the claim of the state is prior. [<ἤ> Wagner (Sch., Thalh.): <τῇ> Sauppe (Bl.): <ἐν> Rehd.: alii alia.]

39. θῦσαι] Cf. *supra* §§ 43, 87, etc.

αἱρεθήσεται] 'shall be taken,' for which ἁλώσεται would be normal in prose: ᾑρέθην regularly = 'was *chosen*.'

41, 42. οὐκοῦν ἅπαντα...πόλιν] 'And so shall all be saved,

so far as lies in *me*: others shall *rule*, but I shall *save*, this city': both lines, however, have been much emended: see Crit. App.—**τοὖν γ' ἐμοί** = τὸ ἕν γ' ἐμοί, *quantum in me est*, 'as far as it rests with me.'

43–45. **ἐκεῖνο δ' οὗ...ἐκβαλεῖ**] 'then again—a matter which toucheth most closely the public weal—no man that lives shall, with my soul's consent, set at naught the ancient ordinances of our sires.'—ἐκεῖνο is an absol. acc. (cf. τοῦτο μὲν...τοῦτο δέ, etc.) which looks forward to and is in apposition with the main statement οὐκ ἔσθ'...ὅστις ἐκβαλεῖ.—**οὗ τὸ πλεῖστον...μέρος**: lit. 'of which the part in the common weal is the greatest': μέρος is said of 'the part assigned to' or 'played by' one in anything: cf. ἐν μέρει (τινὸς) ποιεῖσθαι, ἐν οὐδενὸς εἶναι μέρει, 'to be of no consequence.'— **ἀνήρ**: this, which is Bothe's [Rehd., Sofer: ἄνερ Valck. (Thalh.)] correction, I have adopted with some diffidence for ἄτερ of the MSS. (Turr., Sch., Bl.), which gives the opposite sense to that which is required, and which Rehd. declines to defend on the 'mixture of two constructions' theory, which is the usual solvent in such cases: cf. the well-known crux at the opening of the *Antigone* (l. 4) οὐδὲν γὰρ οὔτ' ἀλγεινὸν οὔτ' ἄτης ἄτερ, which has been variously treated (see C. and A. and Jebb, *ad loc.*) so as to obtain a positive meaning.—**θέσμι'** := νόμιμα, δίκαια, Hesych.: cf. Aesch. *Eum.* 491, Soph. *Ai.* 713.—ἐκβαλεῖ: 'annul,' 'set at naught': cf. Soph. *O.T.* 849 κοὐκ ἔστιν αὐτῷ τοῦτό γ' (sc. τὸ ἔπος) ἐκβαλεῖν πάλιν, *O.C.* 631 τίς δῆτ' ἂν ἀνδρὸς εὐμένειαν ἐκβάλοι | τοιοῦδ';

46. **ἀντ' ἐλάας χρυσέας τε Γ.**] The olive tree and the Gorgon (for which latter see L.S. or Class. Dict.) were the distinctive emblems of Athena, as the trident (τρίαινα) was of Poseidon. It has been suggested that the poet is here thinking of the gilded Gorgon's head on the south wall of the Acropolis (Paus. I. 21. 3).—[ἀντ' ἐλάας, which is Dobree's correction of ἂν τελείας, is truly a *palmaris emendatio.*]

47. **ἐν πόλεως βάθροις**] 'in the heart of the city,' *in sinu urbis*, is perhaps our equivalent.

48. Θρῇξ] subst. used as adj. with λεώς, cf. Eur. *I.T.* 341 Ἕλληνος ἐκ γῆς, and the somewhat similar *Romula gens*, etc. in Latin.

49. Παλλὰς δ' οὐδαμοῦ τιμήσεται] Note that the οὐδ' of l. 46 extends to this clause as well.

50. λοχεύμασιν] plu. for sing.: cf. the similar use of παιδεύματα, Eur. *Hipp.* 11. For the meaning, cf. the use of ὠδίς in Aesch. *Agam.* 1417 παῖδα, φιλτάτην ἐμοί | ὠδῖνα, Eur. *I.T.* 1102 Λατοῦς ὠδῖνα φίλαν.

51. ἀντὶ...ψυχῆς μιᾶς] 'at the price of a single life.'

54. καὶ ῥᾳδίως] i.e. '(in that case) we should both,' etc. For the sentiment, Rehd. cites Eur. *Phoen.* 1017 κακῶν ἂν αἱ πόλεις ἐλασσόνων | πειρώμεναι τὸ λοιπὸν εὐτυχοῖεν ἄν.

c. 25. § 101. ταῦτα] obj. of the thing taught after ἐπαίδευε, with which (as also with ἐποίησε following) supply ὁ Εὐριπίδης as subject.

ἐποίησε] 'he has represented': cf. *supra* § 100 ἃ πεποίηκε λέγουσαν *n*.

τούς γ' ἄνδρας...ἔχειν] (if *women* can bring themselves to behave so) '*men* ought to entertain a quite insuperable affection for their country,' *insuperabilem quandam erga patriam pietatem*: ἀνυπέρβ. is of course predicative.

πρός] 'before,' 'in the eyes of': cf. *infra* § 109 μαρτύρια... ἀναγεγραμμένα ἀληθῆ πρὸς ἅπαντας τοὺς Ἕλληνας.

ὥσπερ Δ.] sc. πεποίηκε generally, or an appropriate tense from the two infins. preceding. The final position of the name gives the same bitter emphasis as *supra* § 44 *n*.

c. 26. § 102. καὶ τῶν Ὁ. παρασχέσθαι ἐπῶν] 'to quote you also some of H.'s poetry,' as inculcating patriotic principles: cf. παρέχεσθαι μάρτυρα, τεκμήριον, etc.—ἐπῶν: of *epic* poetry *par excellence*, cf. Her. II. 117 Ὅμηρος μέν νυν, καὶ τὰ Κύπρια ἔπεα, χαιρέτω, Thuc. I. 3, etc.: the gen. is partitive.

οὕτω γὰρ ὑπέλαβον...σπουδαῖον] For the separation of οὕτω from the adj. which it qualifies, cf. *supra* § 85 οὕτως...εὔνους ἔχοντες διετέλουν *n*.—For the value of the Homeric poems from

§ 102] NOTES 179

the military point of view, which is the one specially intended by
Lycurgus, we may compare the well-known passage of the *Frogs*
(ll. 1034–6), where Aristophanes credits 'the divine Homer' with
having taught τάξεις, ἀρετάς, ὁπλίσεις ἀνδρῶν, and Isocr. *Paneg.*
§ 159 οἶμαι δὲ καὶ τὴν Ὁ. ποίησιν μείζω λαβεῖν δόξαν, ὅτι καλῶς
τοὺς πολεμήσαντας τοῖς βαρβάροις ἐνεκωμίασε, καὶ διὰ τοῦτο βουλη-
θῆναι τοὺς προγόνους ἡμῶν ἔντιμον αὐτοῦ ποιῆσαι τὴν τέχνην ἔν τε
τοῖς τῆς μουσικῆς ἄθλοις καὶ τῇ παιδεύσει τῶν νεωτέρων, ἵνα πολλάκις
ἀκούοντες τῶν ἐπῶν...καὶ ζηλοῦντες τὰς ἀρετὰς τῶν στρατευσαμένων,
τῶν αὐτῶν ἔργων ἐκείνοις ἐπιθυμῶμεν. Against such passages may
be placed the polemic of Plato (*Rep.* 598 D—601 B), where,
denying that the poet writes with knowledge, he asks (600 A),
ἀλλὰ δή τις πόλεμος ἐπὶ Ὁμήρου ὑπ' ἐκείνου ἄρχοντος ἢ ξυμβουλεύ-
οντος εὖ πολεμηθεὶς μνημονεύεται; It does not appear, however,
that Plato's attack did much to shake the position of Homer in
the eyes of those who regarded him 'as at once a universal genius
and the educator of the whole of Greece' (cf. *Ibid.* 606 E).
'The poems of Homer were thought to contain, by precept and
example, everything calculated to awaken national spirit and to
instruct a man how to be καλὸς κἀγαθός' (Sandys on Isocr.
Paneg. l.c.).

ὥστε νόμον ἔθεντο...ῥαψῳδεῖσθαι τὰ ἔπη] 'that they passed a
law that he alone among the poets should have his poems recited
at each quinquennial celebration of the Panathenaea.' Jebb
(*Introd. to Homer*, p. 77) opines that the 'law' here mentioned
by L. was probably as old as 600–500 B.C., limits which would
point to, or admit of, a Pisistratean origin for the ordinance: see
infra.—**καθ' ἑκάστην πεντετηρίδα τῶν Π.**: 'at each quinquennial
celebration of the Panathenaea,' acc. to the Greek mode of
reckoning: the reference is to 'the Great Panathenaea,' Π. τὰ
μεγάλα, held once every four years, in the third year of each
Olympiad)(Π. τὰ μικρά, τὰ κατ' ἐνιαυτόν, a lesser celebration
held annually. A feature of the former, at least, was the procession to the Acropolis, in which was carried the robe, woven by
Athenian maidens, for presentation to the statue of Athena in the

Erechtheum, a ceremony which was represented on the frieze of the Parthenon. Athletic and musical contests (including the recitation of epic poems) also formed part of the festival; and it was with a view to regulating such recitations that the famous traditional 'recension' of the Homeric poems was carried out by Pisistratus—an achievement which a man of Lycurgus' temperament would doubtless have 'counted unto him for righteousness.'

—πεντετηρίδα: so Dobree (Bl., Sofer) for πενταετηρίδα, acc. to Moeris' canon πεντετηρίς· Ἀττικῶς, πενταετηρίς· Ἑλληνικῶς.—

μόνου τῶν ἄλλων ποιητῶν: cf. *supra* § 67 μόνος τῶν ἄλλων πολιτῶν *n.*—ῥαψῳδεῖσθαι τὰ ἔπη: 'that his poems should be recited.' For ῥαψῳδεῖν, ῥαψῳδία, ῥαψῳδός in connexion with epic poetry, see L.S. *s.vv.* and Jebb, *Introd. to Homer*, pp. 76, 77, where he says, *inter alia*: 'The public recitations of the Homeric poems by 'rhapsodes' can be traced back to about 600 B.C., and was doubtless in use from a considerably earlier time...It was further provided [by Hipparchus, son of Pisistratus] that the competing rhapsodes at the Panathenaea should recite consecutive parts of Homer, instead of choosing their passages at random.' The restriction here mentioned would seem to touch what, *pace* the explanations of ῥαψῳδός given by Jebb, *l.c.*, and others, must have been of the essence of the art of the 'rhapsode,' viz. that out of his knowledge of the Homeric poems as a whole he could 'stitch together' such 'cantos' as he would deem most suitable to his particular audience.—For the contemptuous use of ῥαψῳδεῖν (often accompanied by περίειμι, suggestive of the 'wandering minstrel,' as Plat. *Rep.* X. 600 D "Ομηρον...ἢ Ἡσίοδον ῥαψῳδεῖν ἂν περιιόντας εἴων;), cf. Dem. XIV. § 12 οὐδὲν ἀλλ᾽ ἢ ῥαψῳδήσουσιν οἱ πρέσβεις περιιόντες, 'will simply deliver a homily.'

ἐπίδειξιν ποιούμενοι] = ἐπιδεικνύμενοι, 'by way of demonstrating': cf. *supra* § 1 τὴν ἀρχὴν...ποιήσομαι *n.*

οἱ μὲν γὰρ νόμοι κ.τ.λ.] 'for the laws, by reason of their conciseness, do not teach but enjoin what is one's duty, whereas the poets by giving a picture of human life and selecting for their purpose the noblest actions help to influence men by reason and demonstration.'—**μιμούμενοι** in its application to the function of the poet as 'holding up the mirror' to human life is reminiscent of the more technical use of μιμεῖσθαι and μίμησις in Plato and Aristotle, for whom the fine arts generally, including poetry, music, painting and sculpture, are species of 'mimetic': cf. Arist. *Poet. passim*, Plat. *Rep.* 392 C (with Adam's note); Butcher, *Aristotle's Theory of Poetry and Fine Art*[4], c. II. With the language of L. here we may compare Isocr. *Ad Nicoc.* § 43 σημεῖον (that the majority prefer τὰ χαριέστατα to τὰ χρησιμώτατα) δ' ἂν τις ποιήσαιτο τὴν Ἡσιόδου καὶ Θεόγνιδος καὶ Φωκυλίδου ποίησιν· καὶ γὰρ τούτους φασὶ μὲν ἀρίστους γεγενῆσθαι συμβούλους τῷ βίῳ τῷ τῶν ἀνθρώπων.—**ἐκλεξάμενοι**, 'choosing for themselves,' i.e. for their special purpose.—**συμπείθουσιν**: perhaps not so much 'join in influencing' as 'add their influence to other influences' in admonishing men.

§ 103. γάρ] 'for instance.'

ἀλλὰ μάχεσθ' κ.τ.λ.] *Il.* XV. 494–499, with some variations: διαμπερὲς for ἀολλέες, νήπια τέκνα for παῖδες ὀπίσσω, καὶ κλῆρος καὶ οἶκος for καὶ οἶκος καὶ κλῆρος. Quotations like this are notoriously fertile in *variae lectiones*.—For ἀλλά, cf. *infra* § 107. 15 *n*.

βλήμενος ἠὲ τυπείς] The first properly of a *missile*, the second of a *weapon in the hand*, cf. *Il.* XI. 191 ἢ δουρὶ τυπεὶς ἢ βλήμενος ἰῷ, but the distinction cannot always be pressed in Homeric usage.

κλῆρος] "Evidently the right to join in the periodical division of the commonland by lot among members of the community. This is reserved to a man's family after his death. Trans. 'allotment.'" (Leaf and Bayfield *ad loc.*)

c. 27. **§ 104. οὕτως ἔσχον πρὸς ἀρετήν**] But *infra* § 108 οὕτω τοίνυν εἶχον πρὸς ἀνδρείαν οἱ τούτων ἀκούοντες. If the distinction between the tenses is to be pressed, the aor. will describe the *active result* of their hearing: "got such a 'bent' or 'impulse' towards valour ")(their habitual attitude (εἶχον). Goodwin, §§ 55–57.

οἱ γοῦν ἐν Μαραθῶνι] For γοῦν, cf. *supra* §§ 71, 86 *nn*.—

ἐν Μαραθῶνι: the prep. in this phrase is now generally expelled by editors, in accordance, seemingly, with the best Greek usage, which makes Μαραθῶνι a locative; but Cobet's '*nemo umquam veterum ἐν* M. *dixit*' is too sweeping, in the face both of the MSS. and of inscrr. (v. Rehd., App. 1, *ad loc.*). Cf. Her. VI. 111–117, Aeschin. *Ctes.* § 181, etc. On the other hand, ἐν Σαλαμῖνι appears to be the regular expression, though the Aeschin. passage just cited for ἐν M. curiously enough gives τῇ Σαλαμῖνι ναυμαχίᾳ (with τῇ περὶ Σαλαμῖνα as an inevitable variant), and Dem. *F.L.* § 312 shows οἱ Μαραθῶνι καὶ Σαλαμῖνι (κἀν Herwerden).

τὸν ἐξ ἁπάσης τῆς Ἀ. στόλον] An armament 'drawn from the whole of Asia' need not necessarily have been *large*, though this is no doubt the implication. Her. (IX. 27) makes the Athenians boast of having conquered forty-six nations. The actual strength of the Persian fighting force at Marathon, which Her. does not specify and which was grossly exaggerated by later historians, can hardly have exceeded 50,000 to 60,000 men: see some figures in Holm, *History of Greece*, vol. II, p. 25, n. 6.

τῶν μὲν Ἑ. προστάτας, τῶν δὲ β. δεσπότας...λόγῳ...ἔργῳ] A thoroughly Isocratean passage: note the favourite antithesis (λόγῳ...ἔργῳ), the exact balancing of clauses (παρίσωσις), and the assonance (προστάτας...δεσπότας) (παρομοίωσις).

ἐπεδείκνυντο] *prae se ferebant*.

c. 28. § 105. οὕτως ἦσαν...σπουδαῖοι] cf. *supra* §§ 85, 102 *nn*.

ἐν τοῖς ἔμπροσθε χρόνοις] These words (as Dr Verrall points out in his essay on Tyrtaeus, see note *infra*) are ambiguous: (*a*) taking them with πολεμοῦσιν and ἀνεῖλεν, we shall render: 'when the martial L. had in former times a war with the M.,' (*b*) taking them as attributive (= τοῖς ἐν τοῖς ἔμ. χ. Λ. ἀνδρ.) we have: 'when the L., who were in former times first in martial qualities, had a war with the M.' Here, as in many other places, one would give much to know exactly how they were taken by the writer of them.

πολεμοῦσι πρὸς Μ.] This was the 'Second Messenian War,'

§ 106] NOTES 183

which is now dated to about the middle of the 7th cent. B.C. (traditional date 685–668): cf. *supra* § 62 τοῦτο δὲ Μεσσήνην πεντακοσίοις ἔτεσιν ὕστερον...συνοικισθεῖσαν; *n.* [See note on Tyrtaeus, *infra.*]

ἀνεῖλεν ὁ θεός] Cf. *supra* § 84 ἀνελόντος αὐτοῖς τοῦ θεοῦ *n.*

λαβεῖν...νικήσειν] The first infin. represents a *command*, the second a *statement*: 'the god answered that they should take... and thus they would conquer.'

τοῖν ἀφ' Ἡ. γεγ.] The two royal houses of the Agids and Eurypontids at Sparta both traced their descent back to Heracles.

οἳ ἀεὶ βασιλεύουσιν] ἀεί refers here rather to the ancient and unbroken line of the Spartan kings than = 'from time to time.' For the const. τοῖν...οἳ βασιλεύουσι, cf. Xen. *Hell.* v. 4. 19 τὼ δύο στρατηγώ, οἳ (but συνηπιστάσθην following).

§ 106. **Τυρταῖον στρατηγὸν ἔλαβον**] For Tyrtaeus, see Class. Dict. His Athenian origin, in spite of the general consensus of the authorities on this point, seems open to doubt: Bury [*H. G.* (1900), p. 128] opines that he was 'claimed' by the Athenians at a later date, and that the story of the oracle was forthcoming in this connexion. The fragments of his poems have been collected by Bergk, *Poetae Lyrici Graeci*.

[Dr A. W. Verrall makes §§ 102-109 of the speech the basis of two essays [reprinted from the *C. R.* in his *Collected Studies* (Bayfield and Duff)], in which he claims to establish, on the evidence of Lycurgus, (*a*) that Tyrtaeus flourished between the Persian and Peloponnesian wars, (*b*) that the Messenian war with which he was connected was the war of the 5th cent., *c.* 464 B.C., (*c*) that the poetry which passes current under his name cannot possibly belong to such an early date as is usually assigned to it. While I have been much impressed by Dr Verrall's arguments, I have not had the courage to break with the received account of Tyrtaeus' antiquity; and I may add that, wherever the Messenian wars have been in question, I have assumed their historicity and quoted the recognised chronology. In this latter connexion, Dr Verrall remarks: "All...are now agreed...that about these primeval conflicts between the Spartans and Messenians the ancients had no solid information, except what they might rightly or wrongly infer from the poems of Tyrtaeus... The 'first war' and the 'second,' with their dates and episodes, were among the many events of remote antiquity about which the historians of the decadence [Strabo, Diodorus, Pausanias, Athenaeus, Justin] were so much better informed than their authorities." With regard to this pronouncement, it is worth while noting that Lycurgus himself [a first-class (for Dr V.) and an early (comparatively speaking) authority on the point], at another place (§ 62) which does not come within the purview of Dr Verrall's essay, alludes (if we understand him rightly) to an early conquest of Messenia (achieved presumably in a 'primeval conflict') as a matter of universal acceptation, and that not merely as an event of historical inference but as a substantive historical fact, to which he can, and does, assign a date. Whether that date is intrinsically right is another matter: the point is that Lycurgus, in condescending upon it, evidently assumes, with just as much confidence as he does in the case of Tyrtaeus' association (by assumption) with the Messenian war of the 5th cent., that he is speaking of something which is perfectly familiar to his hearers. This, of course, does not touch the question of Tyrtaeus' connexion with one or other of the M. wars; but we are justified (I think) in inferring that, already in the time of Lycurgus, the 'primeval conflicts' between the Spartans and Messenians were so far accepted as historical as to have had some system of chronology worked out for them. We can only speculate as to what information Lycurgus possessed regarding them (other than the chronological glimpse he gives us at the place quoted), and whether, or how far, such information was, as a matter of fact, derived from the poems of Tyrtaeus.]

τὴν περὶ τοὺς νέους ἐπ. συνετάξαντο] 'organised the (well-known) system of supervision for their youth': the Spartan ἀγωγή, or public education (for which see any standard history of Greece), was an elaborate system, the aim of which was to turn out good soldiers. This, like the bulk of Spartan institutions, would be more naturally attributed, we may suspect, by the Spartans themselves to their great reformer, 'Lycurgus.'

εἰς ἅπαντα τὸν αἰῶνα] Cf. *supra* § 7 κατὰ παντὸς τοῦ αἰῶνος, § 62 τὸν αἰῶνα ἀοίκητός ἐστι *n.*

κατέλιπε...ἐλεγεῖα ποιήσας] With the martial elegies of T., and their effect on the course of the Messenian war, we may compare what is recorded of Solon in the matter of the recovery of Salamis (*c.* 570 B.C.): Dem. *F.L.* § 252 τὸν ἴδιον κίνδυνον ὑποθεὶς ('staking his personal safety') ἐλεγεῖα ποιήσας ᾖδε, καὶ τὴν μὲν χώραν <ἂν> ἔσωσε τῇ πόλει, τὴν δ' ὑπάρχουσαν αἰσχύνην ἀπήλλαξεν.—ποιήσας: 'which he had composed': cf. Dem. *l.c.*

§ 107. περὶ τοὺς ἄλλους...λόγον ἔχοντες] *cum ceterorum poetarum nullam rationem habeant*: so Plat. *Tim.* 87 C λόγον ἔχειν περί τινος, and the commoner λόγον τινὸς ποιεῖσθαι, ἐν οὐδενὶ λόγῳ ποιεῖσθαι (esp. in Herod.).

ἐσπουδάκασιν...ἔθεντο] The perf. denotes their standing attitude, 'they exhibit such a regard for him': the aor. represents the passing of the law as a past act.

ὅταν...ἐξεστρατευμένοι ὦσι] 'whenever they have taken the field' is perhaps the nearest English, though it does not quite give the force of the Gk. composite tense. So Andoc. *De Myst.* § 45 Βοιωτοὶ δὲ πεπυσμένοι τὰ πράγματα ἐπὶ τοῖς ὁρίοις ἦσαν ἐξεστρατευμένοι. [ἐξεστ. ὦσι Es (Bl., Sofer): ἐκστρατευόμενοι εἰσι codd.: ἐκστ. ὦσι A. G. Becker (Sch., Rehd., Thalh.): ἐκστ. ἴωσι Heinr. (Turr.).]

καλεῖν] 'should be summoned': cf. *supra* § 16 ἐψηφίσατο ὁ δῆμος...κατακομίζειν *n.*

πρὸ τῆς πατρίδος ἐθέλειν ἀποθ.] Examples of πρὸ=ὑπέρ, 'in defence of,' seem to be quoted mainly from Homer and Herod.: rare in the orators.—ἐθέλειν ἀποθ.: 'ἐθέλω seems especially used of the alacrity and determination of a soldier': Graves on Thuc. IV. 10. 2 ἢν ἐθέλωμέν τε μεῖναι κ.τ.λ., where he quotes from Brasidas' address before the battle of Amphipolis (Thuc. v. 9. 6):

καὶ νομίσατε εἶναι τοῦ καλῶς πολεμεῖν τὸ ἐθέλειν καὶ τὸ αἰσχύνεσθαι καὶ τοῖς ἄρχουσι πείθεσθαι.

οἷα ποιοῦντες...παρ' ἐκείνοις] 'by what sort of poetry people won credit at Sparta.' The sense given to ποιοῦντες (cf. *supra* § 100: so also Rehd. and Sofer) accords best, perhaps, with the context; but the ptcp. might also (I think) refer to the conduct which the poem inculcates)(the conduct of L., 'by what sort of deeds.'—The subject of εὐδοκίμουν is indef., 'people,' *homines*, *on*.

2. **ἄνδρ' ἀγαθόν]** predicative, perhaps, 'like a brave man,' the subject of τεθνάμεναι being indefinite.

περὶ ᾗ πατρίδι] 'for his country': περὶ with the dat. of the thing for which one fights is frequent in Hom. and occurs occasionally in prose: Plat. *Protag.* 314 A περὶ τοῖς φιλτάτοις κυβεύειν (though the idea here is rather different). Thuc. VI. 34 περὶ τῇ Σικελίᾳ ἔσται ὁ ἀγών, which the MSS. give, is corrected by the editors to περὶ τῆς Σικελίας.—ᾗ is of course dat. sing. fem. of the possessive ὅς, ἥ, ὅν, and = τῇ ἑαυτοῦ. So in next line ἦν δ' αὐτοῦ = *suam ipsius*: Soph. *O.T.* 1248 τοῖς οἷσιν αὐτοῦ.

4. **ἀνιηρότατον]** The second syllable of this word is short also in Theognis (πόλλ' ἀνιηρὰ παθών): in Hom. and Soph. always ἀνῑ- (cf. ἀνιάω): see L.S. *s.v.*

6. **κουριδίῃ τ' ἀλόχῳ]** a common Homeric phrase, 'his wedded (lawful) wife')(a concubine, παλλακή, παλλακίς.

7. **τοῖσι...οὕς κεν ἵκηται]** *iis...quoscumque adierit*: τοῖσι is demonstrative and antecedent of οὕς.—ἱκνέομαι regularly with bare acc. in Hom. ("Ολυμπον, Τροίην, δῆμον, etc.), unless indeed the verb here has the meaning of 'supplicate' (= ἱκετεύω), which is quite possible, but the literal sense goes well with πλαζόμενον above.

9. **κατὰ δ' ἀγλαὸν εἶδος ἐλέγχει]** 'and sadly belieth his goodly mien': ἐλέγχω in the Homeric sense of 'disgrace,' 'put to shame' (cf. κάκ' ἐλέγχεα, 'base *reproaches* to your name,' L.S.). —κατὰ...ἐλέγχει may be taken as a tmesis = κατελέγχει (Hes. *Op.* 712 σὲ δὲ μή τι νόον κατελεγχέτω εἶδος), but it must be

remembered that in epic the preps. are in the transitional stage from adverbs, and that their use must be considered accordingly.

10. **ἀτιμίη...ἕπεται**] For the quantity of the penult. of ἀτιμίη, cf. *Od.* XIII. 142 πρεσβύτατον καὶ ἄριστον ἀτιμίῃσιν ἰάλλειν.— ἕπεται, 'attends upon': *Il.* IV. 415 τούτῳ...κῦδος ἅμ' ἕψεται: so also ἄτη, τιμή.—For the sing. predicate with a composite subject, which is felt as making up a single idea, cf. Luc. *Dial. Mort.* 6. 1 ἡ Μοῖρα καὶ ἡ Φύσις διέταξεν: so Livy IX. 11. 4 *tum sponsio et pax repudietur*, Ps. LXXXIV. 2 'my heart and my flesh crieth out.'

11, 12. **εἰ δ'...οὐδεμί' ὥρη...γένεος**] 'as then there is no regard nor respect for a man who is a wanderer, nor for his race after him.'—With the reading in the text, construe : εἰ δ' (οὔτε) ἀνδρὸς ...οὔτ' ὀπίσω γένεος γίγνεται οὐδεμία ὥρη οὐδ' αἰδώς, the suppression of the first οὔτε being paralleled by e.g. Aesch. *Agam.* 532 Πάρις γὰρ οὔτε συντελὴς πόλις κ.τ.λ. See Crit. App.—εἰ οὐ c. indic. in Hom. is so comparatively frequent (*Il.* XV. 162, XX. 129, XXIV. 296; *Od.* II. 274, XII. 382) as to suggest that οὐ was originally normal in protases c. indic. and was afterwards displaced by μή through the use of the latter with the other moods (Monro, *H.G.*², p. 289). As a matter of fact, however, the present passage would stand quite well in Attic, which admits οὐ after εἰ when the latter is virtually=ἐπεί, 'since,' *quoniam, quandoquidem*, as it clearly is here where the substance of the preceding lines is asserted as an established truth. Cf. Andoc. *De Myst.* § 33 εἰ δὲ οὐδὲν ἡμάρτηταί μοι, 'but *since* I have committed no offence,' Dem. *c. Androt.* § 18 εἰ δ' οὐκ ἔξεστι, 'but *seeing that* it is not permissible,' *c. Timocr.* § 53, etc. (See App. C to Cope's *Rhetoric of Aristotle*, vol. I (Sandys), and, generally, Goodwin, §§ 384–387.)—ὥρη, 'regard,' 'consideration' (Att. ὥρα): Her. I. 4 μηδεμίαν ὥρην ἔχειν ἁρπασθεισέων (sc. τῶν γυναικῶν), Soph. *O.C.* 386, *Trach.* 57.

13. **θυμῷ**] 'with spirit,' 'courageously': so often in Hom. ὤτρυνε μένος καὶ θυμὸν ἑκάστου, and cf. θυμός and τὸ θυμοειδές, 'the spirited principle,' in Plato's psychology.

14. ψυχέων] two syllables (*synizesis*).—**μηκέτι** is due to the imperatival force of the hortatory subj., the clause being = θνήσκωμεν μηδὲ φειδώμεθα.

15. ὦ νέοι, ἀλλὰ μάχεσθε] Some think (with Heinrich) that a new fragment begins here.—ἀλλὰ *hortativum* is freq. in Hom. with an imper. or subj.: cf. the quotation *supra* § 103 ἀλλὰ μάχεσθ' ἐπὶ νηυσὶ διαμπερές. The usage no doubt arose after a preceding imperative, which came to be suppressed: 'do not do this, but,' etc.

16. φόβου] in the Homeric sense, practically = φυγῆς preceding.

17. ἐν φρεσὶ θυμόν] 'your heart within your breast,' φρένες being conceived as the physical seat of the θυμός, as often in Hom., θυμὸς ἐνὶ στήθεσσι, ἐν φρεσὶ θυμός, etc. Cf. *supra* § 92 ἐξαφαιρεῖται φρενῶν | τὸν νοῦν τὸν ἐσθλόν *n*.

20. τοὺς γεραιούς] For the short penult., cf. the Aristophanic οἴμοι δειλαῖος at the end of a trimeter, though δείλαιος is also quoted from Soph. and Eur. (not in trimeters), see L.S. *s.v.* The reason was a change in the division of syllables (το-ιουτος for τοι-ουτος), after which the ι disappeared as at the beginning of words. Thus we have οἶος, τοιοῦτος scanned with a short first syllable; ποεῖν alongside of ποιεῖν; ὑός written almost uniformly for υἱός in the 4th cent. B.C., though ὑ- is still scanned as long (Giles, *Comp. Phil.*², § 122. 6).

21. αἰσχρὸν γὰρ δὴ τοῦτο κ.τ.λ.] The ten lines which follow are practically an expansion of Hom. *Il.* XXII. 71–76:

νέῳ δέ τε πάντ' ἐπέοικεν
ἀρηϊκταμένῳ, δεδαϊγμένῳ ὀξέϊ χαλκῷ,
κεῖσθαι· πάντα δὲ καλὰ θανόντι περ, ὅττι φανήῃ·
ἀλλ' ὅτε δὴ πολιόν τε κάρη πολιόν τε γένειον
αἰδῶ τ' αἰσχύνωσι κύνες κταμένοιο γέροντος,
τοῦτο δὴ οἴκτιστον πέλεται δειλοῖσι βροτοῖσιν.

24. κονίῃ] In Hom. the penult. is short in the quadrisyllabic κονίῃσι, long in the trisyllabic forms: in Attic we have -ῐ in dactylic and anapaestic rhythms, but -ῑ in iambics (L.S. *s.v.*).

26. **νεμεσητὸν ἰδεῖν**] 'that moveth indignation to behold': in Hom. νεμεσσητὸν (always in this form, except at *Il.* XI. 649, quoted below) is 'that which stirs righteous indignation': *Il.* III. 410 κεῖσε δ᾿ ἐγὼν οὐκ εἶμι—νεμεσσητὸν δέ κεν εἴη, ''twere enough to make one wroth,' and twice at least (*Il.* IX. 523, *Od.* XXII. 59—in both cases urging the acceptance of an offer), πρὶν δ᾿ οὔ τι νεμεσσητὸν κεχολῶσθαι, 'ere that, 'tis no blame to thee (i.e. no one can feel indignant) that thou should'st be wroth.' At *Il.* XI. 649 we have the word applied to a *person*, αἰδοῖος νεμεσητὸς ὅ με προέηκε πυθέσθαι, where the force seems to be active, 'an austere man,' one whose character it is to be angry at wrong (cf. ἐπιεικτός, 'yielding,' *cautius, gratus*): otherwise 'one to be regarded with awe' (so L.S., but νέμεσις is not found in the sense of 'fear': v. Monro on *Il. l.c.*). [One can only speculate as to what account the writer of this line—to whom the question no doubt never occurred—would have given of its syntax. I have read it as: αἰσχρὰ τά γ᾿ ὀφθαλμοῖς (ἐστι) καὶ νεμεσητὸν ἰδεῖν, lit. 'these things are unseemly to the eyes, and a thing that moveth indignation to behold' (ἰδεῖν epexegetic infin.). But it is possible (I imagine) to take αἰσχρὰ (=αἰσχρόν) and νεμεσητὸν both with ἰδεῖν, and construe: αἰσχρὰ καὶ νεμέσητόν ἐστιν ἰδεῖν τά γ᾿ ὀφθαλμοῖς, where τά γ᾿ is object and ὀφθ. ἰδεῖν go together.]

27. **χρόα γυμνωθέντα**] 'with his body stripped naked': χρόα (χρώς) is acc. of 'respect' or 'of the part affected,' with γυμνωθέντα.

νέοισι] 'a youth': the plural is used in a general sense: we have sings. following.

28. **ὄφρ᾿**] temporal, 'so long as': for omission of ἄν, frequent in epic, lyric and elegiac poetry, cf. Goodwin, *M.T.* § 540.

29. **θηητὸς ἰδεῖν**] *conspiciendus*, 'an object of admiration.'

30. **καλός**] the ᾱ is regular in epic (cf. l. 1): at Theocr. VI. 19 we have τὰ μὴ κᾱλὰ κᾱλὰ πέφανται.

31. **εὖ διαβάς**] of a man standing with legs apart, 'planting himself firmly,' for fighting: cf. Hom. *Il.* XII. 458 εὖ διαβάς, ἵνα μή οἱ ἀφαυρότερον βέλος εἴη, Ar. *Vesp.* 688 ὡδὶ διαβάς (imitating the pose).

32. **στηριχθεὶς ἐπὶ γῆς**] 'firm planted on earth': *Il.* XXI. 241 (of Achilles' combat with Scamander) οὐδὲ πόδεσσιν | εἶχε στηρίξασθαι, 'he could not get a firm footing.'

χεῖλος ὀδοῦσι δακών] a mark of stern determination: the Homeric ὀδὰξ ἐν χείλεσι φύντες, which occurs thrice in *Od.* (I. 381, XVIII. 410, XX. 268), describing, in every instance, the effect of a speech by Telemachus on the suitors, is more specially the sign of *smothered rage*. So Eur. *Bacch.* 621 χείλεσιν διδοὺς ὀδόντας (of Pentheus' rage against the supposed Dionysus).

§ 108. προσέχειν] absol., cf. *supra* § 10, etc.

εἶχον πρὸς ἀνδρείαν] cf. *supra* § 104 οὕτως ἔσχον πρὸς ἀρετήν *n.*

τῆς Ἀττικῆς ἐπέβησαν] 'set foot in A.': so even ἐμβαίνω and ἐπεμβαίνω (Soph. *O.C.* 400, 924), probably through the influence of ἐπιβαίνω, or the gen. may be felt as a partitive.

καταφανῆ ἐποίησαν] For the sentiment, cf. Plato *Menex.* 240 D διδάσκαλοι τοῖς ἄλλοις γενόμενοι, ὅτι...πᾶν πλῆθος καὶ πᾶς πλοῦτος ἀρετῇ ὑπείκει.

ταῖς μὲν τύχαις...ἐχρήσαντο] Cf. *supra* § 48 οὐχ ὁμοίως τῆς τύχης ἐκοινώνησαν.

§ 109. ἑκατέροις ἐπιτύμβια] I have adopted Rehdantz's suggestion for the MSS. ἐπὶ τοῖς ὁρίοις τοῦ βίου, which (as Es points out) cannot well be taken as a metaphor=*in vitae terminis*, while the attempt to see a geographical reference in τοῦ βίου is discounted by the circumstance that the *locale* of the inscrr. is different. Wurm, followed by Blass, reads ἐπὶ τοῖς ἠρίοις, 'on their barrows,' on the strength of Harpocration's ἠρία· Λ. ἐν τῷ κατ' Αὐτολύκου. ἠρία εἰσὶν οἱ τάφοι, but this leaves τοῦ βίου unaccounted for.

πρὸς ἅπαντας τοὺς Ἕ.] πρὸς in this and similar cases seems to combine the meanings of (*a*) 'publicly,' 'openly,' (*b*) 'with reference to,' of the person judging: cf. *supra* § 101 καταισχύνειν πρὸς ἅπαντας τοὺς Ἕλληνας.

ἐκείνοις μέν] 'for them,' i.e. in the case of the L.: the dat. is possessive.

§ 110]　　　　　　NOTES　　　　　　191

ὦ ξεῖν', ἄγγειλον κ.τ.λ.] Her. VII. 228:
　　ὦ ξεῖν', ἀγγέλλειν Λακεδαιμονίοις ὅτι τῇδε
　　κείμεθα τοῖς κείνων ῥήμασι πειθόμενοι.

This 'sublime distich' (Simon. 92) was the work of Simonides of Ceos (c. 560-470 B.C.), 'the unsurpassed master of commemorative epigram' (Macan on Her. *l.c.*). The form in which it is given by Lycurgus (as also by Diod. and Strabo—Strabo also has ὦ ξέν', ἀπάγγειλον) is inferior to the Herodotean, and was apparently that followed by Cicero in his Latin version, *Tusc. Disp.* I. 42:
　　dic, hospes, Spartae nos te hic vidisse iacentes,
　　dum sanctis patriae legibus obsequimur.

Ἑλλήνων προμαχοῦντες κ.τ.λ.] The epigram is also by Simonides (Simon. 93).—χρυσοφόρων: gold, in one form or another, is the inevitable epithet of the oriental, suggesting wealth and luxury.—ἐστόρεσαν: 'laid low': cf. Thuc. VI. 18 ἵνα Πελοποννησίων στορέσωμεν τὸ φρόνημα.

c. 29. § 110. ἀλλ' οὐχ ὁ Λ. πεποίηκεν] sc. ἄξιόν ἐστιν ἐπαίνου, or something similar out of the preceding sentence.

τὴν ἐξ ἅπαντος...δόξαν] 'the accumulated glory of the state from time immemorial.'

δόξετε] 'you will be thought to,' 'will have the reputation.'

θαυμάζοντες] 'admire,' 'reverence': for a strong use of the word, cf. Xen. *Hell.* I. 6. 11 (Callicratidas is speaking of Persian support) δείξομεν τοῖς βαρβάροις ὅτι καὶ ἄνευ τοῦ ἐκείνους θαυμάζειν δυνάμεθα τοὺς ἐχθροὺς τιμωρεῖσθαι, 'even without worshipping them.'

τοῖς παλαιοῖς] So Taylor (Bl., Sofer) for τοῖς πολεμίοις, which does not seem to give good point: τοῖς πολλοῖς s. προγόνοις Rehd.

κεκρίσθαι κάλλιστον] 'are adjudged (the) most honourable (thing)': the perf. infin. denotes the settled attitude: cf. *supra* § 3 ὑπειλῆφθαι, etc.—κάλλιστον: cf. Madvig, § 1 *b*, R. 3.

cc. 30, 31. §§ 111-127. *The way in which your forefathers dealt with traitors is shown by the case (a) of Phrynichus and his would-be defenders, (b) Hipparchus, the son of Charmus, (c) the deserters to Decelea,* (*d*) *the man who died at Salamis: yet Leocrates' crime surpasses these in its enormity. These examples should suffice to prove the temper of our ancestors in this regard, but I should like to remind you of the decree passed by them after the Thirty, proclaiming* 'killing no murder' *in the case even of prospective traitors—and rightly so, for treason is a case where the punishment must anticipate the committal of the act. The psephism of Demophantus, moreover, binds you to punish the traitor by every means in your power. You should not claim to inherit the properties bequeathed you by your ancestors while disclaiming all part in the pledges whereby they safeguarded the public welfare.*

c. 30. **§ 111.** ἔχειν] probably intrans., ὃν τρόπον being then = ὅπως, ' what your attitude should be.'

ἐκείνους τίνα τρόπον ἐλ.] for the 'anticipation,' cf. *supra* § 62 τὴν Τροίαν τίς οὐκ ἀκήκοεν, *n.* and reff. Contrast ἐκεῖνοι...θεωρήσατε ὡς ὠργίζοντο just below.—For the severer methods of the Athens of a previous age, cf. Dem. *F.L.* § 272 τότε μὲν οὕτω σεμνὸν ἦν τὸ δίκαιον καὶ τὸ κολάζειν τοὺς τὰ τοιαῦτα ποιοῦντας (persons like Arthmius of Zelea, a tool of Xerxes, who distributed Persian gold in Greece) ἔντιμον, ὥστε τῆς αὐτῆς ἠξιοῦτο στάσεως τό τε ἀριστεῖον τῆς θεοῦ καὶ αἱ κατὰ τῶν τὰ τοιαῦτ' ἀδικούντων τιμωρίαι [i.e. the στήλη with the decree of execration against A. was placed in a conspicuous position close by the great statue (ἀριστεῖον) of the goddess]· νῦν δὲ γέλως, ἄδεια, αἰσχύνη, εἰ μὴ τὴν ἄγαν ταύτην ἐξουσίαν σχήσετε νῦν ὑμεῖς, *Phil.* III. § 43.

τὴν τιμωρίαν] the 'due' or 'appropriate' punishment.

τὰ καλὰ τῶν ἔργων] a favourite const. with Lycurgus: cf. *supra* §§ 6, 48, 102, 110, *infra* § 133, etc.

ἐνόμιζον] sc. αὐτούς.

§ 112. Φρυνίχου...ἀποσφαγέντος...ὑπὸ 'Α. καὶ Θ.] The Phrynichus mentioned was one of the commanders of the Athenian fleet at Samos and was closely identified with the revolution of the Four Hundred at Athens in 411. He was assassinated on his return from an unsuccessful mission to Sparta in the interests of

§ 112] NOTES 193

the extreme oligarchical party, but accounts differ as to the circumstances of his death and the identity of his murderers. Thucydides (VIII. 92) says that P. πληγεὶς ὑπ' ἀνδρὸς τῶν περιπόλων τινὸς ἐξ ἐπιβουλῆς ἐν τῇ ἀγορᾷ πληθούσῃ καὶ οὐ πολὺ ἀπὸ τοῦ βουλευτηρίου ἀπελθὼν ἀπέθανε παραχρῆμα, and adds that the man who actually struck the blow escaped, but that his accomplice, an Argive, was taken and put to the torture. Plutarch (*Alcib.* 25) calls the assassin Hermon, obviously from a confusion with Ἕρμων τις τῶν περιπόλων mentioned further on in the chap. of Thuc. quoted. The names in Lycurgus agree with those given by Lysias *c. Agorat.* § 71, Thrasybulus of Calydon and Apollodorus of Megara: they fell in with P. as he was taking a walk (βαδίζοντι): T. aimed the blow. We possess the text of a decree, proposed by Erasinides (Hicks and Hill[2], 74), conferring honours on Thrasybulus, and the mention of 'Apollodorus of Megara,' in Lysias περὶ τοῦ σηκοῦ [or. VII] § 4, as receiving a grant of land, is presumably connected with his share in P.'s death. Hicks on the decree quoted reconciles Lycurgus' νύκτωρ with Thuc.'s ἐν τῇ ἀγορᾷ πληθούσῃ by holding that the latter expression is to be understood of the *place*, not the *time*, of the deed; but it is doubtful whether the idea of *time* can be divorced from the Gk. phrase. From a rider attached to Erasinides' decree, we know that the claim of Apollodorus (cf. also Lysias *c. Agorat. l.c.*) was challenged, and on the whole it seems likely, as Arnold says, that 'some zealous friends of the democracy laid claim to a merit with which really they had no concern.' (See Tucker on Thuc. VIII. *l.c.*)—**παρὰ τὴν κρήνην τὴν ἐν τοῖς οἰσύοις**: 'by the fountain in the osier-beds,' presumably within the confines of the marketplace: there being no doubt several κρῆναι, τὴν ἐν τοῖς οἰσύοις is added for purposes of identification.

ληφθέντων] i.q. συλληφθέντων: cf. *supra* § 52 λαβοῦσα ἀπέκτεινε.

ἐξήγαγε] *liberavit*, 'set them free.'

ἀνέκρινε] 'held an inquiry into the matter': cf. ἀνάκρισις, the preliminary investigation of a case before the archon.

ζητῶν] here of a judicial, frequently of a philosophical, inquiry.

προδιδόντα] 'was scheming to betray': conative impf., but possibly = προδότην ὄντα, 'that he was *guilty of treason*' to the state: cf. ἀδικεῖν. Goodwin, § 27.

§ 113. Κριτίου εἰπόντος] 'on the motion of Critias,' who was afterwards chief of 'the Thirty.'

τὸν μὲν νεκρὸν κρίνειν προδοσίας] 'that the dead should be tried for treason': for the active infin., cf. *supra* § 16 ἐψηφίσατο ὁ δῆμος...κατακομίζειν *n*.

κἂν δόξῃ] *si visus sit.*

προδότης ὤν...τεθάφθαι] Cf. Xen. *Hell.* I. 7. 22 νόμος ἐστίν... ἐάν τις τὴν πόλιν προδιδῷ...κριθέντα ἐν δικαστηρίῳ, ἂν καταγνωσθῇ, μὴ ταφῆναι ἐν τῇ Ἀττικῇ, κ.τ.λ.

τά γε ὀστᾶ] γε [Jacob (Bl., Sof.) for τε] implies that the exhumation of the bones was the next best thing after the unjustifiable burial.

ἐξορίσαι ἔξω τῆς Ἀ.] Cf. *supra* § 89 μονώτατος δ' ἂν...ἐξορισθείη τῆς χώρας *n.*, Hyper. *Lycoph.* [or. 1] *ad fin.*

κέηται] this form is quoted also from Plat. *Soph.* 257 C and Xen. *Oec.* 8. 19. [L. S. quote διακέησθε from Isocr. *Antid.* § 278, but the reference should be to § 259.]

τοῦ...προδιδόντος] the same possibilities as in προδιδόντα, *supra* § 112.

§ 114. ἀπολογῶνται] conative, 'seek to defend.'

ἐνόχους...ἐπιτιμίοις] Cf. *supra* § 4 τοὺς ἐνόχους τοῖς...ἐπιτιμίοις *n.*

τὸν διασῴζοντα] 'he that would save' the traitor: Goodwin, § 25.

ἐκ τῶν κινδύνων] This const. seems rarer than the simple gen. with ἀπαλλάττειν.

λαβὲ δ' αὐτοῖς] αὐτοῖς is a 'dativus commodi,' or 'of the person interested in the action,' esp. common, as here, in calling for documents: cf. *supra* § 23 *n*.

§ 115. τούτου τοῦ ψηφίσματος] The demonstrative is usually

§ 116] NOTES 195

omitted in cases like this: see the exx. collected by Rehd., App. 2, p. 155.

ἔπειτα ἐκεῖνοι μὲν...ὑμεῖς δ'] For ἔπειτα, cf. *supra* § 27, and for μὲν...δέ, *supra* § 42 *nn*.

Ἀρίσταρχον καὶ Ἀλεξικλέα] Both of these belonged, like Phrynichus, to the extreme oligarchical party and figure in Thuc.'s account of the revolution of 411 (Thuc. VIII. 90–98). The former is described by Thuc. as ἀνὴρ ἐν τοῖς μάλιστα καὶ ἐκ πλείστου ἐναντίος τῷ δήμῳ, and when the oligarchs were compelled to flee the city, he made himself notorious by betraying the fort of Oenoe on the Boeotian frontier to the enemy (Thuc. VIII. 98; Xen. *Hell.* I. 7. 28). From the latter passage we infer that he had been tried and put to death some time prior to 406 B.C., presumably on the strength of his previous career generally and not on the specific charge assigned by Lycurgus.

αὐτὸ τὸ σῶμα] 'the actual person' of the traitor) (τὰ τοῦ προδότου ὀστᾶ.

ὑποχείριον...τῇ ψήφῳ] Cf. *supra* §§ 2, 27, 91.

§ 116. ἐκεῖνοι μὲν...ὑμεῖς δέ] Cf. *supra* § 42 *n.*

ταῖς ἐσχάταις...μετῆλθον] 'visited with the most severe penalties': μετέρχομαι in this sense (cf. διώκειν, φεύγειν, ἀλίσκεσθαι) suggests the primitive 'avenger of blood': cf. Antiph. I. § 10 ὀρθῶς καὶ δικαίως μετέρχομαι τὸν φονέα τοῦ πατρός, Plat. *Protag.* 322 A Προμηθέα...κλοπῆς δίκη μετῆλθεν.

ὡς οὐδὲν ἀδικοῦντα] 'as if he were entirely guiltless,' i.q. ὡς οὐδὲν ἄδικον ὄντα: Goodwin, § 27.

μὴ δῆτα] sc. τοῦτο ποιήσητε, but the imper. is idiomatically omitted in the Greek.

<οὔτε γὰρ ὅσιον>] See Crit. App.

καὶ γὰρ εἰ μὲν ἓν κ.τ.λ.] 'now had there been (only) one such decree on record, it might have been argued that they passed it in a temper rather than from real conviction': γεγονὸς ἦν ψ. represents the passive of ψ. ποιεῖσθαι, and lays rather more stress than ἐγεγόνει would have done on the *state* as opp. to the *act*: 'were in existence,' 'were on record.'—δι' ἀλήθειαν is explained

13—2

by φύσει just below, the contrast being between the haste of anger (δι' ὀργήν) and their real or settled conviction as to the gravity of the offences.

ὅταν δὲ παρὰ πάντων...τιμωρίαν] *cum tamen de omnibus pariter eandem poenam sumpserint*: ὅταν has the causal sense which frequently attaches to ὅτε and ὁπότε, *quoniam, quando, quandoquidem*: cf. Soph. *O.T.* 918 ὅτ' οὖν παραινοῦσ' οὐδὲν ἐς πλέον ποιῶ, *Ant.* 170.

§ 117. Ἵππαρχον...τὸν Χάρμου] This Hipparchus, acc. to Androtion *ap.* Harpocr., was a relation of the Pisistratids, and was the first victim of the ordinance of ostracism, 487 B.C.: cf. Plut. *Nic.* 11 πρῶτος δὲ (ἐξωστρακίσθη) Ἵππαρχος ὁ Χολαργεύς, συγγενής τις ὢν τοῦ τυράννου. Lycurgus is apparently our only authority for the additional detail concerning him in this passage. [The MSS. give τὸν Τιμάρχου, which some editors correct to Χάρμου, following Harpocr.: Ἵππ. ὁ Χάρμου, ὥς φησι Λυκοῦργος ἐν τῷ κατὰ Λεωκράτους. Others correct Harpocr. from the MSS.; but the Hipparchus intended is no doubt one and the same.]

ἐν τῷ δήμῳ] i.e. before the Assembly, acting as a law-court (Heliaea).

ἔρημον τὸν ἀγῶνα ἐάσαντα] 'having left the case undefended,' 'having let it go by default': so ἐρήμην (sc. δίκην) κατηγορεῖν, ἑλεῖν, ὀφλεῖν, 'be accuser in,' 'win,' 'lose,' an undefended suit.

τοῦτον] For the resumptive pronoun, cf. *supra* §§ 82, 93, etc.

ἐπειδή...οὐκ ἔλαβον...ὅμηρον] 'since they could not lay hands on his person to answer for his guilt': rather an odd use of ὅμηρος, but the sense is clear.

ἐξ ἀκροπόλεως] The article is frequently omitted with this and similar nouns (cf. πόλις, ἀγορά) which are at once common and proper.

συγχωνεύσαντες] 'having melted it down': cf. Dem. *c. Androt.* § 70 φήσας δ' ἀπορρεῖν τὰ φύλλα τῶν στεφάνων...συγχωνεύειν ἔπεισεν.

ποιήσαντες στήλην] The person who had his name so inscribed was στηλίτης: cf. Isocr. *De Big.* § 9 ἐλαύνειν αὐτὸν ἐξ ἁπάσης τῆς Ἑλλάδος καὶ στηλίτην ἀναγράφειν, Dem. *Phil.* III. § 45 ἐτιμωροῦντο οὓς αἴσθοιντο ὥστε καὶ στηλίτας ποιεῖν.

τοὺς ἀλ. καὶ τοὺς πρ.] 'sinners and traitors,' as a class: cf. Andoc. *De Myst.* § 51 ἀναγραφέντας ἐν στήλαις ὡς ὄντας ἀλιτηρίους τῶν θεῶν.—For ἐψηφίσαντο...ἀναγράφειν, cf. *supra* §§ 16, 113, *nn*.

καὶ οἱ ἄλλοι δὲ προδόται] '*and* other traitors *as well*': cf. *supra* § 28 *n*.

§ 118. λαβὲ...ἀναγίγνωσκε] Cf. *supra* § 36 *n*.

καθ' ὅ] 'in pursuance of which.'

ὑπόγραμμα] strictly correct as being *on the base* of the στήλη, but we must be content with 'inscription.'

τοὺς ὕστερον προσαναγραφέντας] 'those who had their names added (πρoς-) later.'

§ 119. τί δοκοῦσιν ὑμῖν] 'what think ye of them?': sc. perhaps γιγνώσκειν out of the following question, but the expression is idiomatic, and is not to be explained simply by the omission of a verb: cf. Aesch. *Ag.* 935 τί δ' ἂν δοκεῖ σοι Πρίαμος, εἰ τάδ' ἤνυσεν; Plat. *Phaedr.* 234 C τί σοι φαίνεται ὁ λόγος; οὐχ ὑπερφυῶς... εἰρῆσθαι;

ὁμοίως ὑμῖν] ὑμῖν depends upon ὁμοίως.

καὶ οὐκ] For the structure of the sentence, cf. *supra* §§ 70, 71 ἆρά γ' ὅμοιοι κ.τ.λ., and notes there. Here we have καὶ οὐκ for the commoner ἀλλ' οὐκ in such cases, and 'instead of' (as at *l.c.*) is again the best equivalent: 'do they appear to you to have held the same views as you with regard to the guilty, instead of pulling down and punishing (as they actually did)?' etc.: or make a new sentence and say, 'Did they not rather pull down?' etc.—**καὶ τὸ σῶμα**: 'the actual person': the statue was the next best thing.—**ὑποχείριον** closely with λαβεῖν, 'get it into their power.'—**τοῦ προδότου...τοῦ προδότου**: Es deletes the first, Blass the second, but Lyc. loves to ring the changes on this word (v. Rehd. *ad loc.*) and probably both are genuine.—**ταῖς ἐνδεχομέναις τιμωρίαις**, 'such penalties as were possible.'

οὐχ ὅπως] The particles here have each a separate force, the negative referring to the general idea of the preceding clause, and giving a formal antithesis to ἀλλ' ἵνα: 'their object was not (simply) to *melt* the statue, but to leave an example,' etc. For sentiment and structure, cf. Dem. *Phil.* III. §41, where after γράμματα τῶν προγόνων...ἀκεῖνοι κατέθεντ' εἰς στήλην χαλκῆν γράψαντες εἰς ἀκρόπολιν (referring to the στήλη of Arthmius, *supra* § 111 *n.*) some MSS. give οὐχ ἵν' αὐτοῖς ᾖ χρήσιμα (καὶ γὰρ ἄνευ τούτων τῶν γραμμάτων τὰ δέοντ' ἐφρόνουν), ἀλλ' ἵν' ὑμεῖς ἔχηθ' ὑπομνήματα...ὡς ὑπὲρ τῶν τοιούτων σπουδάζειν προσήκει.

§ 120. αὐτοῖς] Cf. *supra* §§ 23, 114 *nn.*

τὸ ἕτερον ψήφισμα] Of this decree nothing further seems to be known.

περὶ τῶν εἰς Δ. μεταστάντων] 'concerning absconders to Decelea.' Decelea, which lay due north of Athens on the road to Oropus, was seized and fortified by the Peloponnesians in 413 B.C. (the nineteenth year of the Peloponnesian War), from which time forward it was a great source of annoyance to Athens as a convenient rendezvous for deserters (cf. the name ὁ Δεκελεικὸς πόλεμος which is sometimes applied to the latter part of the war). Another cause of distress was that Athenian corn-supplies, formerly conveyed overland *via* Decelea, had now to be carried round Sunium, which was a slow and expensive business (cf. Thuc. VII. 28; Cornford, *Thuc. Mythist.* p. 33), so that in this respect, as in others, Athens 'was blockaded by the L.' (cf. Thuc. *l.c.* ἀντὶ τοῦ πόλις εἶναι φρούριον κατέστη).

ὅτι περὶ τῶν προδοτῶν...ἐποιοῦντο] 'that the penalties which our ancestors prescribed for traitors were uniform and mutually consistent.'

§ 121. τούτου τοῦ ψηφίσματος] Cf. *supra* § 115 *n.*

ἐπανιὼν ἁλίσκηται] 'should be caught returning' to Athens: the ptcp. of that in which a person is detected is common with this verb, cf. Plat. *Apol.* 29 C ἐὰν δὲ ἁλῷς ἔτι τοῦτο πράττων, Her. I. 112, 209, etc.

ἀπαγαγεῖν...πρὸς τοὺς θεσμοθέτας] 'it should be open to any Athenian to bring them before the thesmothetae': ἀπάγειν was technically said of 'summarily arresting' (cf. ἀπαγωγή) a person,

§ 122]   NOTES   199

whom it was perhaps necessary to take in the act (ἐπ' αὐτοφώρῳ) to make this procedure legitimate (see the argument in Lysias, *C. Agorat.* §§ 85–87). ἀπαγωγή was allowed (1) against 'malefactors' (κακοῦργοι) in the technical application of the term, e.g. thieves (κλέπται), clothes-stealers (λωποδύται), etc.; (2) against persons labouring under any kind of disfranchisement (ἀτιμία), if detected exercising the rights from which the law excluded them; (3) against persons banished either for homicide or political crimes, if they unlawfully returned (κατιέναι) to the country. The Eleven (οἱ ἕνδεκα) had jurisdiction in cases (1) and (2); the Thesmothetae (the six junior archons acting as a college) in (3), as here.—**τὸν βουλόμενον**: the regular phrase of a privilege which any one may claim: cf. the familiar ἐξεῖναι τῷ β., etc.—**παραλαβόντας**: sc. τοὺς θεσμοθέτας.—**τῷ ἐπὶ τοῦ ὀρύγματος**, 'the officer in charge of the pit,' the official style of the executioner at the βάραθρον (outside the Piraic Gate, on the western boundary of the city), into which condemned criminals were thrown: so also ὁ ἐπὶ τῷ ὀρύγματι.

ἔπειτα ἐκεῖνοι μὲν...ὑμεῖς δέ] Cf. *supra* § 115 *n*.

ἐν αὐτῇ τῇ χώρᾳ] Decelea, after all, was on Attic soil.

εἰς Ῥόδον] These words are bracketed here by several editors (as also *supra* §§ 55, 70), on the ground that the *fact* of L.'s flight, not its *destination*, is the important thing: but if Rhodes, as we have reason to suppose, was in bad odour at Athens at the time, the mention of it would create all the greater *invidia* against L.

§ 122. **περὶ τοῦ ἐν Σ. τελευτήσαντος**] The reference is apparently to the story related by Herodotus (IX. 5), who calls the traitor Lycidas, and places the incident *after* the battle of Salamis, when Mardonius was making offers to the Athenians: cf. *supra* § 71 *nn*. Demosthenes, however (*De Cor.* § 204), followed by Cicero (*De Off.* III. 11), gives the name as Cyrsilus, and places the incident *before* the battle, when the Athenians were considering the question of embarking. We can hardly doubt that all three accounts refer to one and the same incident; but whether Herod. or Dem. is correct with the name (which Lyc. does not mention), only the inscr. (as Rehd. observes, App. 3, *ad loc.*) can decide.

περιελομένη τοὺς στεφάνους] 'taking off their crowns,' which they would be wearing as the badge of their office as βουλευταί: crowns were worn also by archons, priests, and by orators in the assembly: cf. Dem. *Mid.* § 17 τὸν ἐστεφανωμένον ἄρχοντα, [Dem.] XXVI. § 5 ὅταν ἀποχειροτονηθῶσί τινες τῶν ἐν ταῖς ἀρχαῖς, παραχρῆμα πέπαυνται ἄρχοντες καὶ τοὺς στεφάνους περιῄρηνται, 'have their crowns taken away from them.' The verb is specially applicable to anything that 'encloses' or 'fits all round' (τεῖχος, στέφανος, δακτύλιος).

εὐγενεῖς γὰρ...ἐκέκτηντο] 'for they were distinguished not only for nobleness of soul but also for the nobleness of the vengeance which they meted out to transgressors' is perhaps the most we can make of the slightly zeugmatic Greek. [εὐγενεῖς Dobree (Sch., Bl.): ἐγγενεῖς Rehd.: συγγενεῖς codd. (Thalh.).]

§ 123. **τί οὖν;**] We may supply δοκεῖτε or ὑμῖν δοκεῖ from the next clause, but τί οὖν is idiomatic (cf. *supra* § 119 *init. n.*), like *quid? quid tandem?* in Latin.

βουλομένοις] 'if you wish.'

μὴ ἀποκτεῖναι] N (Bl., Sofer) has μὴ οὐκ ἀποκ. The question, converted into a statement, is equivalent to οὐ πάτριόν ἐστι Λ. μὴ οὐκ ἀποκτεῖναι, which may be sound Greek, as far as the form goes, but it does not admit of being stated in the positive form πάτριόν ἐστι Λ. μὴ ἀποκ., which is contrary to the speaker's contention.

ὁπότε] causal, like the two ὅτε's following, cf. Lat. *quando*= *quoniam*: cf. Thuc. II. 60 ὁπότε οὖν πόλις μὲν τὰς ἰδίας ξυμφορὰς οἵα τε φέρειν, εἷς δ' ἕκαστος τὰς ἐκείνης ἀδύνατος, πῶς οὐ χρὴ πάντας ἀμύνειν αὐτῇ; Dem. *Ol.* I *init.* ὅτε τοίνυν τοῦθ' οὕτως ἔχει, etc. Cf. *supra* § 116 ὅταν...εἰληφότες ὦσι *n.*

τὴν οἰκουμένην] sc. πόλιν, 'the inhabited city,' 'the city while still inhabited')(ἀνάστατον τὴν πόλιν οὖσαν, through the Persian occupation.

τοὺς ἐπιχειρήσαντας...ἀποστερεῖν] The reference is to οἱ εἰς Δ. μεταστάντες, *supra* §§ 120 sq.—For τῆς παρὰ τοῦ δήμου σωτηρίας, cf. *supra* § 15 τὴν παρ' ὑμῶν...τιμωρίαν *n.*—[The want of an object to ἀποστερεῖν, though not perhaps absolutely necessary to the sense, has been felt by most editors: Reiske supplied ἑαυτοὺς after ἐπιχ., Herwerden τὴν πατρίδα, Blass τὴν πόλιν after σωτηρίας.]

ἐκόλασαν...ἐτιμωροῦντο] κολάζειν of the correction of the offender, τιμωρεῖσθαι of the satisfaction of the offended: Arist. *Rhet.* 1. 10. 17.

§ 124. καὶ ταῦτα] i.e. what I have said already.

γνῶναι] i.q. ἱκανὰ ὥστε ὑμᾶς γνῶναι, 'sufficient to enable you to judge of,' etc.

τῆς στήλης] short for the inscription upon it.

τὸ γὰρ μετὰ πολλῶν...καθίστησι] 'for instruction by (with the help of) numerous examples will enable you to decide with ease.'

μετὰ γὰρ τοὺς τριάκοντα] γὰρ *narrativum*: omit in trans.— 'The Thirty' were installed by the intervention of Lysander, and ruled Athens from Sept. to May, 404–3. Critias and Theramenes were two of the best known members of this body.—Lycurgus appears to be in error in placing the decree of Demophantus, of which he goes on to speak, 'after the Thirty,' as the evidence of the decree itself (cf. Rehd., App. 3, p. 184 *n.*) dates it to July or August, 410, i.e. 'after the *Four Hundred*.' Some suppose that the decree was re-enacted after the downfall of the Thirty, and that the preamble of the original was introduced in the revived measure; but it is as likely as not that the substitution of 'the Thirty' for 'the Four Hundred' is simply another of the historical slips which we have already noticed in the course of the speech (cf. *supra* §§ 62, 70 *sq.*).

οἷα οὐδεὶς...ἠξίωσε] sc. παθεῖν αὐτούς.—ἠξίωσε, 'thought it right': the speaker means that the oppression of the Thirty was not fully endorsed even by Athens' declared enemies, e.g. Sparta and Thebes. [ἠξίωσε is expelled by Dobr. (Sch., Es), but without good reason: ὑπὸ τῶν ξένων, ὑπὸ τῶν πολεμίων, which Sch. and Frohb. respectively substitute for it, give statements which are untrue in point of fact.]

κατεληλυθότες] The verb is technical of the return of exiles. The democrats were led by Thrasybulus, who made Phyle his headquarters: from here he descended and seized the Piraeus: Critias was killed at the battle of Munychia. The democracy was restored *c*. Sept. 403.

ἀπάσας τὰς ὁδοὺς...ἐνέφραξαν κ.τ.λ.] 'blocked up all the avenues to crime, having experience and knowledge of the first moves and methods of attack of those who plan to betray the democracy.'—ἀδικημάτων: here specially of *political* offences.— τὰς ὁδοὺς...ἐνέφραξαν: cf. Isocr. *Areop.* § 40 ἐμφράγματα γὰρ αὐτοὺς [a community with a multiplicity of laws] ποιουμένους τῶν ἁμαρτημάτων πολλοὺς τίθεσθαι τοὺς νόμους ἀναγκάζεσθαι, 'in seeking to raise *barriers against crime*, they are compelled,' etc.; Aeschin. *Ctes.* § 223 οὕτω δὲ ταῖς αἰτίαις ἐνέφραξας τὰς κατὰ σαυτοῦ τιμωρίας, 'barred the penalties against yourself by (counter) charges.'—τὰς ἀρχάς, 'the first occasions,' what they start from, somewhat akin to ἀφορμή: τὰς ἐφόδους, 'ways of approach,' 'methods of attack': the word suggests *grassari*.—τῶν προδιδόντων: cf. *supra* § 112 προδιδόντα τὴν πόλιν *n*.

§ 125. ἐψηφίσαντο γὰρ καὶ ὤμοσαν] The decree of Demophantus, referred to specifically *infra* § 127. It is quoted in full by Andoc. *De Myst.* §§ 96–98, and also mentioned by Dem. *Lept.* § 159. The relevant portion of it, for comparison with Lycurgus here and at § 127, runs as follows: ὁ δὲ ὅρκος ἔστω ὅδε· κτενῶ καὶ λόγῳ καὶ ἔργῳ καὶ ψήφῳ καὶ τῇ ἐμαυτοῦ χειρί, ἂν δυνατὸς ᾦ, ὃς ἂν καταλύσῃ τὴν δημοκρατίαν τὴν Ἀθήνῃσι,...καὶ ἐάν τις τυραννεῖν ἐπαναστῇ ἢ τὸν τύραννον συγκαταστήσῃ, καὶ ἐάν τις ἄλλος ἀποκτείνῃ, ὅσιον αὐτὸν νομιῶ εἶναι καὶ πρὸς θεῶν καὶ δαιμόνων, ὡς πολέμιον κτείναντα τὸν Ἀθηναίων.

ἐάν τις τυραννίδι ἐπιτιθῆται] 'if any one should attempt a tyranny,' i.e. attempt to establish one: cf. Aeschin. *Ctes.* § 235 οὐδεὶς πώποτε ἐπέθετο τῇ τοῦ δήμου καταλύσει, 'attempted the overthrow,' Lysias, or. VI. § 19 ναυκληρίᾳ ἐπιθέμενος τὴν θάλατταν ἔπλει, 'took to shipmastering.'—προδιδῷ...καταλύῃ: conative.

§ 126]   NOTES   203

τὸν αἰσθανόμενον...ἀποκτείναντα] 'whoever detected them should be guiltless of their blood,' lit. 'if he killed him.' With τὸν αἰσθανόμενον cf. the common ὁ βουλόμενος, and *supra* § 121.

καὶ κρεῖττον ἔδοξεν αὐτοῖς...δουλεύειν] 'and they thought it better that those lying under such an imputation should be put to death than that they themselves should have the attempt actually made upon them and be reduced to slavery': the const. in the second half of the sentence is quite normal and must be distinguished from *supra* § 84 Πελοποννησίοις...ἔδοξε...ἐξαναστήσαντας κατανείμασθαι, where ἔδοξε = *visum est*, 'they resolved.'— πειραθέντας I understand as passive (cf. Thuc. VI. 54 πειραθεὶς ὁ Ἁρμόδιος ὑπὸ Ἱππάρχου), which seems slightly more probable than middle (so Rehd., sc. αὐτῶν), in the absence of an accompanying gen.

ἀρχὴν γὰρ οὕτως κ.τ.λ.] 'for they considered that the citizens should simply live in such a way as that no one should so much as incur the suspicion of such crimes.' For the sentiment, cf. Isocr. *Areop.* § 42 (of the Athenians of an earlier time) ταῦτα διανοηθέντες οὐ τοῦτο πρῶτον ἐσκόπουν, δι' ὧν κολάσουσι τοὺς ἀκοσμοῦντας, ἀλλ' ἐξ ὧν παρασκευάσουσι μηδὲν αὐτοὺς ἄξιον ζημίας ἐξαμαρτάνειν.—ἀρχήν, lit. 'to start with,' and so 'at all,' *omnino*, mostly in negative sentences and preceding the negative, as Soph. *Ant.* 92 ἀρχὴν δὲ θηρᾶν οὐ πρέπει τἀμήχανα, 'a hopeless quest should not be made at all.' Also τὴν ἀρχήν, as Dem. *c. Aristocr.* § 93 τὴν ἀρχὴν γὰρ ἐξῆν αὐτῷ μὴ γράφειν, 'he need never have proposed at all,' Her. IV. 25, Isocr. *Antid.* § 272.

§ 126. τοῖς...συνιοῦσι καὶ βουλευομένοις] 'those who meet in council': βουλεύεσθαι, 'deliberate')(βουλεύειν, 'be a member of the βουλή,' but also = βουλεύεσθαι.

ὡς δεῖ] with ὑπόμνημα, 'a reminder of how you ought,' etc. ὡς = *quemadmodum* is less common than ὅπως or ὃν τρόπον.

καὶ διὰ τοῦτο...συνώμοσαν] ἄν τις αἴσθηται explains διὰ τοῦτο: they made the mere detection of the intent a ground for taking extreme measures.—μόνον goes with μέλλοντας.—ἀποκτείνειν: Cobet (Bl.) changes to ἀποκτενεῖν, but (as Rehd. rightly observes *ad loc.*) the whole stress falls on the *act*, not on the *time*. The decree itself, as quoted by Andoc. (ed. Hickie), has ὁμόσαι... ἀποκτείνειν. Curiously enough the provision on which Lyc., whose language reads like a quotation, lays so much stress, is not found in the decree as given by Andocides: see *supra* § 125 *n.*

τῶν μὲν γὰρ ἄλλων κ.τ.λ.] 'for in the case of other offences the penalties should be imposed after the deed, but in the case of treason and subversion of the democracy, before.' For good commentaries on this passage, cf. [Dem.] *c. Aristogit.* B. § 4 διὸ καὶ τὰς τιμωρίας ὁ Σόλων τοῖς μὲν ἰδιώταις ἐποίησε βραδείας, ταῖς δ' ἀρχαῖς καὶ τοῖς δημαγωγοῖς ταχείας, ὑπολαμβάνων τοῖς μὲν ἐνδέχεσθαι καὶ παρὰ τὸν χρόνον [i. e. ὕστερον τοῦ ἀδικήματος] τὸ δίκαιον λαβεῖν, τοῖς δ' οὐκ ἐνεῖναι περιμεῖναι· τὸ γὰρ τιμωρησόμενον οὐχ ὑπέσται τῆς πολιτείας καταλυθείσης, 'there will be no means of vengeance left once the constitution is subverted,' and Sallust, *Cat.* c. 52 (Cato's speech *ad init.*), which almost reads like an imitation of the Greek: '*nam cetera maleficia tum persequare, ubi facta sunt: hoc nisi provideris ne accidat, ubi evenit, frustra iudicia implores: capta urbe nihil fit reliqui victis.*'

παρ' αὐτῶν ἀδικούντων] (to obtain satisfaction) 'from them for the crime': ἀδικούντων is predicative.

κρείττους...γίγνονται...τιμωρίας] 'for they are already beyond the reach of punishment at the hands of the injured': for κρείσσων in this sense, cf. Thuc. III. 84 ἡ ἀνθρωπεία φύσις...ἐδήλωσεν ἀκρατὴς μὲν ὀργῆς οὖσα, κρείσσων δὲ τοῦ δικαίου, 'superior to considerations of right,' Arist. *Pol.* V. 12. 8 φαύλους καὶ κρείττους τῆς παιδείας = οὓς παιδευθῆναι ἀδύνατον (immediately following): v. L.S. *s.v.* κρείσσων, III.

c. 31. § 127. **τῆς προνοίας...τῶν ἔργων**] 'this foresight [which your ancestors displayed] and their practice.'

ἐν τῇ ψήφῳ] *in suffragio ferendo*, 'in giving your vote.'

ἐν τῇ τήμερον ἡμέρᾳ] Cf. *supra* § 2 *n.*

τῆς ἐκείνων τιμωρίας] 'of how they inflicted punishment.'

διομωμόκατε...τῷ ψ. τῷ Δ.] διομωμόκατε: 'you have solemnly sworn,' perhaps: the precise force of this compound is not always easy to determine.—τῷ ψ. τοῦ Δ.: cf. *supra* § 125.—**κτείνειν**: κτενεῖν Cob. (Bl.): cf. *supra* § 126 ἀποκτείνειν συνώμοσαν n.

καὶ λόγῳ καὶ ἔργῳ κ.τ.λ.] For the formula, cf. the extract from the decree quoted *supra* § 125, Aeschin. *Ctes.* § 109 (of the oath of the Amphictyons against the men of Crisa) ὅρκον ὤμοσαν ...βοηθήσειν τῷ θεῷ...καὶ χειρὶ καὶ ποδὶ καὶ φωνῇ καὶ πάσῃ δυνάμει, *Ib.* § 120.

μὴ γὰρ οἴεσθε...κληρονόμοι εἶναι] 'do not *think to be* inheritors of the properties...while you disclaim all portion in the oaths, etc.': οἴεσθε here is virtually = ἀξιοῦτε.

ταύτης δὲ μὴ κ.] For the resumptive δέ, cf. *supra* § 99 ὁ δὲ τῷ θεῷ πιθόμενος τοῦτ' ἔπραξε n.—κληρονομεῖν: cf. *supra* § 88 δικαίως ταύτης (sc. τῆς χώρας) καὶ τεθνεῶτες ἐκληρονόμουν.

c. 32. §§ 128–130. *The Lacedaemonians, whom you will pardon me for quoting once again, showed the same spirit as your ancestors in their treatment of the traitor Pausanias, and in the law which they passed respecting defaulters in their country's defence. This law I shall read to you. Where death is the penalty for cowardice, men will rather face the danger of battle than condemnation by their fellow-countrymen.*

§ 128. μή μοι ἀχθεσθῆτε] A προδιόρθωσις for what he suspects may be unpleasant to his hearers: cf. *supra* § 52 καὶ μηδεὶς μοι θορυβήσῃ. Praise of the institutions of another Greek state, which was expressly forbidden at Sparta, was presumably not encouraged elsewhere.

ἐκ πόλεως εὐνομουμένης] Sparta, with all her faults, was constantly quoted by Athenian statesmen and orators as the model, among cities, of εὐνομία, which, acc. to Aristotle (*Pol.* IV. 8. 6), comprehended 'good laws well obeyed.' *Eunomia*, 'Law and Order,' was the title of a poem by Tyrtaeus. Cf. Thuc. I. 18 ἡ γὰρ Λακεδαίμων...ἐκ παλαιτάτου καὶ εὐνομήθη καὶ ἀεὶ ἀτυράννευτος ἦν, Plat. *Crito* 52 E (the Laws to Socrates) σὺ δὲ οὔτε Λακεδαίμονα προῃροῦ οὔτε Κρήτην, ἃς δὴ ἑκάστοτε φῂς εὐνομεῖσθαι, where Adam remarks: 'What Socrates most admired in Crete and Sparta was their implicit obedience to the law:

they formed the best possible illustration of his principle—τὸ δίκαιον is τὸ νόμιμον.' Also *Prot.* 342 A ff., *Rep.* VIII. 544 C, Xen. *Mem.* III. 5. 15 and IV. 4. 15. 'Few sights are stranger than Plato and Xenophon turning their eyes away from their own free country to regard with admiration the constitution of Sparta....It attracted them because the old order survived there —the citizen absolutely submissive to the authority of the state, and not looking beyond it....Accordingly they saw in Sparta the image of what a state should be; just because it was relatively free from that individualism which they were themselves actively promoting by their speculations in political philosophy.' Bury, *H.G.* (1900), pp. 581–2.

ἀσφαλέστερον] 'with the more certainty.'

τὴν δικαίαν...τὴν εὔορκον] The force of the article with the adjs. depends on the fact that the 'vote,' in the abstract sense, must be for one or other of two things—acquittal or condemnation—the latter being of course, for Lycurgus, ἡ δικαία καὶ ἡ εὔορκος ψῆφος.

Παυσανίαν γὰρ τὸν βασιλέα] The victor of Plataea (479 B.C.), and leader of the confederate Greek fleet against Persia, till the allies disgusted by his conduct transferred the leadership to Athens and incidentally launched her on her imperial career. For his fortunes subsequent to Plataea, see Thuc. I. 94–134. The designation 'king' is not quite accurate, as P. simply succeeded his father Cleombrotus in the guardianship of his cousin Plistarchus, son of Leonidas, for whom he acted as regent from 479 till his death (*c.* 471) (Her. IX. 10); but it makes him all the more effective an example for Lycurgus of the punishment of treason in high places. The account of his death here agrees in the main with that of Thuc. (I. 134): later historians (Nepos, Diodorus, Polyaenus) introduce the inevitable sensational detail about his own mother, who is called Theano, bringing the first stone to wall him up.

τῆς Χαλκιοίκου] sc. θεᾶς, 'the goddess of the Brazen House,' an epithet of Athena Poliouchos at Sparta, of which various

§ 129]   NOTES   207

explanations are given: either (*a*) the temple was made of bronze (so apparently Paus. 10. 5. 5), or (*b*) it contained a bronze image of the goddess (so app. Paus. 3. 17. 3), or (*c*), as Frazer thinks probable (*Pausanias*, vol. III. c. xvii. p. 345), 'the building was merely lined with bronze plates, like the so-called Treasury of Atreus at Mycenae.'

ἀποικοδομήσαντες...ἀποσκευάσαντες] 'walled up the door'... 'pulled off the roof': Thuc. *l.c. μετὰ δὲ τοῦτο τοῦ τε οἰκήματος τὸν ὄροφον ἀφεῖλον καὶ τὰς θύρας...ἀπῳκοδόμησαν, προσκαθεζόμενοί τε ἐξεπολιόρκησαν λιμῷ.*

περιστρατοπεδεύσαντες] the act. form of the verb appears to belong to late writers, e.g. Polybius and Plutarch.

πρὶν ἤ] an 'Ionism' which was abjured by many Atticists: *πρὶν* Es (Bl.). But see Kühner II². 455.

τῷ λιμῷ] hunger, as a form of death (*τῷ*).

§ 129. πᾶσιν ἐπίσημον ἐποίησαν...ὅτι] 'made his punishment a signal proof to all the world, that' etc. [Editors have found difficulty in this const., and either delete *τὴν τιμωρίαν* with Morus (Sch., Es), or change to *τῇ τιμωρίᾳ* Morus (Thalh., Sofer). Rehd. defends the text, quoting Ar. *Thesm.* 684 *πᾶσιν ἐμφανὴς ὁρᾶν ἔσται...ὅτι τὰ παράνομα θεὸς ἀποτίνεται,* Plat. *Crito* 44 D *αὐτὰ δὲ δῆλα τὰ παρόντα νυνί, ὅτι οἷοί τ' εἰσὶν οἱ πολλοὶ κ.τ.λ., Rep.* I. 348 E.]

αἱ παρὰ τῶν θεῶν ἐπικουρίαι] Cf. *supra* §§ 15, 123, etc.

ἀδικοῦσιν] *ἀδικοῦσιν* is bracketed, as might be expected, by some of the editors (Bk., Bl.), but it seems to be Lyc.'s manner to make these idiomatic ellipses more explicit: cf. *supra* §§ 33, 92, and notes.

τῶν ἐκεῖ γεγενημένων] 'of Spartan practice.' [Bl. brackets *γεγ.*]

διαρρήδην λέγοντα ἀποθνῄσκειν] 'expressly prescribing death as the penalty.'

εἰς αὐτὸ τοῦτο...τυγχάνουσι] 'fixing as the due penalty precisely the thing of which they stand most in dread,' i.e. death: they prevent cowardice in facing death by making death the punishment for avoiding it. With τυγχάνουσι supply as subject οἱ μὴ ἐθέλοντες...κινδυνεύειν. Of the two εἰς's, which both seem genuine, the first seems to be used as we say 'to fix something *at* so-and-so': the second may be illustrated from Soph. *O.T.* 980 σὺ δ' εἰς τὰ μητρὸς μὴ φοβοῦ νυμφεύματα. [Hoffmann, followed by Sofer, omits the first εἰς, which simplifies the const.]

καὶ τὴν ἐκ τοῦ πολέμου σωτηρίαν...αἰσχύνης] lit. 'and made a safe return from battle answerable to danger along with disgrace,' i.e. 'subject to' or 'dependent upon' *a degrading trial.* The meaning is: if a man comes out of battle unscathed, he must be prepared to answer the question 'why?,' should it be raised, by submitting to a trial which will fasten disgrace upon him if he fails to make good his defence. In this sense his safety may be said to be ὑπεύθυνος, 'subject to,' 'dependent upon' such a trial, inasmuch as the trial decides whether it has been honourably won. For κίνδυνος in the judicial sense (Lat. *periculum*, O.E. *danger*), cf. τὸν πρὸς τοὺς νόμους (sc. κίνδυνον) in the next §, *supra* § 34 τὸν ὑπὲρ προδοσίας κινδυνεύοντα, and Lysias IX. § 7 τὸν παρ' ὑμῶν κίνδυνον ὑποστάντες, i.e. the prospect of being called to account before a court.

ἀναπόδεικτον] a late word, occurring first in Lyc., 'a tale unsupported by proof': cf. *supra* § 23 ἵνα δὲ μὴ λόγον οἴησθε εἶναι, ἀλλ' εἰδῆτε τὴν ἀλήθειαν.

αὐτοῖς] Cf. *supra* §§ 23, 114, etc.

§ 130. ὁ...παρὰ τῶν πολιτῶν φόβος] *metus, quem iniciunt cives* (Sofer). Cf. *supra* §§ 15, 49 *nn.*

φιλοψυχήσει] a word of poetic complexion: cf. the frag. of Tyrtaeus, l. 18 (*supra* § 107).

ὑποκειμένην] 'is reserved for them': cf. [Dem.] XXXIV. § 19 τιμωρία ὑπόκειται τοῖς τὰ ψευδῆ μαρτυροῦσι. [Corais (Es) would change to ἐπικειμένην, on the analogy of ζημίαν ἐπιτιθέναι (cf. Thuc. II. 24, III. 70), but unnecessarily.]

<ταύτην> τιμωρίαν] 'this as a punishment': cf. *supra* § 79 ταύτην πίστιν δίδωσιν *n.* [<ταύτην> is due to Scheibe (Es, Bl., Sof.): Rehd. (Thalh.) keeping αὐτῷ τιμωρίαν (with the MSS.

except Z) arranges: αὐτῷ τιμωρίαν—οὐδεμίαν γάρ...δειλίας—θάνατον; deleting ἤ.]

δυοῖν κινδύνοιν ὑποκειμένοιν] 'of two dangers which are proposed to them,' slightly different in sense from ὑποκειμένην above.

τὸν πρὸς τοὺς πολεμίους...τὸν πρὸς τοὺς νόμους] sc. κίνδυνον, but with a slight difference of meaning, the first being what one might call the *physical*)(the *judicial*, danger: see previous §. For the sentiment, cf. Isocr. *Paneg.* § 77 δεινότερον ἐνόμιζον εἶναι κακῶς ὑπὸ τῶν πολιτῶν ἀκούειν ἢ καλῶς ὑπὲρ τῆς πόλεως ἀποθνῄσκειν, Aeschin. *Ctes.* § 175 εἰσὶν (sc. φύσεως γραφαί). τίνος ἕνεκα; ἵν' ἕκαστος ἡμῶν τὰς ἐκ τῶν νόμων ζημίας φοβούμενος μᾶλλον ἢ τοὺς πολεμίους ἀμείνων ἀγωνιστὴς ὑπὲρ τῆς πατρίδος ὑπάρχῃ. So Polybius (VI. 37), speaking of Roman discipline, says 'it sometimes happens that men confront certain death at their stations, because, from the fear of the punishment awaiting them at home, they refuse to quit their post.'

cc. 33–34. §§ 131–134. *The conduct of Leocrates is more reprehensible than that of ordinary deserters in the field in that he fled his country without even attempting to defend his own hearth, thus betraying the natural instincts displayed even by the unreasoning animals. In the eyes of the outside world, he is in a worse case than homicides: the man who abandons his own country in the hour of need will not readily lift a finger on behalf of the country of others. More than any other traitor, Leocrates deserves even a severer penalty than death. Other traitors are punished when their crime is only in contemplation: in L.'s case it was a* fait accompli.

§ 131. **ποριζόμενος**] 'seeking to secure.'

ἀλλὰ μόνος οὗτος κ.τ.λ.] 'but L. alone of all men has proved false even to the proper and necessary instincts of nature, which are distinguished even by the unreasoning animals as the greatest and weightiest': οἰκεῖα, what specially or peculiarly appertains to one, Lat. *proprius*: ἀναγκαῖα, 'necessary,' whether in the physical or (as here) in the moral sense: cf. Dem. *c. Steph.* A. [or. XLV] § 53 οὐ γὰρ τοὺς γεγραμμένους νόμους ὁ τοιοῦτος ἄνθρωπος μόνους, ἀλλὰ καὶ τὰ τῆς φύσεως οἰκεῖ᾽ ἀναιρεῖ.—**τοῖς ἀλόγοις ζῴοις**, 'the brutes')('man,' whose distinguishing characteristic is λόγος (rational speech), Arist. *Pol.* I. 2. 10 λόγον δὲ μόνον ἄνθρωπος ἔχει τῶν ζῴων. In modern Greek, curiously enough, ἄλογον is 'a horse.'—**διείληπται**, of the standing attitude, 'have been' and so 'are (as a permanent characteristic) defined': with this, τοῖς ζῴοις is the so-called 'dative of the agent,' which is very closely akin to the possessive dative.

§ 132. τὰ γοῦν πετεινά] is acc. of the object after ἔστιν ἰδεῖν, 'one may see': cf. *supra* § 80 ὅμως ὡς ἴχνος ἔστιν...ἰδεῖν τὴν ἐκείνων ἀρετήν.

ἃ μάλιστα πέφυκε πρὸς τάχος] 'which are best adapted by nature for swiftness,' and so might be expected to offer the less resistance.—For the text, see Crit. App.

οὐδ᾽ ἀγρία γὰρ κ.τ.λ.] The source of the lines is unknown, and Es and Rehd. bracket them as an importation by a later copyist.—**ὄρνις**: so several times in Trag.: cf. Soph. *Ant.* 1021 οὐδ᾽ ὄρνις εὐσήμους ἀπορροιβδεῖ βοάς, but ὄρνῑς in Ar. and normally in Attic: v. Jebb on Soph. *l.c.* and L.S. *s.v.*—**ἠξίωσεν**: 'deigns,' 'expects': gnomic.

ὑπερβέβληκε] absol. 'has so surpassed' in cowardice: cf. Dem. *De Chers.* § 16 κακοδαιμονῶσιν ἄνθρωποι καὶ ὑπερβάλλουσιν ἀνοίᾳ.

§ 133. ἤλαυνεν] supply as subject πᾶσα or ἑκάστη out of οὐδεμία (as frequently): cf. Soph. *Ant.* 263 κοὐδεὶς ἐναργής, ἀλλ᾽ ἔφευγε (sc. ἕκαστος) μὴ εἰδέναι, Dem. *Lept.* § 74 μηδεὶς φθόνῳ τὸ μέλλον ἀκούσῃ, ἀλλ᾽ ἂν ἀληθὲς ᾖ σκοπείτω.—**εἴασε**, of the act of permission: ἤλαυνεν, of their attitude towards him.

οἱ...φόνου φεύγοντες] here, perhaps, in the literal application of the phrase, 'those who flee (their country) for murder,' i.e. anticipate their sentence by going into voluntary exile, as the murderer had the option of doing.

οὐκ ἔχουσιν ἐχθροὺς τοὺς ὑποδ.] 'do not find those who shelter them hostile to them.'

ταχύ γ᾽ ἄν] 'would be in a hurry, I suppose, to' etc.: ironical.

Cf. the idiomatic σχολῇ γε, 'at one's leisure,' and so 'scarcely,' 'hardly': freq. *in apodosi*, Plat. *Rep.* 610 E, etc.

μεθέξουσιν] 'are ready to share.'

ἀξιώσουσι] sc. αὐτήν, i.e. τὴν πόλιν.

§ 134. τῶν πώποτε προδοτῶν] 'of the traitors of all (previous) time': cf. *supra* § 58 *n*. [Es would change to προδόντων on the ground that πώποτε is most frequently joined with a ptcp., but οἱ πώποτε occurs absol., and τῶν πώποτε ἀνθρώπων is quoted from Xen. *Hell.* V. 4. 1.]

εἴ τις μείζων εἴη τιμωρία] The form of the protasis regards the invention of a more severe penalty than death as remotely possible: εἴ τις μείζων ἦν would have denied it. Goodwin, § 410 ff.

μέλλοντες ἀδικεῖν] 'though their crime is only prospective')(διαπεπραγμένος ὅπερ ἐπεχείρησε.

ὅταν ληφθῶσι] See Crit. App.

ὅπερ ἐπεχείρησε] sc. διαπράττεσθαι, but not necessarily, as ἐπιχειρεῖν is found with an object acc.: cf. Plat. *Crit.* 45 C οὐδὲ δίκαιόν μοι δοκεῖς ἐπιχειρεῖν πρᾶγμα, *Phileb.* 57 B.

τὴν πόλιν ἐγκαταλιπών] these words are partly explanatory of ὅπερ, partly predicative with κρίνεται: 'is on his trial for having deserted.'

c. 35. §§ 135-140. *I wonder what plea the speakers on his behalf can possibly put forward for his acquittal: if their friendship with him, they virtually confess their sympathy with his conduct. His dead father, I imagine, whose statue he abandoned to the enemy, would rise up in judgment against him. In this connexion Leocrates may be said to have outraged Zeus Soter, whose name might fairly have been added to the indictment. As to the paid advocates for the defence, remember that these deserve your severest resentment, for their defence of L. is a proof that they would readily share his actions. Some of them will even go the length of seeking to beg him off on the strength of their own public services; but you must discriminate between services which tend merely to the glorification of the individual and those which benefit the state as a whole. No public service is so great as to be entitled to be rewarded with the acquittal of traitors.*

§ 135. θαυμάζω...τῶν...μελλόντων, διὰ τί] θαυμάζω is frequent in the orators c. gen. of the person, followed by a clause introduced by a relative or εἰ, denoting the point in the person's conduct which occasions the surprise (so θαυμάζειν τί τινος, to wonder at something *in* a person): cf. Antiph. or. 1. § 5 θαυμάζω ...τοῦ ἀδελφοῦ, ἥντινά ποτε γνώμην ἔχων ἀντίδικος καθέστηκε πρὸς ἐμέ, Dem. *C. Timocr.* § 66 θαυμάζω δ' αὐτοῦ τί ποτε καὶ τολμήσει λέγειν, Isocr. *Paneg.* § 170 θαυμάζω δὲ τῶν δυναστευόντων...εἰ ...ἡγοῦνται, etc.: also *supra* § 28 καὶ ταῦτα δ', ὦ ἄνδρες, ἐμοῦ θεωρήσατε *n*.

χρῆσθαι] *uti*, 'associate with.'

πρὶν...πρᾶξαι...ἄδηλον ἦν] As far as the form of the sentence goes, we might have had πρὶν...ἔπραξε Λ., ἄδηλον ἦν (= οὐ δῆλον ἦν...πρὶν ἔπραξε): the effect of this would have been to lay stress on the action of L. as the turning-point in people's estimation of his friends' character. But the prominent idea is simply the different estimate of their character *then* and *now*, L.'s action being indicated merely as the dividing line between the two: in other words, the idea of *before* (πρὶν πρᾶξαι) is more prominent than that of *until* (πρὶν ἔπραξε). Goodwin, *M. T.* § 628.

ὁποῖοί τινες ὄντες ἐτύγχανον] we should say simply 'their real character was uncertain': the Greek is reminiscent of Plato's phraseology.

τοῖς αὐτοῖς ἤθεσι χρώμενοι] 'because they are men of like manners.'

πολὺ πρότερον...ἤ] The fusion of the ideas 'before' and 'rather,' which πρότερον exemplifies, is seen in our 'sooner,' 'they would *sooner* die than surrender.' πρότερον, in form and usage, is in fact the exact counterpart of Eng. *rather*, i.e. *rath-er*, 'sooner.'

ἐξαιτητέον] *deprecandum*, 'beg him off': cf. *supra* §§ 20, 67 *nn*.

§ 136]   NOTES   213

§ 136. αὐτῷ] 'I fancy *he would find* his dead father his severest judge': cf. Isocr. *Aeginet*. § 44 οἶμαι γὰρ ἂν αὐτὸν (sc. τὸν πατέρα) πάντων γενέσθαι ταύτῃ χαλεπώτατον δικαστήν.

εἴ τις ἄρ' ἔστιν αἴσθησις...γιγνομένων] 'if indeed the departed [τοῖς ἐκεῖ] have any consciousness of what passes on earth [τῶν ἐνθάδε γιγ.]': this or a practically identical phrase occurs three times in Isocrates (*Evag.* § 2, *Plat.* § 61, *Aeginet.* § 42), but it is perhaps to be regarded here simply as a speculative commonplace with regard to the dead rather than as a trace of Isocratean study on the part of Lycurgus. For a close parallel in Latin, cf. Servius ap. Cic. *Ad Fam*. IV. 5. 6 *quod si qui etiam inferis sensus est*, on which Tyrrell remarks, 'a sad *if*....The words used do not seem to suggest that S. himself believed that consciousness would survive death.' (*Cicero in his Letters*, p. 288.) This observation, *mutatis mutandis*, may fairly be applied to the Greek, which seems equally sceptical in tone. [In Homer, the spirit (ψυχή) of the dead man, in Hades, is a mere 'wraith' (εἴδωλον) of his living self (αὐτός), wherein 'there is no heart at all' (*Il.* XXIII. 103). Socrates, in a famous passage of the *Apology* (40 C), opines that death 'is either the end of all sensation or a migration of the soul from the present sphere into another,' and holds that either of these is good. In Arist. *Eth. Nic.* III. 9. 1115ᵃ 26, on the other hand, it is maintained that death is most formidable just because it *does* end all (φοβερώτατον δ' ὁ θάνατος· πέρας γάρ, καὶ οὐδὲν ἔτι τῷ τεθνεῶτι δοκεῖ οὔτ' ἀγαθὸν οὔτε κακὸν εἶναι, which is quoted by Adam on *Apol. l.c.*]

οὐ τὴν χαλκῆν εἰκόνα] the statue was evidently one of L.'s father himself, dedicated by himself (cf. ἣν ἐκεῖνος ἔστησε κ.τ.λ.): of the circumstances of the dedication we have no knowledge.—

ἔκδοτον κατέλιπε: cf. *supra* § 85.

ἐν τῷ τοῦ Διός] sc. νεῴ or ἱερῷ.—**ἱεροσυλῆσαι...αἰκίσασθαι:** cf. *supra* § 43 τὸ σῶμα παρασχόντα τάξαι τοῖς στρατηγοῖς, etc.

αὐτός] αὐτός may be sound, but οὗτος (Reiske) is tempting with ἐκεῖνος preceding.

τοιούτου γὰρ υἱοῦ...προσαγορεύεται] lit. 'for he is called the father of such a son,' i.e. the character of the son reflects upon the father: people will say, *tel fils, tel père*.

§ 137. διὰ τί οὐκ ἐνέγραψα τοῦτο...προδεδωκέναι] 'why I did not insert this in the impeachment, "betrayal of his father's statue"': προδεδωκέναι (sc. αὐτὸν as subject)...πατρός (or perhaps to ἀνακειμένην) is probably intended to read as an extract from the indictment as it might have been: for the infin. in specifying the charge, cf. the mock indictment in Ar. *Vesp.* 894:—ἐγράψατο | κύων Κυδαθηναιεὺς Λάβητ' Αἰξωνέα, | τὸν τυρὸν ἀδικεῖν ὅτι μόνος κατήσθιεν | τὸν Σικελικόν.—**ἀνακειμένην**: cf. *supra* § 51 ἐν ταῖς ἀγοραῖς ἀθλητὰς ἀνακειμένους n.

ἄξιον <ὄν>] <ὄν> Bekker (Blass).

ἐπιγράψαι] 'to add the name of Z. S. to the bill of indictment,' as a sort of *subscriptor* to the charge: the verb was used of attaching one's name to a decree, etc. as its official mover or supporter: cf. Aeschin. *Ctes.* § 159 ὑμεῖς δὲ οὐδ' ἐπὶ τὰ ψηφίσματα εἰᾶτε τὸ Δημοσθένους ἐπιγράφειν ὄνομα, ἀλλὰ Ναυσικλεῖ τοῦτο προσετάττετε, Plut. *Dem.* 21 τοῖς δὲ ψηφίσμασιν οὐχ ἑαυτόν, ἀλλ' ἐν μέρει τῶν φίλων ἕκαστον ἐπέγραφεν. The addition of the name of Ζεὺς Σωτήρ would have been a good omen for the accused. [ἐγγράψαι Es, ἐγγ. εἰς Cobet.]

§ 138. ἐκπέπληγμαι δὲ...ἐπὶ τοῖς...εἰ λελήθασιν] 'but I am astounded most of all to think that you fail to perceive that those who are in no way connected...but who habitually assist... deserve to meet with,' etc.: the 'anticipatory' structure of the sentence is very characteristic Greek, but requires some recasting in English.—**τοῖς μήτε γένει μήτε φιλίᾳ...μισθοῦ δὲ συναπ.**: 'The private advocate was forbidden to take money. Hence he usually begins by defining the personal interest [kinship, friendship, hatred of the opposite side] which has led him to appear. In the next century [the 4th], at least, the law was not strictly observed; private advocacy was often paid; and it is not rash to suppose that this practice was as old as the frequency of litigation.'—Jebb, *Attic Orators*, vol. I, p. cxxviii, quoting the Lycurgus passage. He adds that 'the real error

§ 139] NOTES 215

both of Greece and of Rome...lay in their refusal to recognise advocacy as a profession.'

ἀδικησάντων] So Bekker (Es, Bl.) for ἀδικημάτων of the MSS.

τοῖς τοιούτοις] dat. of agent with τῶν πεπραγ., but partly, perhaps, with μετάσχοιεν as well: cf. *supra* § 48 *n*. For the sentiment, we may cf. Lysias, *C. Eratosth.* § 41 ἐθαύμασα τῆς τόλμης τῶν λεγόντων ὑπὲρ αὐτῶν (men like E.), πλὴν ὅταν ἐνθυμηθῶ ὅτι τῶν αὐτῶν ἐστιν αὐτούς τε πάντα κακὰ ἐργάζεσθαι καὶ τοὺς τοιούτους ἐπαινεῖν. [τοῖς τοιούτοις Bl. (Sofer): οἱ τοιοῦτοι codd.]

οὐ γὰρ δεῖ κ.τ.λ.] 'for they should not acquire their skill [γεγενῆσθαι] in opposing you, but in championing you and the laws,' etc. δεινός here, as often, of rhetorical 'cleverness' or 'skill': cf. the familiar δεινὸς λέγειν. The word has usually the added connotation of 'over-cleverness,' 'uncanniness,' and is freq. in the orators in a quasi-disparaging sense: cf. Lysias, *C. Theomnest.* [or. X] § 9 περὶ τοῦτο γὰρ δεινὸς εἶ, 'you are a past-master at this business,' Plat. *Euthyph.* 3 C Ἀθηναίοις γάρ...οὐ σφόδρα μέλει, ἄν τινα δεινὸν οἴωνται εἶναι, 'clever above his fellows,' 'out of the ordinary.'—For the reading, see Crit. App.

§ 139. οὐκέτι...ἤδη] logical, 'are not content with seeking to mislead you...but will actually go the length of expecting,' etc.

ταῖς αὐτῶν λῃτουργίαις] 'on the strength of the public services which they themselves have performed.' At Athens, λῃτουργίαι were certain state burdens which the richer citizens discharged at their own expense. They may be classified as (*a*) 'recurrent' or 'ordinary' (ἐγκύκλιοι), such as the χορηγία, γυμνασιαρχία, ἑστίασις, (*b*) 'periodic' at longer intervals, such as the θεωρίαι or sacred embassies to the great festivals, (*c*) 'extraordinary' or required at uncertain times: of these the most important was the τριηραρχία. The χορηγία and the τριηραρχία are noticed more in detail below: for the others mentioned, see L.S. *s.vv.*—

ἐξαιτεῖσθαι: cf. *supra* § 20 τὰς δεήσεις τῶν ἐξαιτουμένων *n*.—

ἐφ' οἷς: οἷς is most probably masc.: cf. *supra* § 138 *init.* ἐκπέπληγμαι...ἐπὶ τοῖς...προσήκουσι.—καὶ μάλιστα, *vel maxime*.

εἰς γὰρ τὸν ἴδιον οἶκον κ.τ.λ.] 'for after compassing them [the λητουργίαι] for (the glorification of) their own private families, they demand of you public favours,' i.e. concessions in matters affecting the interests of the state: cf. καταχαρίζεσθαι τὰ δίκαια, 'give judgment by private interest,' Plat. *Apol.* 35 C.

ἱπποτρόφηκεν] (so Es for ἱπποτετρ- of the MSS.): *Anglicè*, 'has been a patron of the turf.' The keeping of race-horses was in ancient, as in modern, times a mark of wealth: cf. Isocr. *De Big.* § 33 ἱπποτροφεῖν ἐπιχειρήσας, ὃ τῶν εὐδαιμονεστάτων ('the wealthiest') ἔργον ἐστί, Dem. *De Cor.* § 320 καὶ μέγας καὶ λαμπρὸς ἱπποτρόφος, 'a grand gentleman' (Drake). So Herodotus (VI. 35) describes Miltiades, son of Cypselus, as being οἰκίης τεθριπποτρόφου, 'of a family that kept a four-horse chariot for racing,' and Thuc. (VI. 15) speaks of Alcibiades as one who ταῖς ἐπιθυμίαις μείζοσιν ἢ κατὰ τὴν ὑπάρχουσαν οὐσίαν ἐχρῆτο ἔς τε τὰς ἱπποτροφίας καὶ τὰς ἄλλας δαπάνας. So καθιπποτροφεῖν τὴν οὐσίαν, 'to squander one's fortune in keeping horses.'

κεχορήγηκε] 'has performed the office of choregus,' who defrayed the cost of providing, training and dressing a chorus for the dramatic festivals at Athens: the χορηγοί were nominated from the φυλαί in turn, but the burden might be imposed (after the Peloponnesian War) on two persons jointly (cf. τριηραρχία). The χορηγία was perhaps the chief, and the most spectacular, of the λητουργίαι (see above), and afforded an opportunity for the display of munificence.—**δεδαπάνηκεν**: 'has defrayed the expense of.'

αὐτὸς μόνος...τοὺς ἄλλους οὐδὲν ὠφελῶν] But the victors themselves claimed, perhaps with some reason, that the state benefited by their reflected glory: cf. Alcibiades' defence of himself in Thuc. VI. 16 ὧν γὰρ πέρι ἐπιβόητός εἰμι, τοῖς μὲν προγόνοις μου καὶ ἐμοὶ δόξαν φέρει ταῦτα, τῇ δὲ πατρίδι καὶ ὠφελίαν. οἱ γὰρ Ἕλληνες καὶ ὑπὲρ δύναμιν μείζω ἡμῶν τὴν πόλιν ἐνόμισαν τῷ ἐμῷ διαπρεπεῖ τῆς Ὀλυμπίαζε θεωρίας, πρότερον ἐλπίζοντες αὐτὴν καταπεπολεμῆσθαι, διότι ἅρματα μὲν ἑπτὰ καθῆκα κ.τ.λ., 'entered seven teams for the chariot race.'...καὶ ὅσα αὖ ἐν τῇ πόλει χορηγίαις ἢ ἄλλῳ τῳ λαμπρύνομαι, τοῖς μὲν ἀστοῖς

§ 139] NOTES 217

φθονεῖται φύσει, πρὸς δὲ τοὺς ξένους καὶ αὕτη ἰσχὺς φαίνεται, Lysias, or. XIX. § 63 (the defendant is quoting his father's services) ὅσα γὰρ ἔξω τῶν ἀναγκαίων ἐπεθύμησεν ἀναλίσκειν, πάντα φανήσεται τοιαῦτα ὅθεν καὶ τῇ πόλει τιμὴ ἔμελλεν ἔσεσθαι. αὐτίκα ('for instance') ὅτε ἵππευεν, οὐ μόνον ἵππους ἐκτήσατο λαμπροὺς ἀλλὰ καὶ ἀθλητάς, οἷς ἐνίκησεν Ἰσθμοῖ καὶ Νεμέᾳ, ὥστε τὴν πόλιν κηρυχθῆναι καὶ αὐτὸν στεφανωθῆναι. The glory shed on their native cities by the winners at the great games is the burden of Pindar's odes.

τετριηράρχηκε] The function of the τριήραρχος was the fitting out of a trireme, of which the state supplied the hull (and usually the oars and rigging), and keeping the ship in repair for a year, during which period the τριήραρχος was also responsible for the command of the vessel, though not necessarily in his own person. The trierarchy was the most important of the extraordinary λητουργίαι (see note *supra*). Originally the burden was imposed on one person, after 405 B.C. on two, after 358 (?) on the trierarchic symmories (συμμορίαι). These were the 1200 richest citizens, divided into twenty 'symmories' or boards of sixty members each; and each 'symmory' was sub-divided into so many groups (συντέλειαι), which might consist of as many as fifteen or sixteen members each, and which were each charged with the duty of providing a ship. This arrangement bore hard on the poorer members of such a group, who contributed individually the same amount as a wealthier colleague (Dem. *De Symm.* or. XIV). About 340 B.C. this abuse was removed by a reform of Demosthenes which made the amount payable by each member proportional to his taxable property: a single wealthy citizen might thus be required to provide two ships by himself, instead of bearing, as previously, only the sixteenth part of the cost of one (Dem. *De Cor.* §§ 102–108).

τείχη τῇ πατρίδι περιέβαλεν] Perhaps a compliment to Demosthenes: cf. Macan, *Herod*. VII–IX, vol. II. p. 41 *n*.—The usage of περιβάλλω admits either τείχη τῇ πατρίδι περιβαλεῖν or τείχεσι τὴν πατρίδα: cf. *circumdo*.—τῇ πατρίδι, 'his native *city*,' as often.

συνευπόρησε] 'has helped to contribute.'

§ 140. τῶν ἐπιδεδωκότων] 'of those who have made a voluntary contribution': ἐπιδιδόναι was said of contributing a 'benevolence' towards state necessities: the 'benevolence' was ἐπίδοσις, 'a giving over and above.'

τὴν εὐπορίαν τῶν δεδαπ.] Cf. Antiph. *Tetr.* Α. γ. § 8 αἱ δ' εἰσφοραὶ καὶ χορηγίαι εὐδαιμονίας ἱκανὸν σημεῖόν ἐστι, where εὐδαιμονία = 'wealth': cf. note on ἱπποτρόφηκεν, *supra* § 139.

ὥστ' ἐξαίρετον ἀξιοῦν λαμβάνειν...τιμωρίαν] 'as to claim to win *the remission of* punishment for traitors as a special favour': so we must translate the somewhat pregnant Greek, τὴν κατὰ τῶν προδιδόντων τιμωρίαν being equivalent to τὸ μὴ τιμωρεῖσθαι τοὺς προδιδόντας, 'the non-punishment of traitors.' We may compare Aeschin. *Ctes.* § 196 οἱ γὰρ ἀγαθοὶ στρατηγοί...ἐξαιτοῦνται τὰς γραφὰς τῶν παρανόμων, 'try to obtain *the rejection of* suits for παράνομα as a personal favour.'—ἐξαίρετος, of something 'picked out' from the number, Lat. *eximius*, and so 'special,' 'peculiar': Lysias, or. x. § 3 τούτῳ μόνῳ Ἀθηναίων ἐξαίρετόν ἐστι καὶ ποιεῖν καὶ λέγειν παρὰ τοὺς νόμους, 'he alone has the special privilege,' Dem. *c. Aristocr.* § 181 Καρδιανῶν πόλιν, ἣν ἐν ἁπάσαις ταῖς συνθήκαις ἐξαίρετον αὐτῷ γέγραφεν, 'has defined as his special prerogative.'

ἀνόητον] sc. εἶναι.

ὥστε φιλοτιμεῖσθαι...ἠφάνισεν] 'as that, while ambitious for the honour of the state, he should seek to succour the defendant, by whom he was the very first to have his ambitions effaced': there would be no question of being ambitious for the honour of the state, when L., so far as in him lay, would have ruined the state itself.

εἰ μὴ νὴ Δία κ.τ.λ.] 'unless, save the mark, it be the case that the interests of these men [the would-be defenders of L.] and their country are not identical': εἰ μὴ introduces here an ironical hypothesis, like *nisi forte* in Latin, the second μὴ adheres closely to ταὐτά: *nisi forte istis et patriae non eadem conveniunt*.

c. 36. §§ 141–145. *I could wish that an exception to the customary rule which forbids the presence of your wives and children* *in court were made in a case like this, so that the victims of Leocrates' treason might whet you against the traitor. As their representatives you must pass sentence upon their betrayer. It is intolerable that Leocrates should have the assurance to claim equal treatment in the city which he deserted, under the very eyes of those who have mourned the heroes of Chaeronea—heroes whose fate has never cost him a pang. To what can he appeal? Laws, walls, gods, temples, citizens—he has betrayed them all! Both old and young will unite to pass sentence upon him. Surely you cannot by the same vote convict of madness the men who died for freedom, and pronounce Leocrates the traitor to be of sound mind! Leocrates' return is not that of an ordinary exile—it is that of a man who would have turned Attica into a sheep-walk.*

§ 141. ἐχρῆν] For the potential impf. indic. without ἄν (cf. ἔδει, προσῆκεν, etc.), implying a denial of the action of the infin. ['it ought to be lawful for you'...(but it is not)], see Goodwin, §§ 415 ff.

εἰ καὶ περὶ οὐδενὸς ἄλλου] οὐδενὸς for μηδενός, which we should have expected, is difficult (cf. two exx. taken at random from Lysias: or. XIX. § 1 εἰ καὶ μὴ δεινὸς πέφυκα, XXXII. § 11 εἰ καὶ πρότερον μὴ εἴθισται), and I do not find this particular passage dealt with by any of the authorities on Gk. syntax I have been able to consult. The explanation of οὐδενὸς here must be sought (I think) in the positive quality of the concession introduced by εἰ καί: 'although ('as is well known,' 'which is a notorious fact') it is customary in no other case.' Cf. *supra* § 62 *n*.

παῖδας καὶ γυναῖκας παρακαθισαμένους...δικάζειν] 'to let their wives and children sit by them in court': for the combination of middle with reflexive pronoun, cf. *supra* § 70 τὴν σωτηρίαν αὐτοῖς ἔμελλον πορίζεσθαι.—It was of course quite usual for *defendants*, for the opposite purpose to that indicated by the speaker here, to bring their wives and children into court: the technical word for this was παραστήσασθαι (Lys. XX. § 35, Aeschin. *Ctes*. § 154, Dem. *Mid*. § 187), or ἀναβιβάζεσθαι (Andoc. *De Myst*. § 148, Isocr. *Antid*. § 321, Plat. *Apol*. 34 C, etc.).

ἀλλ' οὖν γε] This combination is frequent in introducing an apodosis which constitutes an exception to, or a qualification of a concession contained in a protasis either expressed or implied: the word on which the emphasis falls is normally enclosed between ἀλλ' οὖν and γε: cf. Isocr. *Philip.* § 85 καὶ γὰρ ἦν ἐλλίπω τι...ἀλλ' οὖν ὑπογράψειν γ' οἶμαι κ.τ.λ., 'yet at least I think I can trace,' etc., Dem. *Phil.* III. § 30 καὶ μὴν κἀκεῖνό γ' ἴστε, ὅτι ὅσα μὲν ὑπὸ Λακεδαιμονίων ἢ ὑφ' ἡμῶν ἔπασχον οἱ Ἕλληνες, ἀλλ' οὖν ὑπὸ γνησίων γ' ὄντων τῆς Ἑλλάδος ἠδικοῦντο, 'it was at any rate genuine sons of Hellas who wronged them' (as opp. to Philip, who is a 'barbarian'). The combination undivided (as here) is much more rare, but in Isocr. XX. § 14 we have: ἐπειδὴ δ' οὐχ οἷόν τ' ἐστὶν αἰσθέσθαι (since it is impossible to detect wicked men before being injured by them)...ἀλλ' οὖν γ' ἐπειδὰν γνωρισθῶσι, προσήκει...μισεῖν τοὺς τοιούτους κ.τ.λ. [Es (Bl.) changes to ἀλλ' οὖν περὶ προδοσίας γε.]

οὕτως] resuming (as often) the content of a preceding ptcp. (here περὶ προδοσίας κρίνοντας).

τοῦτο πράττειν] i.e. τοὺς δικαστὰς δικάζειν π. καὶ γ. παρακαθισαμένους.

ἐν ὀφθαλμοῖς ὄντες καὶ ὁρώμενοι] ὁρώμενοι, if genuine, must be felt to be more definite than ἐν ὀφθ. ὄντες, but the expression is admittedly redundant. [Blass (with Es) brackets καὶ ὁρώμενοι.]

τοῦ κοινοῦ παρὰ πᾶσιν ἐλέου] 'the universal attribute of pity.'

πικροτέρας τὰς γνώσεις...παρεσκεύαζον] 'that (ὅπως) they might have rendered your findings against the culprit more severe': γνῶσις, of a *judicial* inquiry, Lat. *cognitio*: Dem. *De Cor.* § 224 τὰς τῶν δικαστηρίων γνώσεις.—ὅπως...παρεσκεύαζον: lit. 'in order that they might (now) be rendering': a secondary tense of the indic. is so used with ἵνα and ὅπως in final clauses depending upon a postulate which can no longer be fulfilled: cf. Plat. *Protag.* 335 C ἀλλὰ σὲ ἐχρῆν ἡμῖν συγχωρεῖν, ἵνα συνουσία ἐγίγνετο, 'you ought to have given way to us, so that our conference might (now) be proceeding' (but you did not give way, so it is not proceeding): Goodwin, § 333. [παρεσκεύαζον Es (Bl.): παρασκευάζωσιν codd. The latter, if more unusual after ἐχρῆν, is defensible on the supposition that the speaker vividly transfers the purpose from the sphere of unreality to that of actuality.]

ἀναγκαῖον] sc. ἐστιν.

τὸν προδότην αὐτῶν] 'the man who betrayed them.'

§ 142. ὅταν νομίζῃ] causal, *cum putet*: a variant for εἰ νομίζει or τὸ νομίζειν δεῖν Λεωκράτη: cf. *supra* §§ 116, 123 *nn*.

ὁ μὴ κινδυνεύσας] 'a man who shunned the peril': generic. Cf. *supra* §§ 27, 43.

ἥκῃ] Steph. (Bl.): ἥκει codd.

ἱερῶν θυσιῶν ἀγορᾶς κ.τ.λ.] i.e. everything from which a person in his position was held εἴργεσθαι: cf. Antiph. *De Chor*. § 4 νόμῳ εἴργεσθαι πόλεως ἱερῶν ἀγώνων θυσιῶν, *supra* § 65 εἶργον τῶν νομίμων *n*. [θυσιῶν Tayl. (Sch., Bl., Thalh.): ὁσίων Reiske (Bk., Rehd.): οὐσιῶν codd.]

ὑπὲρ ὧν τοῦ μὴ καταλυθῆναι] These words *may* be construed as follows: ὑπὲρ ὧν, 'on behalf of which,' τοῦ μὴ κ., 'so that they should not be abolished'—a perfectly natural and normal construction. I cannot persuade myself, however, that τοῦ μὴ καταλυθῆναι is independent of ὑπέρ; in other words, that the writer of these words did not feel them to be the exact equivalent, in syntax as well as in meaning, of the rendering which occurs most naturally to us, viz. 'in defence of the non-abolition of which,' or (which is the same thing) 'to prevent the abolition of which,' this *final* use of ὑπέρ with the infin. being easily paralleled from Aeschin. *Ctes*. § 1 τὰς δεήσεις αἷς κέχρηνταί τινες ὑπὲρ τοῦ τὰ μέτρια καὶ τὰ συνήθη μὴ γίγνεσθαι ἐν τῇ πόλει (=ἵνα μὴ γίγνηται), Dem. *De Cor*. § 204: Goodwin, § 802. The obvious objection to this interpretation, viz. that it postulates the possibility of writing τὸ μὴ καταλυθῆναι τῶν νόμων for 'the non-abolition of the laws,' is discounted (I think) by the presence of the relative, which must come early in the clause. Thus while ὑπὲρ τοῦ μὴ ταῦτα καταλυθῆναι is quite easy, ὑπὲρ τοῦ μὴ ἃ κ. is impossible, with the result that the relative is displaced and brought close to the preposition, where it appears, as was almost inevitable, in the genitive. This I believe to be the true explanation of the construction. [I had written this note before discovering that Rehd. (App. 2 *ad loc.*) takes substantially the same view. He opines that this const. was a mannerism of Apollodorus, 'a peculiarly artistic stylist,' who was also a political partisan of Demosthenes and Lycurgus. The examples, however, which Rehd. cites from Dem., viz. XLV. 34, [Dem.] LIX. 112, 114, are, to my mind, less convincing, for the trajection of ὑπέρ, than the present passage of Lyc.]

ἡ πόλις ἔθαψαν] For the 'sense construction,' cf. *supra* § 87 ἡ πόλις...ἔδοσαν *n*.

οὐδὲ τὰ ἐλεγεῖα...ᾐδέσθη] Cf. *supra* § 45 οὐδὲ τὰς θήκας παριὼν ᾐσχύνθη.

ἀναστρέφεσθαι] *versari*: Xen. *Hell.* VI. 4. 16 λιπαροὺς καὶ φαιδροὺς ἐν τῷ φανερῷ ἀναστρεφομένους, 'moving about in public.'

§ 143. αὐτίκα μάλ'] αὐτίκα μάλα is idiomatic, μάλα intensifying αὐτίκα, 'he will be begging you *just in a moment* to hear him': cf. Plato, *Protag.* 318 B εἰ αὐτίκα μάλα μεταβαλὼν τὴν ἐπιθυμίαν ...ἐπιθυμήσειεν, 'if he should change his desire *on the spot*' (Adam's *n. ad loc.*), *Gorg.* 469 D, *Crat.* 384 B. Note that the words are always in this order: αὐτίκα δὴ μάλα is a frequent variant.

ποίους; οὕς] The general structure of this and the next paragraph, consisting of short pithy answers to questions put by the speaker anticipating the adversary's line of defence, is of a type common in perorations.

ἐᾶσαι] sc. ἀξιώσει. [ἐᾶσαι Reiske: ἐάσετε codd.]

ποίοις; ἃ μόνος] This brilliant resolution of the desperate ποιησάμενοι of the MSS. is due to Reiske.

σώσοντας] Cf. *supra* § 17 οὓς αὐτίκα σώσοντας ἑαυτόν...ἐπικαλέσεται *n*.

τοὺς νεώς...τὰ ἕδη...τὰ τεμένη] Cf. *supra* § 1 *n*.

δεήσεται καὶ ἱκετεύσει...τίνων;] τίνων must be regarded as depending on δεήσεται, which is felt as the emphatic verb, καὶ ἱκετεύσει forming a sort of parenthesis, for ἱκετεύω is normally construed with the acc.: cf. 'Ροδίους ίκετευέτω immediately following. ίκετεύειν ύμῶν (*infra* § 150), where ύμῶν can hardly be taken with τὴν χώραν καὶ τὰ δένδρα, is exceptional and perhaps poetic.

οἷς τὸν αὑτὸν ἔρανον...οὐκ ἐτόλμησε] 'men with whom he could not bring himself to make an equal contribution to the public safety': οἷς depends on τὸν αὑτόν, and is compressed for ὧν τῷ ἐράνῳ τὸν αὑτὸν ἔρανον κ.τ.λ. For ἔρανος, cf. *supra* § 22 τοὺς ἐράνους διενεγκεῖν *n*.

§ 144. πότερον...ἀλλ' οὐδέ] For ἀλλά in questions put and answered by the speaker, cf. Andoc. *De Myst.* § 148, which Hickie (*ad loc.*) describes as the *locus classicus* in Greek literature in this connexion, and which, he adds, is regularly quoted as such in grammars. But not with better reason than Lysias, XXIV. §§ 24, 25, which 'out-ἀλλά's' the Andoc. passage, and Lysias, XXX. §§ 26, 27 is deserving of honourable mention.

γηροτροφηθῆναι] a moral and legal duty of children towards their parents: cf. *supra* § 94.

οὐδ' ἐν ἐλευθέρῳ...παρέδωκεν] 'no, nor did he suffer them, so far as he was concerned, to have burial in the free soil of their country': ἐλευθέρῳ is of course predicative, but it is difficult to give it this force in trans.: the meaning is that L. did his best to enslave his country. For ἔδαφος, 'ground,' 'soil,' cf. Dem. *De Chers.* § 39 (of Philip) ἐχθρὸς ὅλῃ τῇ πόλει καὶ τῷ τῆς πόλεως ἐδάφει, 'the very ground on which it stands,' Aeschin. *Ctes.* § 134 οὐκέτι περὶ τῆς...ἡγεμονίας ἀγωνίζεται (sc. ἡ πόλις), ἀλλ' ἤδη περὶ τοῦ τῆς πατρίδος ἐδάφους, 'the very soil of our country.'— ταφῆναι...παρέδωκεν: cf. Her. VI. 103 τῇσι αὐτῇσι ἵπποισι νικῶν παραδιδοῖ Πεισιστράτῳ ἀνακηρυχθῆναι.—**τὸ καθ' αὑτὸν μέρος**: cf. *supra* § 17 *n*.

ἡ τῶν νεωτέρων] sc. ἡλικία.

§ 145. ἐξουσίαν] ἐξ., as often, of improper freedom, 'licence': cf. *supra* § 12 τὴν γὰρ ἐξ. ταύτην δεδώκατε τοῖς ἐνθάδ' εἰσιοῦσι.

τὸν δῆμον καὶ ὑμᾶς] 'the body politic')('you, as individuals.'

οὐ γὰρ μόνον νῦν...κατέρχονται] 'for it is not merely a case of an exile returning' (νῦν—supposing you let L. go unpunished).—

οἱ φεύγοντες: the plural here is used to put a general case.—
κατέρχονται: technical in this sense: cf. *supra* § 124 μόλις εἰς
τὴν ἑαυτῶν κατεληλυθότες.

φυγὴν...καταγνούς] Cf. *supra* § 22 οὕτως αὐτοῦ κατεγνώκει
ἀίδιον φυγήν.

οἰκήσας ἐν Μ. ἐπὶ προστάτου] Cf. *supra* § 21 *n*.

πλείω πέντ' ἢ ἓξ ἔτη] The duration of L.'s sojourn abroad is
given *supra* § 21 as πλείω ἢ πέντε ἔτη, § 56 πέντε ἔτη, § 58 ἓξ ἔτη.
[Es considers that a copyist who had before him πλεῖν (so Es, as
supra § 21) ἢ ἓξ ἔτη introduced πέντε from his memory of §§ 21,
56: πλείω ἢ πέντε ἔτη (as § 21) Auger (Rehd.).]

ἀναστρέφηται] Cf. *supra* § 142 ἡγεῖται δεῖν ἀναστρέφεσθαι *n*.

μηλόβοτον τὴν 'Α. ἀνεῖναι] 'to turn Attica into a sheep-walk':
cf. Isocr. *Plat.* § 31 (of Theban animosity) οὐ δυστυχησάντων
ὑμῶν [after Aegospotami] μόνοι τῶν συμμάχων ἔθεντο τὴν ψῆφον,
ὡς χρή...τὴν χώραν ἀνεῖναι μηλόβοτον ὥσπερ τὸ Κρισαῖον πεδίον;

σύνοικος ὑμῶν] we might expect ὑμῖν, but cf. Soph. *Ant.* 451
ἡ ξύνοικος τῶν κάτω θεῶν Δίκη. [ὑμῖν Herwerden.]

γίγνεται] Rehd. (Bl.): γενήσεται Melanchth. (Sch., Turr.,
Sof.): γεγένηται Thalh.: γένηται codd.

c. 37. §§ 146–148. *Before concluding, I should like to quote you
the decree of the people 'concerning piety.' I have denounced
the guilty party to you: with you rests the responsibility of
punishing him as he deserves. Be assured that each one of you,
though giving his vote in secret, will make his mind open to the
gods. Consider that by your single verdict you are pronouncing
sentence on all the most heinous crimes, of all of which Leocrates
stands guilty—treason, overthrow of the democracy, impiety, ill-
treatment of parents, desertion. By showing him mercy, you will
expose yourselves to the vengeance of heaven.*

§ 146. βραχέα...εἰπὼν καταβῆναι] 'to say a few words
more...and to cite the decree of the people...before stepping
down': a good example of a case where the stress, in Greek,
falls on the ptcp. Of the decree 'concerning piety' nothing
further is known.

§ 147] NOTES 225

τὸν ἀφανίζοντα] either (*a*) 'him who would obliterate' (conative) or (*b*) 'him who has obliterated,' the present denoting the 'standing characteristic' as in ἀδικεῖν, προδιδόναι = ἄδικος, προδότης εἶναι.—**ταῦτα πάντα**: i.e. all the clauses of the decree just quoted.

κολάσαι...τιμωρήσασθαι] the first, of the reformation of the offender; the second, of the satisfaction of the offended: Arist. *Rhet.* I. 10. 1369 b διαφέρει δὲ τιμωρία καὶ κόλασις· ἡ μὲν γὰρ κόλασις τοῦ ποιοῦντος ἕνεκά ἐστιν, ἡ δὲ τιμωρία τοῦ πάσχοντος, ἵνα ἀποπληρωθῇ.

τὰ γὰρ ἀδικήματα κ.τ.λ.] 'for crimes, so long as they are untried, lie at the door of the perpetrators, but as soon as the trial has taken place, at the door of those who fail to punish them as they deserve': the force of παρὰ c. dat. here seems to be that of 'resting with,' 'chargeable upon,' as *apud* and *penes* are occasionally used in Latin.

κρύβδην...φανεράν] a common sentiment in the orators: cf. Lysias *c. Eratosth.* § 91 μηδ' οἴεσθε κρύβδην <εἶναι> τὴν ψῆφον· φανερὰν γὰρ τῇ πόλει τὴν ὑμετέραν γνώμην ποιήσετε, or. VI. § 53 ποῖον δημότην χρὴ τούτῳ χαρισάμενον κρύβδην φανερῶς τοῖς θεοῖς ἀπεχθέσθαι; or. XV. § 10, Dem. *F. L.* § 239 οὐ γὰρ εἰ κρύβδην ἐστὶν ἡ ψῆφος, λήσει τοὺς θεούς, κ.τ.λ.

§ 147. ὑπὲρ ἁπάντων...μίαν ὑμᾶς ψῆφον] 'that you are passing a single verdict on all the greatest and most heinous forms of crime,' i.e. though you only vote once, your vote has reference to a multiplicity of crimes, of which (as he explains) L. is guilty. For ὑπέρ, cf. *supra* § 9 τὴν ὑπὲρ τῶν τοιούτων τιμωρίαν *n.*

ἐν τῇ τήμερον ἡμέρᾳ] cf. *supra* § 2 *n.*

προδοσίας] This and the following genitives are in app. with ἀδικημάτων above.

τὰ τεμένη τέμνεσθαι] The collocation of the words is no doubt helped by the fact that τέμενος belongs to the same root as τέμνω ('a place cut off' from common use, Lat. *templum*): τέμνεσθαι here of course = 'be ravaged,' 'laid waste.'

τοκέων δὲ κακώσεως] 'maltreatment of parents' was a specific

P. L. 15

offence under Athenian law, and might be the subject of an εἰσαγγελία which was brought before the chief archon: see notes to § 1. Note the poetic τοκέων = γονέων. For the text after κακώσεως, see Crit. App.

λιποταξίου...ἀστρατείας] 'desertion'...'shirking of service': both were subject to γραφή. Properly λιποταξίου (which occurs only as gen. with γραφή, ἔνοχος, etc., though Cobet restores λιποτάξιον for λιποταξίαν of codd. at Dem. Mid. § 166) would be said of desertion in actual battle, ἀστρατεία of failing to take one's place in the ranks when placed upon the military list, the latter only of which might be held to be applicable to the case of Leocrates. For a discussion of the point, see Lysias c. Alcib. I [or. XIV] §§ 1–8, where the speaker contends that λιποταξία includes non-appearance in the ranks as well as falling out in presence of the enemy: Lys. l.c. § 6 ἀκούετε, ὦ ἄνδρες δικασταί, ὅτι περὶ ἀμφοτέρων κεῖται (sc. ὁ νόμος), καὶ ὅσοι ἂν μάχης οὔσης εἰς τοὐπίσω ἀναχωρήσωσι, καὶ ὅσοι ἂν ἐν τῇ πεζῇ στρατιᾷ μὴ παρῶσι. From Lyc.'s language in the present passage we should certainly infer that the two terms covered pretty much the same ground.

παρασχὼν τὸ σῶμα τάξαι] Cf. supra § 43 n.

§ 148. ἔπειτα] admirantis vel indignantis, 'after all that': Xen. Mem. I. 4. 11 ἔπειτ' οὐκ οἴει φροντίζειν (τοὺς θεοὺς τῶν ἀνθρώπων); supra § 27 n.

τούτου τις] note the indef. τις, which has the effect of throwing more weight upon τούτου.

τῶν κατὰ π. ἀδικημάτων] 'deliberate crimes': cf. ἐκ προνοίας in τὰ ἐκ πρ. τραύματα, 'wounding with intent,' and supra § 38 κατὰ τὴν τούτου προαίρεσιν n.

καὶ τίς οὕτως] Dobr. (Bl., Sof.): καὶ τοσοῦτον codd.

σῴζων...ἐλεήσας] 'by seeking to save'...'by showing him pity.'

προαιρήσεται] Bekker would omit this, on the ground that it disturbs the symmetry of the passage without helping the sense.

χάριν θέμενος] 'by doing him a favour': a common Gk. phrase.

§ 149] NOTES 227

ὑπεύθυνος εἶναι...τιμωρίᾳ] sc. προαιρήσεται, 'to expose himself to the vengeance of heaven.'

§§ 149, 150. *On behalf of my country and the laws, I have conducted the case honestly and straightforwardly, confining myself strictly to the point at issue. Reflect that, by acquitting Leocrates, you are condemning your country to death and slavery, and that your votes, according to the use you make of them, mean either the destruction or the salvation of your native city. Consider that a cry goes up to you from the very land—from harbours and arsenals, shrines and temples—and make Leocrates a signal example of the fact that tears and compassion do not weigh more with you than the vindication of the laws and the public weal.*

§ 149. ἀποδέδωκα τὸν ἀγῶνα] 'I have conducted my case' is perhaps the most we can make of this: the speaker regards the prosecution as something committed to his charge, which he has 'duly delivered' (cf. *reddo*): ἀπολαμβάνω is the correlative.

οὔτε τὸν ἄλλον...βίον διαβαλών] 'without either attacking his life in general,' which was an all too common practice in Athenian courts: cf. the amenities exchanged between Aeschines and Demosthenes (Aeschin. *Ctes.* §§ 51-53, Dem. *De Cor.* §§ 257-266), etc.

ἔξω τοῦ πράγματος] cf. *supra* § 11 *n*.

τὸν Λεωκράτους] [τὸν] Rehd. : τοῦ Es.

καὶ δυοῖν καδίσκοιν...τὸν μὲν προδοσίας, τὸν δὲ σωτηρίας] 'and that of the two urns which are set out, one is for betrayal, the other for safety': the method of voting here described appears to be the older and simpler one, according to which *two* voting-urns were provided, one for condemnation and one for acquittal, called respectively ὁ πρότερος and ὁ ὕστερος, Ar. *Vesp.* 986-991 : cf. Phrynichus, Μοῦσαι, quoted by Harp. *s.v.* καδίσκος (Mein. *Com. Frag.* 2. 593), ἰδού, δέχου τὴν ψῆφον. ὁ καδίσκος δέ σοι | ὁ μὲν ἀπολύων οὗτος, ὁ δ' ἀπολλὺς ὁδί, and each dicast was provided with *one* ψῆφος, which was dropped into one or other of the urns. According to the later method described by Aristotle, Ἀθ. Πολ.

col. 36, ll. 14-22, there were still two urns, one of bronze and one of wood, but each dicast was furnished with *two* ψῆφοι, one with a hollow cylinder (ἡ τετρυπημένη), for condemnation, the other with a solid (ἡ πλήρης), for acquittal: these held between the finger and thumb were indistinguishable to the onlookers: the dicast dropped whichever he wanted to use into the bronze urn, which was called ὁ κύριος (the 'operative' or 'deciding'), the wooden (ὁ ἄκυρος) being reserved for the ψῆφος which was unused. At the conclusion of the voting, the contents of the κύριος were emptied out, the perforated and the solid ballots were counted, and the verdict was declared accordingly. The latter method secured secrecy of voting: it is difficult to see how the former could have done so. For a discussion of the subject, and the authorities bearing upon it, see the exhaustive note of Wyse on Isaeus v. 17 *s.vv.* ἐξεραθεισῶν [*alii* ἐξαιρεθεισῶν] τῶν ψήφων, and Sandys on 'Αθ. Πολ. col. 35, 22 *sqq*.

φέρεσθαι] passive: cf. Aeschin. *Ctes.* § 233 ἡ γὰρ ψῆφος ἀφανὴς φέρεται. —**ὑπὲρ ἀναστάσεως**: cf. *supra* § 9 τὴν ὑπὲρ τῶν τοιούτων τιμωρίαν *n*.

§ 150. ἐὰν...ἀπολύσητε] *si absolveritis.*

προδιδόναι...ψηφιεῖσθε] 'you will vote for the betrayal of,' etc.: so ψηφίζεσθαι βοηθεῖν, etc.

παρακελεύσεσθε] 'you will encourage' (others): παρακελεύσασθαι· προτρέψασθαι Hesych.

ἱκετεύειν ὑμῶν] Cf. *supra* § 143 δεήσεται καὶ ἱκετεύσει...τίνων; *n*.

τὰ δένδρα]. The reference is no doubt especially to the olive-trees, an important state asset: cf. *supra* § 43 ὅθ' ἡ μὲν χώρα τὰ δένδρα συνεβάλλετο *n*.

τοὺς λιμένας <καὶ> τὰ νεώρια] The appeal of the 'harbours' and the 'dockyards,' important sources of Athens' strength, is specially pertinent in the mouth of Lycurgus, who had increased the fleet and completed an arsenal during his administration: see Introd. p. xx. So Lysias *c. Eratosth.* § 99 appeals to the judges ὑπὲρ τῶν νεωρίων, ἃ καθεῖλον (sc. οἱ τριάκοντα). [<καὶ> is added by

§ 150] NOTES 229

Scheibe (Es, Thalh.), who postulates either this or the asyndetic τοὺς λ. τὰ ν. τὰ τ. (Bl.) as the proper form.]

παράδειγμα ποιήσατε Λ.] Cf. with the conclusion Lysias, XXVIII. § 11 ἀλλὰ παράδειγμα πᾶσιν ἀνθρώποις ποιῆσαι καὶ μήτε κέρδος μήτε ἔλεον μήτ' ἄλλο μηδὲν περὶ πλείονος ποιήσασθαι τῆς τούτων τιμωρίας.

ὅτι οὐ πλέον ἰσχύει] depending on παράδ. π. Λ., 'make him a (warning) example (of the fact) that,' etc. [καί, which the MSS. give before ὅτι, is deleted by the editors generally (with Morus): Rehd. defends it in an elaborate excursus, App. 2, pp. 162 *sqq.*]

ὑπέρ] Lycurgean, for the simple genitive: cf. *supra* § 9 τὴν ὑπὲρ τῶν τοιούτων τιμωρίαν, [Dem.] XXVI. § 12 εἰς τὴν ὑπὲρ τῆς πατρίδος σωτηρίαν.

σωτηρίας] so the MSS., and intrinsically probable as supplying the desiderated *vox fausta* with which to conclude. [τιμωρίας Reiske (Sch., Bl.).]

CRITICAL APPENDIX

§ 8. The MSS. give: ὥστε μήτε κατηγορίαν μήτε τιμωρίαν ἐνδέχεσθαι εὑρεῖν ἀξίαν, μηδὲ ἐν τοῖς νόμοις ὡρίσθαι τιμωρίαν ἀξίαν τῶν ἁμαρτημάτων, with ὥστε...εὑρεῖν ἀξίαν recurring *infra* § 9 after γενήσεσθαι. The passage has been variously emended: Bekker brackets μήτε κατηγορίαν...εὑρεῖν ἀξίαν, Baiter and Sauppe μήτε τιμωρίαν, Rehdantz τιμωρίαν ἀξίαν. I have followed Blass, with the change of μηδὲ...μηδ' to μήτε...μήτ'.

§ 13. <τοιούτου> Nicolai (Rehd., Sofer): ἄνευ τοῦ ἀλόγου, G. Herm., Turr.; ἀδ. γάρ ἐστι καὶ ἀνόητον λόγῳ Thalh.; totum locum ἀδύνατον...ψῆφον secl. Bekk. (Sch.).

§ 14. οἳ ἴσασι...ὄντα. I have followed Blass in transposing (with Franke and Scheibe) this clause from its position in the MSS. after ἠκηκόεσαν *infra*, where it is awkward (as seems necessary) to refer οἳ to τὴν οἰκουμένην.

§ 19. ὡς καὶ μεγάλα...μετέχων αὐτῆς. The MSS. give ὡς καὶ μεγάλα καὶ βλάβους εἴη: βεβλαφὼς pro καὶ βλάβους, Sauppe (Blass, Thalh.): καταβεβλαφὼς Jenicke (Rehd.): μεγάλου βλάβους αἴτιος εἴη Corais: μεγάλου αἴτιος βλάβους εἴη Franz.—μετέχων αὐτοῖς codd. praeter N (Franz, Saupp., Scheib., Thalh.): αὐτὸς Jenicke: αὐτῆς N (cf. § 58) (Blass, Rehd.).

§ 26. The MSS. give τὴν Ἀθηνᾶν ὡς τὴν χώραν εἰληχυῖαν ὁμώνυμον αὐτῇ κ.τ.λ. τιμῶντες ante τὴν Ἀ. volunt Taylor, Es: ὡς τὴν χώραν τῆς Ἀ. εἰληχυίας Blass: τῇ Ἀ. ὡς τὴν χ. εἰληχυίᾳ Corais (Schöne, Rehd., Thalh.).—ὁμώνυμον αὐτῇ Cor.: secl. Blass: αὐτῇ secl. Schöne, Thalh.: αὐτὴν Rehd.

§ 28. After **οἰκέτας**, half a line is wanting in A: ἡ προκλήσεις προκλῆσοι ἄξιόν ἐστι N: ἧς ἀκοῦσαι ἄξιόν ἐστιν ci. Blass.

§ 29. τὸν παρὰ τῶν συνειδότων. τῶν (τὸν A) πάντων συνειδότων ABN: τὸν πάντα Doberenz: τὸν πάντ' αὐτῷ Scheib. (Rehd.)

CRITICAL APPENDIX 231

[but, as Blass rightly remarks, the article cannot be omitted with the ptcp.]: τὸν τῶν πάντ' αὐτῷ Herw.: τὸν πάντων σαφέστατον ἔλεγχον Reiske (Thalh.): τὸν παρὰ τῶν συνειδότων Schoem. (Bl.).

§ 38. After οἱ ναοί, the MSS. give τῶν ἱερέων, which is probably an importation due to a misunderstanding of the const. of ἔρημοι ...τῶν τειχῶν immediately following. Heinrich (Sch., Bl., Thalh.) deletes the words: Rehd. defends them.

§ 39. τῷ <στρατῷ> scripsi. τῷ ALP: τῷ <δήμῳ> Ald., Bk. (Sch.): utrumque deletum volunt Osann., Turr.; τῷ <στρατοπέδῳ> Meier, prob. Rehd.: ἀρτίως Blass.—προσήγγελτο Es (Bl.): προσηγγέλλετο ALP.

§ 43. ὅθ' ἡ μὲν χώρα...τὰ ὅπλα. I have followed Blass (Sofer) in transposing this clause from its place in the MSS. after τὴν τῆς πόλεως σωτηρίαν *infra*.

§ 45. μηδὲ συνενεγκεῖν. μηδὲ ξυνεγκεῖν AB, μηδὲ ξυνενεγκεῖν LP (Rehd.), μ. συνενεγκεῖν Z: μηδὲν ξυνενεγκεῖν Cor.: μηδὲ ξυνεισενεγκεῖν Mätz.: μηδὲ ξυνεπενεγκεῖν Sch., prob. Es (sec. Thuc. II. 34 ἐπιφέρει τῷ αὐτοῦ ἕκαστος ἤν τι βούληται): μηδὲ ξυνεξενεγκεῖν Dobree (Bl.), deletis verbis μηδ' ἐπ' ἐκφορὰν ἐλθεῖν: μηδ' ἐξενεγκεῖν Thalh.

§ 46. The MSS. give τοὺς τοιούτους τῶν δημοσίων ἀγῶνας (Rehd., Thalh.), Rehd. explaining τῶν δημοσίων as 'the state interests,' *res publica*, and pointing out that the arrangement τοὺς τοιούτους ἀγῶνας τῶν δημοσίων (which we should have expected) would postulate the supplying of ἀγώνων with δημοσίων. Otherwise ἀγῶνες is to be understood in the sense of the ἀγωνιζόμενοι λόγοι of Isocr. (XV. 48), 'Privatprocessreden')('Staatsprocessen.' On the whole, I prefer the reading in the text, which is due to Reiske (Turr., Sch., Bl., Es): τῶν τοιούτων τοὺς δ. ἀγῶνας Mätz.: τοῖς τοιούτοις τοὺς δ. ἀγῶνας Franke.

§ 49. As Rehd. remarks (App. I, p. 109), there is a good deal that is unusual, both in expression and arrangement, in this and the following paragraph, which have probably suffered from the incorporation in them of reminiscences of famous *Epitaphii* which were much handled in the schools.

CRITICAL APPENDIX

(*a*) ἃ γὰρ ἆθλα...ταῦτ' ἀμφότερα Cor., Dobr. (Bl.): τὰ γὰρ ἆθλα...ταῦτα γὰρ ἀμφότ. codd.: ταῦτα δὲ Auger, Bekk.: ταῦτ' ἄρα Rosenberg (Rehd.).

(*b*) μόνους γὰρ τοὺς κ.τ.λ. μόνους does not seem wanted if ἡττῆσθαι is understood (as seems most natural in its context) of *military* defeat: Rehd., who attempts a reconstruction of the whole passage, considers that μόνους arose out of ἀμύνοντες ^{μενοι} *supra*, and that the original ran...ὑπὲρ τῆς ἐλευθερίας ἀμυνόμενοι· τοὺς γὰρ ἐν τοῖς πολέμοις κ.τ.λ.

§ 51. The MSS. give καὶ δι' ἃ οὐκ ἀλόγως ἐπετήδευον, which has been variously emended so as (*a*) to supply an object to ἐπετήδευον, (*b*) to define more precisely the force of ἐπίστασθε. I have adopted Blass's <ἀνδρείαν> after ἀλόγως, taking δι' ἃ... ἐπετήδευον in a causal relation to ἐπίστασθε (see explanatory note). Other suggestions are: καὶ νὴ Δία οὐκ ἀλ. ἐπ. ταῦτα· ἐπίστασθε γὰρ Cor.: καὶ νὴ Δία ταῦτ' οὐκ ἀλ. ἐπ., ἐπεὶ ἐπίστασθε Herw.: ἃ νὴ Δία οὐκ ἀλ. ἐπ.· ἐπίστασθε γὰρ ci. Rehd.

§ 67. ἀλλ' εἰς τὸ πρᾶγμα codd. (Sch., Rehd., Sofer): ἀλλ οἷον τὸ πρᾶγμα Bekker: ἀλλ' εἰ (Tayl.) τὸ πρ. μέγα Dobr.: ἀλλ' εἰς τὸ πρᾶγμα <ἀποβλέψεσθε> ci. Frohb., prob. Thalh.

§ 73. The probabilities for and against the genuineness of ἔστησαν seem to be about equally balanced: I have followed Meutzner (Bl., Thalh.) in bracketing it: Turr., Sch., Rehd. retain it.

§ 76. <ὡς> οὐδὲν ποιήσων. The MSS. give οὐδὲν ποιήσειν (Sch., Rehd., Thalh.), which, if defensible, is at least an exceptional const. with παρασκευάζεσθαι, which seems to be found only with (*a*) the infin. present or aorist, (*b*) fut. ptcp., with or without ὡς (Rehd., App. 2, *ad loc.*): ποιήσων Frohb.: <ὡς>... ποιήσων Es (Bl.).

§ 80. ὅμως ὡς ἴχνος. I have adopted Rehd.'s suggestion for ὅμως ἰσχνῶς of the MSS., which has been very variously emended: ἱκανῶς Cor.: ἰσχυρῶς Dind.: συχνῶς Sch.: ἴχνος...τῆς...ἀρετῆς M Haupt. (Bl.): alii alia.

CRITICAL APPENDIX 233

§ 85. κατακλησθέντες ἐπολιορκοῦντο καὶ διεκαρτέρουν εἰς τὴν πατρίδα.—διακαρτερεῖν εἰς τὴν πατρίδα, 'to stand staunchly by one's country' (see expl. note) is perhaps somewhat difficult (though Lyc. has other unusual examples of εἰς, cf. § 129); but it seems intolerably harsh to join (with Rehd.) κατακλησθέντες with εἰς τὴν π. Es (Bl.) would delete ἐπολιορκοῦντο καί, which no doubt makes κατακλ....εἰς τὴν π. easier, though even then the rhythm of the sentence is in favour of joining εἰς with διεκαρτέρουν.

§ 86. κατὰ τὰς πύλας ὑποδύντα.—After considering the passage in all its bearings, I am inclined to believe that ὑποδύντα (which I once thought might conceal something like ὑπὸ νύκτα— a *time* note) is sound, and that the corruption lies in κατὰ τὰς πύλας. I put forward the following suggestions for what they are worth.

(i) φρύγανα συλλέγειν (added to the general testimony that Codrus took the disguise of a *woodman*: εὐτελεῖ σκευῇ ὡς ξυλιστής Schol. Platon., ὑλοτόμου ἐσθῆτα λαβών Suidas) points to ὕλας for πύλας. We should then have, (*a*) with κατά, 'taking shelter (secreting himself: ὑποδύντα used absol.) near (in the neighbourhood of) the woods,' (*b*) with κᾆτα (Madvig), 'and then taking cover *in* the woods' (τὰς ὕλας being here direct obj. of ὑποδύντα: cf. *subire*). In either case, the action of ὑποδύντα (as well as of λαβόντα) is strictly antecedent in time (as the tense itself shows) to that of συλλέγειν (see expl. note): during the time when φρ. συλλέγειν could be predicated of him, C. was, and intended himself to be, easily seen.

(ii) ὑποδύεσθαι is capable of two other meanings, either of which seems pertinent for the present passage: (*a*) to 'put on' *shoes* [cf. Ar. *Vesp.* 1158, where RV give ὑπόδυθι...τὰς Λακωνικάς, with ὑποδύσασθαι and ὑποδυσάμενος at ll. 1159, 1168 respectively, though it is true that Scaliger and Hirschig changed all three to corresponding forms of ὑποδεῖσθαι (ὑποδοῦ, ὑποδησ-), which are now adopted by the editors], (*b*) to 'put on' *a certain character* (cf. Plat. *Gorg.* 464 C ἡ κολακευτική...προσποιεῖται εἶναι τοῦθ' ὅπερ ὑπέδυ, Arist. *Metaph.* III. 2. 19 οἱ σοφισταὶ ταὐτὸν ὑποδύονται σχῆμα τῷ φιλοσόφῳ).

Assuming that ὑποδῦναι could have been said by Lycurgus in the sense of (*a*), and reading Madvig's κᾆτα, I see in πύλας an additional detail of Codrus' 'make up': λαβόντα πτωχικὴν στολήν...κᾆτα τὰς ἀρβύλας (τὰς ἁπλᾶς?—cf. Dem. LIV. 34 ἁπλᾶς ὑποδέδενται) ὑποδύντα κ.τ.λ. ἀρβύλη is defined by L.S. as 'a strong shoe...a half-boot, used by country-people, hunters, travellers'; with (*b*), I suggest that the original may have run: λαβόντα πτ. στολὴν...ταύτην ὑποδύντα κ.τ.λ., 'assuming, I say, this disguise,' etc.: Lyc. is partial to the resumptive οὗτος (cf. §§35, 42, 46, 82, 93, 117). If TAYTHN (ταύτην) came to look like, or was misread as, TAYTHI (ταύτηι, ταύτῃ), κατὰ τὰς πύλας might very well be a gloss which attempted to explain the latter word.

§ 88. ἀρά γ' ὁμοίως. I have adopted Corais' (Es, Bl., Sofer) ἀρά γε for ὁρᾶτε of the MSS., which Scheibe (Rehd., Thalh.) retains (ὁρᾶτε εἰ Ald.). ὁρᾶτε (rarer than ὁρᾷς) thus used initially is felt (acc. Rehd., App. 2, p. 151) as a statement, not as a question, and is without influence on the construction, as in Lucian, πῶς δεῖ ἱστ. γρ. § 27 ὁρᾷς, ὅμοιος οὗτος ἐκείνῳ. The idiom, however, appears to be distinctly rare *in prose*. On the other hand, ἀρά γε seems to have an affinity for ὅμοιος in introducing an ironical question, cf. § 70 ἀρά γ' ὅμοιοι, § 119 ἀρά γ' ὁμοίως, which passages may perhaps be regarded as creating an *à priori* case for ἀρά γε here. Palaeographically, as Es points out, ΑΡΑΓΕ and ΟΡΑΤΕ would be easily confused.

§ 93. εἰ ταῦτὰ σημεῖα...φαίνονται codd.(Sch.): φαίνοιντο Steph.: φαίνοιτο Heinrich (Bl., Sofer): φαίνοιτ' ὄντα Rehd.: ταῦτὰ <τὰ> σημεῖα (Melanchth.)...φαίνονται Thalh.: ταῦτὰ <τὰ> σ....φαίνοι Reiske (Sauppe): σημαίνοι pro σημεῖα, del. φαίν., Nicolai.

§ 100. Eur. *Erechth.* l. 3. The line has been variously completed: I have adopted Meineke's <λέγω> (see expl. note). χρόνῳ δὲ πολλῷ δρῶσι, δυσγενέστεροι B (sec. Osann.) et vett.

CRITICAL APPENDIX 235

edd.: χρόνῳ δὲ δρῶσι, <δρῶσι> δ—ρον Heinrich: δ—ροι φύσιν G. Herm.: alii alia.

l. 41. τοὖν γ' ἐμοὶ Heinr. (Turr., Sch., Thalh.): τοὺν ἐμοὶ Reiske: γοῦν ἐμοὶ Bk.: σύν γ' ἐμοὶ Bl.: γοῦν τ' ἐμοὶ codd. etiam οὔκουν...σωθήσεται; Dind.

l. 42. ἄρξουσί τ' AN, ἄρξουσιν M, deinde ἄλλοι τήνδ' (sive τὴν δ') ἐγὼ σώσω πόλιν codd.: ἄρξουσιν ἄλλοι, τήνδ' ἐγὼ σώσω πόλιν Dind. (Thalh., Sof.): ἄρξουσί τ' ἄλλοις τήνδ' ἐγὼ οὐ δώσω πόλιν Jenicke: ἄρξ. τ' ἄλλοις τήνδε γ' οὐ σώσω πόλιν Blass. Hunc et priorem versum ita ponit Rehdantz:

οὐκοῦν ἅπανθ' ἃ τοὐπ' ἐμοὶ σωθήσεται
ἄρξουσιν ἄλλοι, τὴν δ' ἐγὼ σώσω πόλιν.

§ 107. Tyrtaeus, ll. 11, 12.

**εἰ δ' οὕτως ἀνδρός τοι ἀλωμένου οὐδεμί' ὥρη
γίγνεται οὐδ' αἰδώς, οὔτ' ὀπίσω γένεος.**

οὐδ' αἰδὼς M (Bk., Turr., Sch.): οὔτ' αἰδὼς libri et vulg. ‖ οὔτ' ὀπίσω τέλος ABN: εἰσοπίσω τελέθει Ald. (Bk., Turr.): οὔτ' ὀπίσω γένεος Ahrens (Bl., Sofer): ἐξοπίσω s. τοὐξοπίσω γένεος Sch.: οὔτ' ὄπις οὔτ' ἔλεος Bergk (Rehd., Thalh.).

For the second half of the line, I have adopted Ahrens' οὔτ' ὀπίσω γένεος as against Bergk's οὔτ' ὄπις οὔτ' ἔλεος, the objection to which is, ceteris paribus, that αἰδὼς...ὄπις...ἔλεος seem to overload the whole line somewhat with the same idea. With Ahrens' reading, however, it seems necessary to adopt, in the first half, οὐδ' αἰδὼς (with M): otherwise οὔτε...οὔτε (Bl., Sofer) connect heterogeneous elements in a way for which I can find no parallel. Reading then οὐδ' αἰδώς, and punctuating as in the text for the sake of clearness, we have: εἰ δ' (οὔτε) ἀνδρὸς...οὔτ' ὀπίσω γένεος οὐδεμία ὥρη γίγνεται οὐδ' αἰδώς, which I submit is normal and intelligible Greek (see explanatory note).

On the other hand, the double οὔτε, subdividing the preceding οὐδεμία, is thoroughly characteristic Greek, and tempts one to suppose that οὔτε...οὔτε is sound. Is it possible that the true reading is:

γίγνεται οὔτ' αὐτοῦ οὔτ' ὀπίσω γένεος?

It will be granted that οὔτ' ὀπίσω γένεος, if sound and not directly pointing to a preceding αὐτοῦ, at least goes very well with it (cf. the familiar ἐξώλη εἶναι αὐτὸν καὶ γένος in imprecations in the orators *passim*, and § 79 of the speech, ἀλλ' εἰ μὴ αὐτός, οἱ παῖδές γε καὶ τὸ γένος ἅπαν κ.τ.λ.). I do not think that the hiatus resulting from the reading of αὐτοῦ, coming where it does in the line, is an insuperable objection (cf. Theognis 478 οὔτε τι γὰρ νήφω, οὔτε λίην μεθύω); and it may be observed, further, that this very hiatus (assuming that Tyrtaeus wrote αὐτοῦ) would very naturally have suggested the mending of the metre by the substitution of a word like αἰδώς which did not offend. In any case, it will be agreed that a place like ΟΥΤΑΥΤΟΥΟΥ would be, on the face of it, a likely source of corruption.

§ 116. ὑμῖν οὔτε πάτριον codd.: ὑμῖν οὔτοι πάτριον N² (Schaub): ὑμῖν οὕτω πάτριον Ald. (Bk.). ‖ ψηφίζεσθαι NM: ψηφίζεσθε cett. (Sch., Thalh.).—A great many remedies have been proposed. οὐδὲ γὰρ πάτριον Franke, ὃ ὑμῖν οὐδὲ πάτριον Sch., οὐ γὰρ ὑμῖν πάτριον Es, ὑμῖν οὔ γε πάτριον Rehd., <οὔτε γὰρ νόμιμον (s. εἰθισμένον)> ὑμῖν οὔτε π. Cohn, <οὔτε γὰρ ἔμφυτον> ὑμῖν κ.τ.λ. prob. Bl. (Sofer): ὑμεῖς· οὐδὲ γὰρ πάτριον Jenicke. The most attractive of all is Rehd.'s μὴ δῆτα, ὦ ἅ. δ., οὕτω τῶν τε πατέρων ἀναξίως καὶ ὑμῶν αὐτῶν ψηφίζεσθε, which he does not, however, introduce into his text. Needless, and useless, as it may appear to add to the above list, I have ventured to write <οὔτε γὰρ ὅσιον>, on the ground that, if an adjective is missing, ὅσιος seems as likely as any other on the lips of Lycurgus.

§ 132. The MSS. give τὰ γοῦν ζῷα πετεινὰ μάλιστα πέφυκε πρὸς (τὸ AN) τάχος ἃ ἔστιν ἰδεῖν.—ζῷα del. G. Hermann (Sch., Bl., Thalh.): <ἅ> ante μάλιστα add. R. (Sch., Bl., Thalh.): <ἅ> πετεινὰ Rehd.: τάχος, ἔστιν dist. R. (edd. omn.).

§ 134. ὅταν ληφθῶσι Contius (Rehd., Bl., Thalh.): καταληφθῶσι G. Herm. (Sch.): συλληφθῶσι Halm (Turr.): ὅταν μὴ (δὴ N²) ληφθῶσι ANpr. μὴ is difficult and contrary to the sense: the omission of it at least cuts the knot, but there is some force in van Es's criticism :...'quod (sc. ὅταν μὴ λ.) explicari nequit;

quam ob causam alius aliam viam corrigendi ingressus est, omnes tamen in eo convenientes in his vocabulis latere elocutionem quae optime hoc modo redditur "cum deprehenduntur." sed Lycurgus nonnumquam insulsus et futilis est, ne talia eum dixisse credamus. quis umquam maleficus non deprehensus poenas luit? puto Lycurgum scripsisse: "dum reliqui in animo habentes peccare poenas patiuntur *eorum, quae non perpetraverunt,*" quod recte opponitur Leocrati τῷ διαπεπραγμένῳ ὅπερ ἐπεχείρησε.' Is it possible that ὅταν μὴ ληφθῶσι may have been developed from ὅταν μὴ φθῶσι, a (somewhat superfluous) gloss on μέλλοντες ἀδικεῖν?

§ 138. The MSS. give οὐ γὰρ δὴ καθ' ὑμῶν γεγενῆσθαι δεινόν: δεῖ pro δὴ Bekker (edd. omn.): γενέσθαι δεινοὺς Dobr. (prob. Es): οὐ γὰρ δεῖ μὴ καθ' ὑμῶν γεγενῆσθαι μόνον, ἀλλ' ὑπὲρ ὑμῶν κ.τ.λ. Rehd., who considers that δεῖ μὴ became δή, and that δεινὸν arose from μόνον with δεῖ superscribed.

§ 147. The MSS. give ὅτι τὰ μνημεῖα κ.τ.λ. Most editors follow Morus in deleting ὅτι (Turr., Sch., Bl., Thalh.) as a ptcp., and not a finite verb, follows: others suppose that a finite verb such as εἴληπται or ἤλεγκται (Reiske), ἐξελήλεγκται or ἐφευρέθη (Duke) has fallen out. Rehd. suggests the change of ὅτι to ἄτε.

INDEX A. PROPER NAMES

(*The numbers refer to the Sections*)

Ἄγλαυρος, 77
Ἀδείμαντος, 70
Ἀθηνᾶ, 1, 17, 26, 75
Ἀθῆναι, 26, 84
Αἰγινῆται, 70
Αἴτνη, 95
Ἀλέξανδρος, 71
Ἀλεξικλῆς, 115
Ἀμύντας, 22 sqq.
Ἄνδρος, 42
Ἀντιγένης, 22
Ἀπολλόδωρος, 112
Ἄρειος πάγος, 12, 52
Ἄρης, 77
Ἀρίσταρχος, 115
Ἀσία, 42, 62, 72 sq., 104
Ἀττική, 85, 108, 113, 115, 145
Αὐξώ, 77
Αὐτόλυκος, 53
Ἀχαρνεύς, 23

Βοιωτία, 47

Γοργώ, 100 (46)

Δεκέλεια, 120 sq.
Δελφοί, 84, 93, 99
Δημόφαντος, 127

Εἰρηνίς, 17
Ἕκτωρ, 103
Ἐνυάλιος, 77
Ἐπίδαυρος, 42
Ἐρεχθεύς, 98
Ἐτεόνικος, 70

Εὔμολπος, 98, 100
Εὐριπίδης, 100
Εὐρυμέδων, 72
Εὐρώπη, 73

Ζεύς, 77: (ὁ σωτήρ), 17, 136 sq.

Ἡγεμόνη, 77
Ἤπειρος, 26
Ἡρακλῆς, 105

Θαλλώ, 77
Θερμοπύλαι, 108
Θρᾶκες, 98
Θρασύβουλος, 112
Θρῇξ, 100 (48)

Ἵππαρχος ὁ Χάρμου, 117

Καλλίστρατος, 93
Κέως, 42
Κηφισός, 98, 100
Κιλικία, 72
Κλεόμαντις, 85, 87
Κλεοπάτρα, 26
Κόδρος, 84 sqq.
Κόρινθος, 26
Κριτίας, 113
Κυάνεαι, 73

Λακεδαιμόνιοι, 42, 61, 105, 108 sq., 120, 128
Λευκάς, 26
Λεωκράτης, 1 et pass.
Λυσικλῆς, 23

INDEX A. PROPER NAMES

Μακεδόνες, 42
Μαραθών, 104, 109
Μέγαρα, 21, 25 sq., 56, 90, 145
Μενέλαος, 24
Μεσσήνη, 62
Μεσσήνιοι, 105
Μῆδοι, 109
Μητρῷον, 66

Ξέρξης, 68, 71, 80
Ξυπεταιών, 22

Ομηρος, 102

Παλλάς, 100 (49)
Παναθήναια, 102
Παυσανίας, 128
Πειραιεύς, 18, 37
Πελοποννήσιοι, 42, 84 sq., 87
Πέρσης, 128
Πλαταιαί, 80
Ποσειδών, 98
Πραξιθέα, 98

Ῥόδιοι, 14, 18, 143

Ῥόδος, 14, 18 sq., 21, 55, 70, 121

Σαλαμίς, 68, 70, 73, 122
Σικελία, 95
Σπάρτη, 105

Τιμοχάρης, 23 sq.
Τροζήν, 42
Τροία, 62
Τρῶες, 103
Τυρταῖος, 106 sq.

Ὑπερείδης, 36

Φάσηλις, 73
Φιλόμηλος, 24
Φοινίκη, 72
Φρύνιχος, 112
Φυρκῖνος, 19

Χαιρώνεια, 16, 45, 142, 144
Χαλκίοικος, 128
Χάρμος, 117
Χιόνη, 98
Χολαργεύς, 24

INDEX B. SUBJECTS

Advocacy as a profession, 138
Areopagus, history and functions of, 12
Athenian Empire, duration of, 72
Athens, reputation of for piety, 15
Athletes, disparaging reference to, 51
'Autochthony' of Athenians, 41, 83, 100 (7, 8)

Blindness, mental, 92
Bury, *H.G.*, quoted, 10, 73, 106, 128

Callias, Peace of, 73
Corn, importation and exportation of, 27

Dead, commonplaces in praise of the, 46 *sqq*.
— speculation regarding the, 136
Death penalty, inadequacy of, 8
Decree: of Demophantus, 125 *sq*.
— of Hyperides, 16, 36 *sqq*.
— concerning absconders to Decelea, 120 *sq*.
— concerning Hipparchus, 117 *sqq*.
— concerning Phrynichus, 113 *sqq*.
— concerning 'the man who died at Salamis,' 121

Decree: 'concerning piety,' 146

'Epheby,' at Athens, 76
Evidence, admission of, at trials, 20

Gorgias of Leontini quoted, 48 *n*.
Grote, *H.G.*, quoted, 73

Holm, *H.G.*, quoted, 73, 104
Homer as an educator, 102
— law regulating recitations of, *ibid*.
— quoted, 103
Horsekeeping as a sign of wealth, 139

Inaccurate history, 62, 70 *sqq*., 80, 124, 128
Interest, rates of, 23
Irrelevant pleading in courts, 11

Law, inadequacy of the, to cover every offence, 9
Legislation, process of, 7 *n*.
Livy quoted, 40, 107

Messenian Wars, chronology of, 62, 106 *nn*.
Military age at Athens, 39

Oath: of Ephebi, 76 *sqq*.
— Plataean, 80 *sqq*.

Prayer at opening of speech, 1 *n*.

INDEX B. SUBJECTS

Rhetorical exaggeration, 62, 73

Sallust quoted, 126
Senatus consultum ultimum quoted, 37
Severity of ancient legislators, 65 *sq.*
Slaves, challenge to surrender, 28
— enfranchisement of, 41
— evidence of, under torture, 28 *sqq.*

Sparta, quoted for good government, 128
Symmories, trierarchic, 139 *n.*

Verrall on Tyrtaeus, quoted, 106 *n.*
Voting, method of, at trials, 149

Witnesses, summoning of to depose, 20
Wives and children in court, 141

INDEX C. GRAMMAR AND LANGUAGE

Accusative: in absol. phrases, 17, 26, 45, 61, 73, 78, 92, 100, 144; cognate, 100 (1); of extent or compass of action, 2, 9, 11, 26, 41, 46, 52, 65, 78; *induendi*, 40; internal, 51; modal, 60, 67, 77, 111; of part affected, 107 (27); agreeing with implied subject of infin., 61; secondary acc. of space traversed, 70; of thing asked for, 139; of thing taught, 101; of thing taken away, 97

'Anticipation,' 62, 90, 96, 111, 138

Aorist: gnomic, 79, 100 (29, 33), 132; inceptive, 21, 25, 104; in sense of perf., 68; aor. infin. c. εἰκός and ἐλπίς, 60

Article: coupling two separate classes, 90; demonstrative, 107 (7); of something well known, 51, 95; omitted in certain formulae, 87; omitted with certain nouns, 117; with neut. adj. = abstract noun, 10, 33

Asyndeton, 33, 150 *n*.

Attraction of Relative, 26, 77

Chiasmus, 93

Dative, of agent, 14, 69, 108, 131, 138; ethic (in calling for documents, etc.), 23 *sq.*, 28, 114, 120, 129; of interest or person affected, 26, 99, 109, 136; of recipient, 18; modal, 25, 30; of point of predication, 40; depending on verbal force of noun, 63; with ἔνοχος, 4, 53, 114, etc.

Dual, followed by plural relative, 105

Emphatic position of words, 18, 44, 101

Future Indic. in final clause, 31

Future Participle, final, 17, 143; c. article, 4

Genitive, of characteristic, 6; of charge, 133; of definition, 25; objective, 10, 29, 46, 141; partitive, 6, 9, 18, 48, 111; of price, 22, 23, 138; of separation, 65, 98; of source, 15; of person in whom something is praised, blamed, etc., 28, 135; c. ἀθῷος, 79; c. ἀλλότριος, 46; c. ἀμφισβητεῖν, 98; c. ἐπιβαίνω, 108; c. ἐπώνυμος, 88; c. ἱκετεύω, 150; c. σύνοικος, 145

INDEX C. GRAMMAR AND

Hiatus, avoidance of, 7, 58

Indirect Question, form of *recta* retained in, 66, 84
Infinitive: Active or Middle idiomatic in decrees, 16, 107, 113, 117; absolute, 71; epexegetic, 62, 95, 100 (37), 107 (26, 29), 110; final, 100; as gerundive, 34, 43 *sq*., 47, 87, 100 (4, 39), 136, 147; in indictments, 137; of inner object, 100; in relative clause in *Or. Obl.*, 96; of respect or limitation, 91; c. αἰτίαν ἔχειν, 53; c. λαγχάνω, of official bodies, 54; c. φεύγειν, 'shrink from,' 32; perf. infin. of 'standing attitude,' 3, 110; pres. infin. in impf. tense, 64, 86, 95; with verbs of swearing, 126 *sq*.

Isocratean structure, 3, 104

Masculine participle joined with nouns of different gender, 30
Masculine pronoun referring to nouns of different gender, 29
Middle with reflexive pronoun, 43, 70, 141
Mixed Conditional, 66

Negative: affecting whole clause, 51, 65, 100 (49); generic, 8, 11, 43, 44, 49, 138, 142; trajected, 58
Neuter Adjective in Predicate, 110

Omission: of imperative, 116; of infin., 119; of subst. verb, 61; of subject, 19, 23

Parataxis: see under μὲν...δέ, Index D
Participle: absol. acc. of, after ὥσπερ, 90; conative, 49, 53, 71, 112 *sqq*., 124, 131, 146, 148; concessive, 35, 41, 58, 80, 82, 101; conditional, 10, 13, 52, 66, 100 (21), 123, 125; coupled by τε...καί with finite verb, 100; of impf., 17, 36; agreeing with accusatival subject of infin., 84; in protasis, 60, 90, 91; main stress falling upon, 28, 36, 146; 'like to be...,' 70, 95; with article denoting a class, 2; with subst. verb, 36, 52, 68, 107, 116; with φανερὸν ποιεῖν, 50
Plural: of abstract nouns, 6, 18, 20, 48, 64, 75, 140; of pronoun, referring to collective sing., 42; for singular (poetic), 100 (50); in sense of general sing., 107 (27), 145; verb with collective sing. subject, 87, 142
Poetic words in Lycurgus, 4, 7, 82, 99, 130, 147
Prepositions used for simple case: see παρά, ὑπέρ (Index D); 'pregnant' use of, 25
Present Indicative, with force of perfect, 29, 37; historic, 23, 85
Pronoun, emphatic, 53, 107; unemphatic in emphatic position, 58; reflexive, with middle, 43, 70, 141; resumptive, 35, 42, 46, 82, 93, 117

Redundant Expression, 39, 46, 87, 119, 141

Relative clause substituted for second adjective, 16; for articular infin. or εἴ τις, 100 (1)

Singular verb, with composite subject, 38, 107 (10); agreeing with nearer subject, 33, 79
Subject supplied out of preceding negative, 133
Subjunctive: conative, 58, 114, 125; 'vivid,' 26; without ἄν in relative clause, 100 (11)
Synizesis, 100 (7, 15), 107 (14)

'Trajected' const. of verb, 43, 143

Variation of declension, 15, 38; of idiomatic phrases, 17, 33, 92, 129
Verbal adjective (gerund), 67, 135

INDEX D. GREEK WORDS

ἀγών, 'trial,' 5, 7, 13 sq., 90; ἀγῶνες δημόσιοι, 7, 46
ἀθλῆται, 51
ἀθῷος, c. gen. 79; absol. 144
αἱρεθήσεται, 'shall be taken,' 100 (39)
αἰτίαν ἔχειν, c. infin. 53; absol. 125
αἰών: τὸν αἰῶνα, in sempiternum, 62; εἰς ἅπαντα τὸν αἰ. 106; ἐξ ἅπ. τοῦ αἰ. 110; κατὰ παντὸς τοῦ αἰ. 7
ἀκτή, 17, 55
ἁλίσκεσθαι, 'be convicted,' 12, 114; 'be caught,' 121
ἀλιτήριος, 117
ἀλλά, hortativum, 103, 107 (15); in question and answer, 144; ἀλλὰ μήν, 53; ἀλλ' οὐ, 'instead of,' 71; ἀλλ' οὖν γε, 141
ἀλλότριος, c. gen. 46
ἄλλως, 'merely,' 100 (27)
ἅμα...καί, 29, 31, 50
ἀμύνειν, rare for ἀμύνεσθαι, 49
ἀμφισβητεῖν, c. gen. 98; ἀμφ. περί, 108
ἄν, repeated, 57, 74; omitted with ὅστις c. subj., 100 (11), om. with ὄφρα c. subj., 107 (28)
ἀναβαίνειν, of witnesses, 20
ἀναιρεῖν, of oracle, 84, 105
ἀνακεῖσθαι, of statues, 51, 137
ἀνακρίνειν, 112
ἀναρπάζεσθαι, 31

ἀνάστασις, 'ruin,' 149
ἀνάστατος, 60 sqq., 81, 123
ἀναστρέφεσθαι, versari, 142, 145
ἀντί, 'at the price of,' 100 (51); ἀνθ' ὧν, 76
ἄξιον (ἐστι), 'worth while,' 25, 28, 58, 75, 80, 96, 100, 122
ἀπάγειν, of summary arrest, 121
ἀπαλλάττειν ἐκ, 114
ἀπό, 'with' (of money), 22
ἀποβλέπειν πρός, 10, 12, 64, 66, 100
ἀποδιδόναι, reddere, 20, 22, 53, 149; c. infin., 'empower,' 93
ἀποδόσθαι, 'sell')(πωλεῖν, 22
ἀπολαμβάνειν, 'duly receive,' 24
ἀπολύειν, 'quash,' 56
ἀποστερεῖν, c. acc. rei, 97; c. gen., 59, 110, 123, 129, 147
ἄρα, 'one must conclude,' 27, 54, 78, 145
ἀρά γε, ironical, 70, 88, 119, 123
ἀρά, 'curse,' 31
ἀργύριον, 'cash,' 23
ἀρείω, 'better,' 77
ἀρετή, 'fruits of valour,' 48; 'reputation for valour,' 49
ἁρμόζει, convenit, 95
ἁρμός, 100 (12)
ἀρχήν, omnino, 125
ἀσέβεια, 147
ἀσεβεῖν εἰς, 76; ἀσ. περί, 129

INDEX D. GREEK WORDS 247

ἀστρατεία, 147
ἄστυ: τὸ ἄστυ τῆς πόλεως)(ὁ Πειραιεύς, 18
ἄτιμος, 41
αὐτίκα μάλα, idiomatic, 143
αὐτοῦ, 'on the spot,' 18
αὐτόχθων, 41, 100 (8)
ἀφίστασθαι, 98; τοσοῦτον ἀφέστηκα τοῦ...ὅσον, *tantum abest ut...ut*, 30
ἀφορᾶν, 'view from afar,' 17
ἀφορία, 'famine,' 84
ἀφορμή, 'capital,' 26

βάθρον: ἐν πόλεως βάθροις, *in sinu urbis*, 100 (47)
βασανίζειν, 28 *sqq.*
βίᾳ, 'in spite of,' 70
βλάπτειν, of mental hurt, 92
βουλευτήριον, 124, 126
βουλή: ἡ β. οἱ πεντακόσιοι, 37; ἡ ἐν Ἀρείῳ πάγῳ β., 52
βωμός, ὁ τῶν δώδεκα θεῶν, 93

γάρ, *narrativum*, 16, 124; introducing substance of τεκμήριον, 61; 'for instance,' 103
γεγραμμένα, τά, *capita accusationis*, 5
γεραιός, 107 (20)
γῆ καὶ ὕδωρ, 71
γηροτροφεῖν, 144
γίγνεσθαι, of time, 21
γνώμη)(νοῦς, 92; γνώμην ἀποφήνασθαι, 11
γνῶσις, 'finding,' 141
γονεῖς pro γονέας, 15, 96, 97
γοῦν, introducing illustration of general principle, 71, 86, 95, 104
γραφὴ παρανόμων, 7

δέ, *in apodosi*, 99, 127
δέ γε, 93

δεινός, of rhetorical skill, 31, 138
δεινότης, 31 *sq.*
δεκατεύω, 'betithe,' 81
δένδρα, τά, 43, 150
δή, *igitur*, 54
δημόσιοι ἀγῶνες, v. ἀγών
δημοτικός, 29
διά: διὰ τέλους, 16; δι' ἀπορρήτων, *clam*, 85; δι' ἐργασίαν, 15; δι' ὀργήν, δι' ἀλήθειαν, 116
διακαρτερεῖν εἰς, 85
διαλαμβάνω, 'define,' 131
διάνοια, in plural, 75
διαρρήδην, 129
διαφέρειν, c. gen., *praestare*, 12, 15, 83, 108: absol. 89; ἐράνους, 'pay off loans,' 22
διαφοραί (πεσσῶν), 100 (9)
διεσκευασμένος, 37
δικάζειν)(δικάζεσθαι, 7 *n.*
διομνύναι, 127
διπλᾶ θαἰμάτια ἐμπεπορπημένοι, 40

ἐάτωσαν, 63
ἐβουλόμην ἄν, *vellem*, 3
ἐγγράφειν, 76, 137
ἐγκαταλείπειν, *derelinquere*, 2, 5, 8, *et pass.*
ἔδαφος, 'soil,' 144
ἔδος, 1, 143
ἐθέλειν, of ready obedience, 107
εἰ: εἰ δεῖ, apologetic, 49, 61: εἰ καί)(καὶ εἰ, 62, 95, 141; εἰ μή, *nisi forte*, 140; εἰ οὔ, *in protasi*, 107 (11, 12), 141
εἰκότως, 47 *n.*
εἰκών, of Hipparchus, 117; of Leocrates' father, 136 *sq.*
εἴπερ, 66, 100 (19), 101
εἴργειν τῶν νομίμων, 65

INDEX D. GREEK WORDS

εἰς: 'for' (of purpose), 53; 'against' (of sinning), 76, 94, 124; c. διακαρτερεῖν, 85; c. λογίζεσθαι, 67; c. τάσσειν and φοβεῖσθαι, 129
εἰσαγγελία, 5, 30, 137
εἰσαγγέλλειν, 1
εἰσαγώγιμος, 100 (10)
εἰσιέναι, 'appear in court,' 11 sq.
εἶτα, 'and then,' 66; in question, 78
ἐκ: 'by' (of means), 35; 'composed of,' 62; 'prescribed by,' 4, 8, 34
ἕκατι = ἕνεκα, 100 (14)
ἐκβάλλειν, *inritum reddere*, 100 (45)
ἔκδοτον ποιεῖν, 59; παραδοῦναι, 85; καταλιπεῖν, 136
ἐκεῖ)(ἐνθάδε, 136
ἐκεῖνο, appositional, 100 (43)
ἐλάα, emblem of Athena, 100 (46)
ἐλεγεία, of Tyrtaeus, 106; of inscriptions, 142
ἔλεγχος, 'scrutiny,' 'test of veracity,' 28, 30, 33; διδόναι, 28; φεύγειν, 29, 30, 34; 'conviction,' 46
ἐμβάλλειν εἰς τὴν ἀγοράν, 5
ἐμμένειν ἐν, 82 n.
ἐμπορία, 'trade,' 55, 57; 'merchandise,' 57
ἐμφράττειν, 124
ἐν, 'among,' 14; instrumental, 30; 'in the power of,' 52; ἐν γειτόνων, 21; ἐν Μαραθῶνι, 104
ἐνδέχεσθαι, 'be possible,' 8; αἱ ἐνδεχόμεναι τιμωρίαι, 119
ἐνεστηκώς, 'present,' 7
ἐνίστασθαι, 'institute,' 31
ἔνοχος, 'amenable (liable) to,' 4, 5, 9, *et pass.*

ἐνταῦθα, of motion, 33
ἐξαγώγιμος, 26
ἐξαίρετος, 140
ἐξαιτεῖσθαι, 'beg off,' 20, 135
ἐξανιστάναι, 84
ἐξόμνυσθαι, 'swear disclaimer,' 20
ἐξορίζειν, 89, 113, 115
ἐξουσία, *licentia*, 12, 145
ἔξω τοῦ πράγματος, 11, 13, 149
ἔπειτα, 'after all this,' 27, 115, 121, 148
ἐπεξελθεῖν, 'punish,' 146
ἐπερωτᾶν, *terminus technicus* of consulting oracle, 84
ἔπη, 'epic poetry,' 102, 104
ἐπί: c. gen., 'in charge of,' 44, 121; 'engaged in,' 58; 'in the case of,' 64; of condition, ἐπὶ προστάτου, 145; c. dative, of occasion or cause, 27, 39, 63, 78, 138; of that on which penalty is imposed, 65; τὸ ἐπὶ τούτῳ μέρος, *quod ad eum attinet*, 45; c. acc., of purpose, 45, 57
ἐπὶ γήρως ὁδῷ, 40
ἐπιβαίνω, c. gen., 'set foot on,' 108
ἐπιγράφειν, 137
ἐπιδημεῖν, 14, 39
ἐπιδιδόναι, of voluntary contribution, 140
ἐπίδοξος, 'expected,' 9
ἐπίκτητος)(φύσει προσήκων, 48
ἐπιμέλεια, ἡ περὶ τοὺς νέους, at Sparta, 106
ἐπίσημος, followed by ὅτι, 129
ἐπιτίθεσθαι τυραννίδι, 125
ἐπιτίμιον, 'penalty,' 8, 65; plural, 4, 114
ἐπίτιμος, 41
ἐπιτρέπειν, 'allow,' 13, 58, 77, 115

INDEX D. GREEK WORDS

ἐπιτύμβιος, 109
ἐπωβελία, 7 n.
ἐπωνυμία, 25
ἐπώνυμος, 88
ἔρανος, 22, 143
ἐργασία, 15, 55, 58
ἔρημος, 'unprovided for,' 17; 'undefended,' 117
εὖ διαβάς, 107 (31)
εὐαγγελίζεσθαι, 18
εὐδαιμονία, 4, 61, 127, 149, 150
εὐηκοεῖν, *dicto audiens esse*, 77
εὔκλεια, poetic, 82, 100 (33)
εὔνοια, in plu., 48
εὐνομεῖσθαι, of Sparta, 128
εὐσεβῶν χῶρος, in Sicily, 96
ἔφηβοι, 76
ἔχειν, 'involve,' 6; 'have to wife,' 22 *sq.*
ἐχρῆν, *oportuit*, 141

ζητεῖν, of judicial inquiry, 112

ἦ που, 71; *in apod.*, with ὅπου preceding, *ibid.*
ἡλικίαι, αἱ, of age for military service, 40
ἦν, *licuit*, 40 *sq.*
ἥρωες, 1

θαυμάζειν, 'admire,' 110; c. gen. of person, 135
θέσθαι τὰ ὅπλα, 'take up arms,' 43; θ. τὴν ψῆφον, 'vote,' 13, 128; χάριν θ., 'show favour,' 148
θεσμοθέται, 121
θεσμός, 77
θορυβεῖν, *acclamare*, 52

ἰαμβεῖα, 92, 100
ἰδιώτης, 'private individual,' 14, 79; 'a layman,' 31
ἱδρῦσθαι, 1, 25, 77

ἱερά: τὰ πάτρια, 77; τὰ πατρῷα, 8, 25, 38, 56; λαβόντες τὰ ἱερά, 20; ἱερὰ καὶ ὅσια, 77
ἱκετεύειν, c. gen., 150; c. acc., 143
ἱπποτροφεῖν, 139
ἴστωρ, 'witness,' 77
ἴχνος, 'outline,' 80
ἰών, poetic, 99

καδίσκος, 149
καθέστηκε, a stronger ἐστί, 4, 8
καί: intensive, 19, 65, 90; after ἤ, 14; μικροὶ καὶ οἱ τυχόντες, 37
καί...δέ, 'and...too,' 28, 117
καὶ δὴ καί, 95
καὶ μάλιστα, *vel maxime*, 139
καὶ μήν, 79, 100 (32), 134
καὶ πῶς; 35
καὶ ταῦτα, 'and that too,' 12, 32
καλεῖν, as συνήγορος, 43
κανών, *norma*, 9
κατά, c. gen., of time, κατὰ παντὸς τοῦ αἰῶνος, *in sempiternum*, 7; 'concerning,' καθ' ὑμῶν ἀπαγγελία, 14; 'against,' 138; c. acc., of occupation, κατὰ ταύτην τὴν ἐργασίαν, κατ' ἐμπορίαν, 55 *sqq.*; κατὰ φύσιν, 'naturally,' 32; κατὰ τὸ ἑαυτοῦ μέρος, 97
καταβαίνειν, to Piraeus, 37; from the βῆμα, 146
κατάγειν τὰ πλοῖα, 18
κατέρχεσθαι, of exiles, 124, 145
κατηγορεῖν, 'be the accuser of,' 19
κατοικεῖσθαι (passive), 95
κέηται, 113
κινδυνεύειν, in judicial sense, 34
κίνδυνος, of judicial danger, 129 *sq.*
κινεῖν, of sacred things, 25

INDEX D. GREEK WORDS

κληρονομεῖν, 88, 127
κλητεύειν, 20
κοινός, 'public,' 6, 11, 29, 46, *alib.*; 'common to all,' 60; τὰ κοινά, 'the public interest,' 3
κολάζειν)(τιμωρεῖσθαι, 123, 146
κραίνειν, in oath, 77
κρείττων, 'beyond the reach of,' 126
κρήνη, ἡ ἐν τοῖς οἰσύοις, 112
κρίνω, 'put on trial,' 1, 134, 137
κρίσις, 'trial,' 4, 6, 12, 31, 117, 146; 'decision,' 'verdict,' 7, 9, 124
κρύβδην)(φανερός, 146
κύριος, 'having control of,' 56, 59, 146

λάβοιν = λάβοιμι, 100 (6)
λαγχάνειν, of tutelar deity, 26; of 'duly elected' bodies, 54
λαμβάνειν = συλλαμβάνειν, 52, 112; 'judge,' 66
λέμβος, 'cock-boat,' 17
ληξιαρχικὸν γραμματεῖον, 76
λητουργία, 139
λιποταξίου, 147
λόγος, 'an idle tale,' 23, 129; ἔσται λόγος, 'will be talked about,' 14; λόγον ἔχειν περί τινα, *rationem alicuius habere*, 107; λόγος)(ἔργον, 71, 127, 145; λόγῳ)(ἔργῳ, 104, 116, 123; λόγῳ)(τοῖς δ' ἔργοισιν, 100 (13)
λοχεύματα, 'offspring,' 100 (50)

μακρὸν πλοῖον, 73
μέγας, 'important,' 7, 29
μέλλω, const. of, 66 *n*.
μέν, 'isolated,' 57, 66
μὲν ... δέ, 'though ... yet,' 'whereas...*you*,' 8, 12, 42, 53, 82, 110, 115 *sq.*, 121, 140
μέρος, 'importance,' 100 (43); τὸ καθ' αὑτὸν μέρος, etc., v. under τό
μεταλλάσσειν : τὸν βίον, 50; τὸν τόπον, 69; χώραν, 86
μεταπίπτειν, *in deterius*, 50; *in melius*, 60
μετέρχομαι, 'punish,' 116
μετέχειν : τῶν ἱερῶν, 5, 142; τῆς πεντηκοστῆς, 19, 58; τινός τινι, 48 *n*.
μὴ δῆτα, 116
μὴ ὅτι...ἀλλά, 94
μηλόβοτον ἀνεῖναι, 145
μιμεῖσθαι, of poetry, 102
μόνος τῶν ἄλλων, 67, 102
μονώτατος, 88 *sq.*
μῦθος, dramatic, 100

ναοί, 38
νεμεσητόν, 107 (26)
νεώρια, 150
νεώς, 1, 25, 43, etc.
νομίζειν, 'adopt,' 'make customary,' 75
νόμιμος, 'customary,' 141; τὰ νόμιμα, 'customary rites,' 25 *sq.*, 59, 97, 147
νομοθέται, 7 *n*., 64; νομοθέται)(δικασταί, 9
νόμος, *re* Homeric recitations, 102; νόμος)(ψήφισμα, 7 *n*.
νῦν δέ, 'as it is,' 3

ὁ ἐπὶ τοῦ ὀρύγματος, 121
ὃ καὶ...εἰ, 56; c. infin. clause following, 82
ὀθνεῖος, 'alien,' 25
οἴεσθαι = ἀξιοῦν, 127
οἰκουμένη, ἡ, 'the world,' 15; opp. to ἀνάστατος, 123
ὀλίγοι, 'a few,' 51

INDEX D. GREEK WORDS

ὅμηρος, 'surety,' 117, 127
ὅμως, adhering to ptcp., 75
ὅπλα, τὰ ἱερά, 76; θέσθαι τὰ ὅπλα, 43
ὁπότε, causal, 123
ὅπου, with ἢ που following, 71
ὅπως, final with impf. indic., 141
ὀρθός, *metu erectus*, 39
ὅρκος, ephebic, 76; Plataic, 80 *sq*.
ὄρνῑς, 132
ὅς, *suus ipsius*, 107 (2, 3)
ὅσια καὶ ἱερά, 78
ὅστις = εἴ τις or articular infin., 100 (1)
ὅταν, causal, 116, 142
ὅτε, causal, 123
ὅτι, initial, 'in proof that,' 19
οὐδὲ εἷς, 49 *n*.
οὐδὲ πώποτε, 58 *n*.
οὐδὲν ἕτερον ἤ, 33
οὐδὲν πρότερον ἀδικοῦσιν ἤ, 129
οὐδὲν πρότερον ποιοῦσιν ἤ, 92
οὐκ ἔστιν ἥτις = οὐδεμία, 44
οὗτος, more emphatic than αὐτός, 3, 28, 117, 126, 150; prospective, 14, 28, 68, 79, 107 (21), 126; resumptive, 35, 42, 46, 82, 93, 117; as predicate, 9, 79 *sq*., 130
οὕτως, followed by ὅς, 69; separated from noun, 85, 105; resuming a ptcp., 141
οὐχ ὅμοιος, 'quite different,' 14, 48
οὐχ ὅπως, *non ut*, 119
ὄφρα = ἕως ἄν, 107 (28)

παρά, c. gen., often for simple gen. (subjective), 15, 26, 97, 123, 129, 130, 148; c. dat., of person judging, 3, 12, 32, 54; of responsibility resting with, 146; c. acc., of that upon which a result depends, 63 (*bis*), 64, 66
παράγειν, 32, 92
παράδειγμα, 'warning example,' 27, 150
παραδιδόναι, of slaves, 32, 34
παρακαθίζεσθαι, 141
παρακελεύεσθαι, 150
παρακρούεσθαι, 139
παραλογισμός, 31
παρασκευή, in plu., 'tricks' (of defendants), 20; (of speech), 31
παραστάτης, 77
παρέχεσθαι, of witness or evidence, 23, 102, 146
πάτριος: πάτρια ἔθη, 25; ἱερὰ τὰ πάτρια, 77; νόμιμα, 59, 129; absol., 26, 116, 123
πατρίς, 'native city,' 17, 139
πατρῷος)(πάτριος)(πατρικός, 25 *n*.; ἱερὰ τὰ πατρῷα, 8, 25, 38, 56
πεντετηρίς)(πενταετηρίς, 102 *n*.
πεντηκοστή, ἡ, 19, 58
πέρας ἔχειν, 60
περί, c. gen., ἐξετάζειν περί, 66; σπουδάζειν περί, 107; περὶ πολλοῦ, πλείονος—v. ποιεῖσθαι; c. dat., of that for which one fights, 107 (2); c. acc., of time, περὶ δείλην ὀψίαν, 17
περιαιρεῖσθαι, 'deprive oneself of,' 35; 'take off,' 122
περιβάλλειν, *circumdare*, 139
περιέστηκεν ἐς τοῦτο, 'things have come to this,' 3
περιρρεῦσαι, 96
περιφθείρεσθαι, 40
πεσσοί, 100 (9)
πέφυκε, 4, 66, 132
πίστις, 'pledge': π. διδόναι, 79 *n*., 127

INDEX D. GREEK WORDS

ποιεῖν, 'dramatise,' 100 sq.; 'compose,' 106 sq.
ποιεῖσθαι, c. object noun, 1, 5, 11, 12, 14, 28, 30, 63, 73, 96, 102, 120, 146; περὶ πολλοῦ, 15; περὶ πλείονος, 10, 20, 81
ποιητός, 'adopted,' 48
πόλεος, metri causa, 100 (21)
ποῦ; 'how?,' 78
πρᾶγμα, res de qua agitur, 11, 13, 90 sq., 149
πρὶν ἤ, 128
πρό, 'in preference to,' 100 (30); 'for' (in defence of), 107
προαγαγέσθαι (εἰς ἔλεον), 33
προαίρεσις, 38, 148
προβούλευμα, 7 n.
προκαλεῖσθαι, 'challenge,' c. cog. acc., 28
πρόκλησις, 28 sq., 36; π. δέχεσθαι, 29
πρός, c. acc., of various relationship, 'before,' 'in the eyes of,' 101, 109; 'in face of,' 82; 'concerning,' 'connected with,' 129, 130; (adapted) 'to,' 132
προσαγορεύειν, 'designate,' 9, 18, 26, 96; salutare, 45
προσέχειν, 'attend to,' c. dat., 10, 75; absol., 86, 108
προσπίπτειν, 'attack,' 86
προστάτην ἔχειν, 21; πρ. νέμειν, ib. n.; ἐπὶ προστάτου οἰκεῖν, 145; προστάται, 'leaders,' 'champions,' 61, 104
πρότερον, 'sooner' (rather), 135 n.
πρόφασις, 'ground,' 6; 'pretext,' 20, 33
πρυτανεῖον: ἐν πρ. σίτησις, 87
πρῶτα μέν, folld. by ἔπειτα, 100 (5)

πρῶτον μέν, folld. by ἔπειτα, 19, 55
πτήσσειν (τὸν τῶν ἐπιόντων φόβον), 49
πυλίς, 17, 55
πυνθάνομαι, in anteoccupatio, 55
πωλεῖν, 'advertise for sale,' 56
πώποτε, c. noun (τῶν π. προδοτῶν), 134

ῥαψῳδεῖν, 102 n.
ῥῆσις, 100
ῥήτωρ, 'professional speaker,' 31
ῥύαξ πυρός, 'an eruption,' 95

σημεῖον, 90, 93
σθένειν = δύνασθαι, of equivalence, 100 (20)
σιτηγεῖν, 26, 27
σκῆψις, 33
στεφανῖται ἀγῶνες, 51
στέφανος, 'crown of glory,' 50, 100 (34); worn by senators, 122
στήλη, inscribed with names of traitors, 117, 124
στοιχεῖν, 'stand in rank,' 77
συγχωνεύειν, 117, 119
συκοφαντεῖν, of vexatious prosecution, 13, 31
συμβουλεύειν)(συμβουλεύεσθαι, 11 n., 59
συμφέρειν, 'help to collect,' 45
συνατυχεῖν, 131
συνέδριον (of Areopagus), 12, 54
συνευπορεῖν, 139
συνέχειν, 'embrace,' 'concern,' 7; 'hold together,' 79
συνήγορος, 59, 63
συνθῆκαι, 'bond,' 23 sq.; 'covenant,' 73

INDEX D. GREEK WORDS

σύνοιδα, 29, 30, 90; οἱ συνειδότες, 'accomplices,' 29
συνοικίζειν, 62
σύνοικος, c. gen., 145
σφόδρα, 'precisely,' 9
σχῆμα, 'mere figure,' 100 (27)
σώτειρα ('Αθηνᾶ), 27
σωτήρ (Ζεύς), 17, 136

τάξις, 'ordinance,' 4; 'duty,' 'rôle,' 20, 37; 'post,' 76
τὰς χιλίας ὀφλεῖν, 7 n.
τάσσειν εἰς, 'fix at,' 129
ταχύ, ironical, 133
τε, misplaced, 56; long in arsi before ῥ, 100 (15)
τεκμήριον)(σημεῖον, 90
τέμενος, 1, 143, 147
τήμερον: ἐν τῇ τήμερον ἡμέρᾳ, 1, 127, 147
τί οὖν; 123
τὸ ἐπὶ τούτῳ μέρος, 45
τὸ καθ' αὑτὸν μέρος, 17, 144
τὸ καθ' ἑαυτόν, 26
τὸ τούτου μέρος, 78
τοιοῦτος)(τηλικοῦτος, 2, 43; τοσαῦτα καὶ τηλικαῦτα, 26
τοκέων κάκωσις, 147
τόκος, 'interest,' 23
τολμᾶν, 'bring oneself to,' 43, 101, 131
τοῦτο μέν...τοῦτο δέ, 62
τρίαινα, symbol of Poseidon, 100 (47)
τριάκοντα, οἱ, 124
τριηραρχεῖν, 139
τροφεῖα, 53
τυγχάνειν: τῶν νόμων, 93; τιμωρίας, ib.
τύραννος, ὁ, 51
τυχόντες, οἱ, 'ordinary,' 37, 62

ὑγρότης (τοῦ ἤθους), 33
ὑπεκδῦναι, 86 n.

ὑπεκθέσθαι, 25, 53
ὑπέρ, c. gen., often = περί, 7, 34, 35, 40, 147, 149; periphrastic for simple gen., 9, 150; c. acc., of age, 'over,' 39
ὑπὲρ ὧν τοῦ μὴ καταλυθῆναι, 142 n.
ὑπερβάλλω, abs. 'surpass,' 133
ὑπεύθυνος, 'subject to,' 129, 148
ὑπό, c. dat., 'at the mercy of,' 2, 27
ὑπόγραμμα, 'inscription,' 118
ὑποδῦναι, 86
ὑποκεῖσθαι, 130
ὑπομένειν, 'stand' (one's trial), 90, 117
ὑπωμοσία, 7 n.

φανερὸν ποιεῖν, c. ptcp., 50
φέρε γάρ, introducing question, 66
φέρειν, 'pay' (interest), 23; τὴν ψῆφον, v. ψῆφος
φερόμενος, modal ptcp., 59
φεύγειν, c. infin., 'shrink from,' 32; φόνου, 133
φιλάνθρωπος, humanus, 3
φιλονεικία (-νικία), 5
φιλοψυχεῖν, 130
φοβεῖσθαι εἰς, 129
φορτίον ἄρασθαι, 96 n.
φρένες: ὁ νοῦς τῶν φρενῶν,92 n.; ἐν φρεσὶ θυμός, 107 (17)
φυλακή, 'defence,' 17, 37, 47; plural, 'defences,' 'defence forces,' 16, 38

χαλκοτύπος, 58
χάρις, 'favour,' 135, 139, 140; plural, 20, 139; χάριτας χαρίζεσθαι, 100 (1); χάριν θέσθαι, 148
χεῖλος ὀδοῦσι δακών, 107 (32)

INDEX D. GREEK WORDS

χορηγεῖν, 139
χρηματίζειν)(χρηματίζεσθαι, 37 n.
χρῆσαι, of oracle, 99
χρῆσθαι, 'experience,' 42 ; 'associate with,' 135
χρησμός, 'solemn utterance,' 92
χωρία, *loci*, 31
χωρὶς τούτων, *praeterea*, 31, 56

ψήφισμα, 7 n.

ψῆφος : ἐν τῇ ψήφῳ, *in suffragio ferendo*, 127 ; τὴν ψῆφον θέσθαι, 13, 128 ; τὴν ψῆφον φέρειν, 7, 11, 12 sq., 146 sq. ; passive, 149
ψυχαγωγεῖν, 33

ὥσπερ, c. acc. absol. of personal verb, 90
ὥστε, 'introductory,' c. infin., 97
ὥστε οὐ, c. infin., 3
ᾤχετο, as perf., 68

Made in the USA
Monee, IL
03 May 2026

49437830R00164